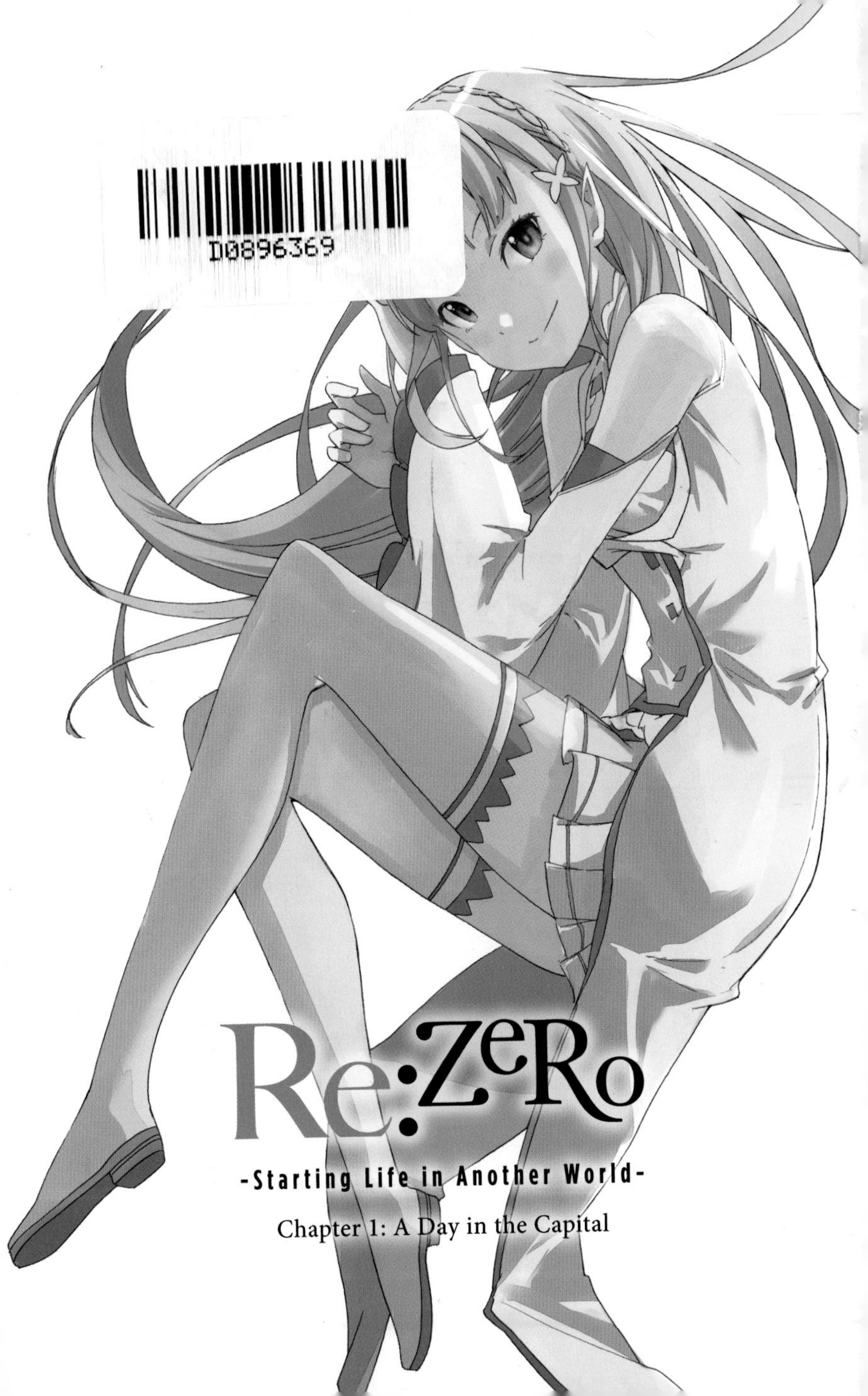

Re:ZeRo

-Starting Life in Another World-

Chapter 1: A Day in the Capital

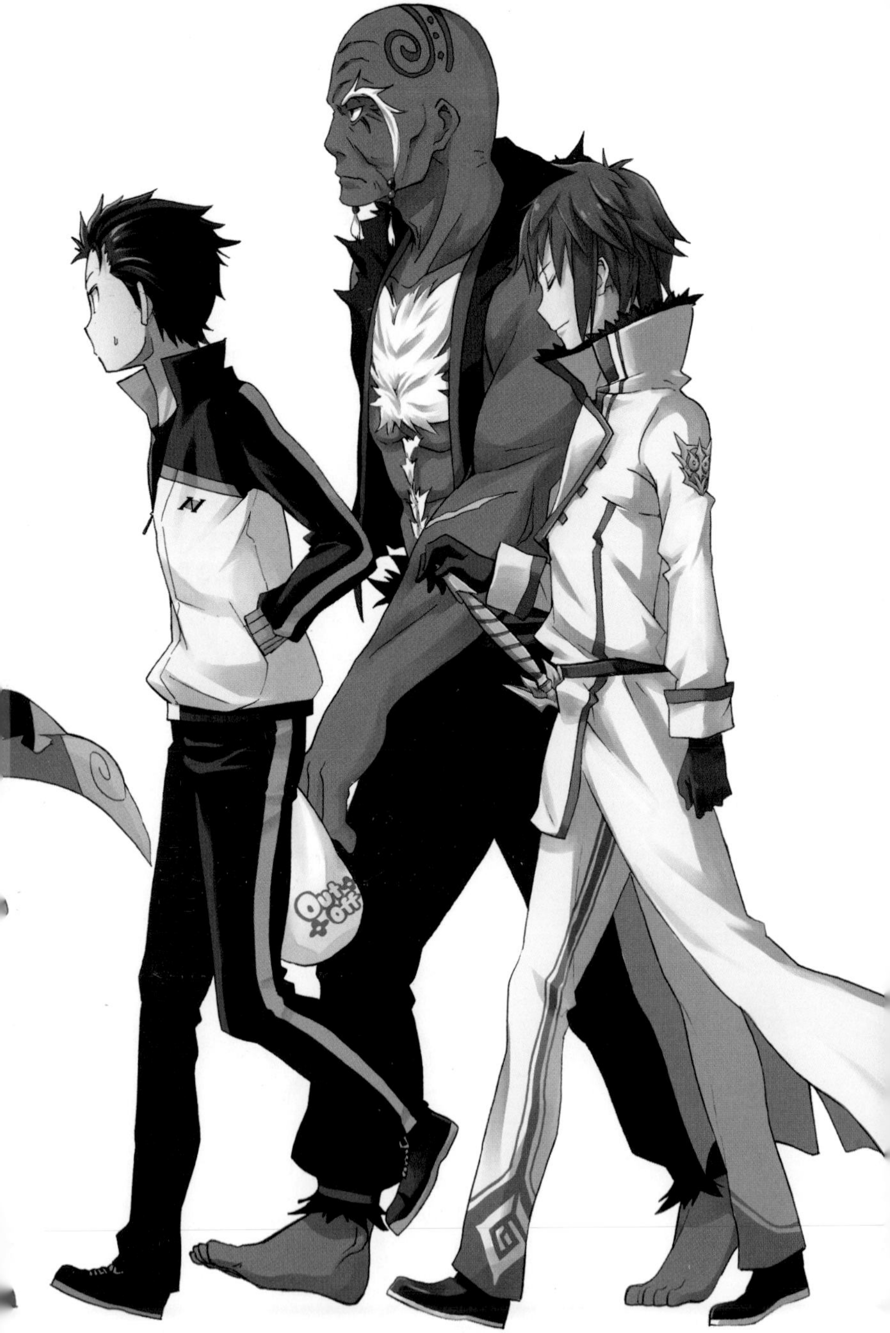

Episode 6: Ending and Beginning
Re: ZERO -Starting Life in Another World-
Chapter 1: A Day in the Capital

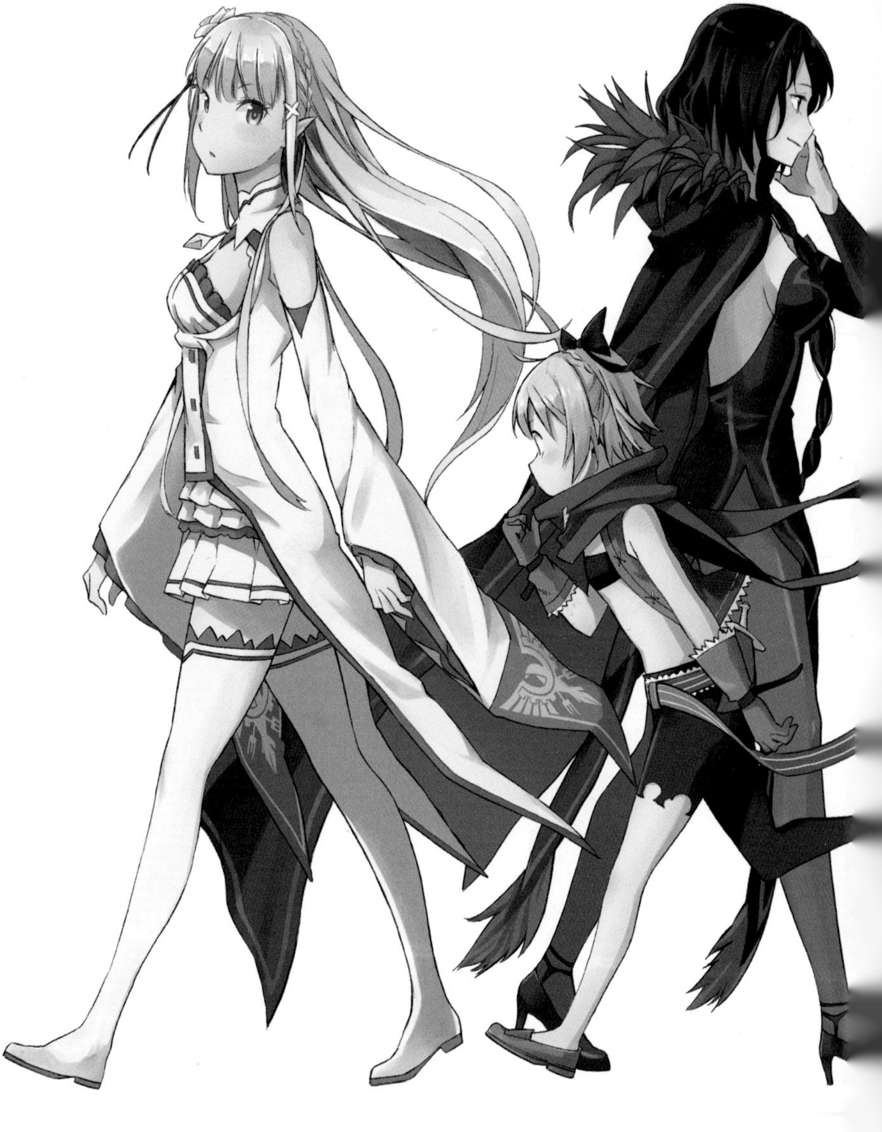

Re:ZERO -Starting Life in Another World-

Chapter 1: A Day in the Capital

The only ability Subaru Natsuki gets when he's summoned to another world is time travel via his own death. But to save her, he'll die as many times as it takes.

Contents

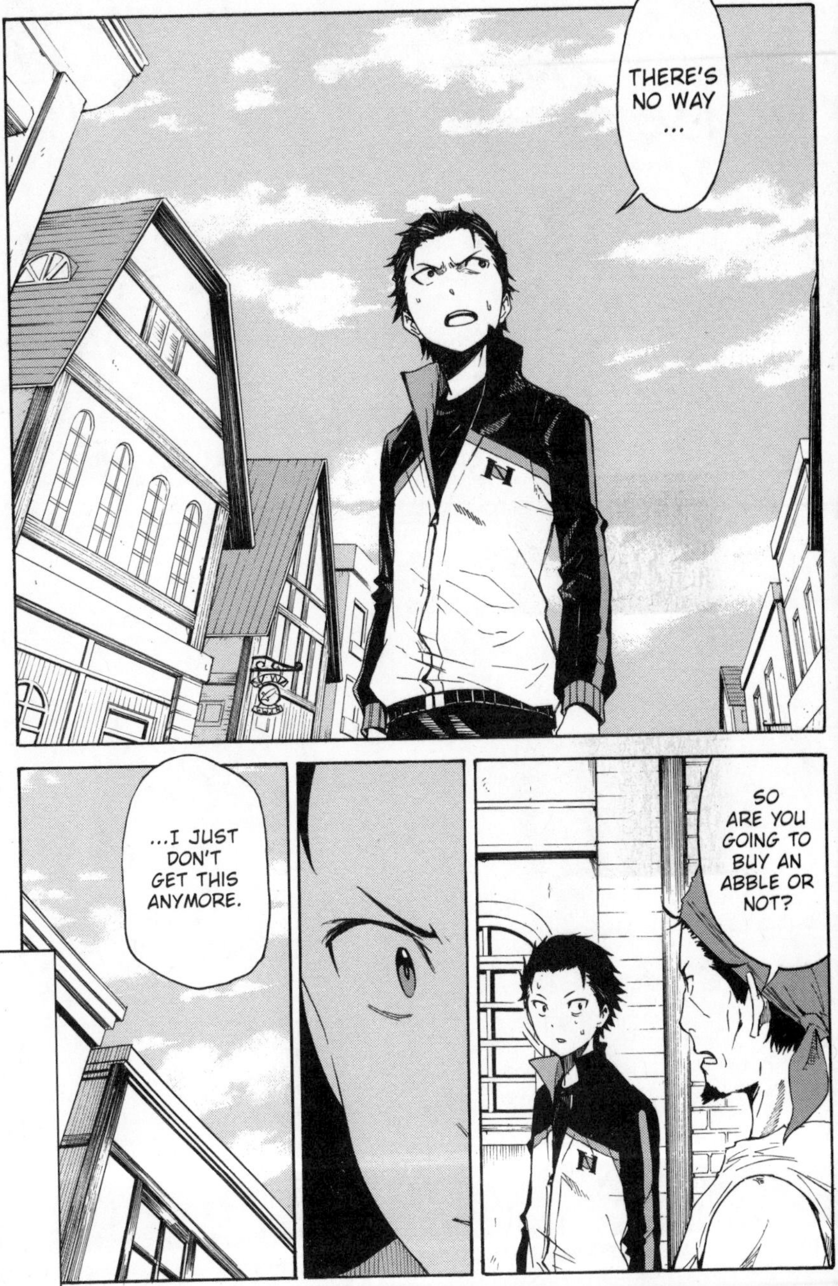
THERE'S NO WAY ...
SO ARE YOU GOING TO BUY AN ABBLE OR NOT?
...I JUST DON'T GET THIS ANYMORE.

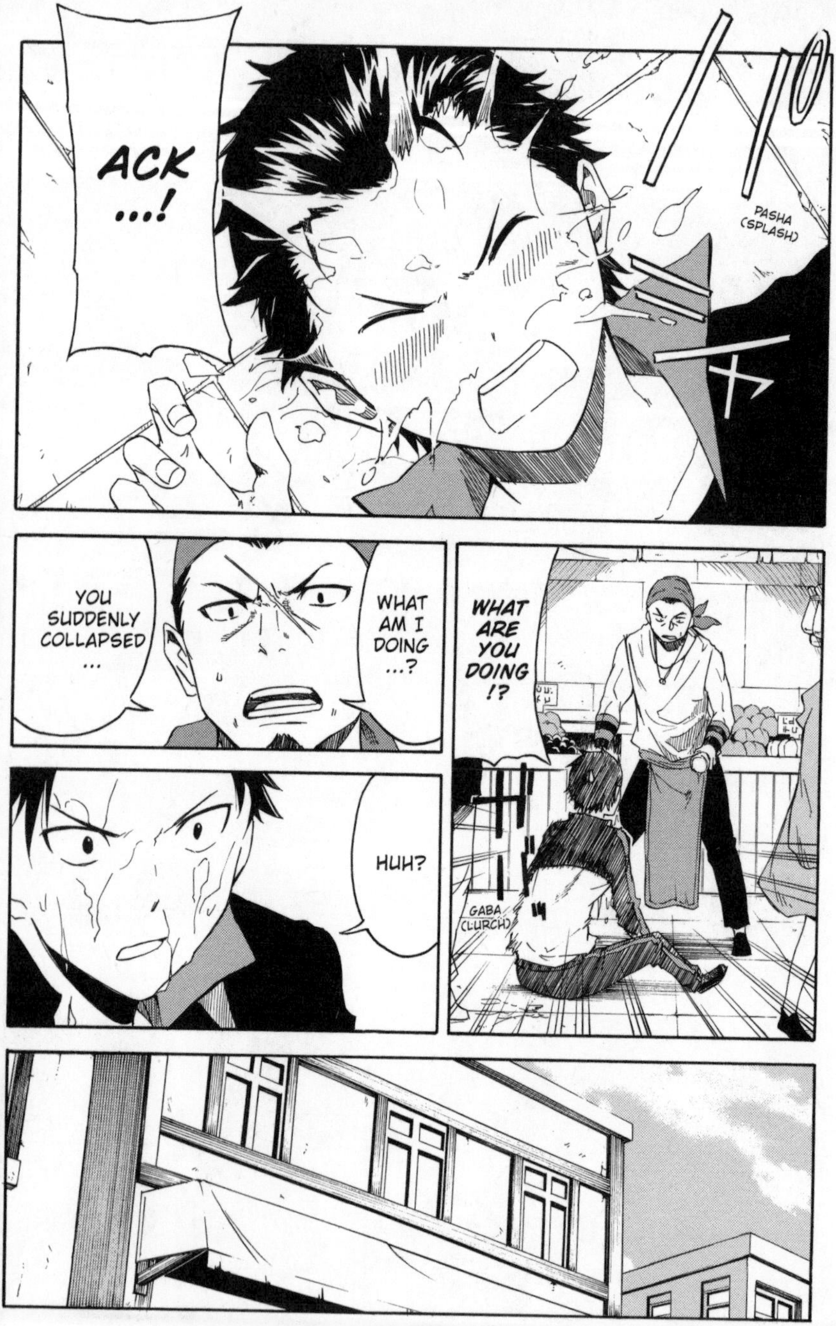

PASHA (SPLASH)
ACK ...!
WHAT ARE YOU DOING !?
GABA (CLURCH)
WHAT AM I DOING ...?
YOU SUDDENLY COLLAPSED ...
HUH?

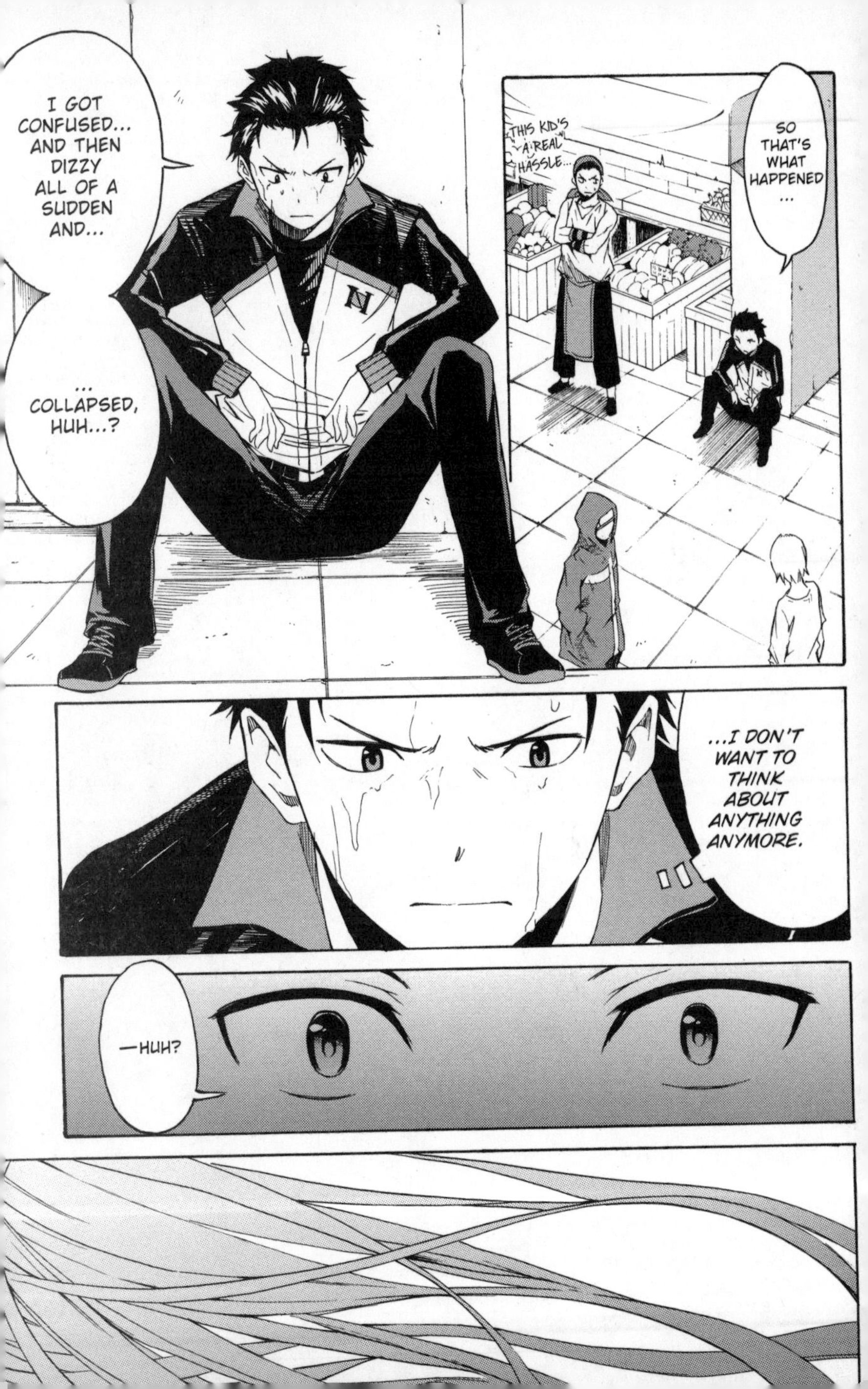
SO THAT'S WHAT HAPPENED...
THIS KID'S A REAL HASSLE...
I GOT CONFUSED... AND THEN DIZZY ALL OF A SUDDEN AND...
...COLLAPSED, HUH...?
...I DON'T WANT TO THINK ABOUT ANYTHING ANYMORE.
—HUH?

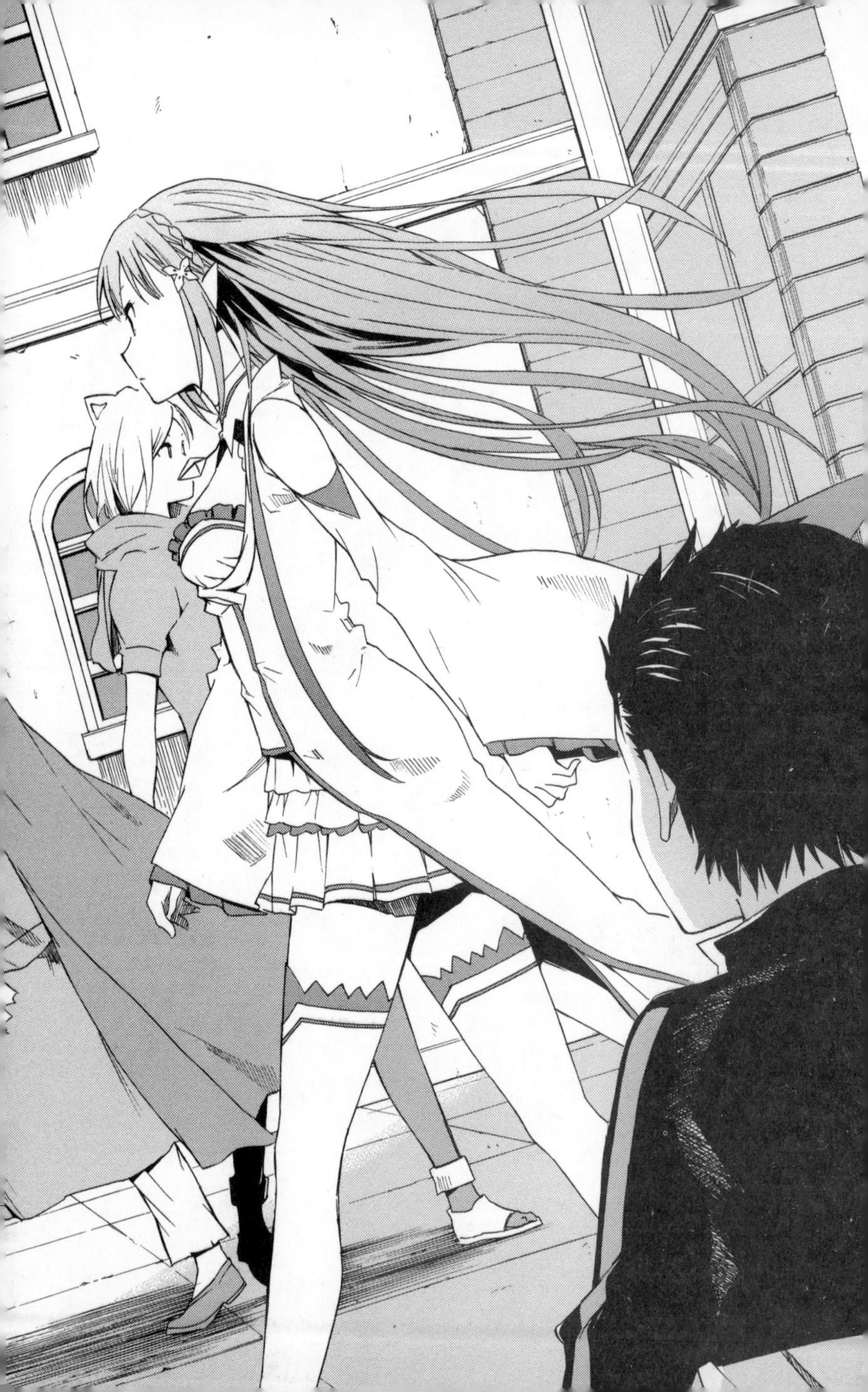

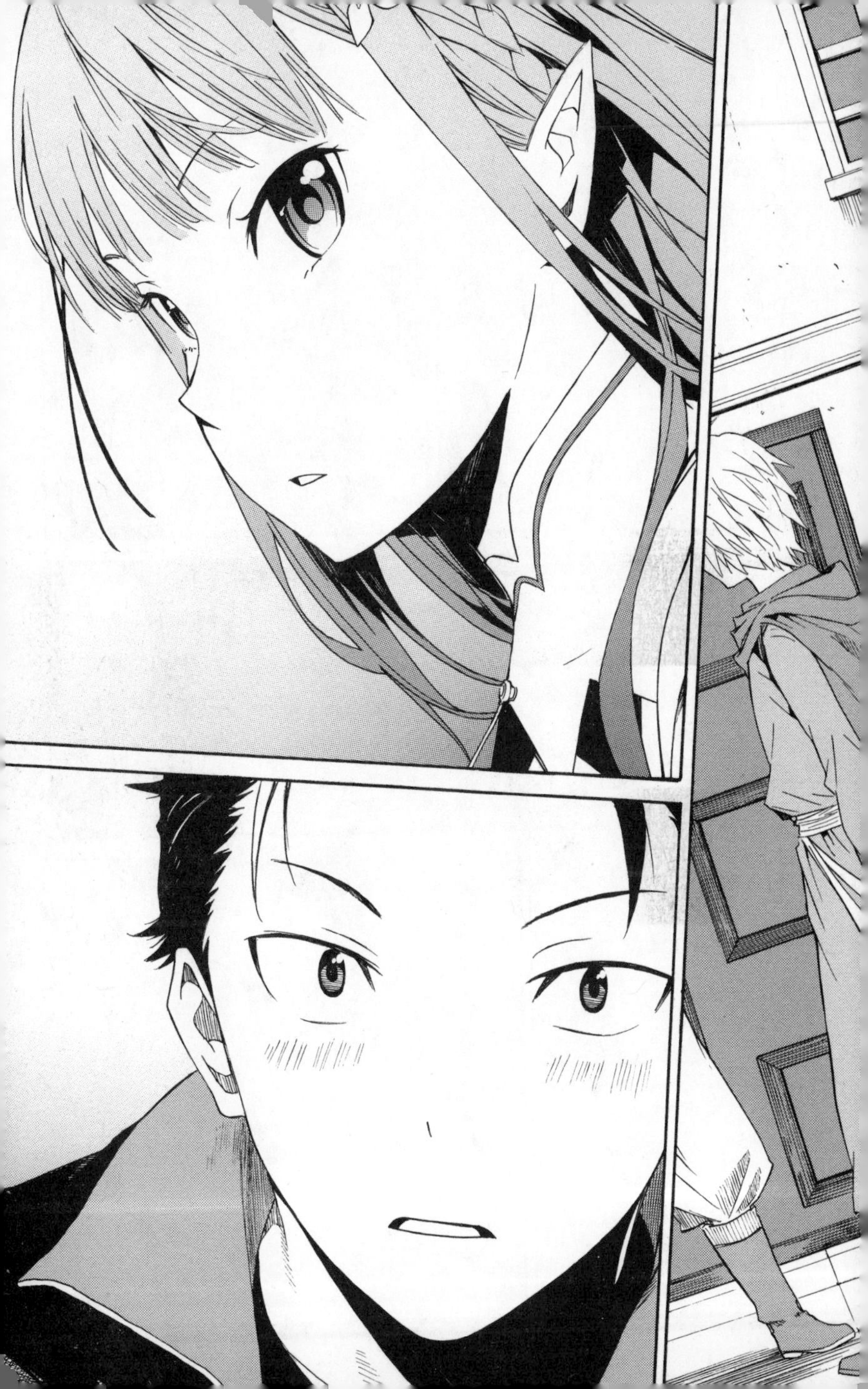

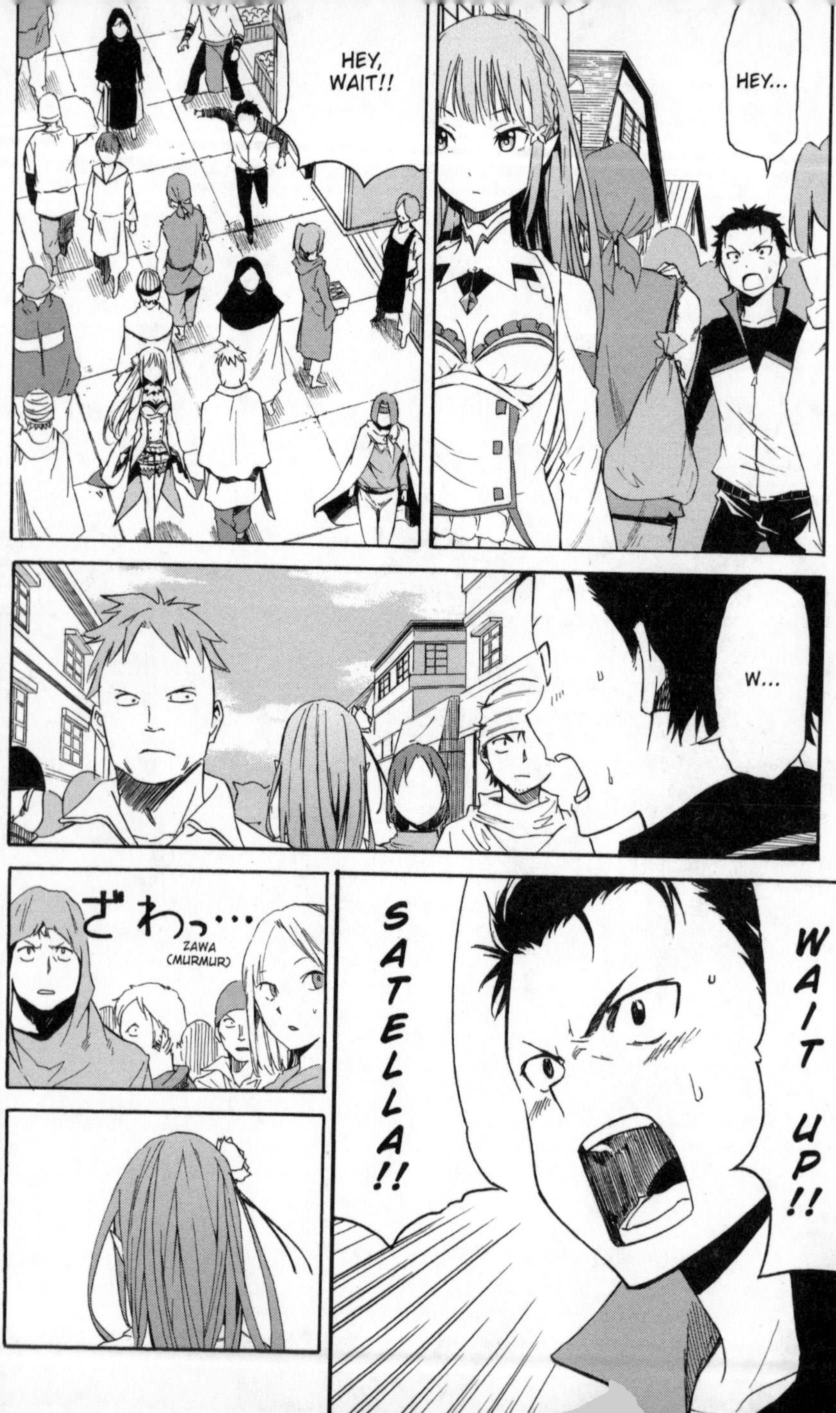
HEY...
HEY, WAIT!!
W...
WAIT UP!!
SATELLA!!
ざわっ…
ZAWA (MURMUR)

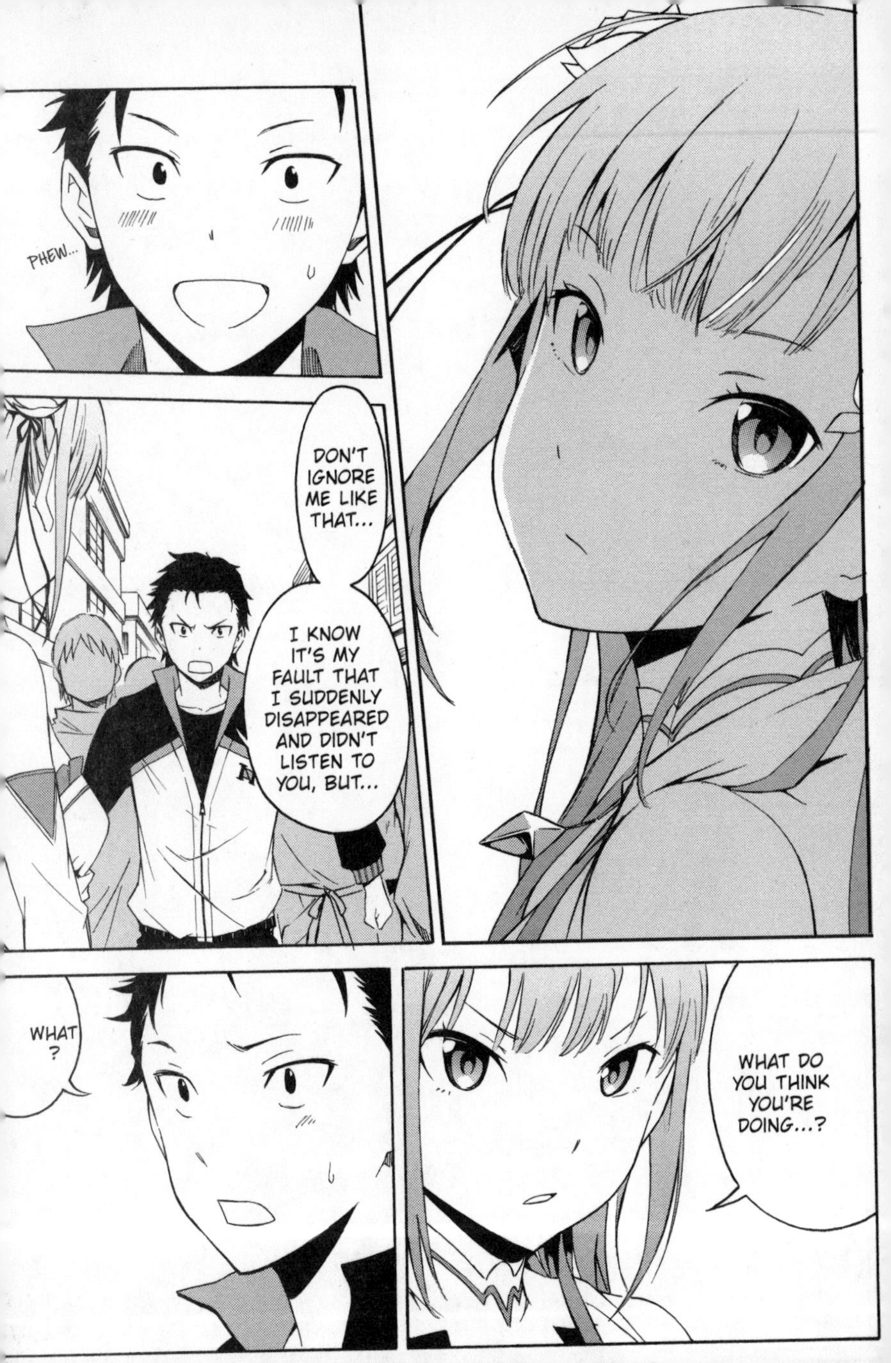
PHEW...
DON'T IGNORE ME LIKE THAT...
I KNOW IT'S MY FAULT THAT I SUDDENLY DISAPPEARED AND DIDN'T LISTEN TO YOU, BUT...
WHAT DO YOU THINK YOU'RE DOING...?
WHAT?

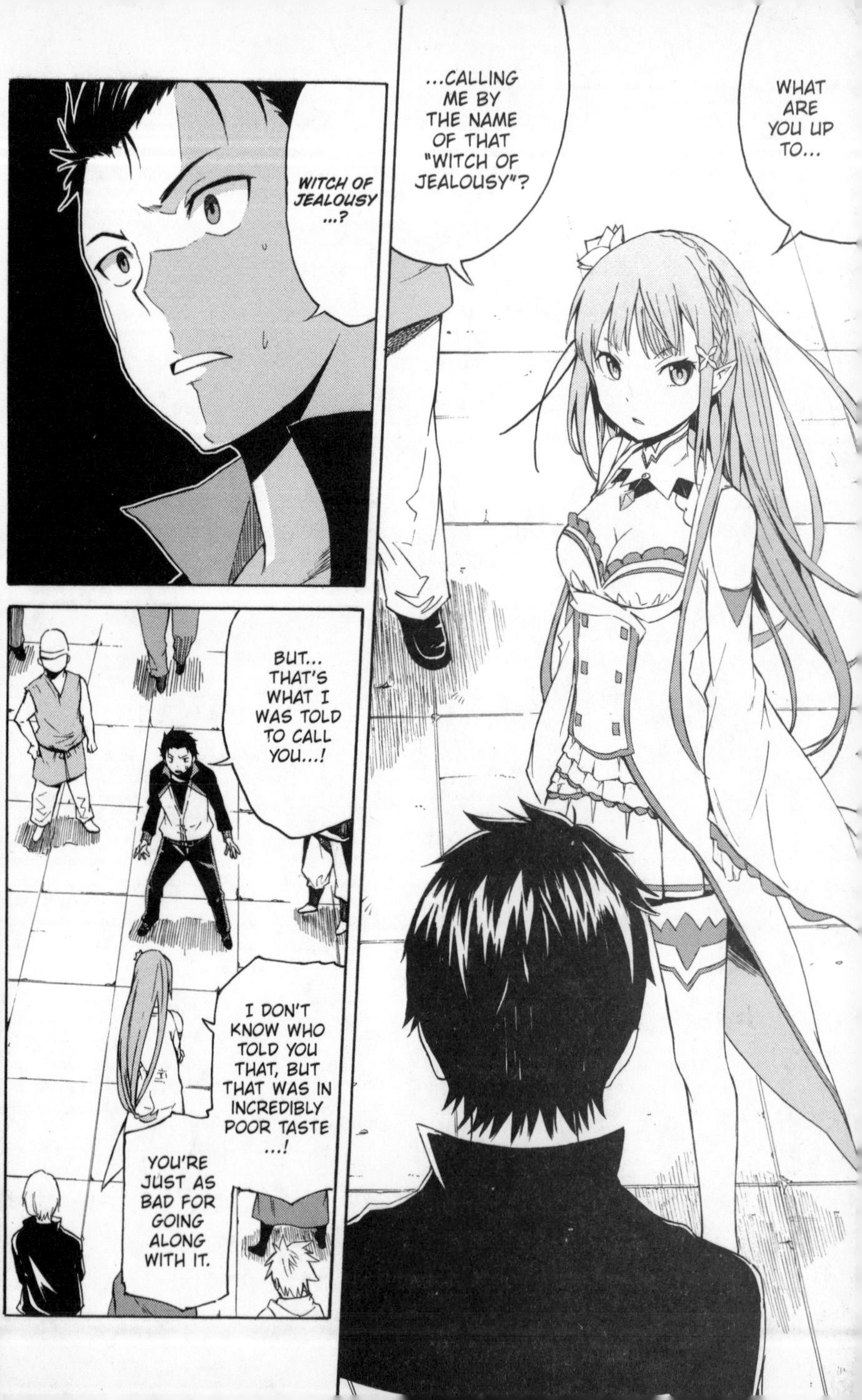
WHAT ARE YOU UP TO...
...CALLING ME BY THE NAME OF THAT "WITCH OF JEALOUSY"?
WITCH OF JEALOUSY ...?
BUT... THAT'S WHAT I WAS TOLD TO CALL YOU...!
I DON'T KNOW WHO TOLD YOU THAT, BUT THAT WAS IN INCREDIBLY POOR TASTE ...!
YOU'RE JUST AS BAD FOR GOING ALONG WITH IT.

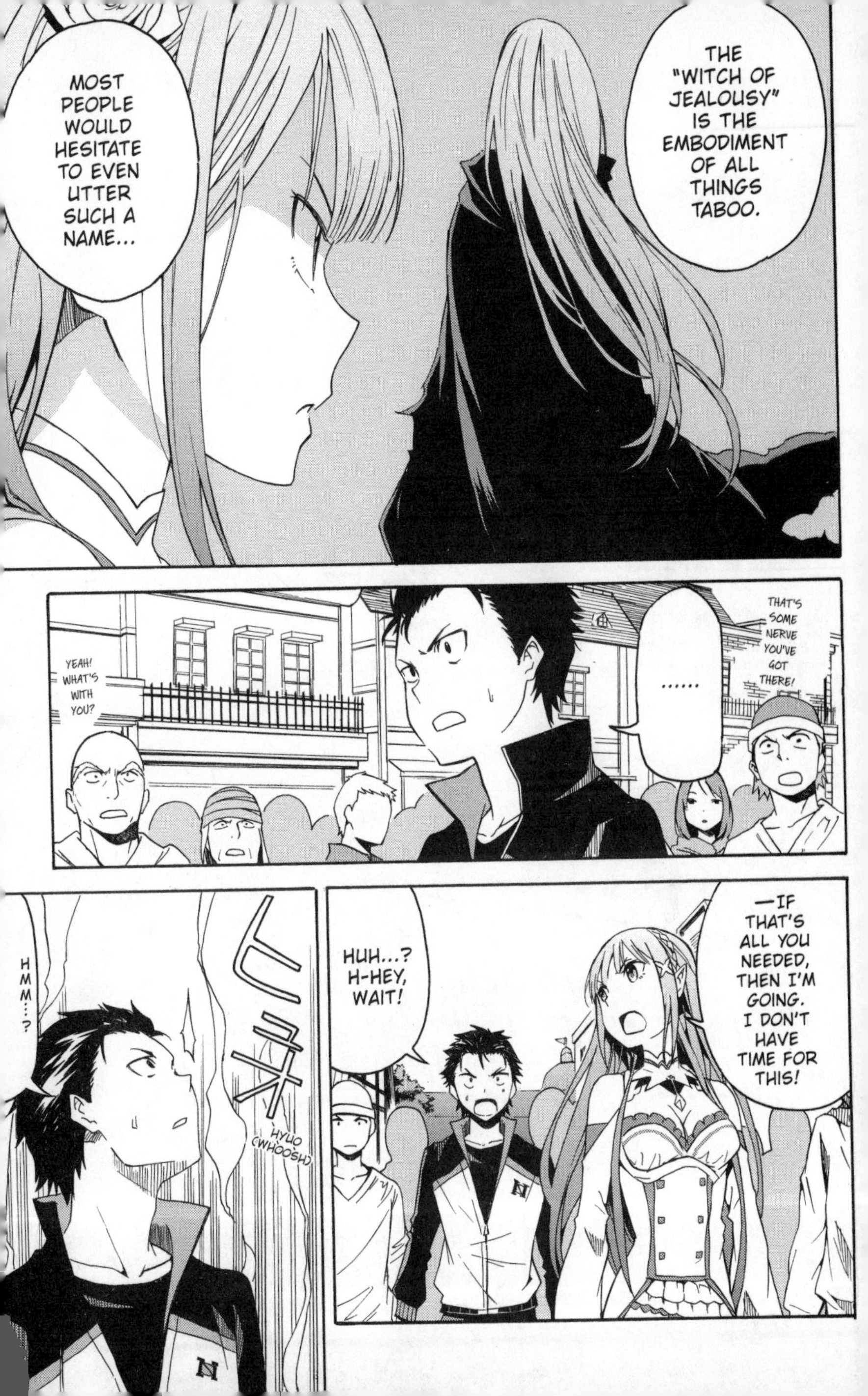
THE "WITCH OF JEALOUSY" IS THE EMBODIMENT OF ALL THINGS TABOO.
MOST PEOPLE WOULD HESITATE TO EVEN UTTER SUCH A NAME...
THAT'S SOME NERVE YOU'VE GOT THERE!
......
YEAH! WHAT'S WITH YOU?
—IF THAT'S ALL YOU NEEDED, THEN I'M GOING. I DON'T HAVE TIME FOR THIS!
HUH...? H-HEY, WAIT!
HYUO (WHOOSH)
HMM...?

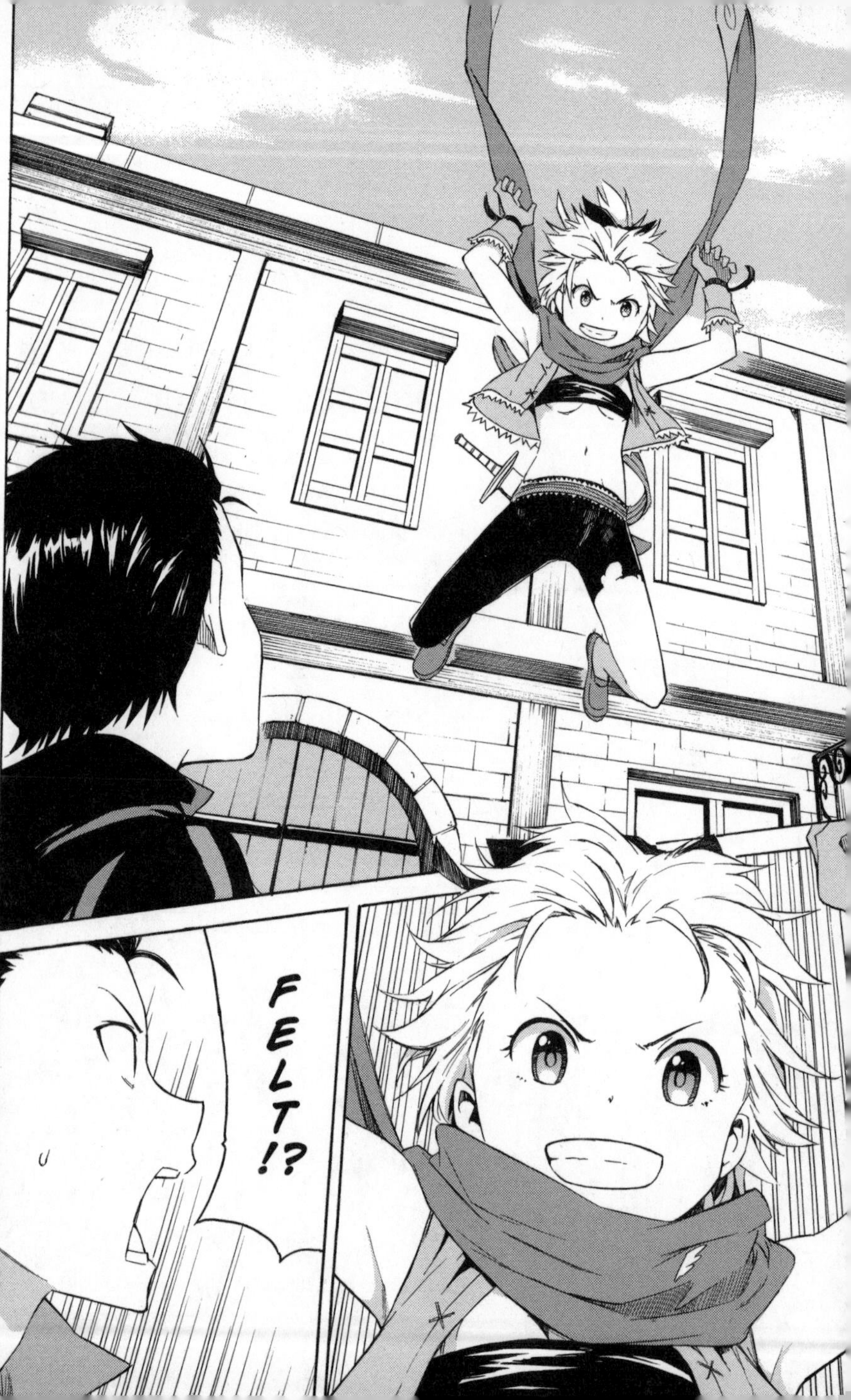
FELT!?

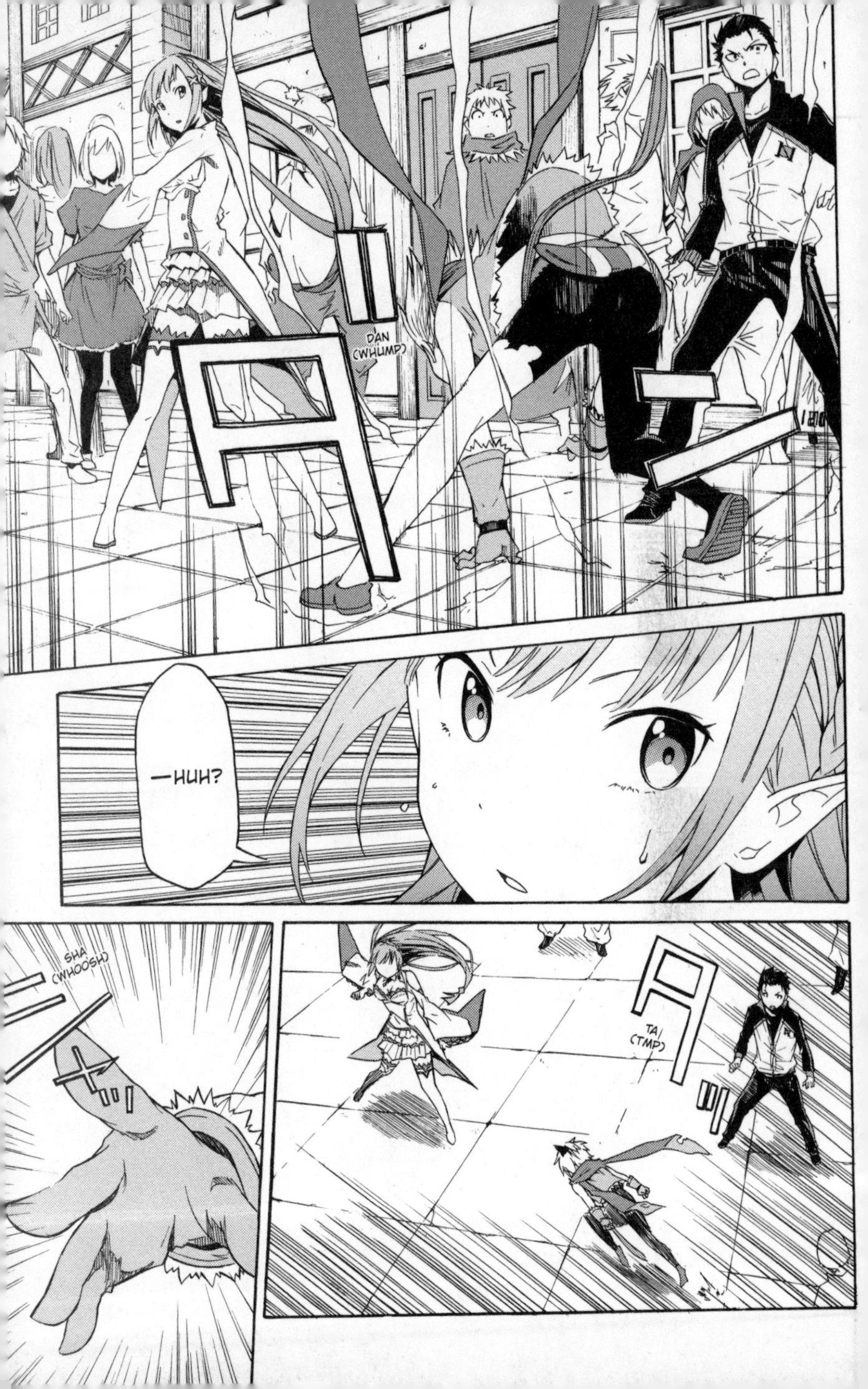
DAN (WHUMP)
—HUH?
TA! (TMP)
SHA (WHOOSH)

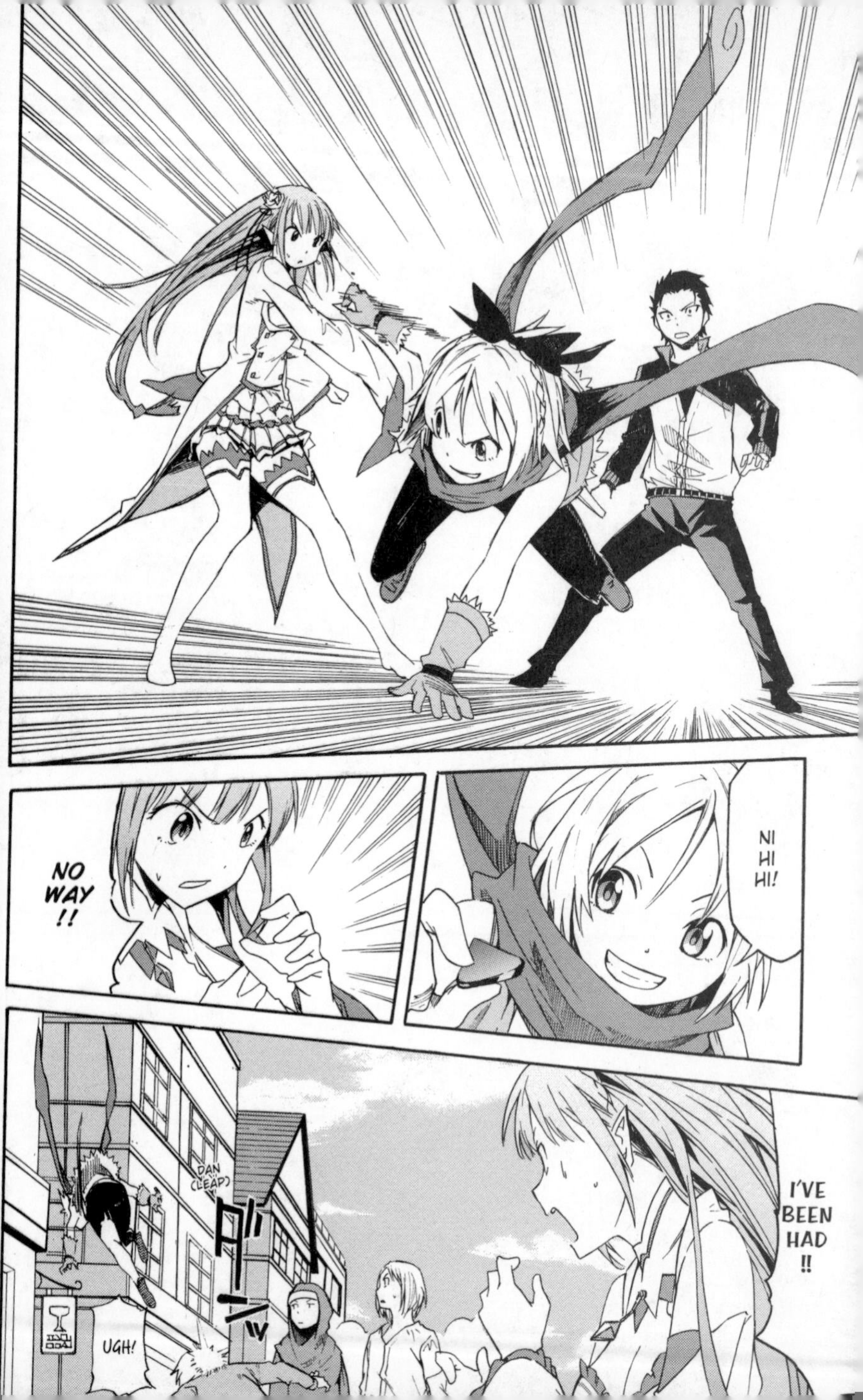
NI HI HI!
NO WAY !!
I'VE BEEN HAD !!
DAN (LEAP)
UGH!

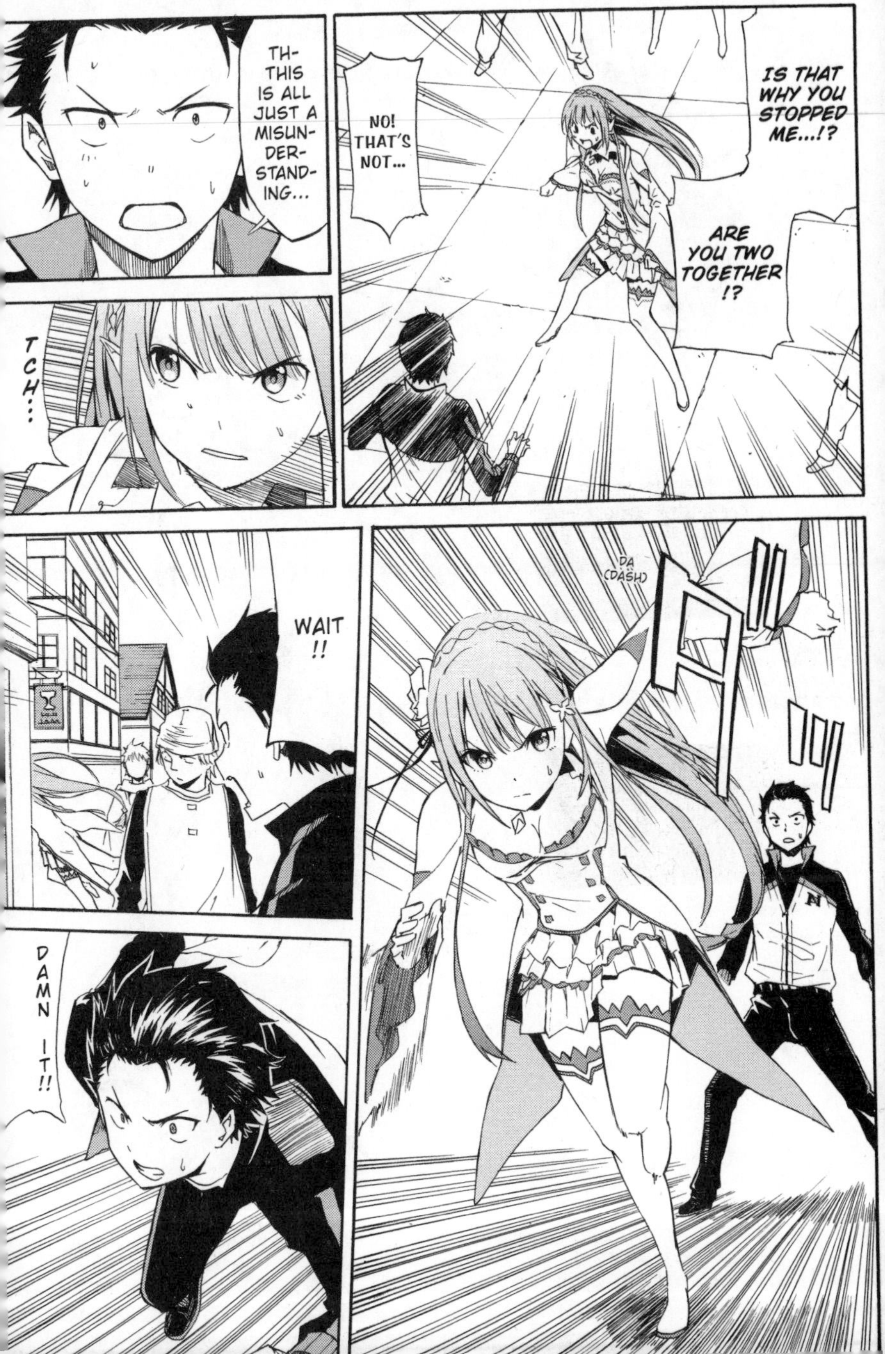
IS THAT WHY YOU STOPPED ME...!?
ARE YOU TWO TOGETHER !?
NO! THAT'S NOT...
TH-THIS IS ALL JUST A MISUNDERSTANDING...
TCH...
DA (DASH)
WAIT !!
DAMN IT!!

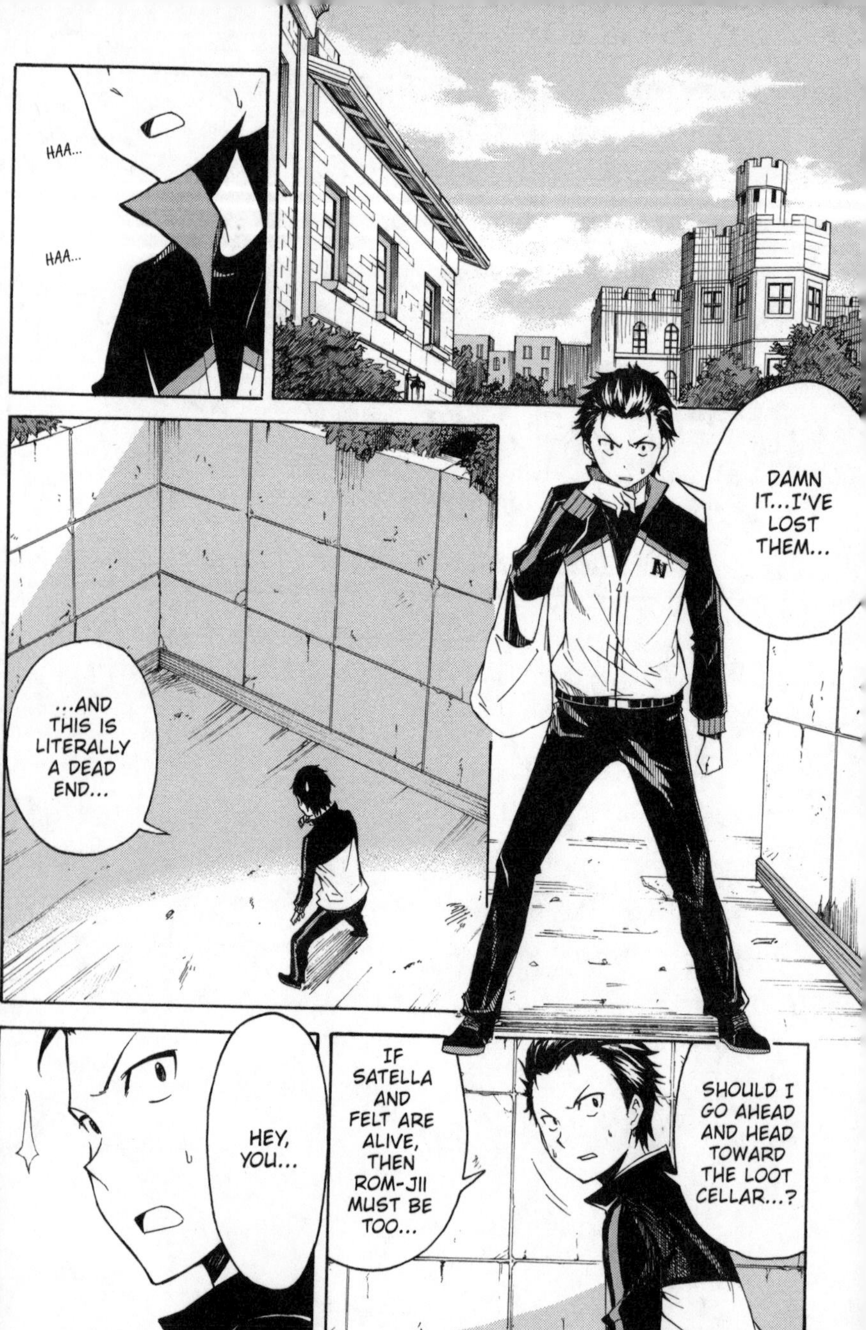
HAA...
HAA...
DAMN IT...I'VE LOST THEM...
...AND THIS IS LITERALLY A DEAD END...
SHOULD I GO AHEAD AND HEAD TOWARD THE LOOT CELLAR...?
IF SATELLA AND FELT ARE ALIVE, THEN ROM-JII MUST BE TOO...
HEY, YOU...

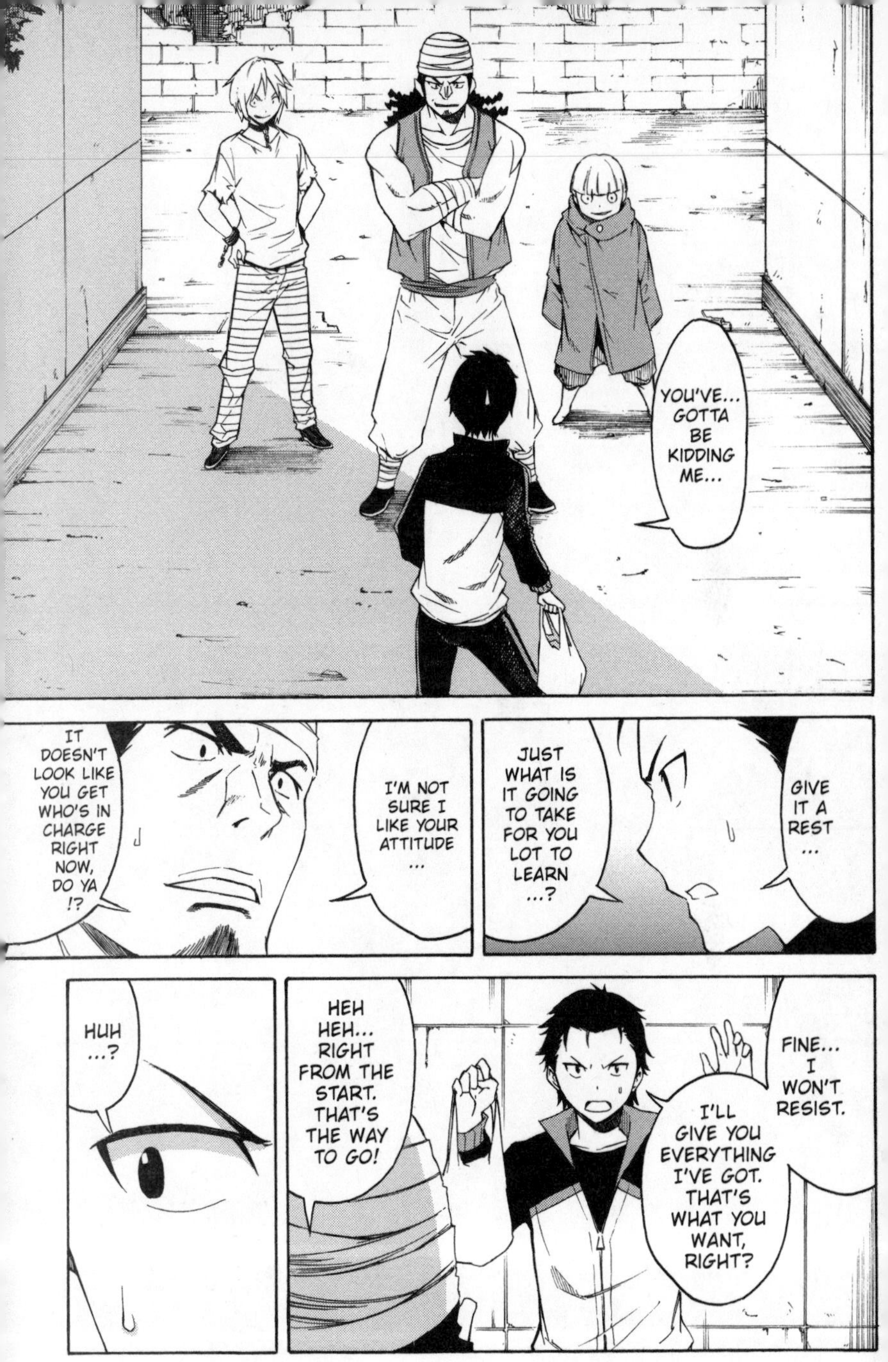

YOU'VE... GOTTA BE KIDDING ME...
GIVE IT A REST ...
JUST WHAT IS IT GOING TO TAKE FOR YOU LOT TO LEARN ...?
I'M NOT SURE I LIKE YOUR ATTITUDE ...
IT DOESN'T LOOK LIKE YOU GET WHO'S IN CHARGE RIGHT NOW, DO YA !?
FINE... I WON'T RESIST.
I'LL GIVE YOU EVERYTHING I'VE GOT. THAT'S WHAT YOU WANT, RIGHT?
HEH HEH... RIGHT FROM THE START. THAT'S THE WAY TO GO!
HUH ...?

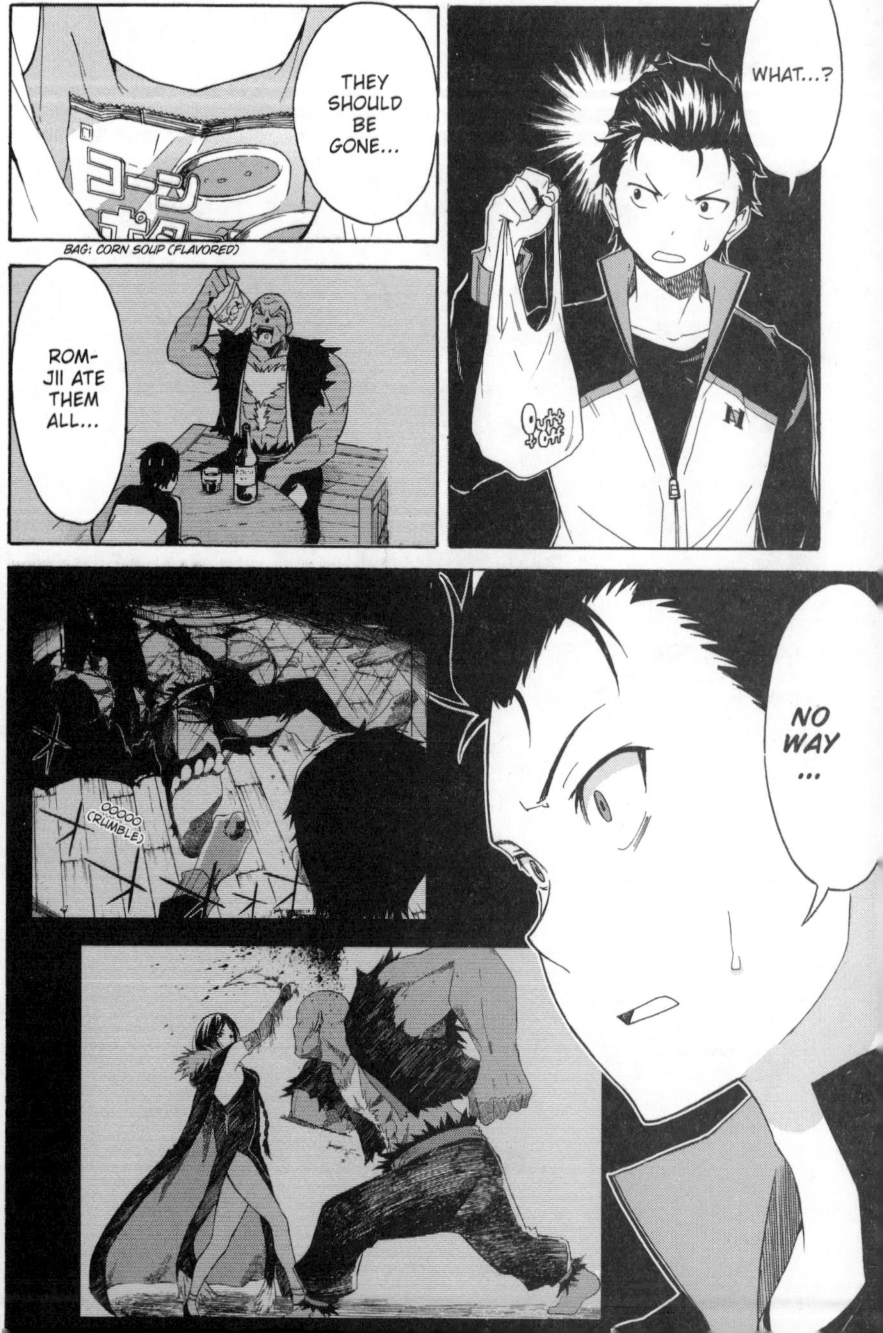
WHAT...?
THEY SHOULD BE GONE...
BAG: CORN SOUP (FLAVORED)
ROM-JII ATE THEM ALL...
NO WAY ...
OOOOO (RUMBLE)

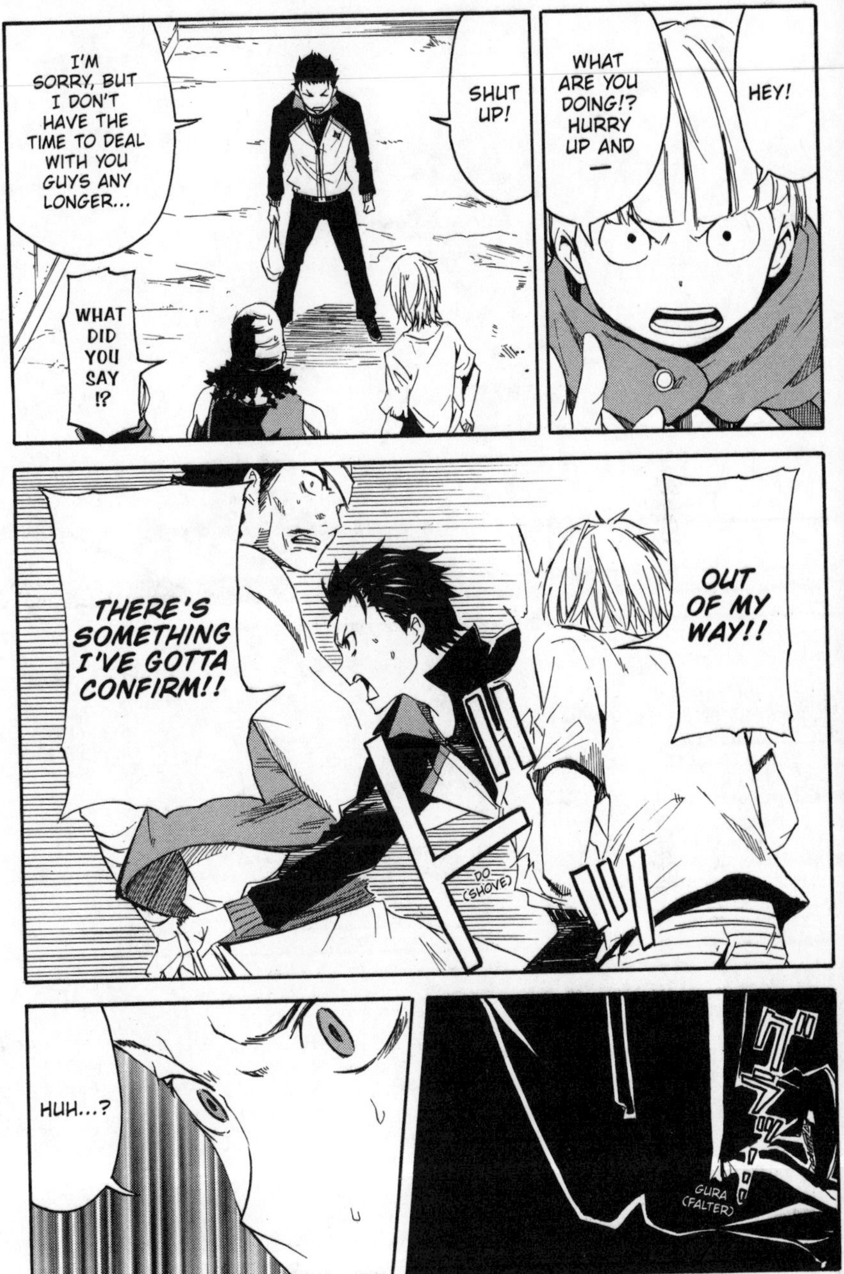
HEY!
WHAT ARE YOU DOING!? HURRY UP AND —
SHUT UP!
I'M SORRY, BUT I DON'T HAVE THE TIME TO DEAL WITH YOU GUYS ANY LONGER...
WHAT DID YOU SAY !?
OUT OF MY WAY!!
THERE'S SOMETHING I'VE GOTTA CONFIRM!!
DO (SHOVE)
GURA (FALTER)
HUH...?

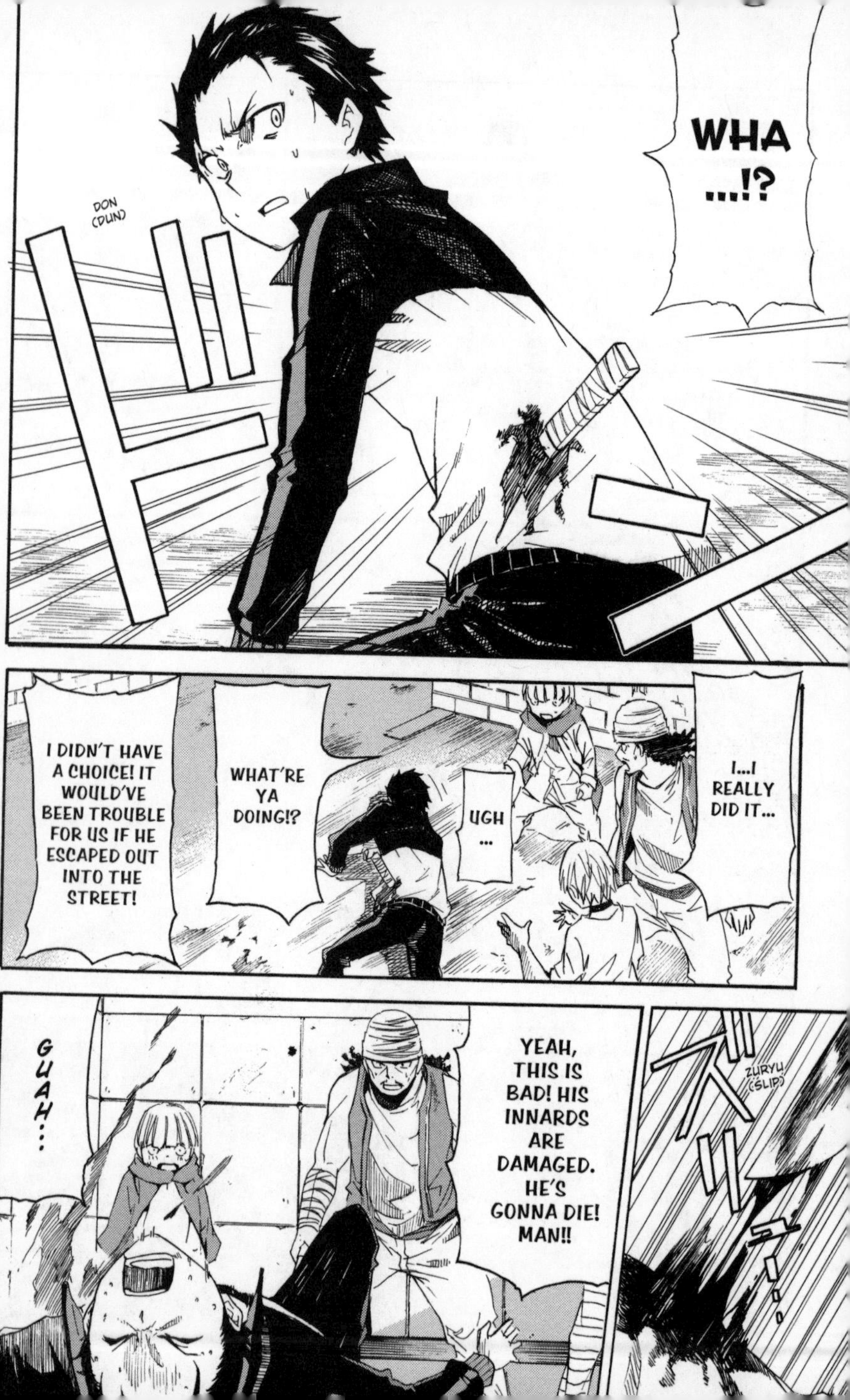
WHA ...!?
DON (DUN)
I...I REALLY DID IT...
UGH ...
WHAT'RE YA DOING!?
I DIDN'T HAVE A CHOICE! IT WOULD'VE BEEN TROUBLE FOR US IF HE ESCAPED OUT INTO THE STREET!
ZURYU (SLIP)
YEAH, THIS IS BAD! HIS INNARDS ARE DAMAGED. HE'S GONNA DIE! MAN!!
GUAH...

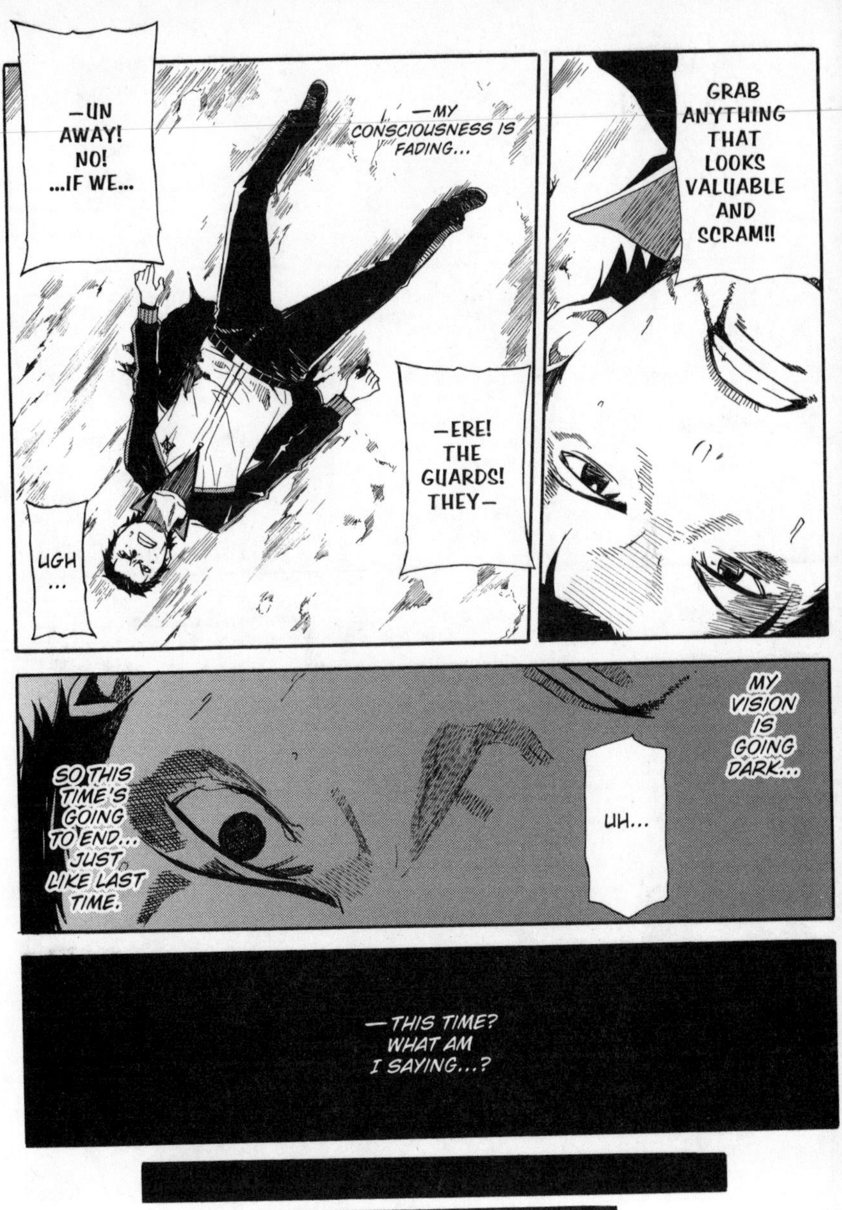
GRAB ANYTHING THAT LOOKS VALUABLE AND SCRAM!!
—MY CONSCIOUSNESS IS FADING...
—UN AWAY! NO! ...IF WE...
—ERE! THE GUARDS! THEY—
UGH...
MY VISION IS GOING DARK...
UH...
SO THIS TIME'S GOING TO END... JUST LIKE LAST TIME.
—THIS TIME? WHAT AM I SAYING...?

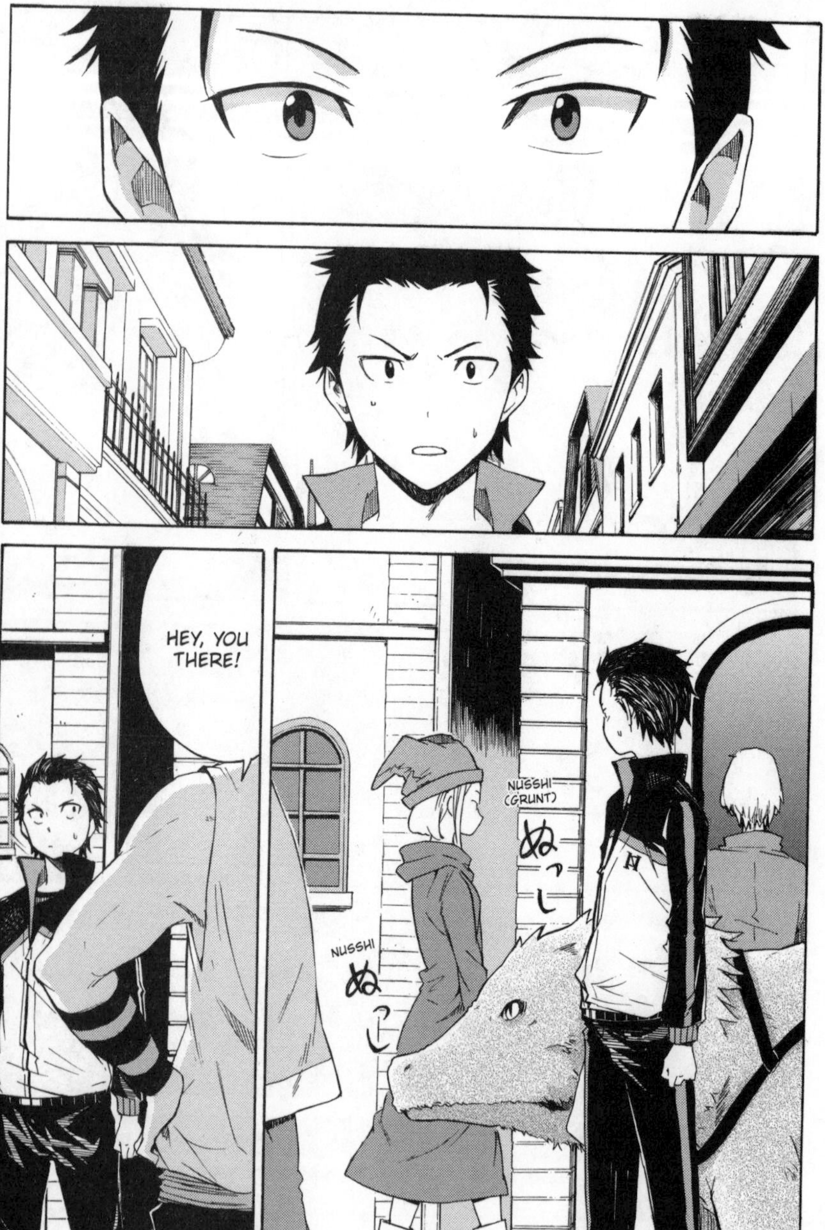
HEY, YOU THERE!
NUSSHI (GRUNT)
ぬっし
NUSSHI
ぬっし

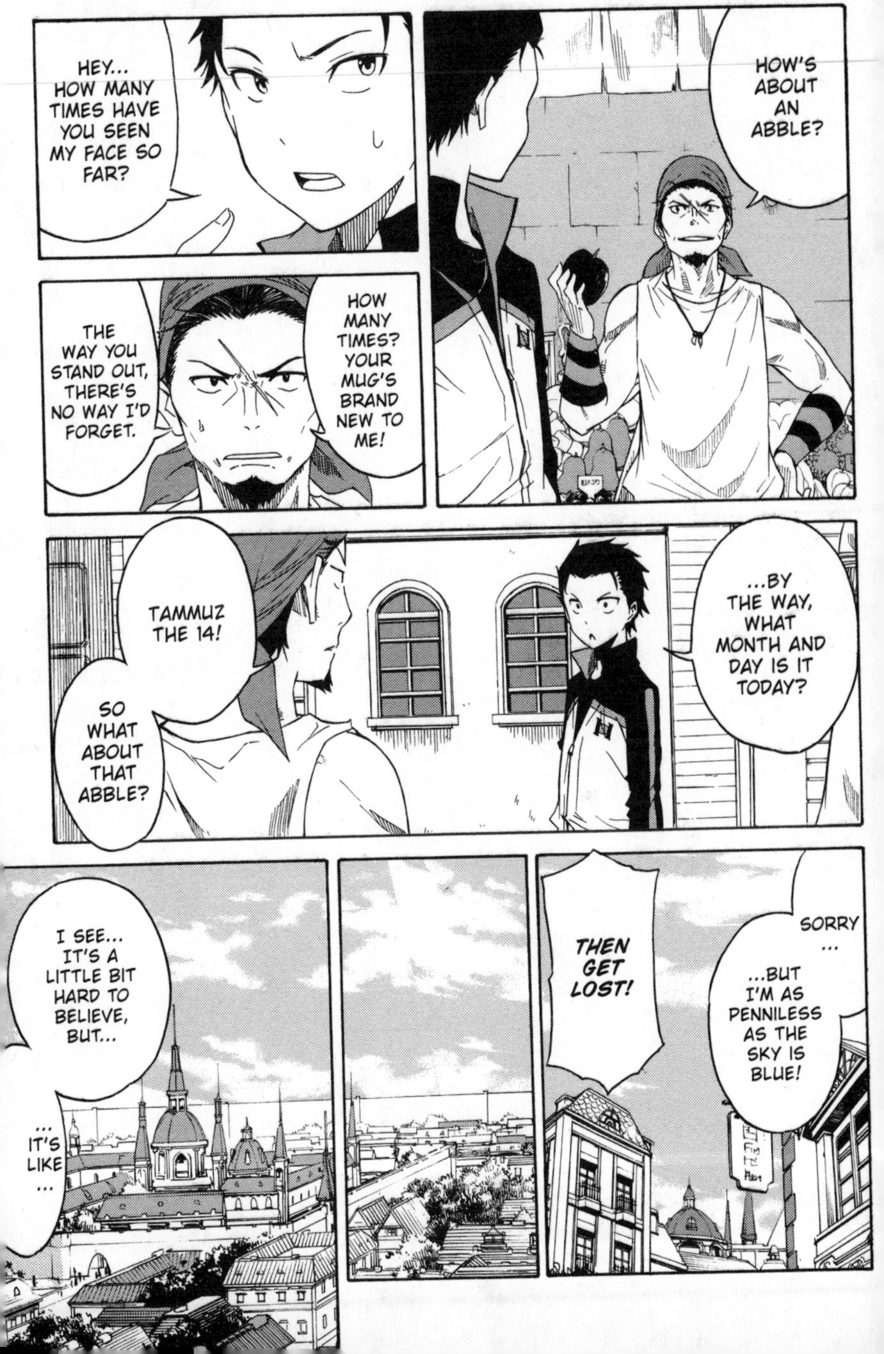
HOW'S ABOUT AN ABBLE?
HEY... HOW MANY TIMES HAVE YOU SEEN MY FACE SO FAR?
HOW MANY TIMES? YOUR MUG'S BRAND NEW TO ME!
THE WAY YOU STAND OUT, THERE'S NO WAY I'D FORGET.
...BY THE WAY, WHAT MONTH AND DAY IS IT TODAY?
TAMMUZ THE 14!
SO WHAT ABOUT THAT ABBLE?
SORRY...
...BUT I'M AS PENNILESS AS THE SKY IS BLUE!
THEN GET LOST!
I SEE... IT'S A LITTLE BIT HARD TO BELIEVE, BUT...
...IT'S LIKE...

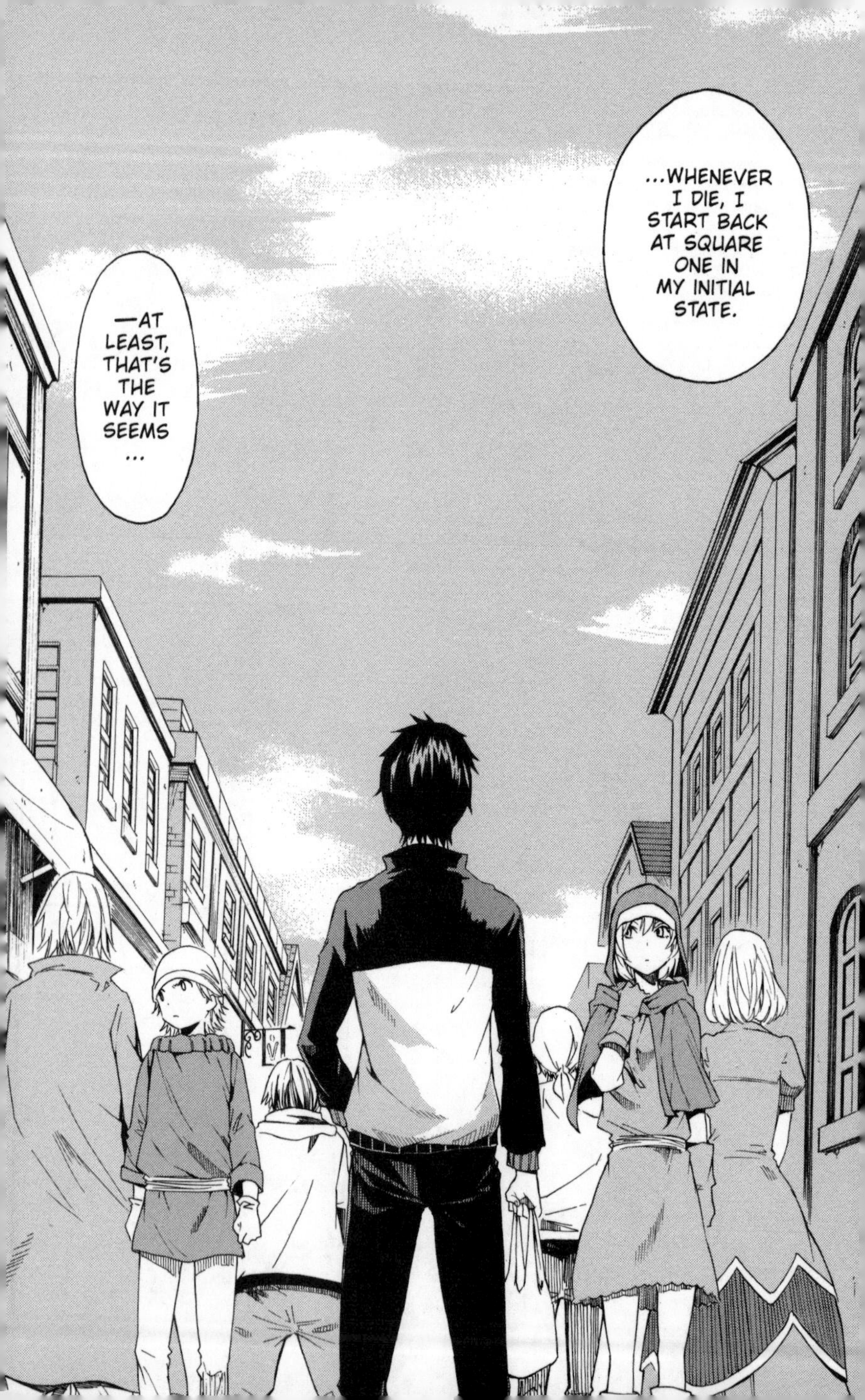
...WHENEVER I DIE, I START BACK AT SQUARE ONE IN MY INITIAL STATE.
—AT LEAST, THAT'S THE WAY IT SEEMS...

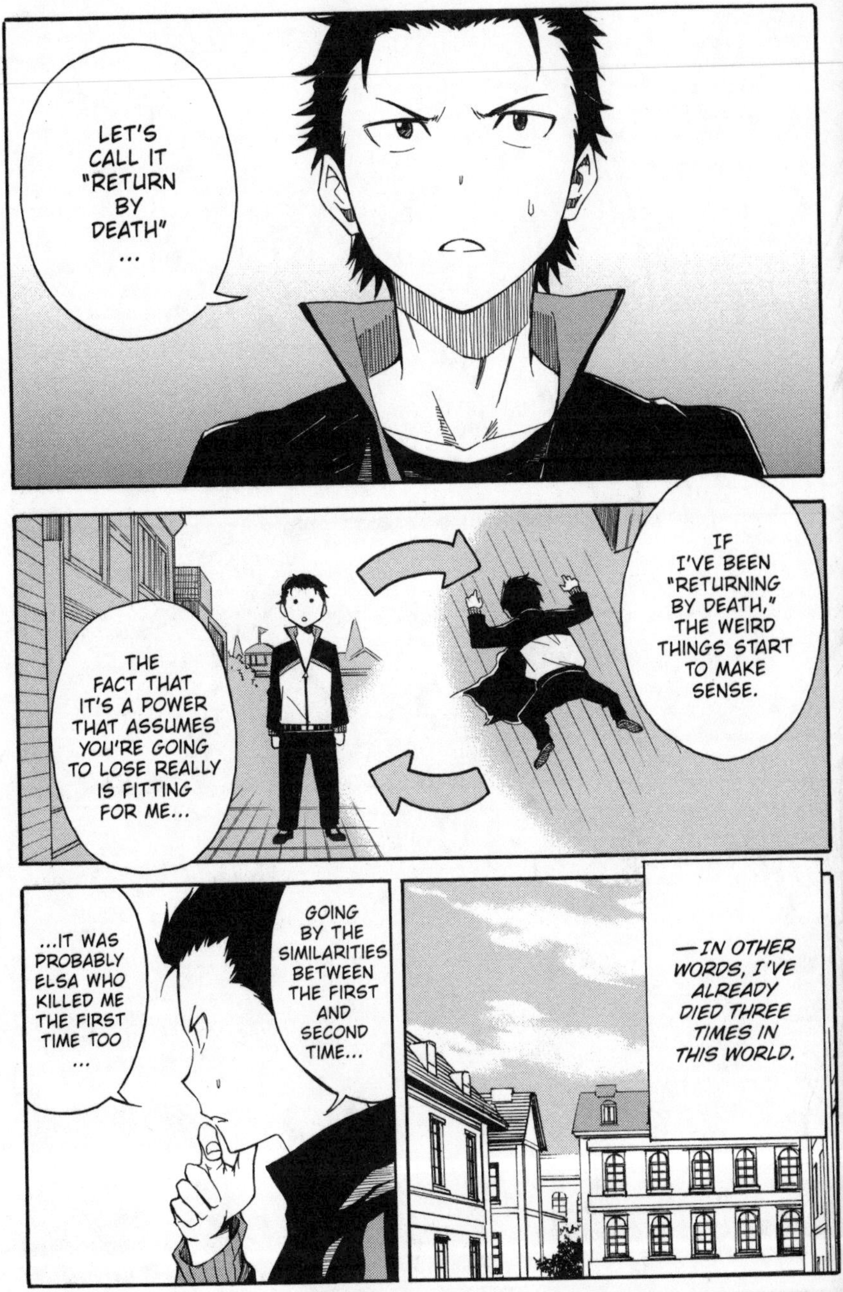
LET'S CALL IT "RETURN BY DEATH" ...
IF I'VE BEEN "RETURNING BY DEATH," THE WEIRD THINGS START TO MAKE SENSE.
THE FACT THAT IT'S A POWER THAT ASSUMES YOU'RE GOING TO LOSE REALLY IS FITTING FOR ME...
—IN OTHER WORDS, I'VE ALREADY DIED THREE TIMES IN THIS WORLD.
GOING BY THE SIMILARITIES BETWEEN THE FIRST AND SECOND TIME...
...IT WAS PROBABLY ELSA WHO KILLED ME THE FIRST TIME TOO ...

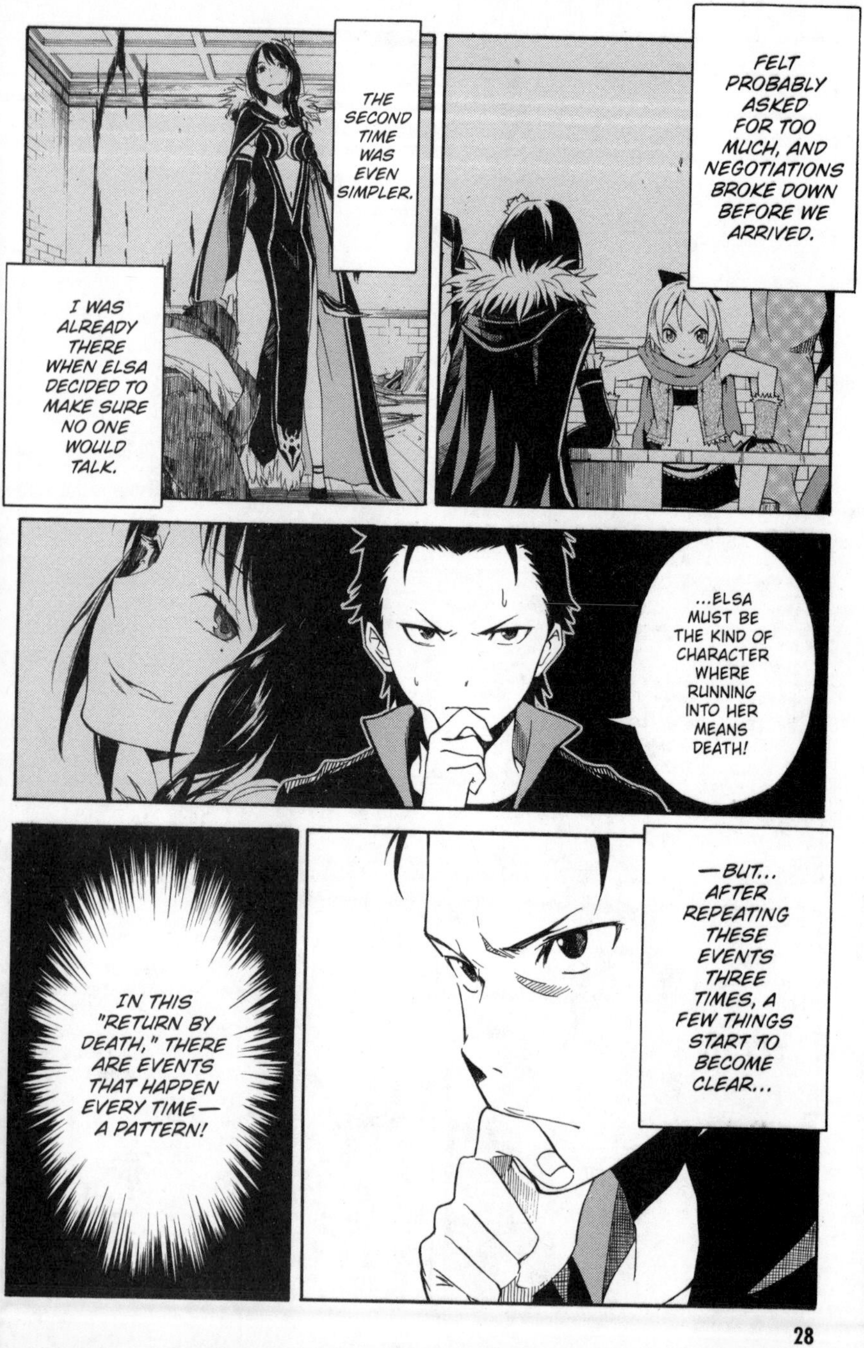
FELT PROBABLY ASKED FOR TOO MUCH, AND NEGOTIATIONS BROKE DOWN BEFORE WE ARRIVED.
THE SECOND TIME WAS EVEN SIMPLER.
I WAS ALREADY THERE WHEN ELSA DECIDED TO MAKE SURE NO ONE WOULD TALK.
...ELSA MUST BE THE KIND OF CHARACTER WHERE RUNNING INTO HER MEANS DEATH!
—BUT... AFTER REPEATING THESE EVENTS THREE TIMES, A FEW THINGS START TO BECOME CLEAR...
IN THIS "RETURN BY DEATH," THERE ARE EVENTS THAT HAPPEN EVERY TIME—A PATTERN!

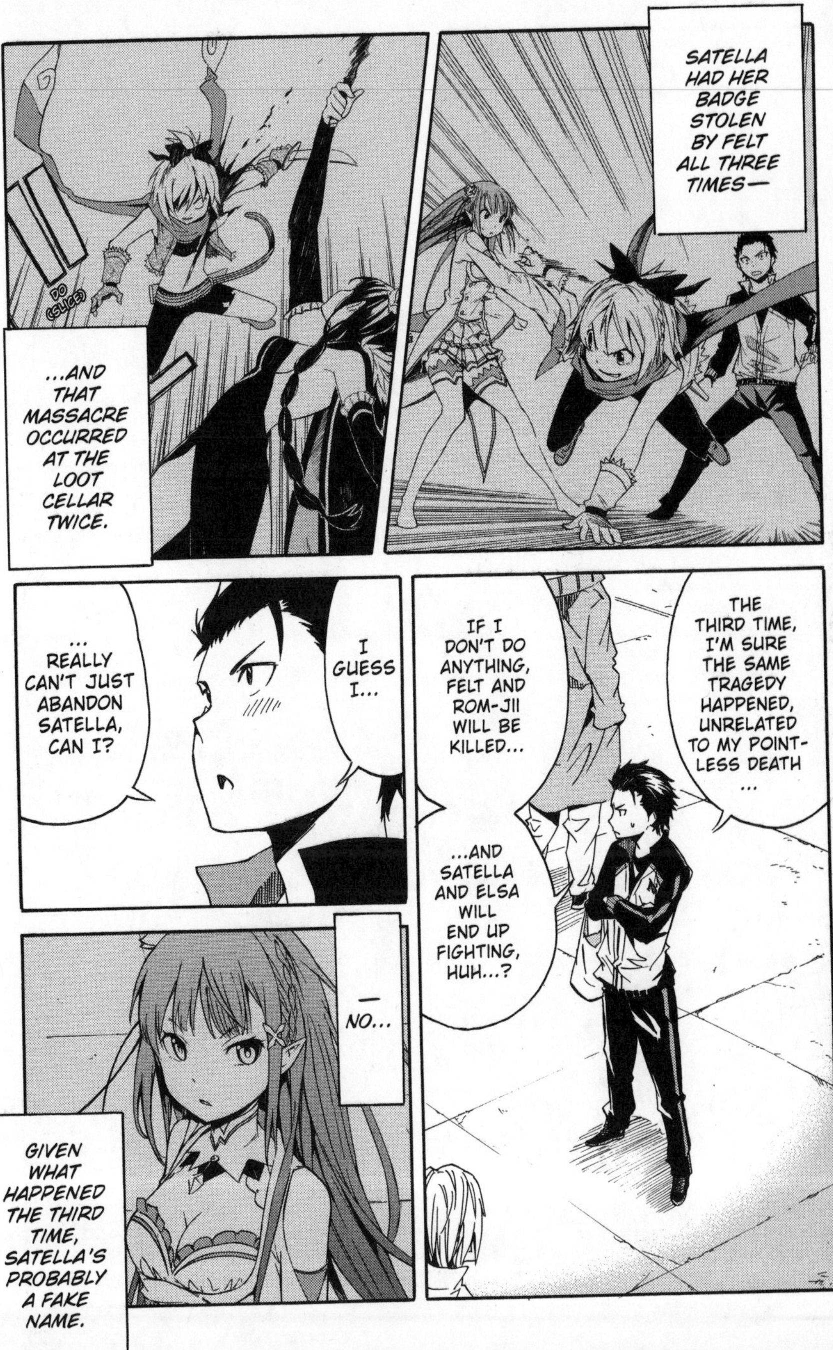
SATELLA HAD HER BADGE STOLEN BY FELT ALL THREE TIMES—
DO (SLICE)
...AND THAT MASSACRE OCCURRED AT THE LOOT CELLAR TWICE.
THE THIRD TIME, I'M SURE THE SAME TRAGEDY HAPPENED, UNRELATED TO MY POINTLESS DEATH ...
IF I DON'T DO ANYTHING, FELT AND ROM-JII WILL BE KILLED...
...AND SATELLA AND ELSA WILL END UP FIGHTING, HUH...?
I GUESS I...
...REALLY CAN'T JUST ABANDON SATELLA, CAN I?
—NO...
GIVEN WHAT HAPPENED THE THIRD TIME, SATELLA'S PROBABLY A FAKE NAME.

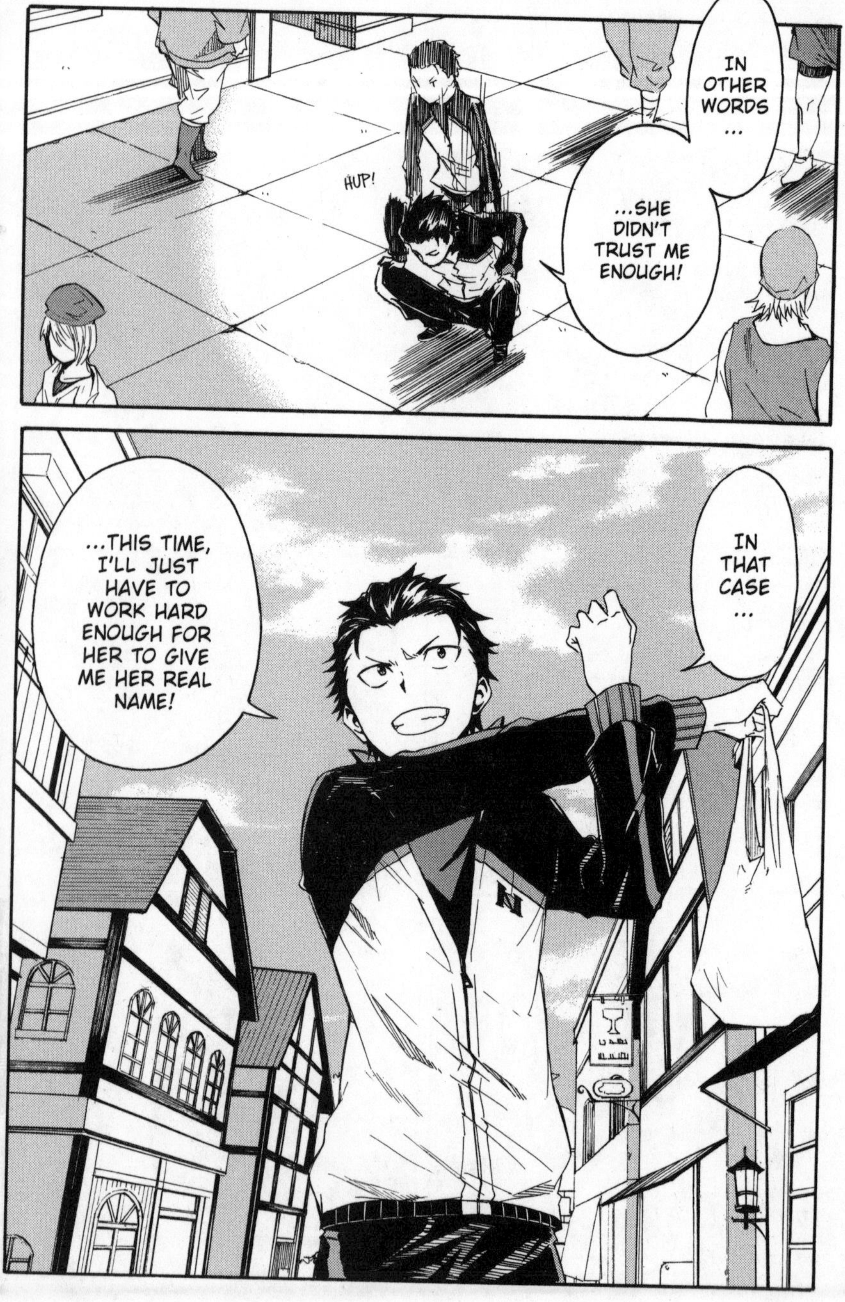
IN OTHER WORDS...
...SHE DIDN'T TRUST ME ENOUGH!
HUP!
IN THAT CASE...
...THIS TIME, I'LL JUST HAVE TO WORK HARD ENOUGH FOR HER TO GIVE ME HER REAL NAME!

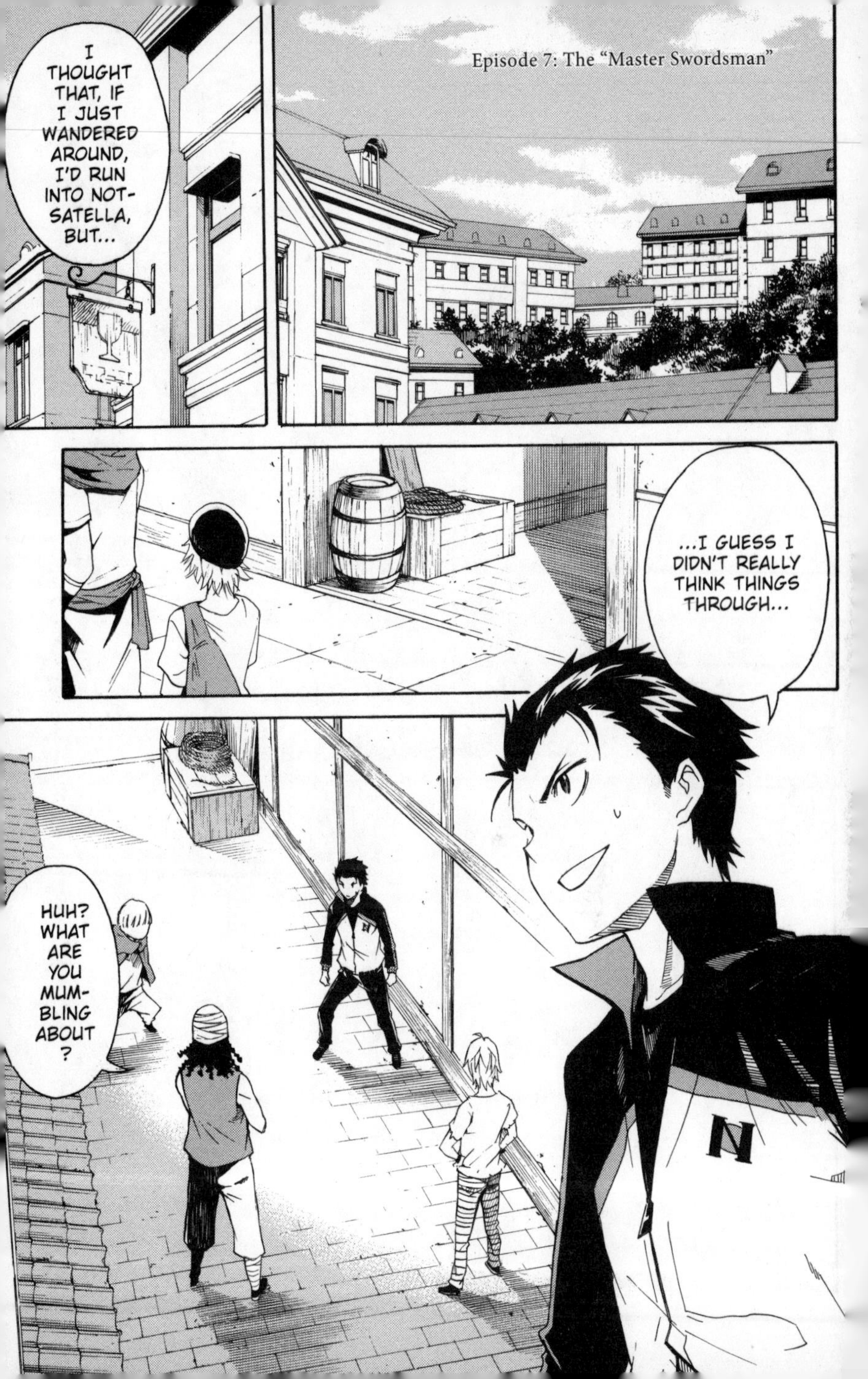
Episode 7: The "Master Swordsman"
I THOUGHT THAT, IF I JUST WANDERED AROUND, I'D RUN INTO NOT-SATELLA, BUT...
...I GUESS I DIDN'T REALLY THINK THINGS THROUGH...
HUH? WHAT ARE YOU MUMBLING ABOUT?

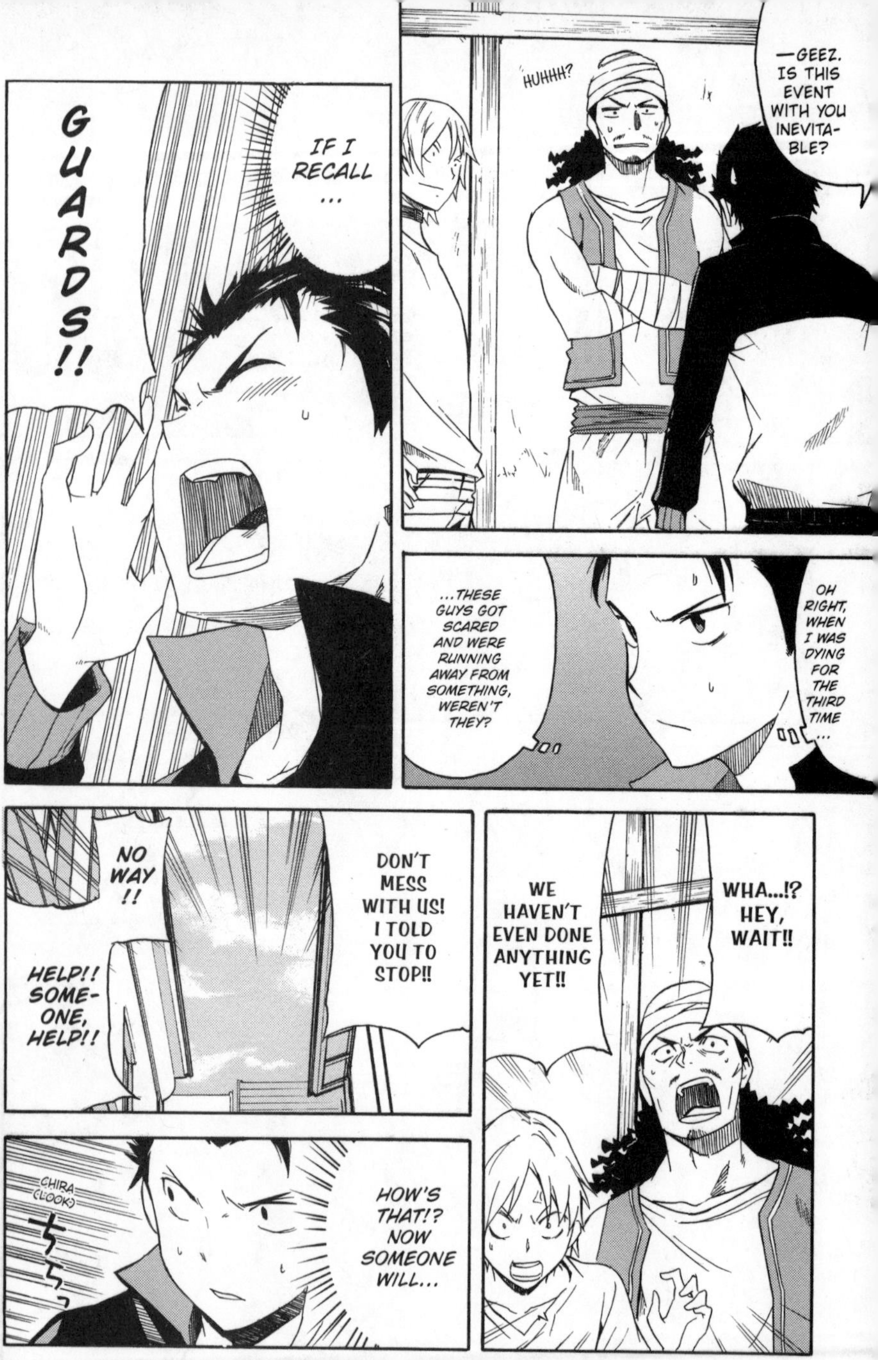
—GEEZ. IS THIS EVENT WITH YOU INEVITA-BLE?
HUHHH?
OH RIGHT, WHEN I WAS DYING FOR THE THIRD TIME...
...THESE GUYS GOT SCARED AND WERE RUNNING AWAY FROM SOMETHING, WEREN'T THEY?
IF I RECALL...
GUARDS!!
WHA...!? HEY, WAIT!!
WE HAVEN'T EVEN DONE ANYTHING YET!!
DON'T MESS WITH US! I TOLD YOU TO STOP!!
NO WAY!!
HELP!! SOME-ONE, HELP!!
HOW'S THAT!? NOW SOMEONE WILL...
CHIRA (LOOK)

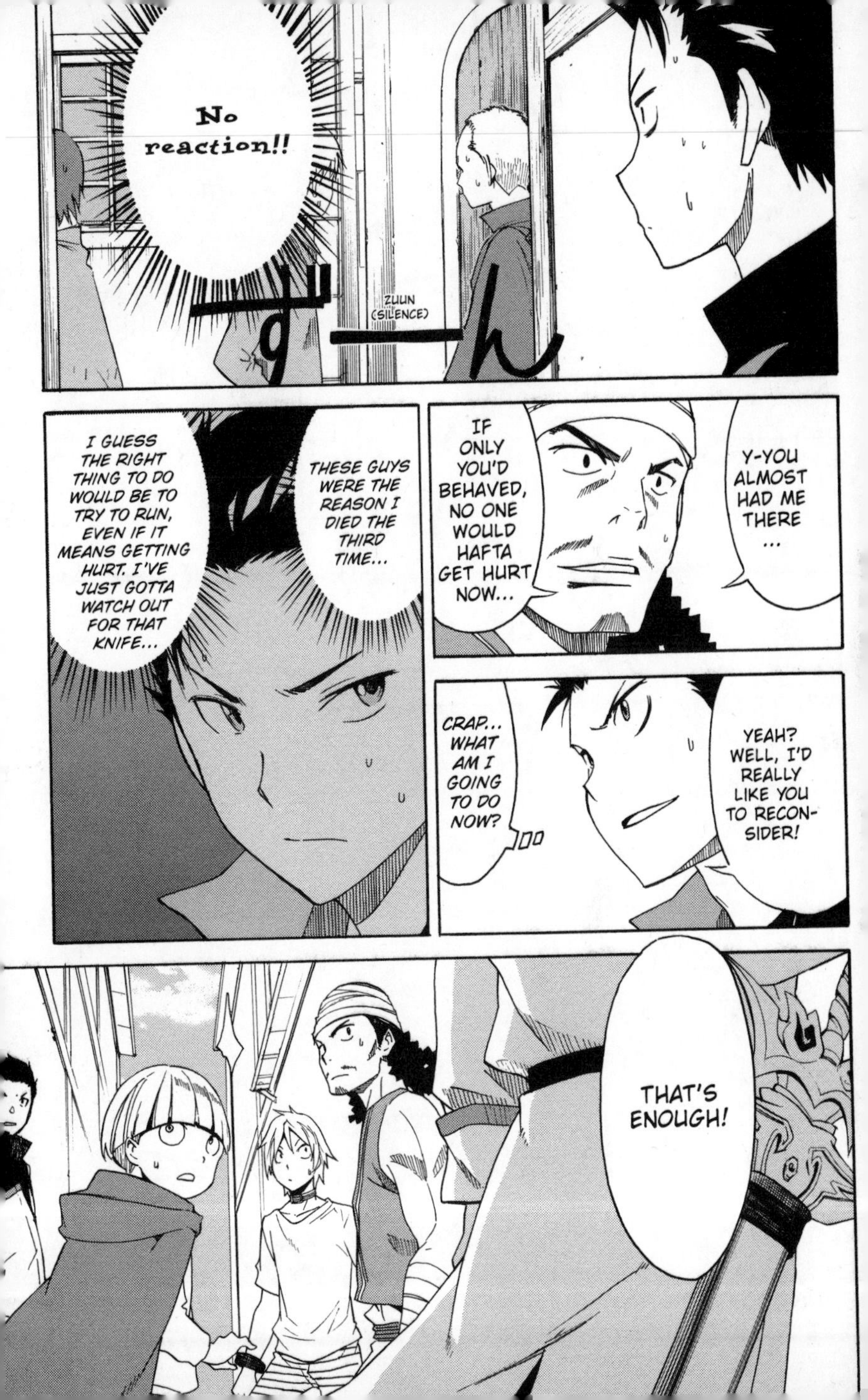
No reaction!!
ZUUN (SILENCE)
Y-YOU ALMOST HAD ME THERE ...
IF ONLY YOU'D BEHAVED, NO ONE WOULD HAFTA GET HURT NOW...
YEAH? WELL, I'D REALLY LIKE YOU TO RECON-SIDER!
CRAP... WHAT AM I GOING TO DO NOW?
THESE GUYS WERE THE REASON I DIED THE THIRD TIME...
I GUESS THE RIGHT THING TO DO WOULD BE TO TRY TO RUN, EVEN IF IT MEANS GETTING HURT. I'VE JUST GOTTA WATCH OUT FOR THAT KNIFE...
THAT'S ENOUGH!

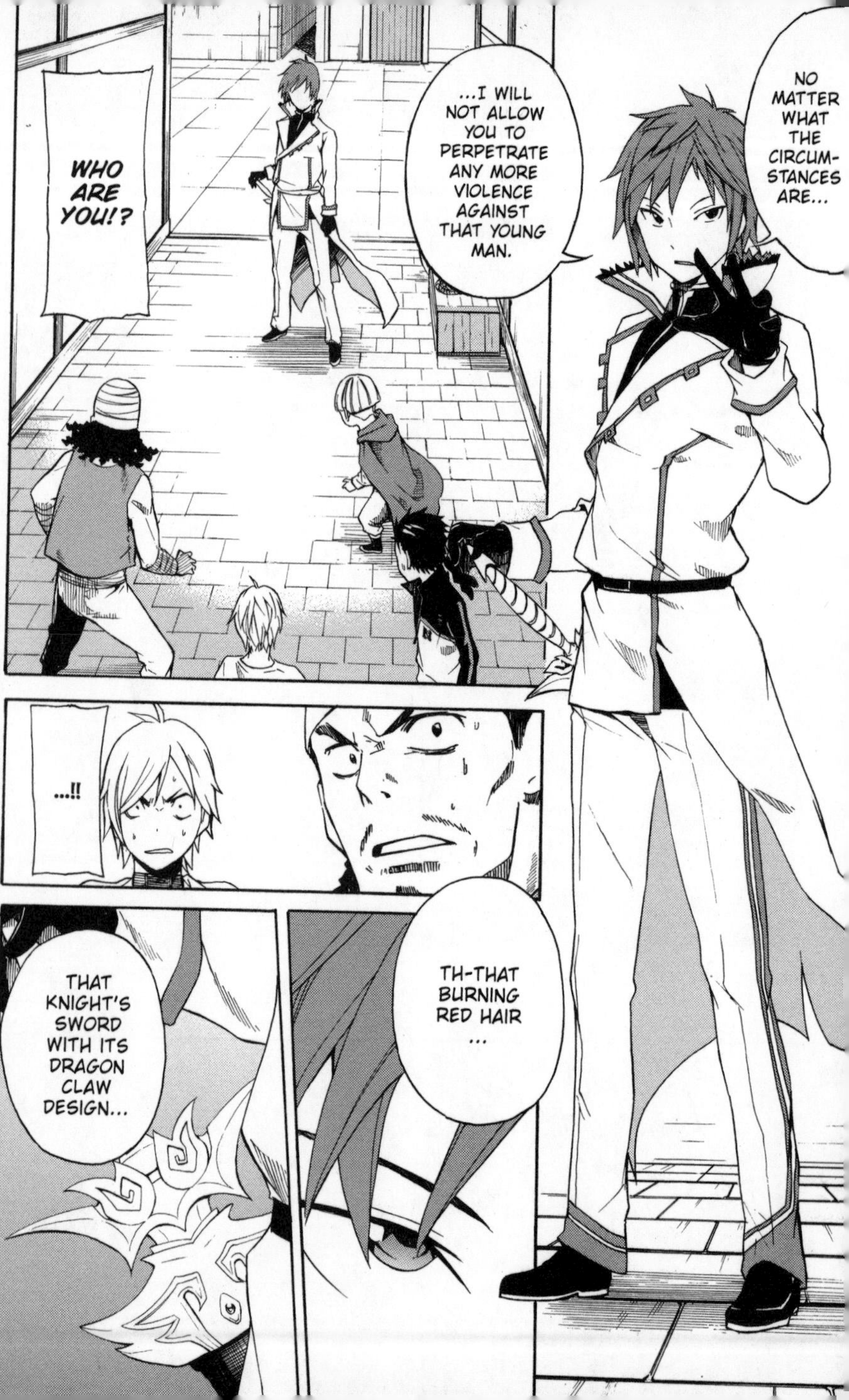
NO MATTER WHAT THE CIRCUM-STANCES ARE...
...I WILL NOT ALLOW YOU TO PERPETRATE ANY MORE VIOLENCE AGAINST THAT YOUNG MAN.
WHO ARE YOU!?
...!!
TH-THAT BURNING RED HAIR ...
THAT KNIGHT'S SWORD WITH ITS DRAGON CLAW DESIGN...

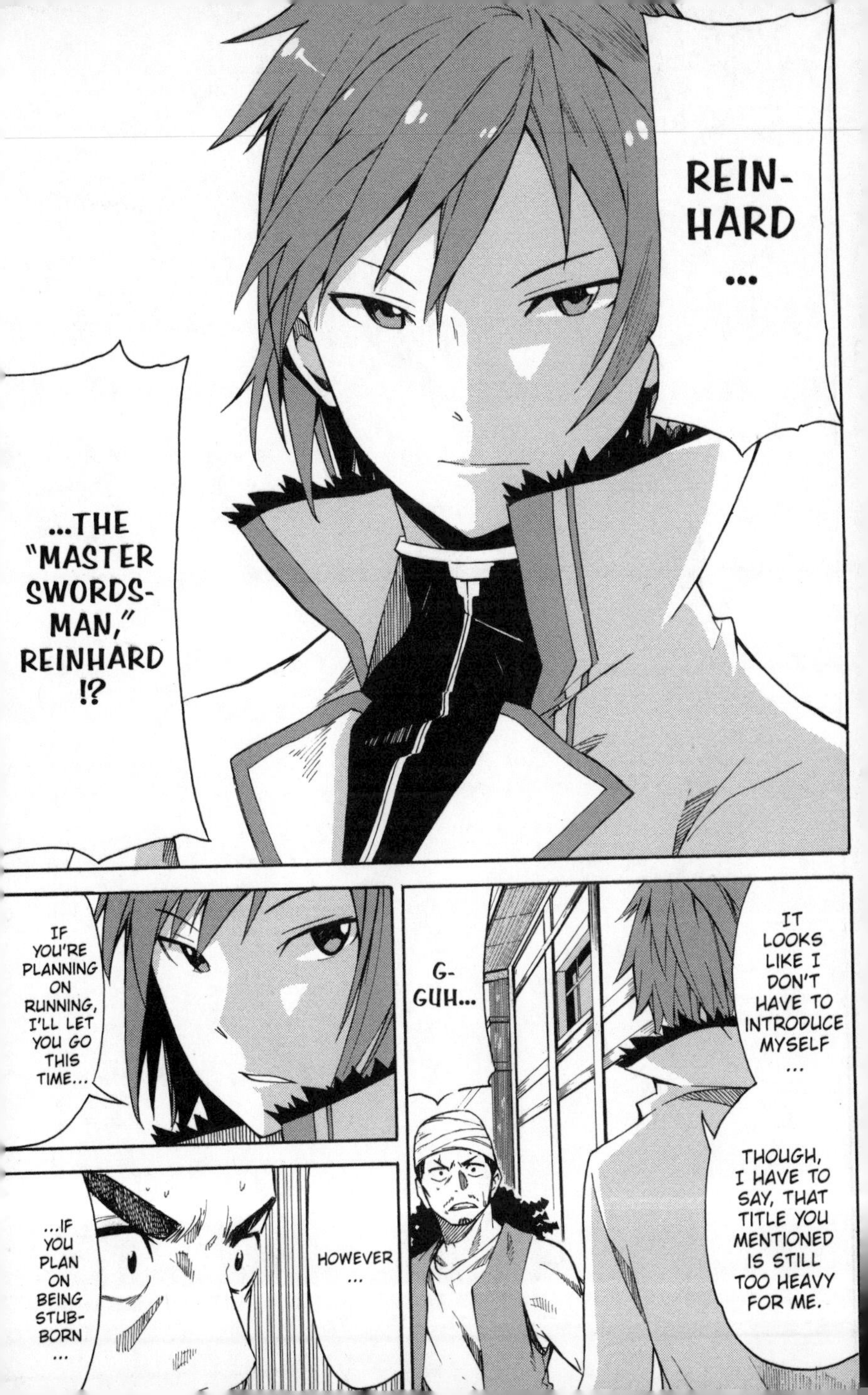
REIN-HARD...
...THE "MASTER SWORDS-MAN," REINHARD !?
IT LOOKS LIKE I DON'T HAVE TO INTRODUCE MYSELF...
G-GUH...
THOUGH, I HAVE TO SAY, THAT TITLE YOU MENTIONED IS STILL TOO HEAVY FOR ME.
IF YOU'RE PLANNING ON RUNNING, I'LL LET YOU GO THIS TIME...
HOWEVER...
...IF YOU PLAN ON BEING STUB-BORN...

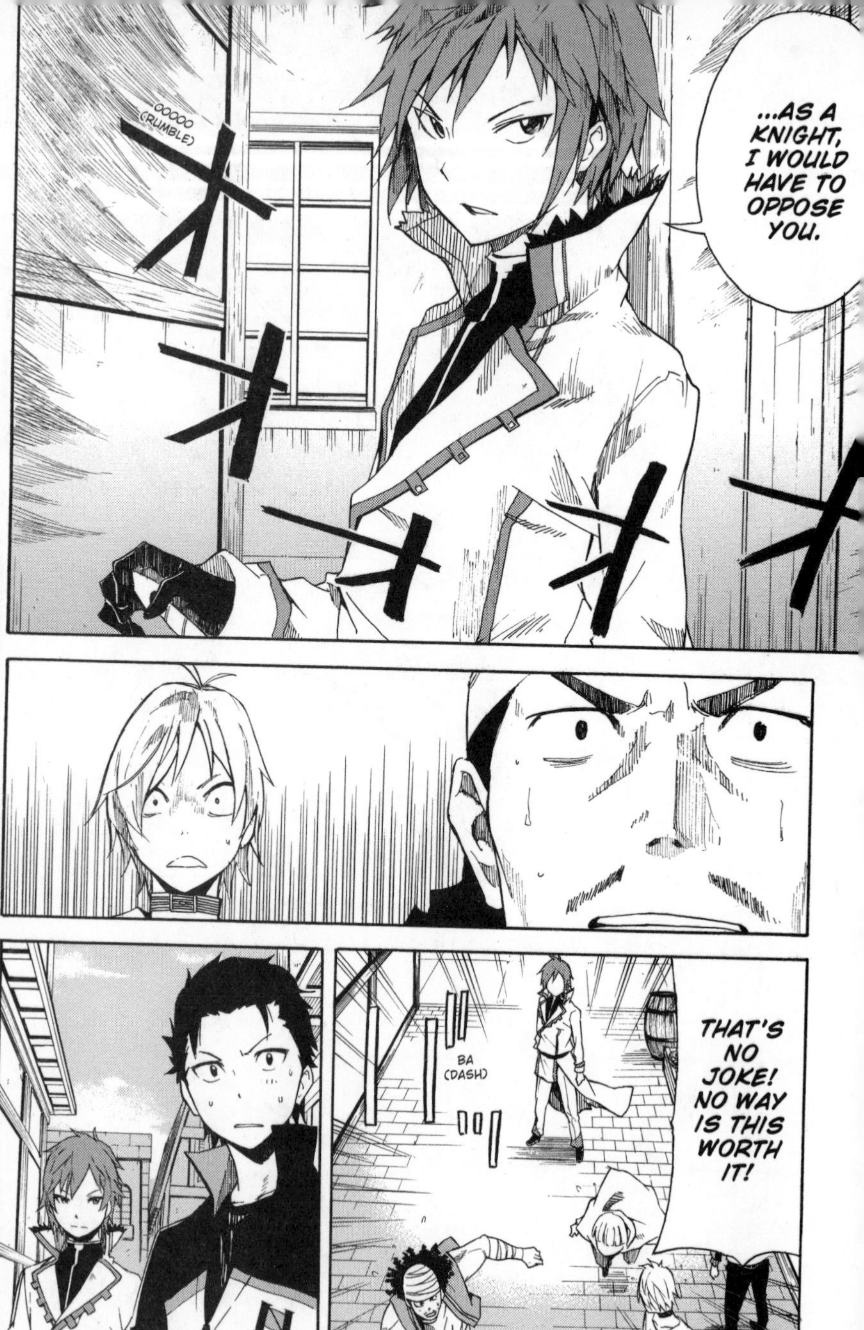
...AS A KNIGHT, I WOULD HAVE TO OPPOSE YOU.
OOOOO (RUMBLE)
THAT'S NO JOKE! NO WAY IS THIS WORTH IT!
BA (DASH)

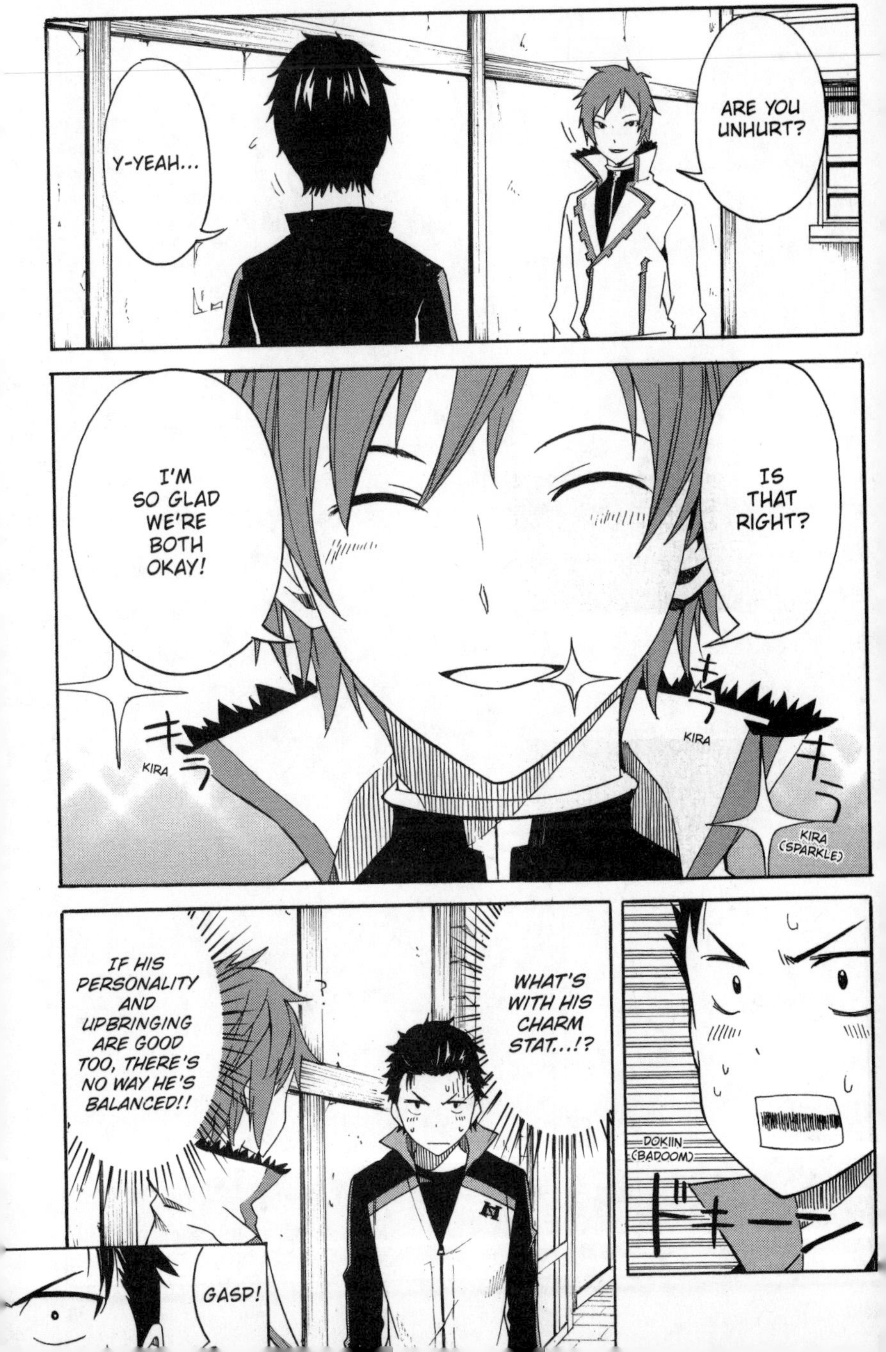
ARE YOU UNHURT?
Y-YEAH...
IS THAT RIGHT?
I'M SO GLAD WE'RE BOTH OKAY!
KIRA
KIRA (SPARKLE)
KIRA
DOKIIN (BADOOM)
WHAT'S WITH HIS CHARM STAT...!?
IF HIS PERSONALITY AND UPBRINGING ARE GOOD TOO, THERE'S NO WAY HE'S BALANCED!!
GASP!

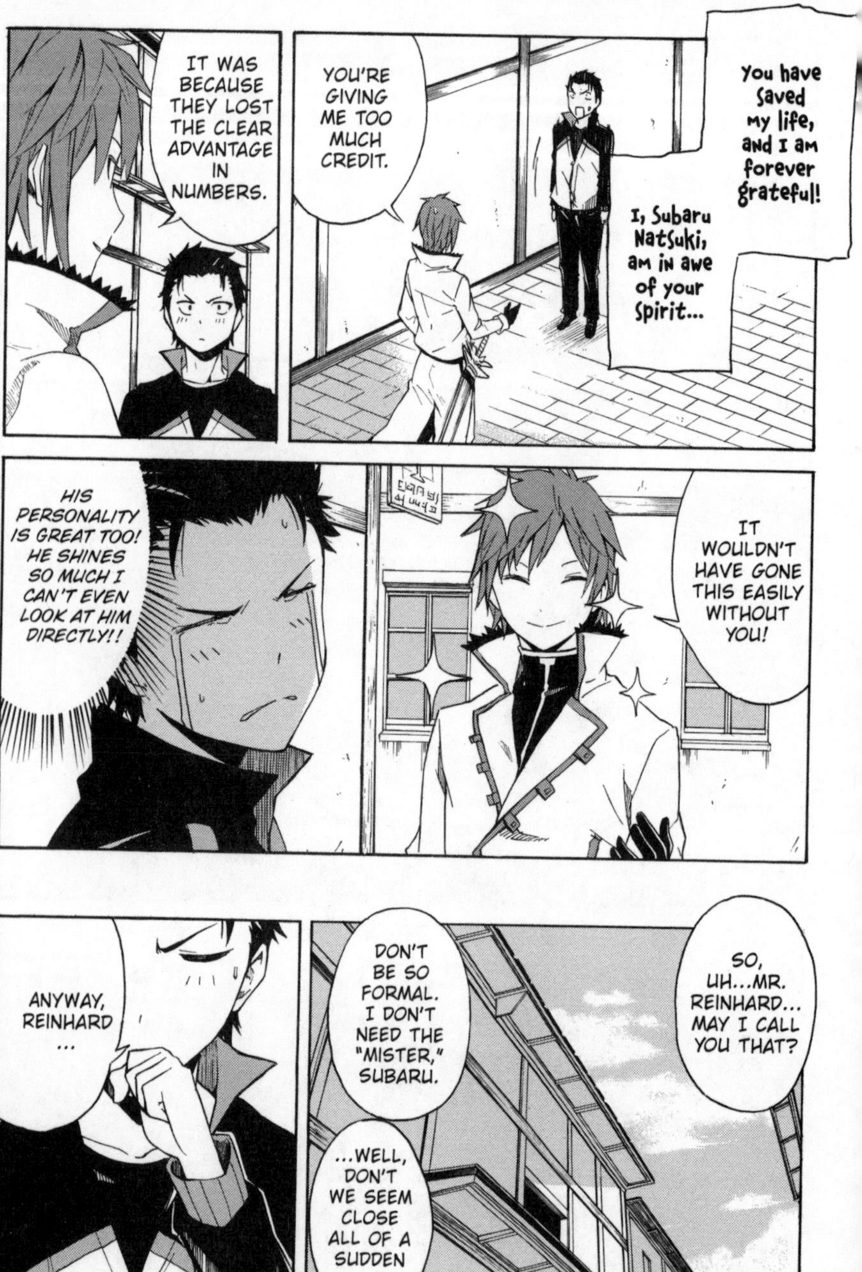
You have saved my life, and I am forever grateful!
I, Subaru Natsuki, am in awe of your Spirit...
YOU'RE GIVING ME TOO MUCH CREDIT.
IT WAS BECAUSE THEY LOST THE CLEAR ADVANTAGE IN NUMBERS.
IT WOULDN'T HAVE GONE THIS EASILY WITHOUT YOU!
HIS PERSONALITY IS GREAT TOO! HE SHINES SO MUCH I CAN'T EVEN LOOK AT HIM DIRECTLY!!
SO, UH...MR. REINHARD... MAY I CALL YOU THAT?
DON'T BE SO FORMAL. I DON'T NEED THE "MISTER," SUBARU.
...WELL, DON'T WE SEEM CLOSE ALL OF A SUDDEN...?
ANYWAY, REINHARD...

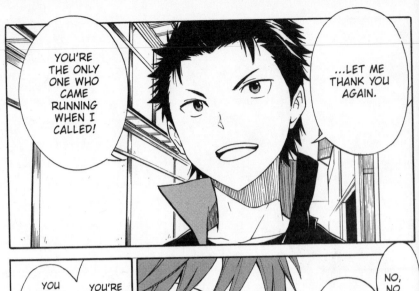

...LET ME THANK YOU AGAIN.
YOU'RE THE ONLY ONE WHO CAME RUNNING WHEN I CALLED!
NO, NO ...
AS A GUARD, I JUST DID WHAT'S EXPECTED OF ME.
YOU'RE A GUARD, REINHARD?
YOU DON'T LOOK LIKE ONE AT ALL...
HMM... IT'S MORE LIKE MY IMAGE OF A GUARD IS A LOT GRUNGIER ...
I GET THAT A LOT. I KNOW I'M LACKING THE STERNNESS OF AN AUTHORITY FIGURE...
...AND TODAY, I'M OFF DUTY, SO I'M NOT WEARING MY UNIFORM.
NOW THAT I THINK OF IT, THEY DID CALL YOU "MASTER SWORDS-MAN"...

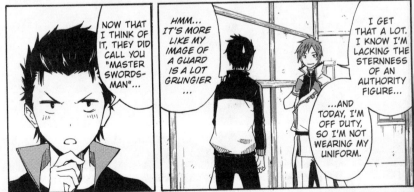

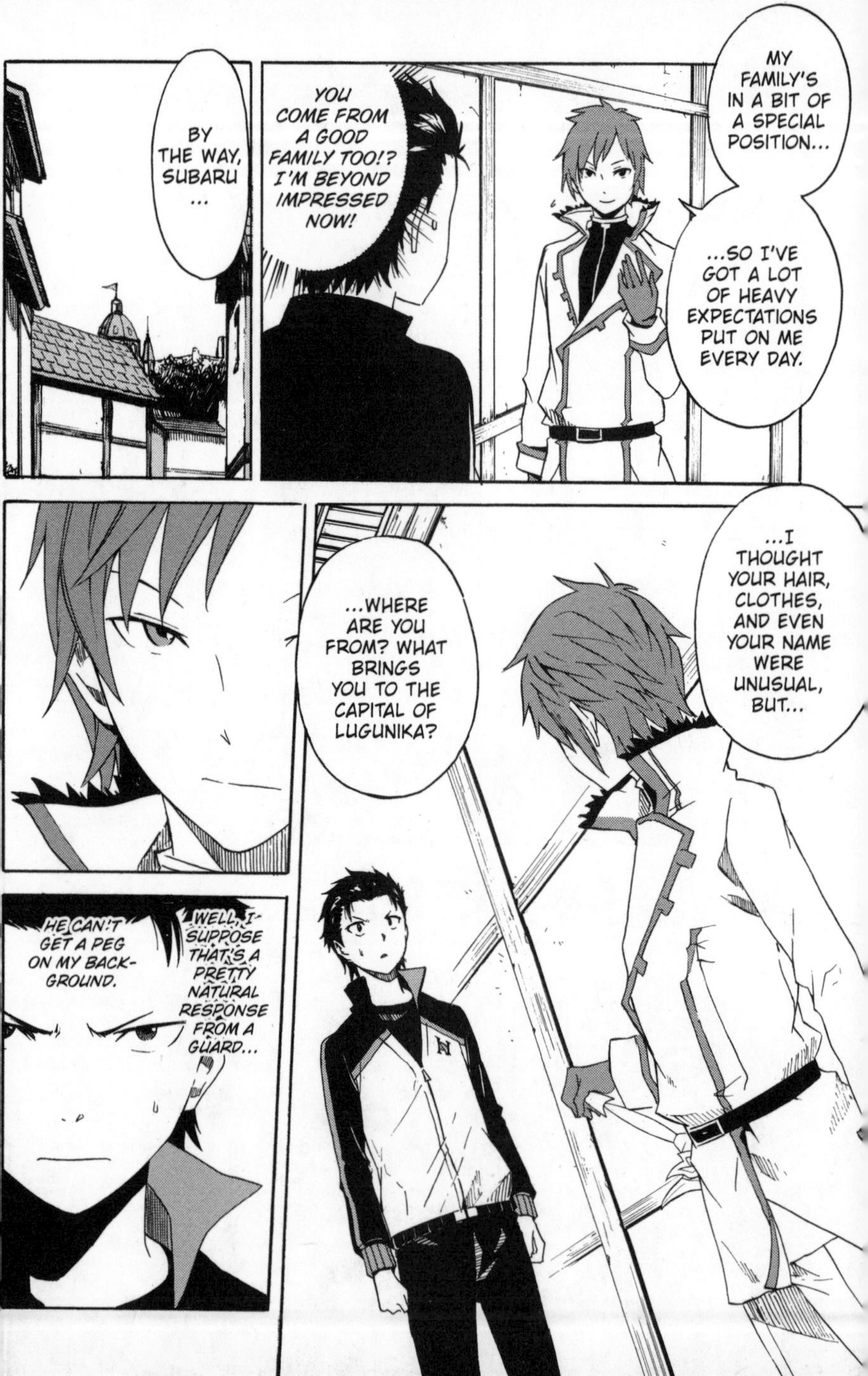
MY FAMILY'S IN A BIT OF A SPECIAL POSITION...
...SO I'VE GOT A LOT OF HEAVY EXPECTATIONS PUT ON ME EVERY DAY.
YOU COME FROM A GOOD FAMILY TOO!? I'M BEYOND IMPRESSED NOW!
BY THE WAY, SUBARU ...
...I THOUGHT YOUR HAIR, CLOTHES, AND EVEN YOUR NAME WERE UNUSUAL, BUT...
...WHERE ARE YOU FROM? WHAT BRINGS YOU TO THE CAPITAL OF LUGUNIKA?
WELL, I SUPPOSE THAT'S A PRETTY NATURAL RESPONSE FROM A GUARD...
HE CAN'T GET A PEG ON MY BACK-GROUND.

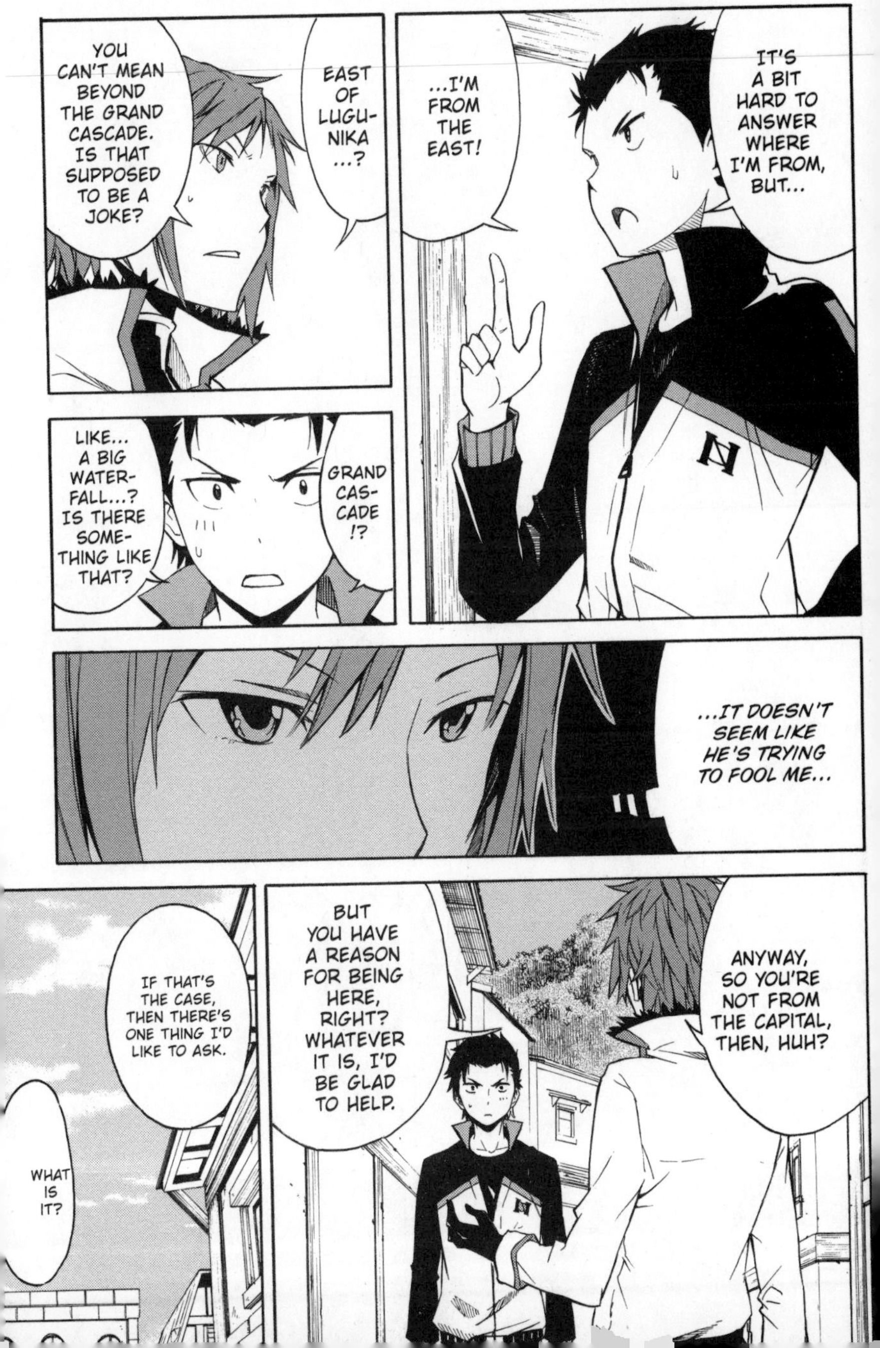
IT'S A BIT HARD TO ANSWER WHERE I'M FROM, BUT...
...I'M FROM THE EAST!
EAST OF LUGU-NIKA...?
YOU CAN'T MEAN BEYOND THE GRAND CASCADE. IS THAT SUPPOSED TO BE A JOKE?
GRAND CAS-CADE!?
LIKE... A BIG WATER-FALL...? IS THERE SOME-THING LIKE THAT?
...IT DOESN'T SEEM LIKE HE'S TRYING TO FOOL ME...
ANYWAY, SO YOU'RE NOT FROM THE CAPITAL, THEN, HUH?
BUT YOU HAVE A REASON FOR BEING HERE, RIGHT? WHATEVER IT IS, I'D BE GLAD TO HELP.
IF THAT'S THE CASE, THEN THERE'S ONE THING I'D LIKE TO ASK.
WHAT IS IT?

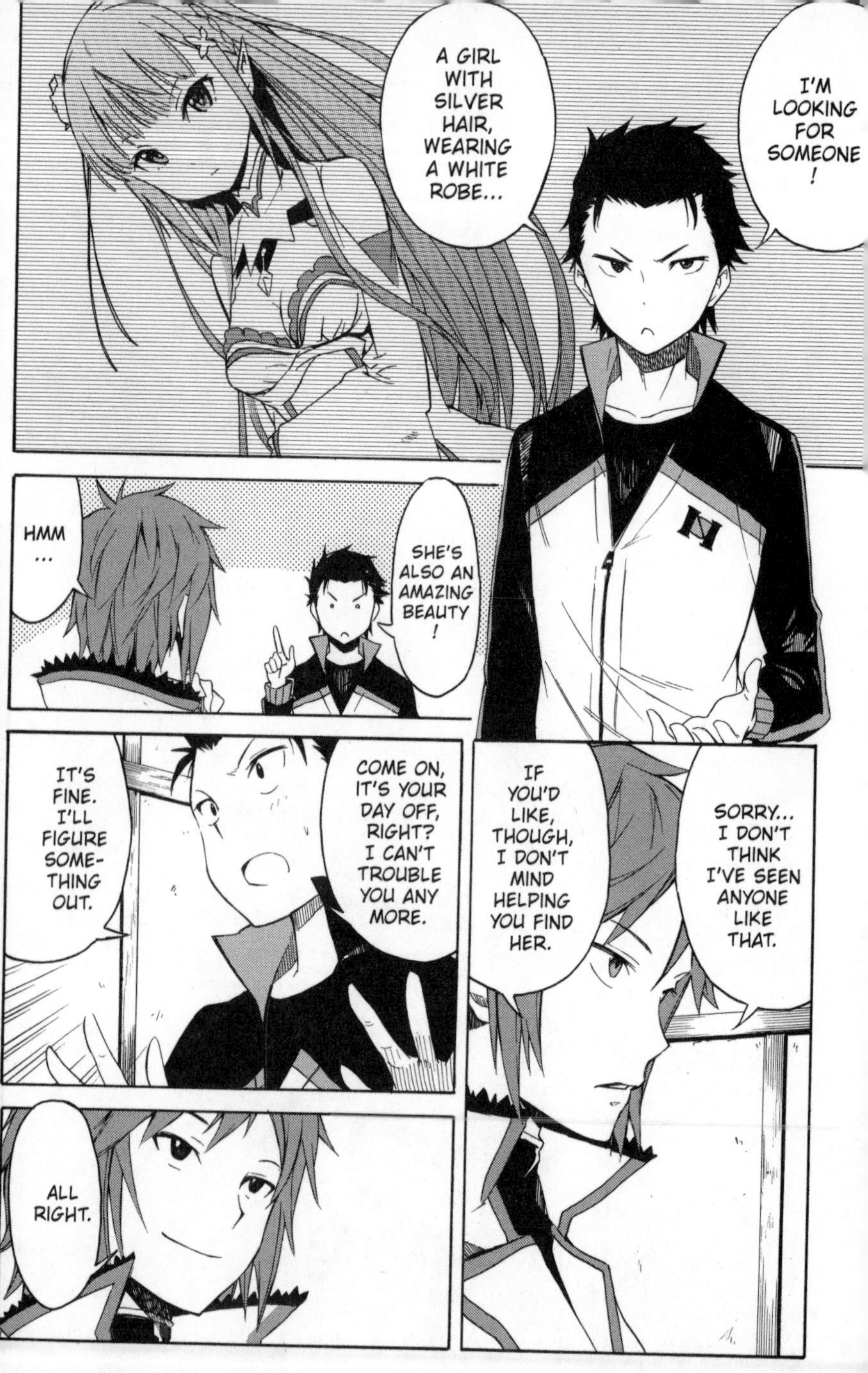
I'M LOOKING FOR SOMEONE!
A GIRL WITH SILVER HAIR, WEARING A WHITE ROBE...
SHE'S ALSO AN AMAZING BEAUTY!
HMM...
SORRY... I DON'T THINK I'VE SEEN ANYONE LIKE THAT.
IF YOU'D LIKE, THOUGH, I DON'T MIND HELPING YOU FIND HER.
COME ON, IT'S YOUR DAY OFF, RIGHT? I CAN'T TROUBLE YOU ANY MORE.
IT'S FINE. I'LL FIGURE SOMETHING OUT.
ALL RIGHT.

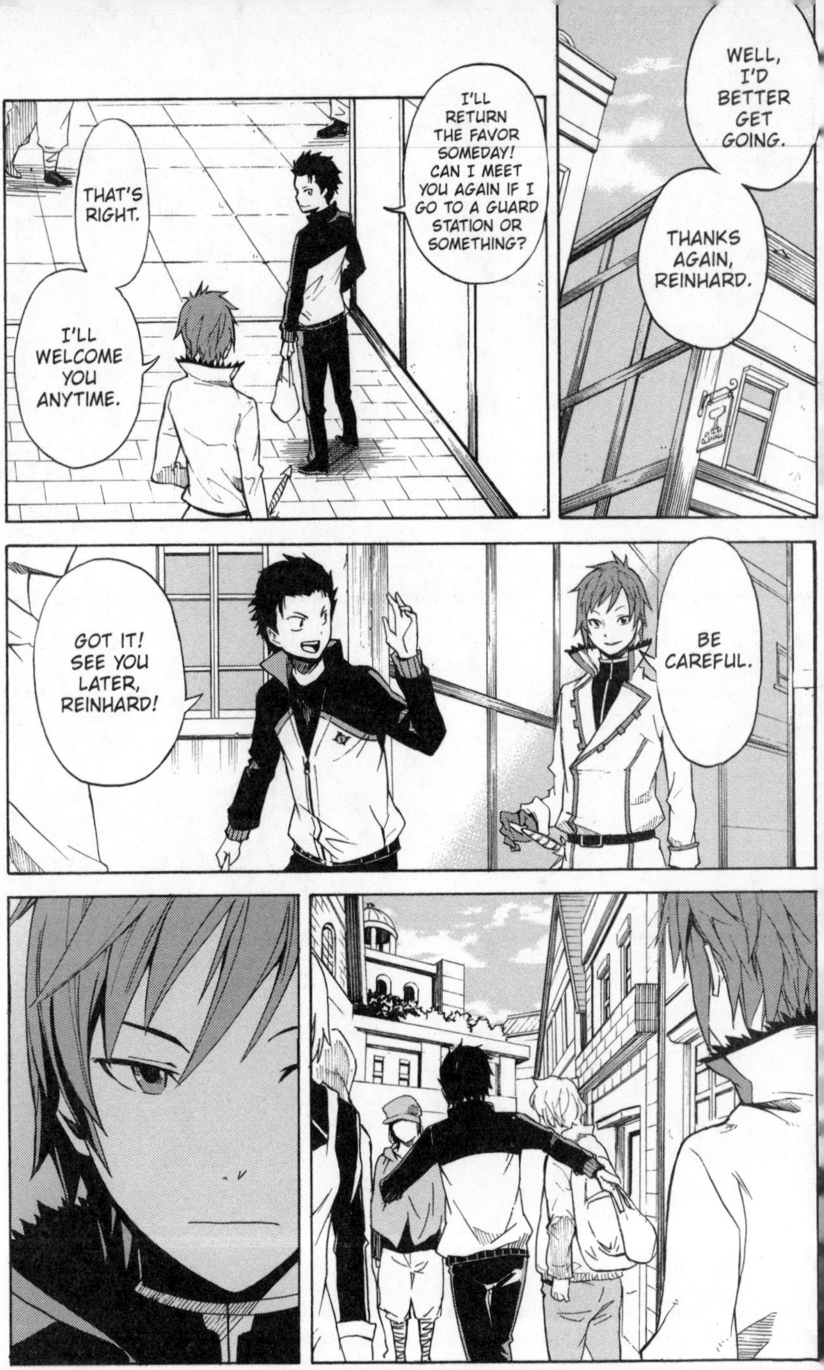
WELL, I'D BETTER GET GOING.
THANKS AGAIN, REINHARD.
I'LL RETURN THE FAVOR SOMEDAY! CAN I MEET YOU AGAIN IF I GO TO A GUARD STATION OR SOMETHING?
THAT'S RIGHT.
I'LL WELCOME YOU ANYTIME.
BE CAREFUL.
GOT IT! SEE YOU LATER, REINHARD!

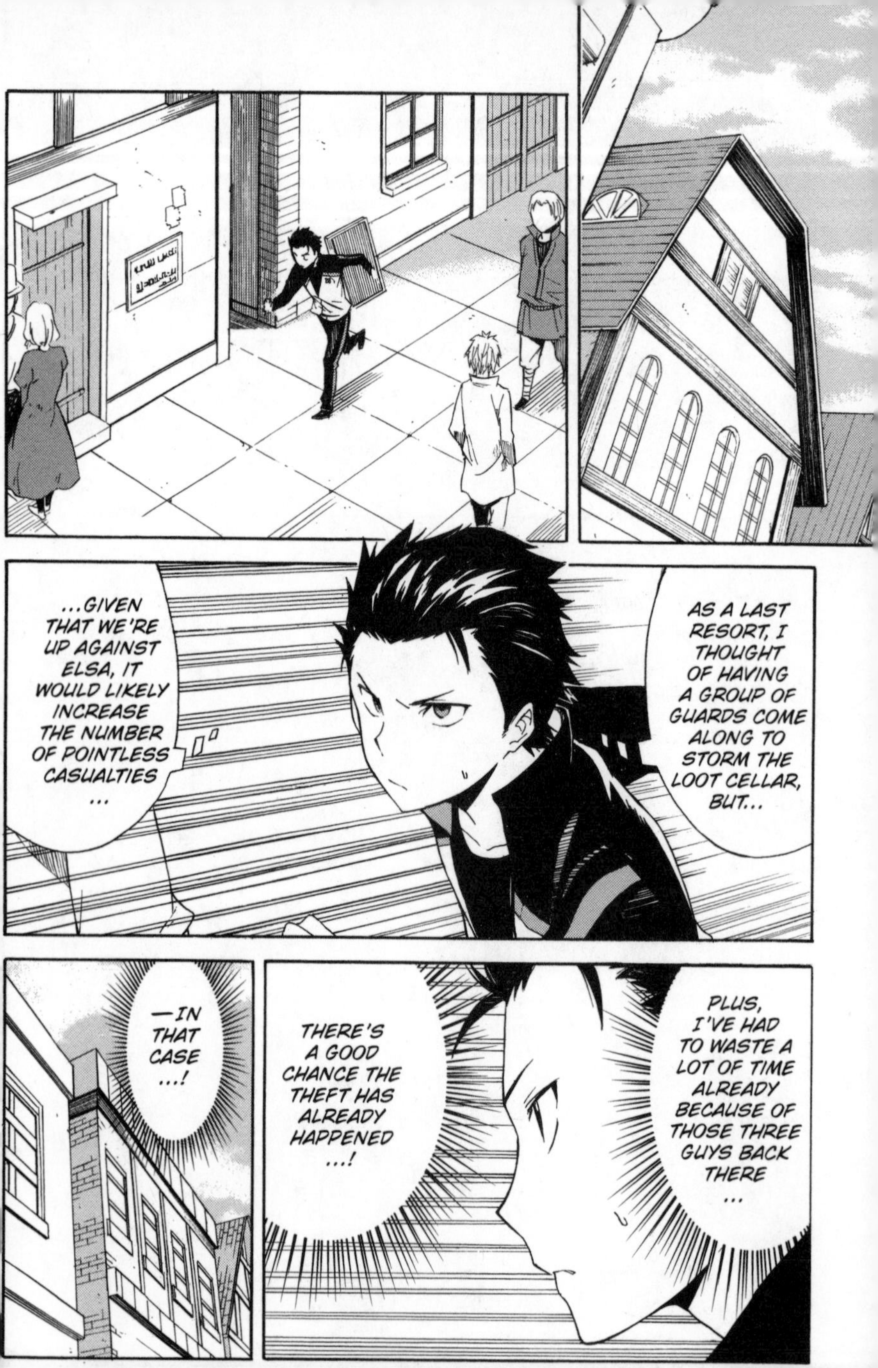
AS A LAST RESORT, I THOUGHT OF HAVING A GROUP OF GUARDS COME ALONG TO STORM THE LOOT CELLAR, BUT...
...GIVEN THAT WE'RE UP AGAINST ELSA, IT WOULD LIKELY INCREASE THE NUMBER OF POINTLESS CASUALTIES...
PLUS, I'VE HAD TO WASTE A LOT OF TIME ALREADY BECAUSE OF THOSE THREE GUYS BACK THERE...
THERE'S A GOOD CHANCE THE THEFT HAS ALREADY HAPPENED...!
—IN THAT CASE...!

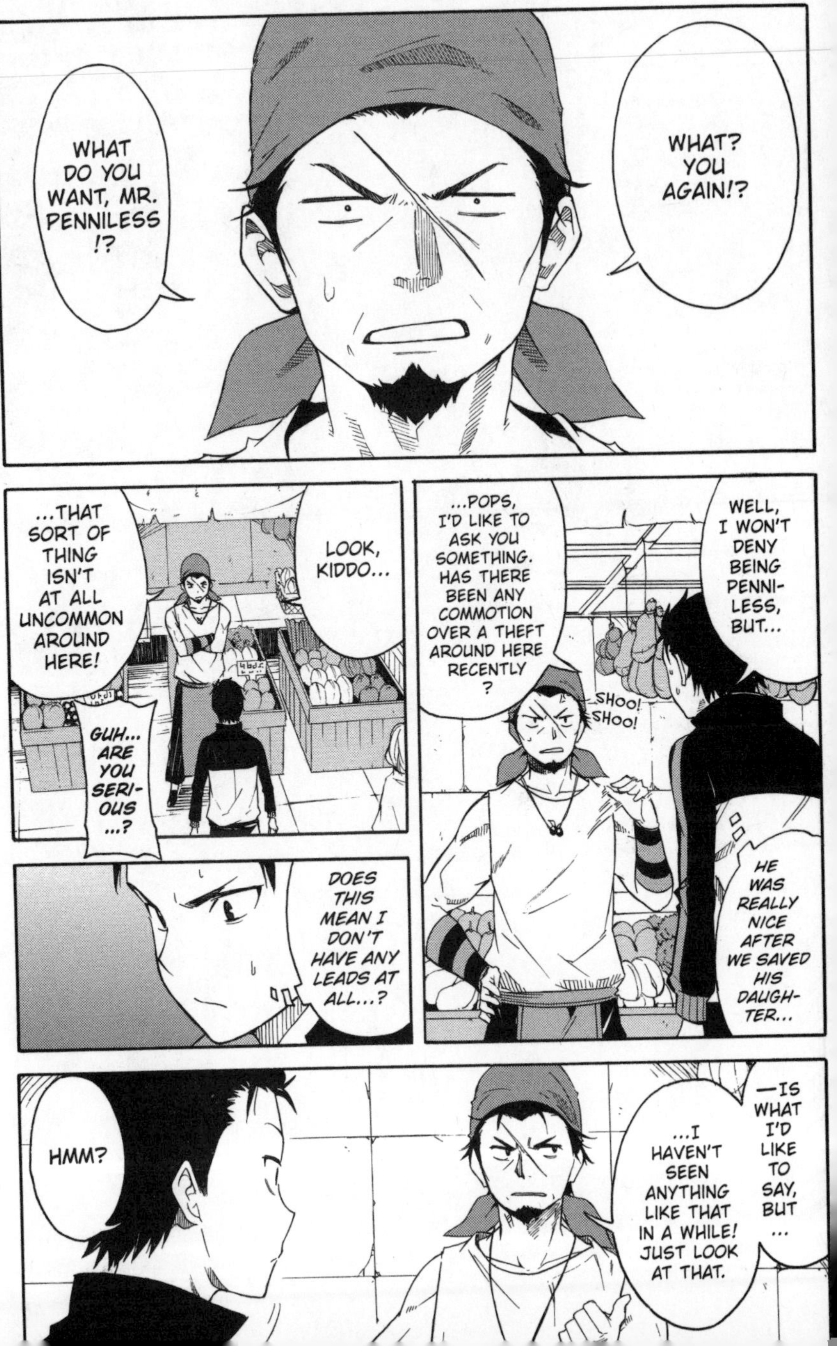
WHAT? YOU AGAIN!?
WHAT DO YOU WANT, MR. PENNILESS!?
WELL, I WON'T DENY BEING PENNILESS, BUT...
...POPS, I'D LIKE TO ASK YOU SOMETHING. HAS THERE BEEN ANY COMMOTION OVER A THEFT AROUND HERE RECENTLY?
SHOO! SHOO!
HE WAS REALLY NICE AFTER WE SAVED HIS DAUGHTER...
LOOK, KIDDO...
...THAT SORT OF THING ISN'T AT ALL UNCOMMON AROUND HERE!
GUH... ARE YOU SERIOUS...?
DOES THIS MEAN I DON'T HAVE ANY LEADS AT ALL...?
...I HAVEN'T SEEN ANYTHING LIKE THAT IN A WHILE! JUST LOOK AT THAT.
—IS WHAT I'D LIKE TO SAY, BUT...
HMM?

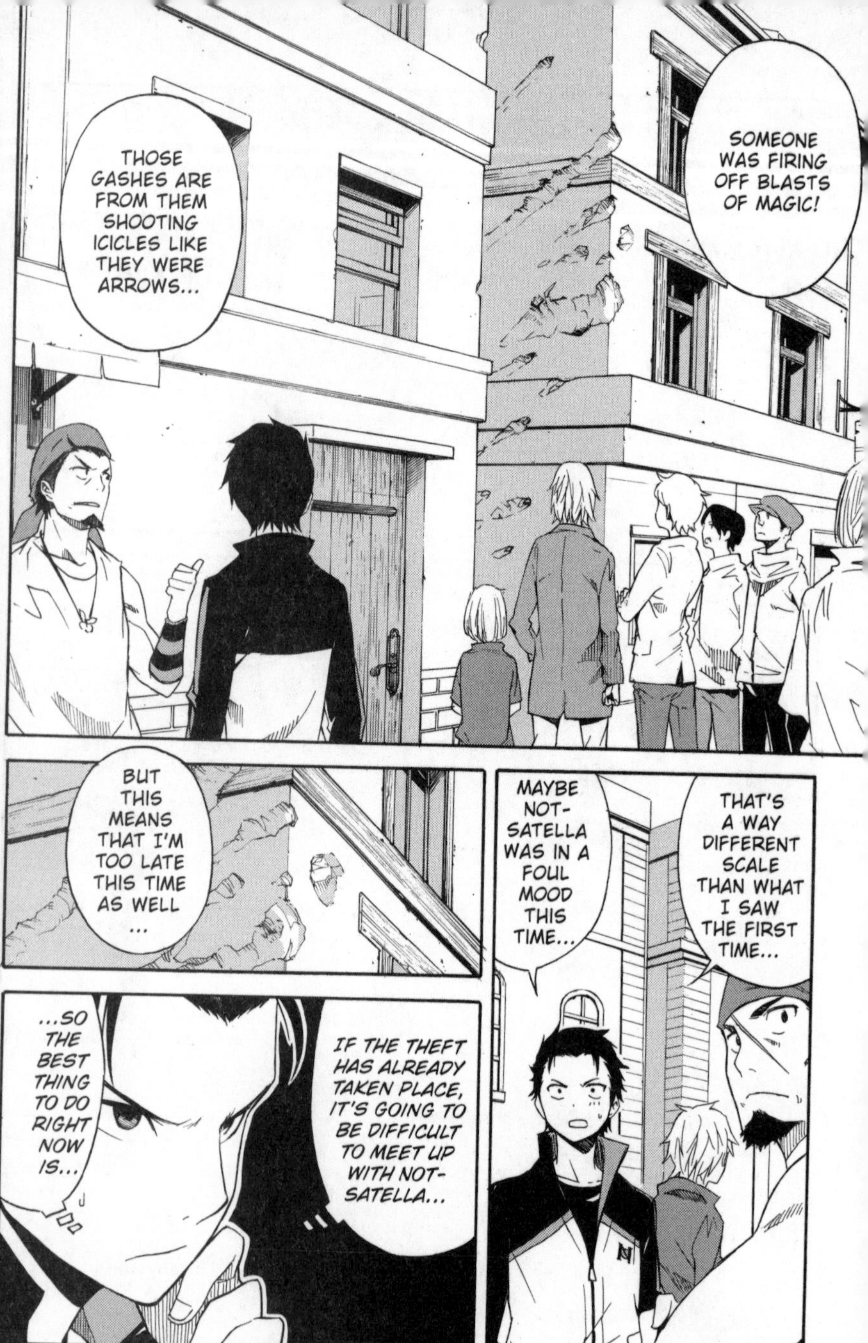
SOMEONE WAS FIRING OFF BLASTS OF MAGIC!
THOSE GASHES ARE FROM THEM SHOOTING ICICLES LIKE THEY WERE ARROWS...
THAT'S A WAY DIFFERENT SCALE THAN WHAT I SAW THE FIRST TIME...
MAYBE NOT-SATELLA WAS IN A FOUL MOOD THIS TIME...
BUT THIS MEANS THAT I'M TOO LATE THIS TIME AS WELL ...
IF THE THEFT HAS ALREADY TAKEN PLACE, IT'S GOING TO BE DIFFICULT TO MEET UP WITH NOT-SATELLA...
...SO THE BEST THING TO DO RIGHT NOW IS...

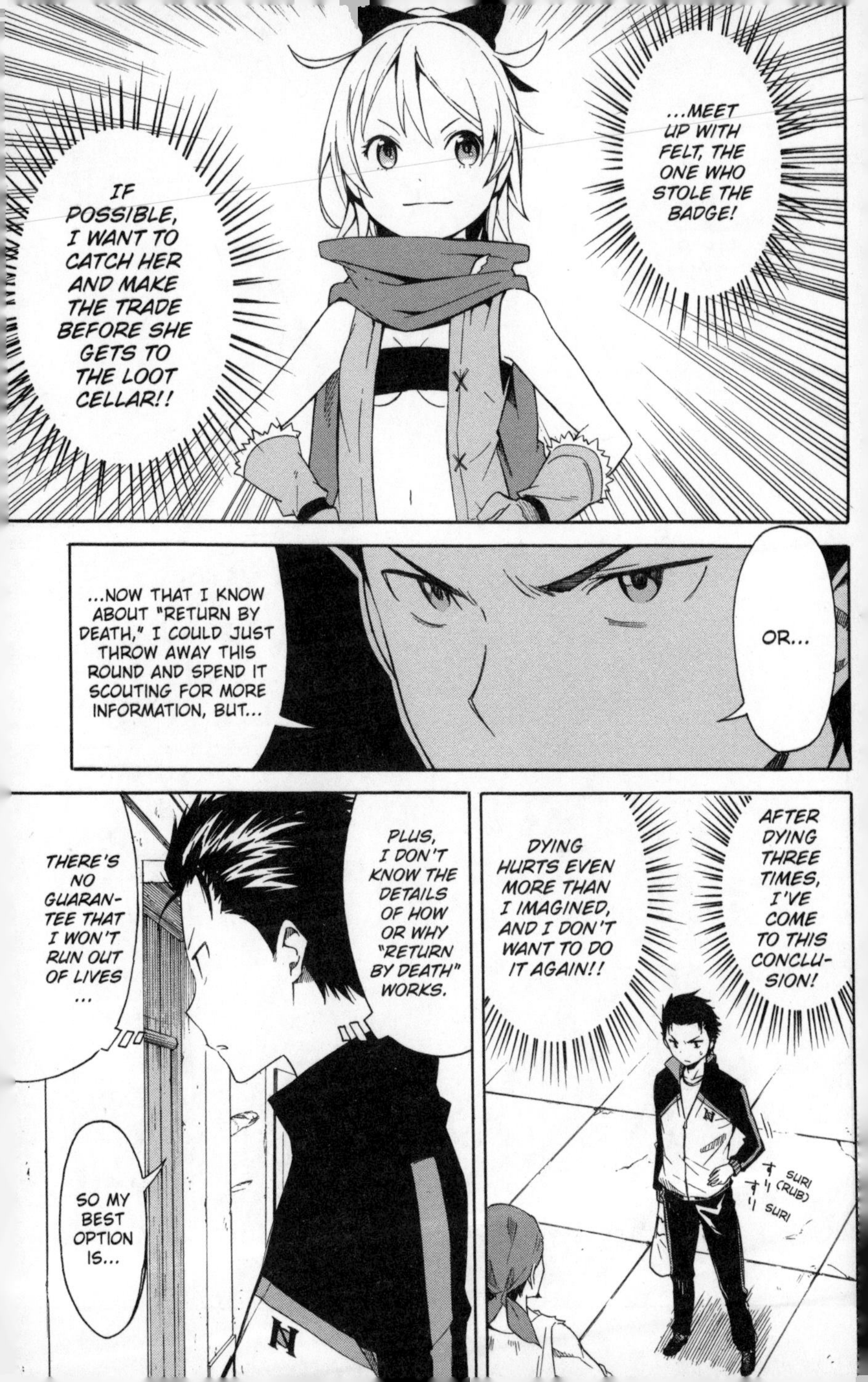
...MEET UP WITH FELT, THE ONE WHO STOLE THE BADGE!
IF POSSIBLE, I WANT TO CATCH HER AND MAKE THE TRADE BEFORE SHE GETS TO THE LOOT CELLAR!!
OR...
...NOW THAT I KNOW ABOUT "RETURN BY DEATH," I COULD JUST THROW AWAY THIS ROUND AND SPEND IT SCOUTING FOR MORE INFORMATION, BUT...
AFTER DYING THREE TIMES, I'VE COME TO THIS CONCLUSION!
DYING HURTS EVEN MORE THAN I IMAGINED, AND I DON'T WANT TO DO IT AGAIN!!
SURI (RUB)
SURI
PLUS, I DON'T KNOW THE DETAILS OF HOW OR WHY "RETURN BY DEATH" WORKS.
THERE'S NO GUARANTEE THAT I WON'T RUN OUT OF LIVES...
SO MY BEST OPTION IS...

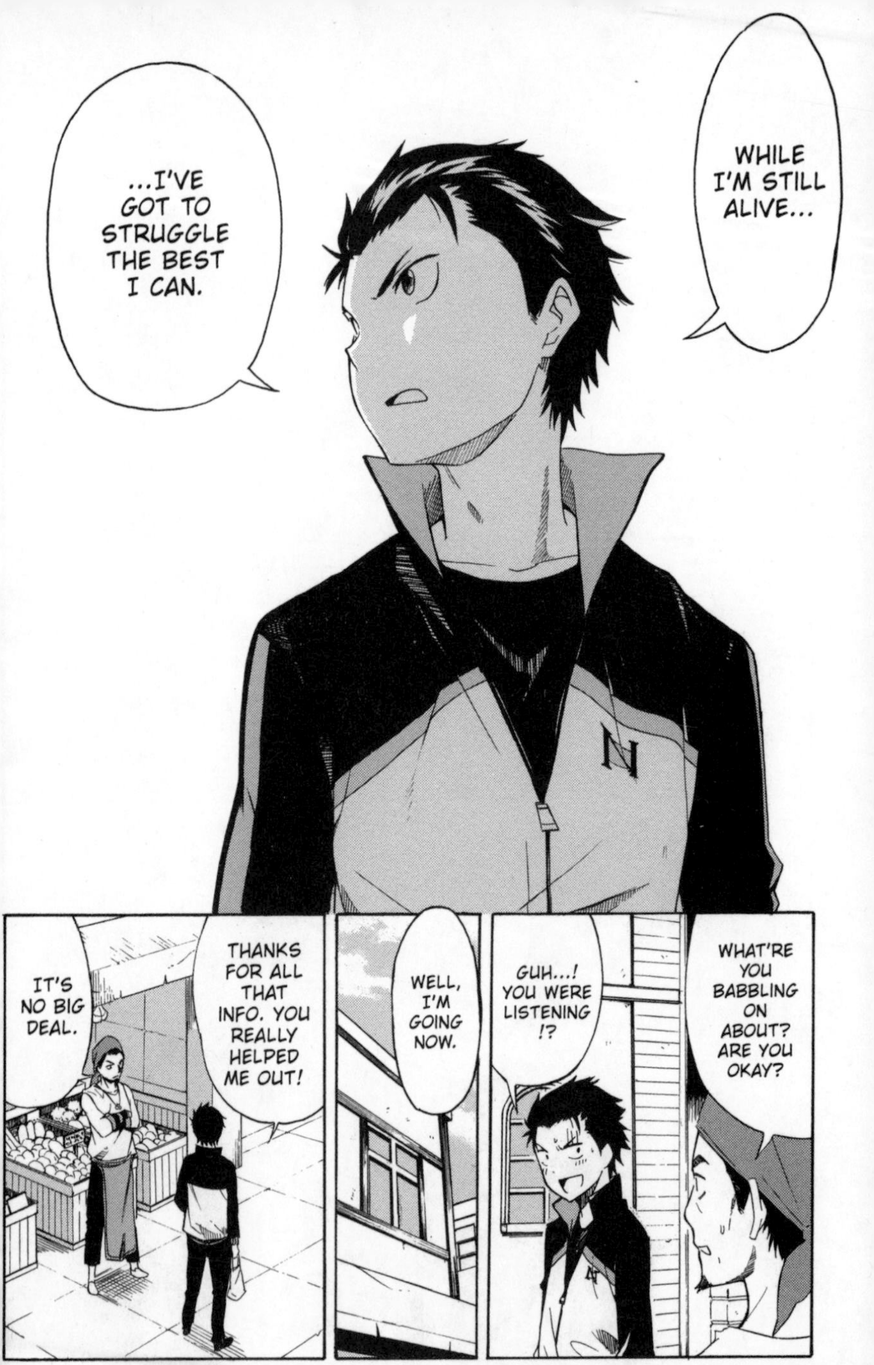
WHILE I'M STILL ALIVE...
...I'VE GOT TO STRUGGLE THE BEST I CAN.
WHAT'RE YOU BABBLING ON ABOUT? ARE YOU OKAY?
GUH...! YOU WERE LISTENING!?
WELL, I'M GOING NOW.
THANKS FOR ALL THAT INFO. YOU REALLY HELPED ME OUT!
IT'S NO BIG DEAL.

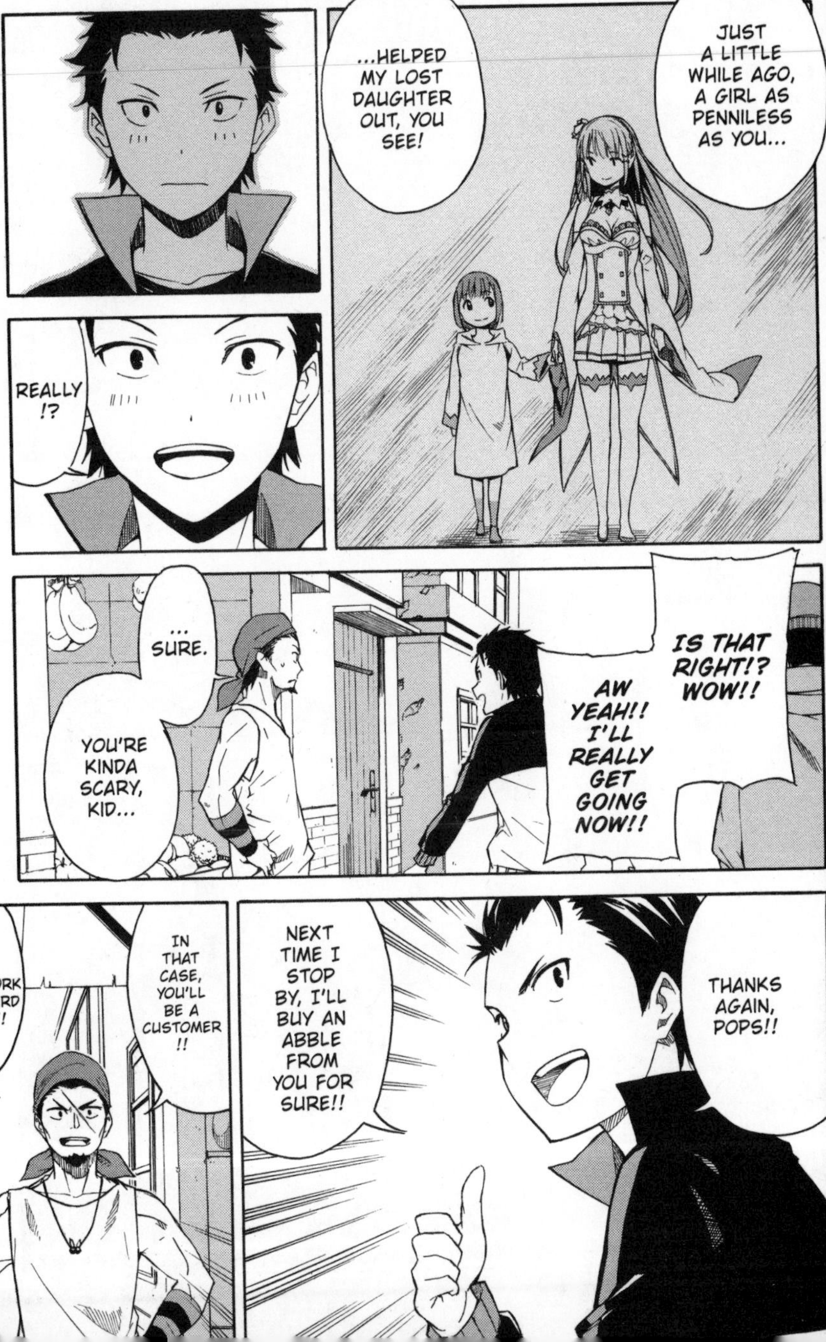
JUST A LITTLE WHILE AGO, A GIRL AS PENNILESS AS YOU...
...HELPED MY LOST DAUGHTER OUT, YOU SEE!
REALLY!?
IS THAT RIGHT!? WOW!!
AW YEAH!! I'LL REALLY GET GOING NOW!!
... SURE.
YOU'RE KINDA SCARY, KID...
THANKS AGAIN, POPS!!
NEXT TIME I STOP BY, I'LL BUY AN ABBLE FROM YOU FOR SURE!!
IN THAT CASE, YOU'LL BE A CUSTOMER!!
WORK HARD!!

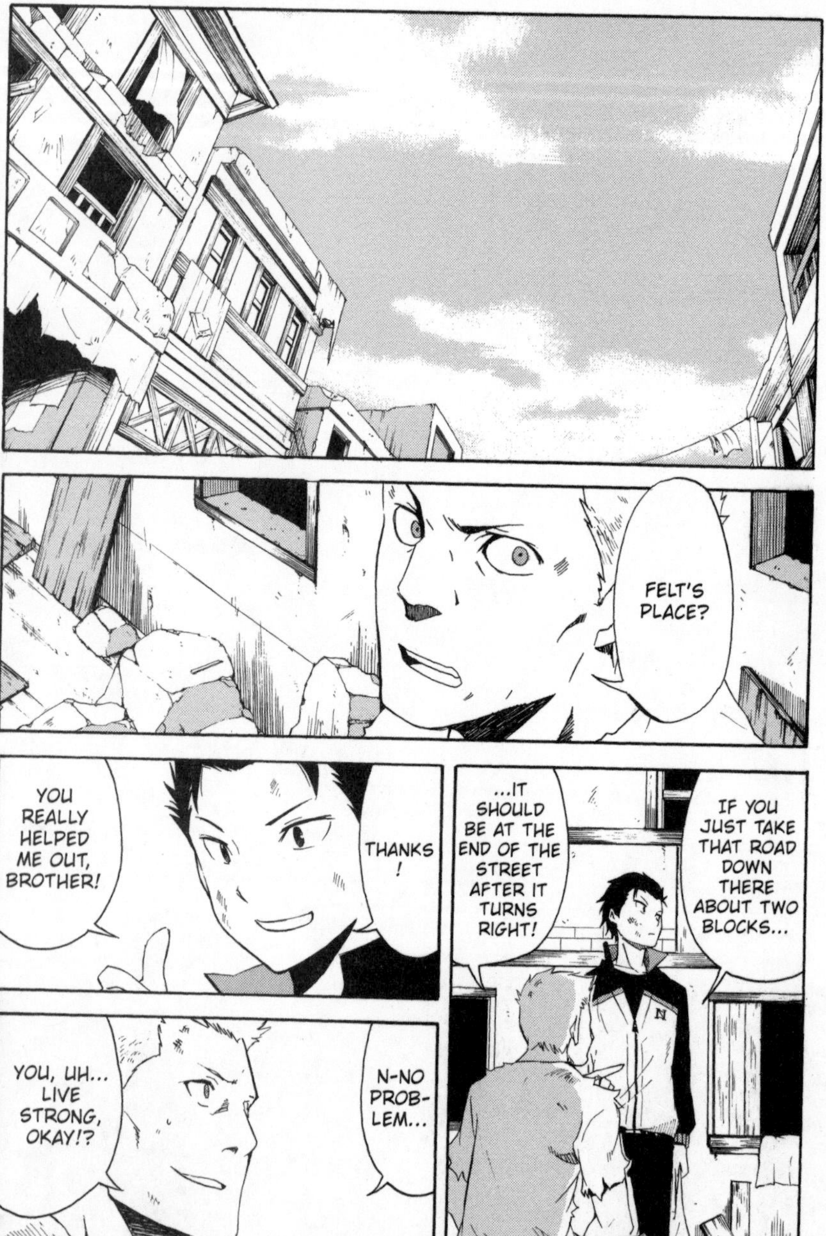
FELT'S PLACE?
IF YOU JUST TAKE THAT ROAD DOWN THERE ABOUT TWO BLOCKS...
...IT SHOULD BE AT THE END OF THE STREET AFTER IT TURNS RIGHT!
THANKS!
YOU REALLY HELPED ME OUT, BROTHER!
N-NO PROB-LEM...
YOU, UH... LIVE STRONG, OKAY!?

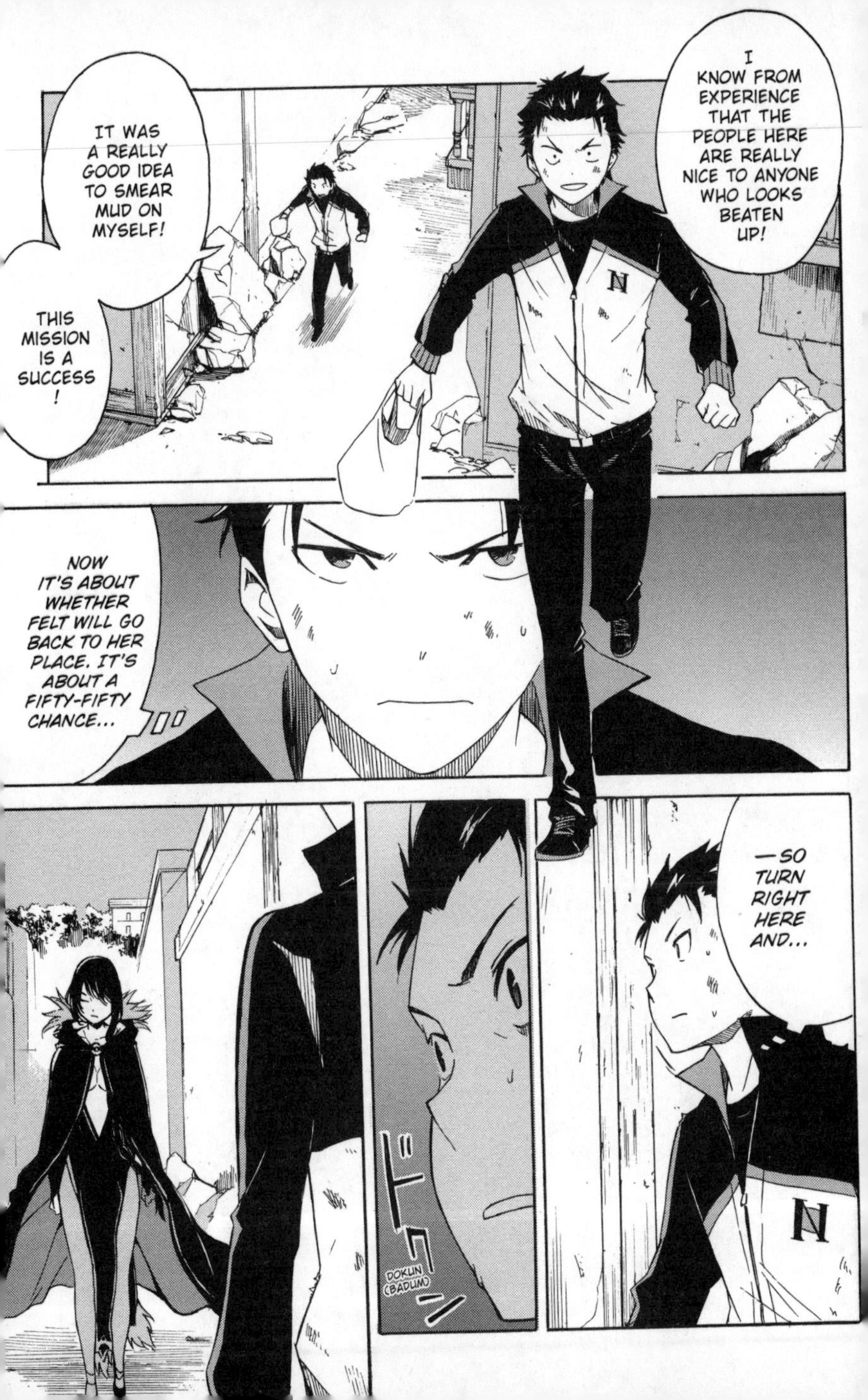
I KNOW FROM EXPERIENCE THAT THE PEOPLE HERE ARE REALLY NICE TO ANYONE WHO LOOKS BEATEN UP!
IT WAS A REALLY GOOD IDEA TO SMEAR MUD ON MYSELF!
THIS MISSION IS A SUCCESS!
NOW IT'S ABOUT WHETHER FELT WILL GO BACK TO HER PLACE. IT'S ABOUT A FIFTY-FIFTY CHANCE...
—SO TURN RIGHT HERE AND...
DOKUN (BADUM)

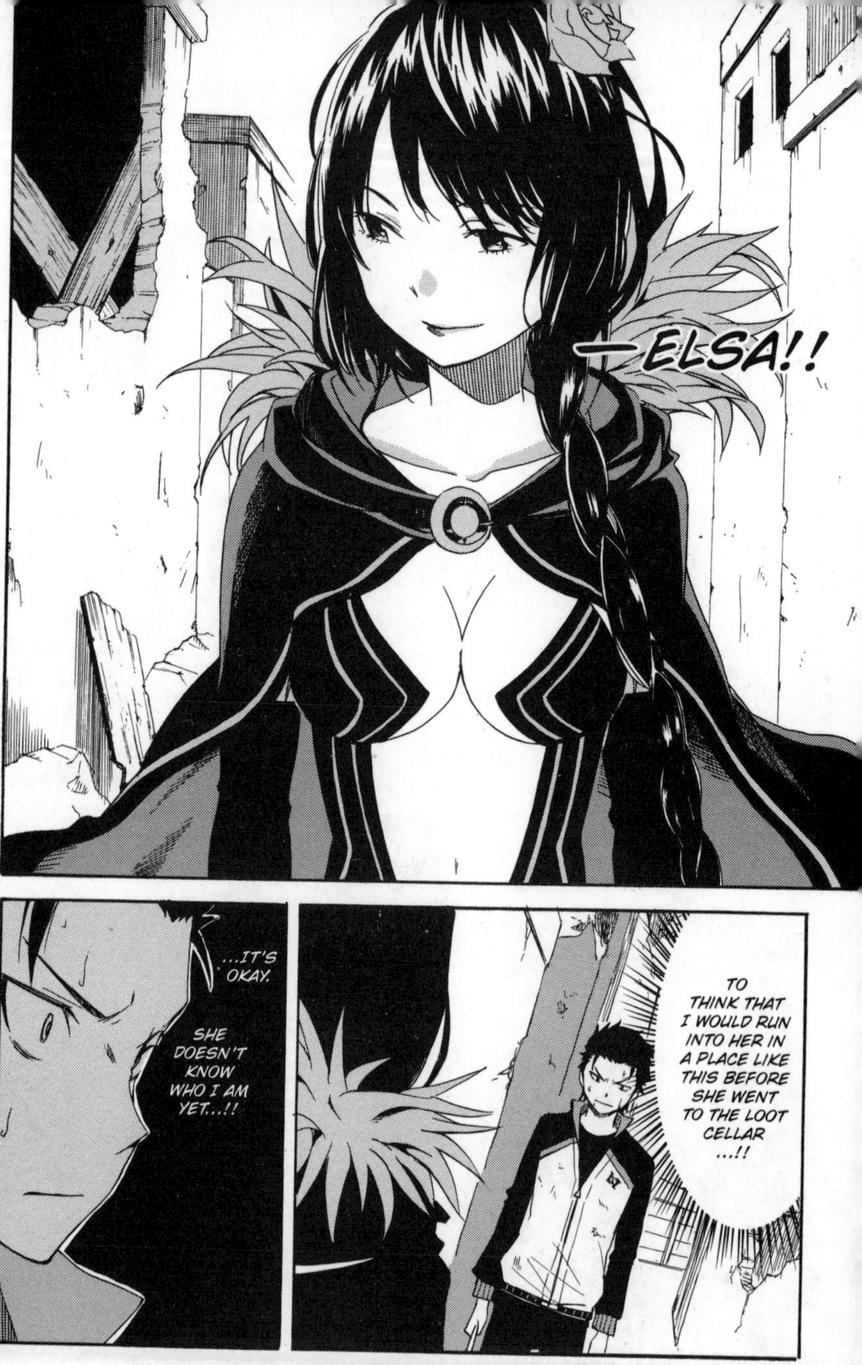
—ELSA!!
TO THINK THAT I WOULD RUN INTO HER IN A PLACE LIKE THIS BEFORE SHE WENT TO THE LOOT CELLAR ...!!
...IT'S OKAY.
SHE DOESN'T KNOW WHO I AM YET...!!

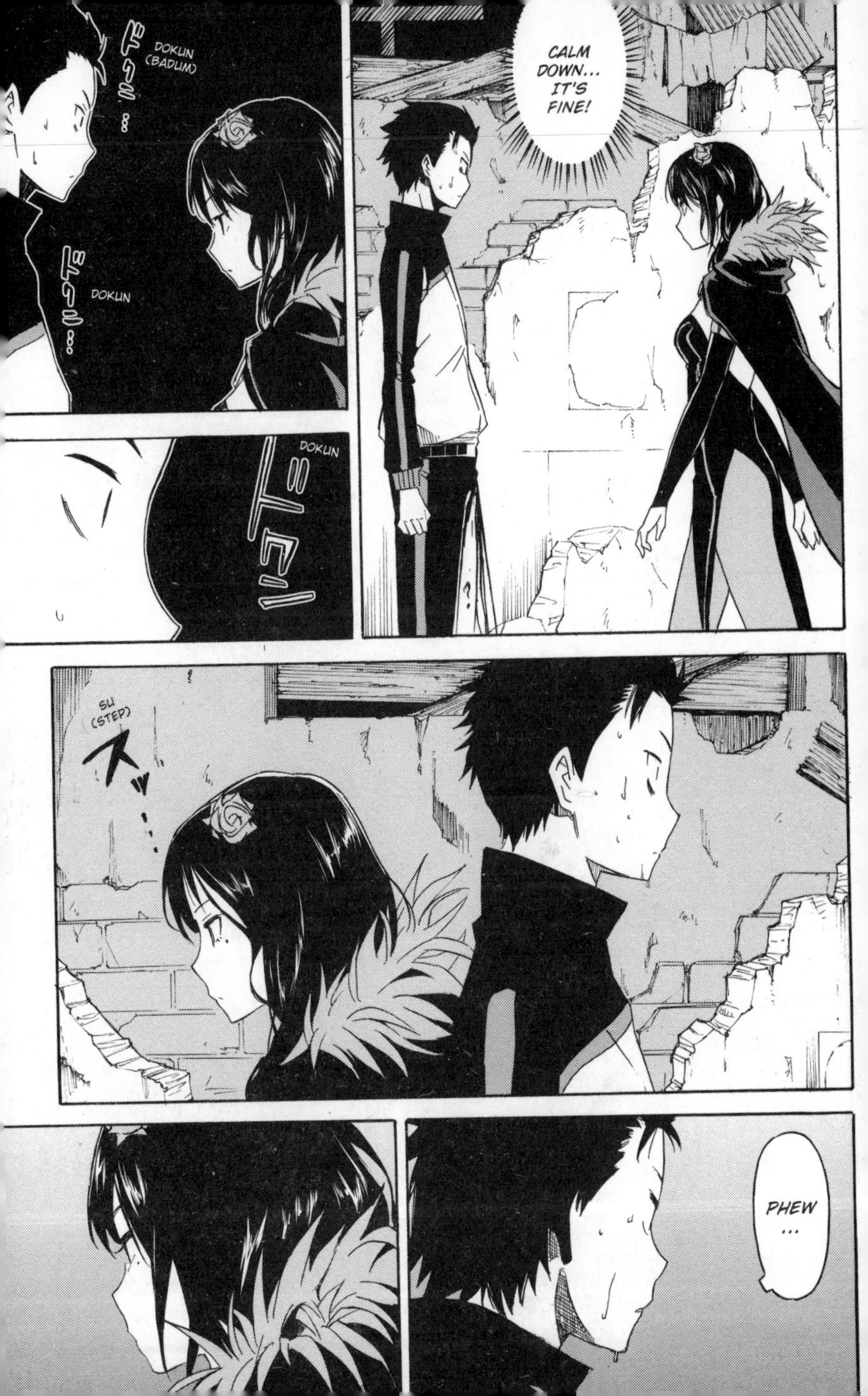
CALM DOWN... IT'S FINE!
DOKUN (BADUM)
ドクン…
DOKUN
ドクン…
DOKUN
ドクン
SU (STEP)
スッ…
PHEW...

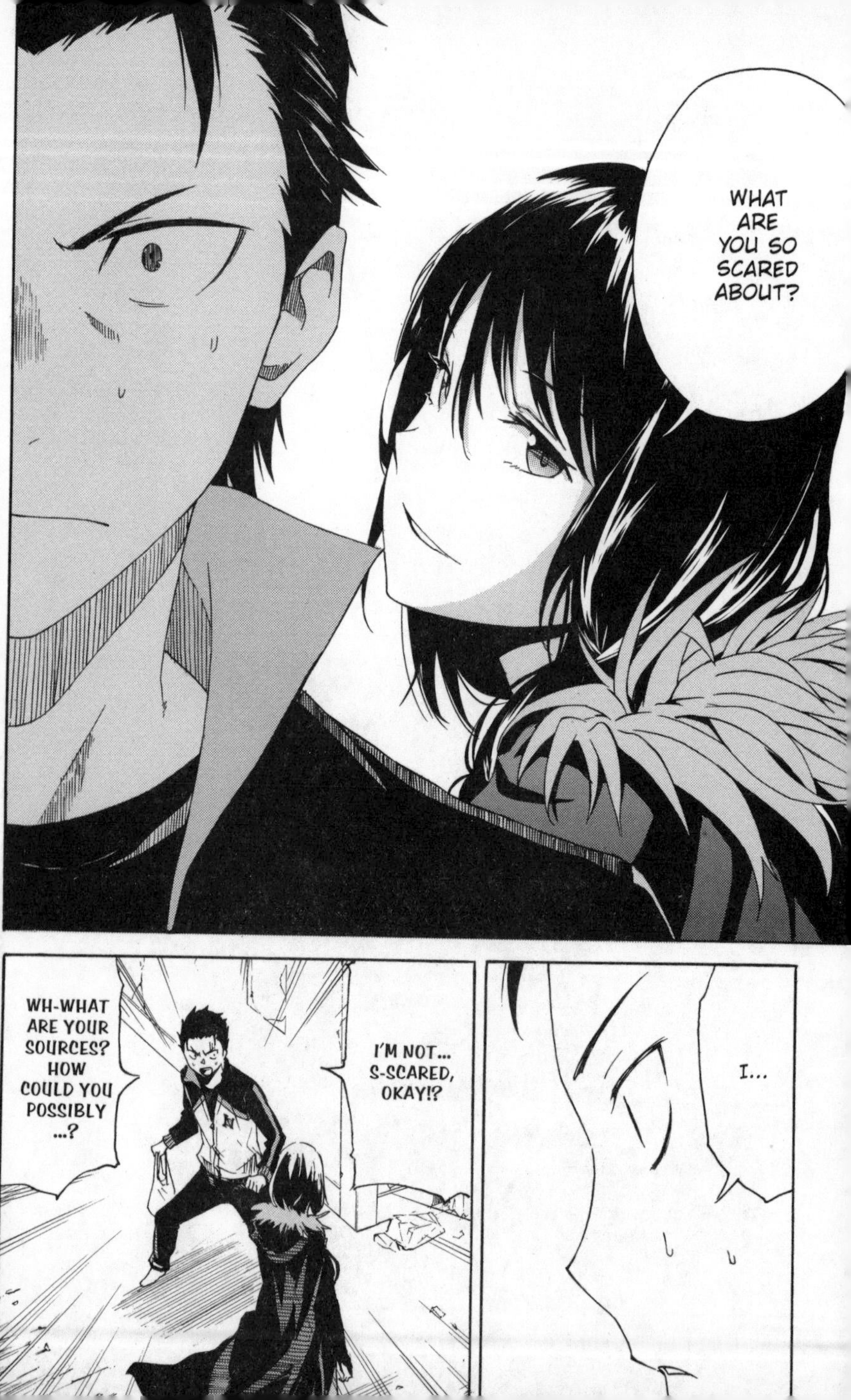
WHAT ARE YOU SO SCARED ABOUT?
I...
I'M NOT... S-SCARED, OKAY!?
WH-WHAT ARE YOUR SOURCES? HOW COULD YOU POSSIBLY ...?

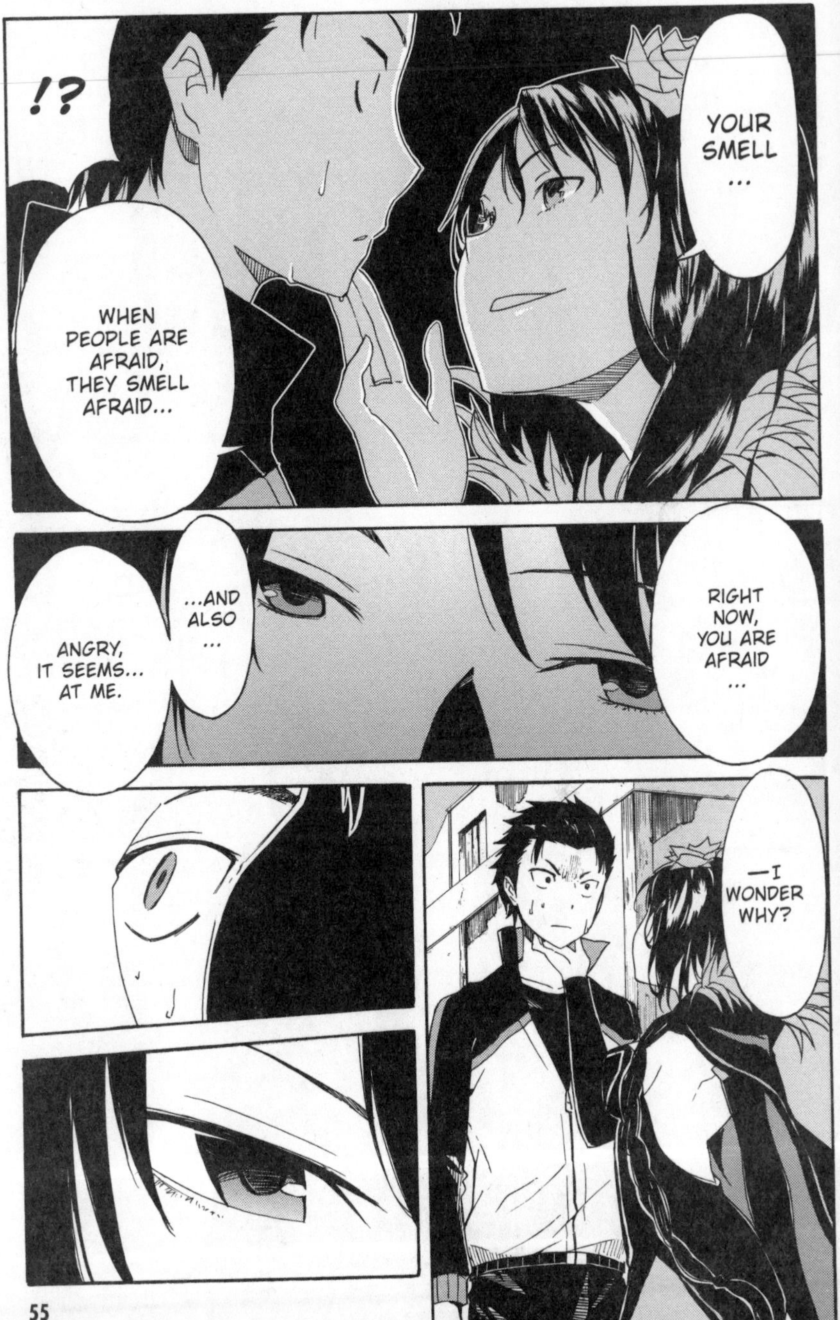

YOUR SMELL ...
!?
WHEN PEOPLE ARE AFRAID, THEY SMELL AFRAID...
RIGHT NOW, YOU ARE AFRAID ...
...AND ALSO ...
ANGRY, IT SEEMS... AT ME.
—I WONDER WHY?

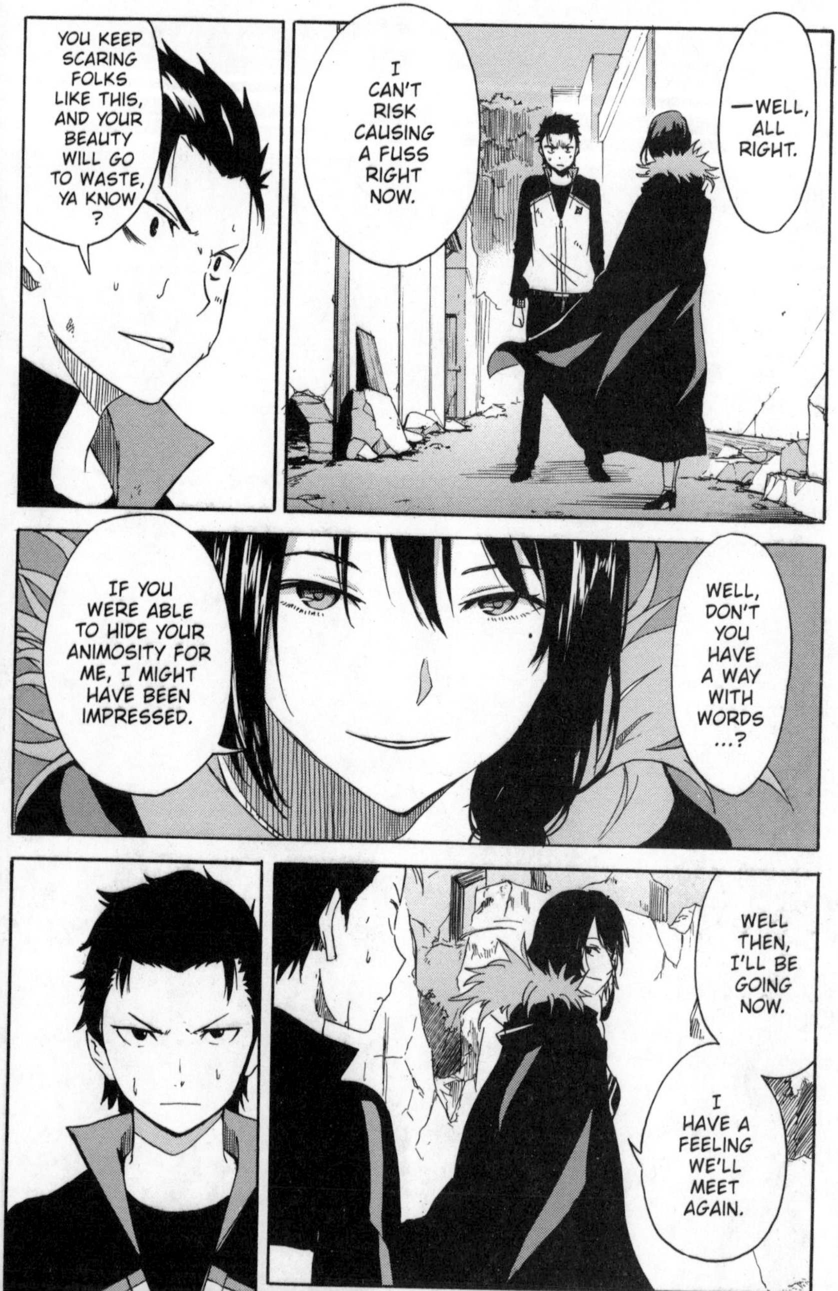
—WELL, ALL RIGHT.
I CAN'T RISK CAUSING A FUSS RIGHT NOW.
YOU KEEP SCARING FOLKS LIKE THIS, AND YOUR BEAUTY WILL GO TO WASTE, YA KNOW?
WELL, DON'T YOU HAVE A WAY WITH WORDS...?
IF YOU WERE ABLE TO HIDE YOUR ANIMOSITY FOR ME, I MIGHT HAVE BEEN IMPRESSED.
WELL THEN, I'LL BE GOING NOW.
I HAVE A FEELING WE'LL MEET AGAIN.

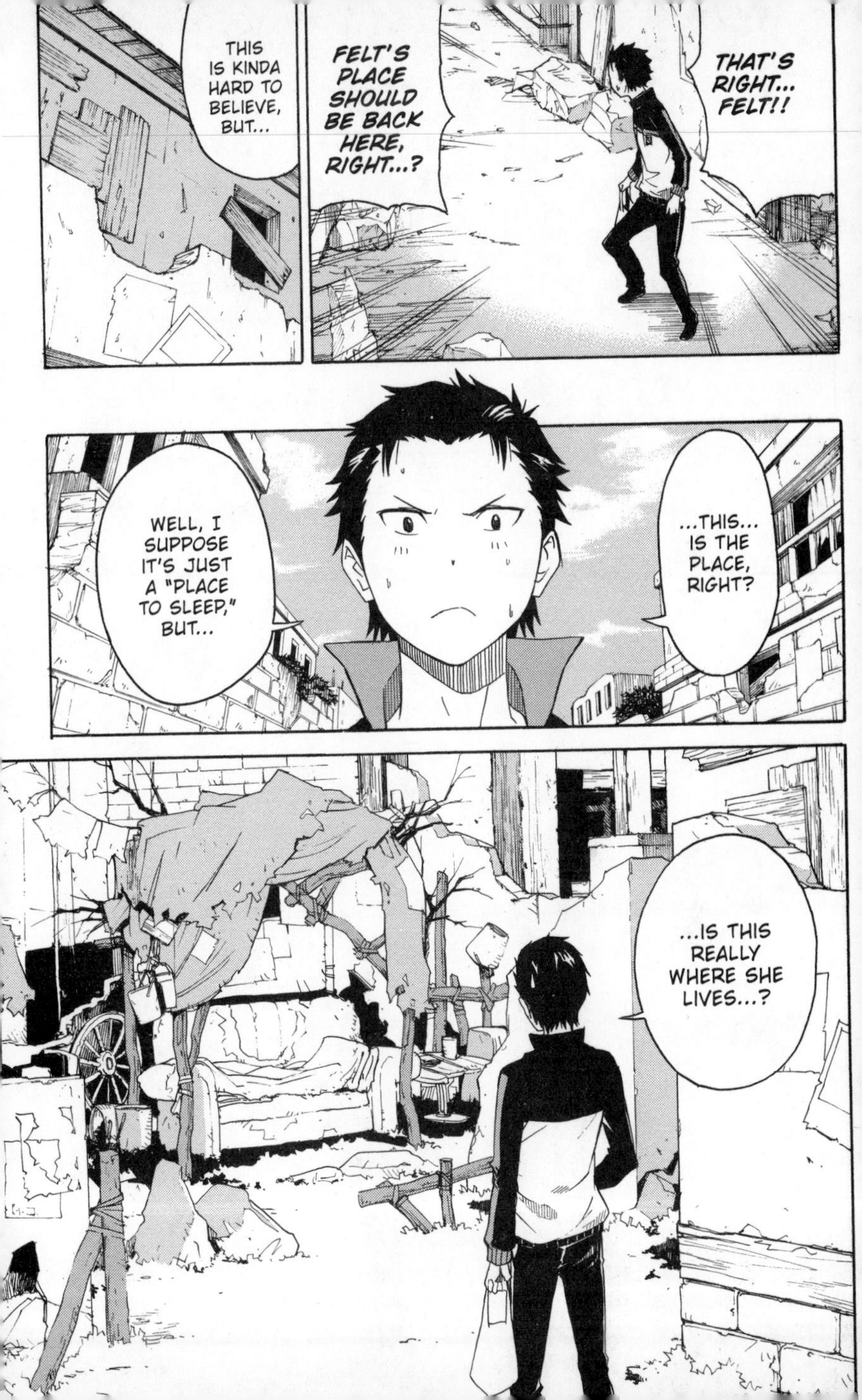
THAT'S RIGHT... FELT!!
FELT'S PLACE SHOULD BE BACK HERE, RIGHT...?
THIS IS KINDA HARD TO BELIEVE, BUT...
...THIS... IS THE PLACE, RIGHT?
WELL, I SUPPOSE IT'S JUST A "PLACE TO SLEEP," BUT...
...IS THIS REALLY WHERE SHE LIVES...?

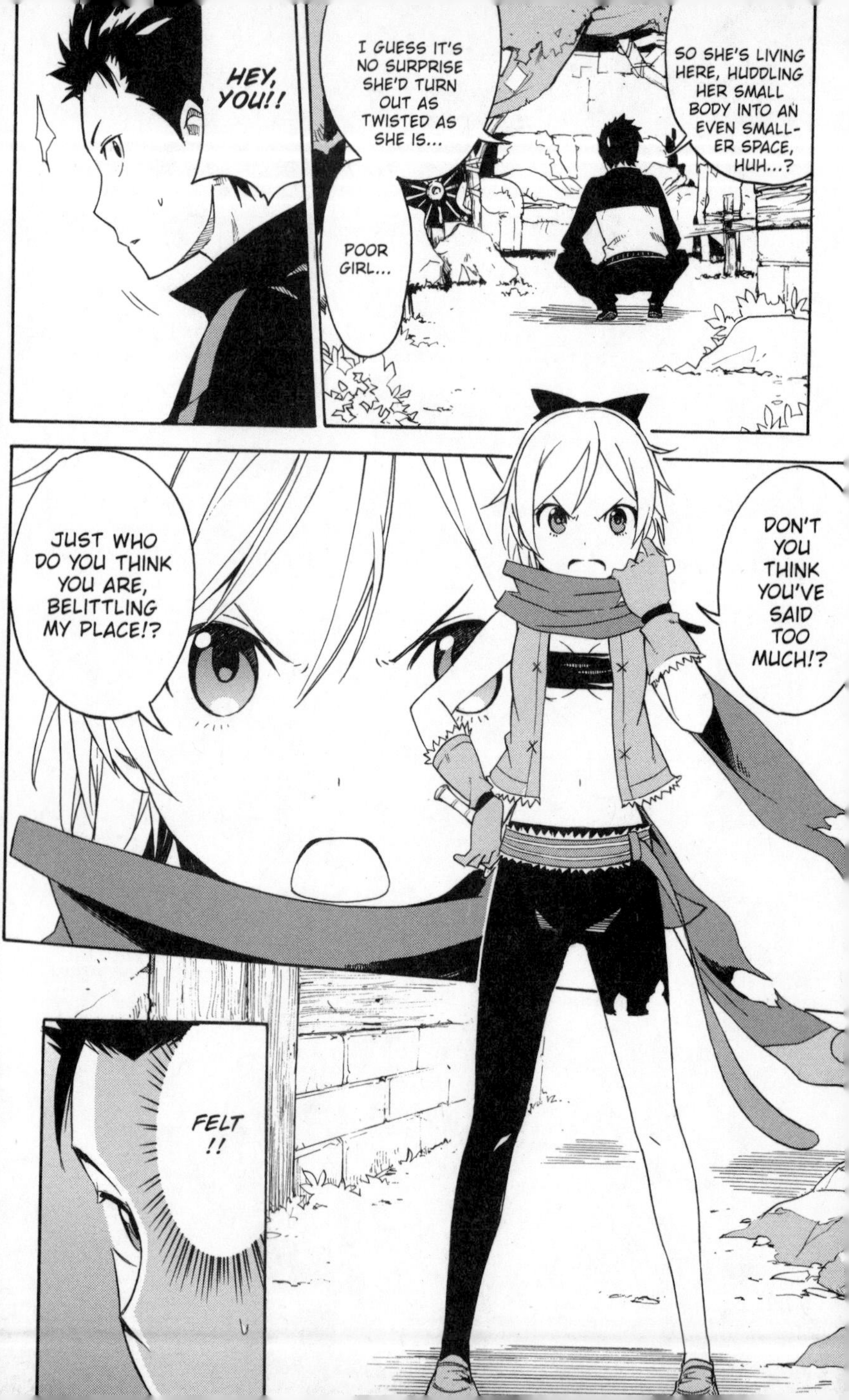
SO SHE'S LIVING HERE, HUDDLING HER SMALL BODY INTO AN EVEN SMALLER SPACE, HUH...?
I GUESS IT'S NO SURPRISE SHE'D TURN OUT AS TWISTED AS SHE IS...
POOR GIRL...
HEY, YOU!!
DON'T YOU THINK YOU'VE SAID TOO MUCH!?
JUST WHO DO YOU THINK YOU ARE, BELITTLING MY PLACE!?
FELT!!

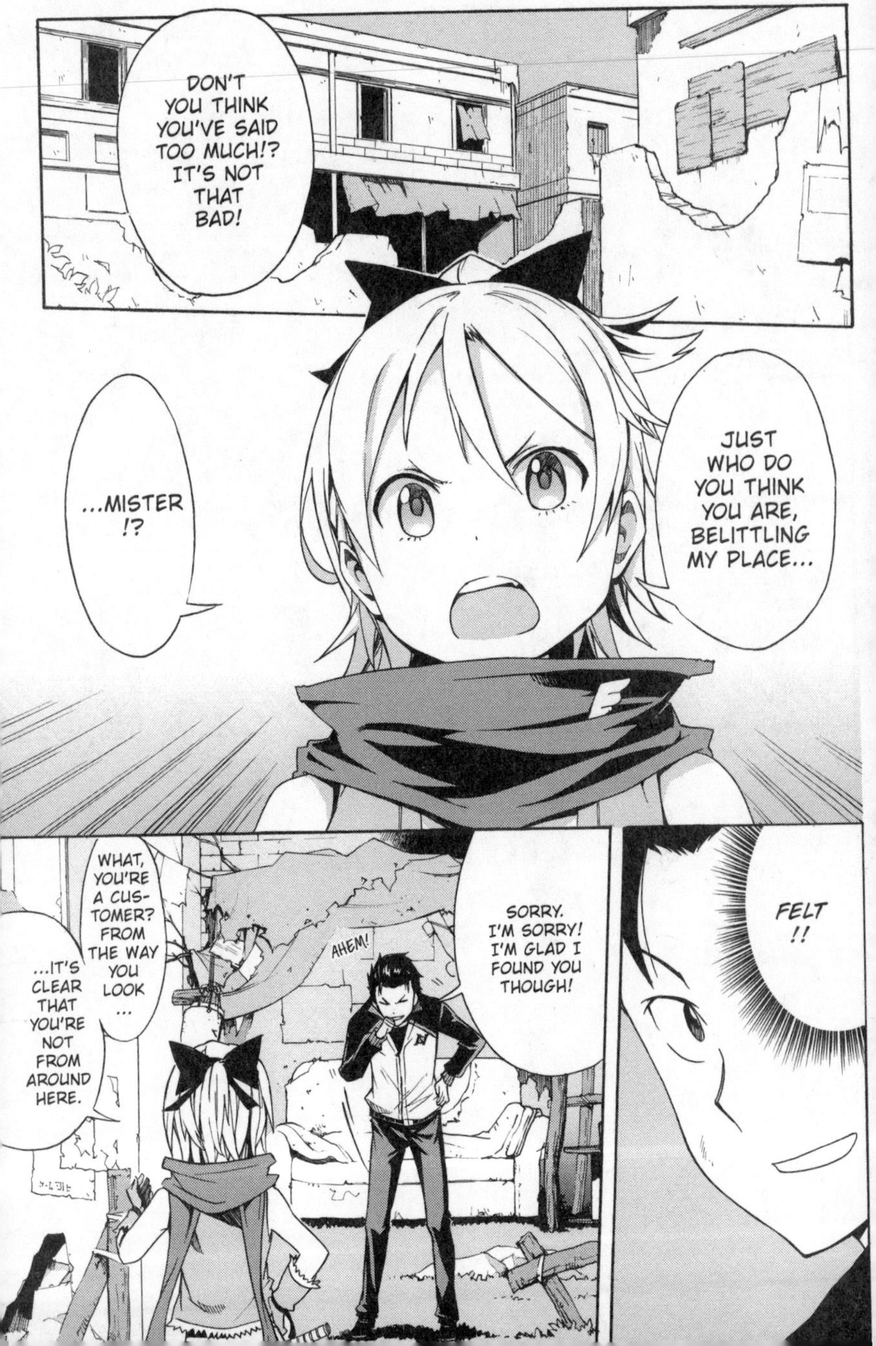
DON'T YOU THINK YOU'VE SAID TOO MUCH!? IT'S NOT THAT BAD!
JUST WHO DO YOU THINK YOU ARE, BELITTLING MY PLACE...
...MISTER !?
FELT !!
SORRY. I'M SORRY! I'M GLAD I FOUND YOU THOUGH!
AHEM!
WHAT, YOU'RE A CUS-TOMER? FROM THE WAY YOU LOOK ...
...IT'S CLEAR THAT YOU'RE NOT FROM AROUND HERE.

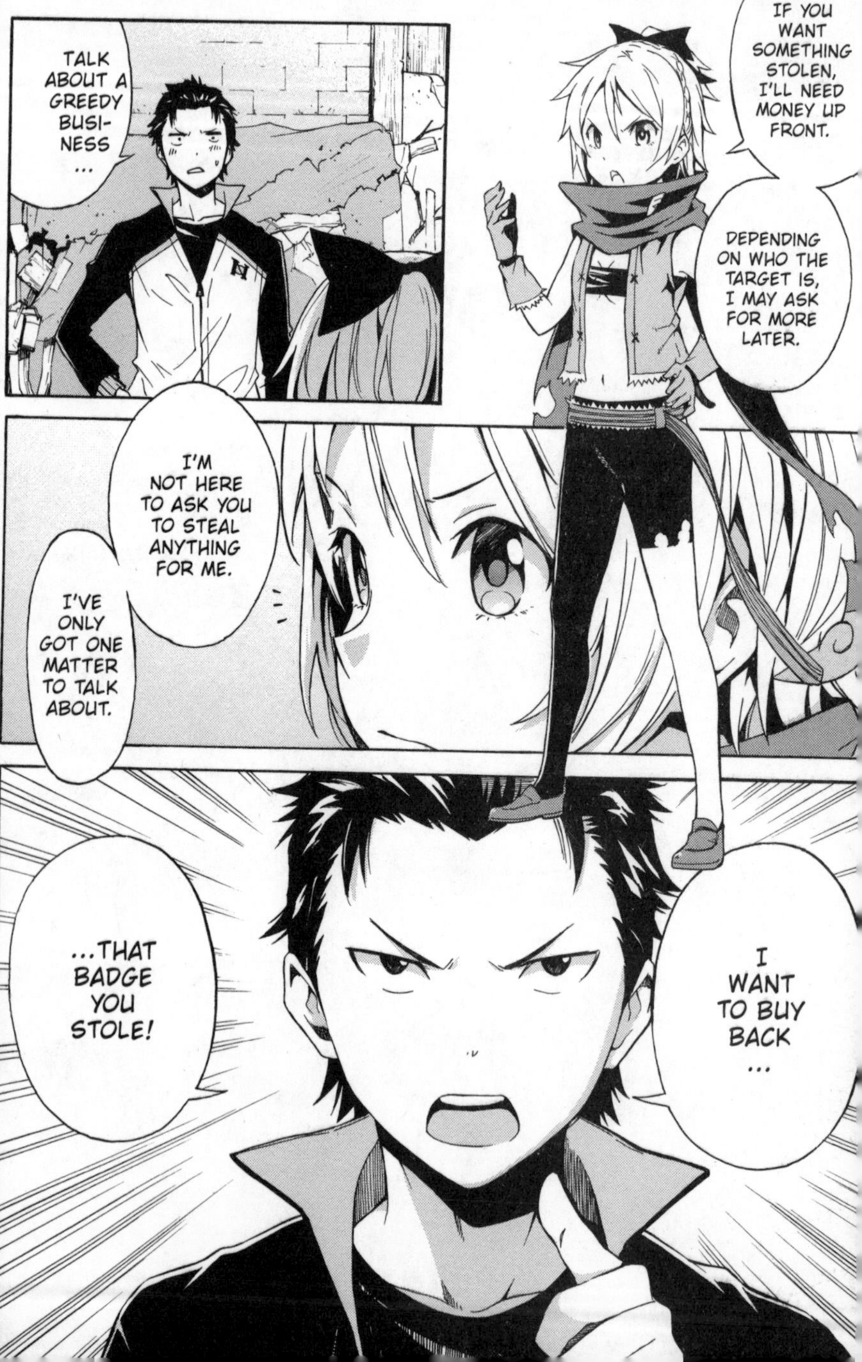
IF YOU WANT SOMETHING STOLEN, I'LL NEED MONEY UP FRONT.
DEPENDING ON WHO THE TARGET IS, I MAY ASK FOR MORE LATER.
TALK ABOUT A GREEDY BUSI-NESS...
I'M NOT HERE TO ASK YOU TO STEAL ANYTHING FOR ME.
I'VE ONLY GOT ONE MATTER TO TALK ABOUT.
I WANT TO BUY BACK...
...THAT BADGE YOU STOLE!

Episode 8: Negotiations in the Slums

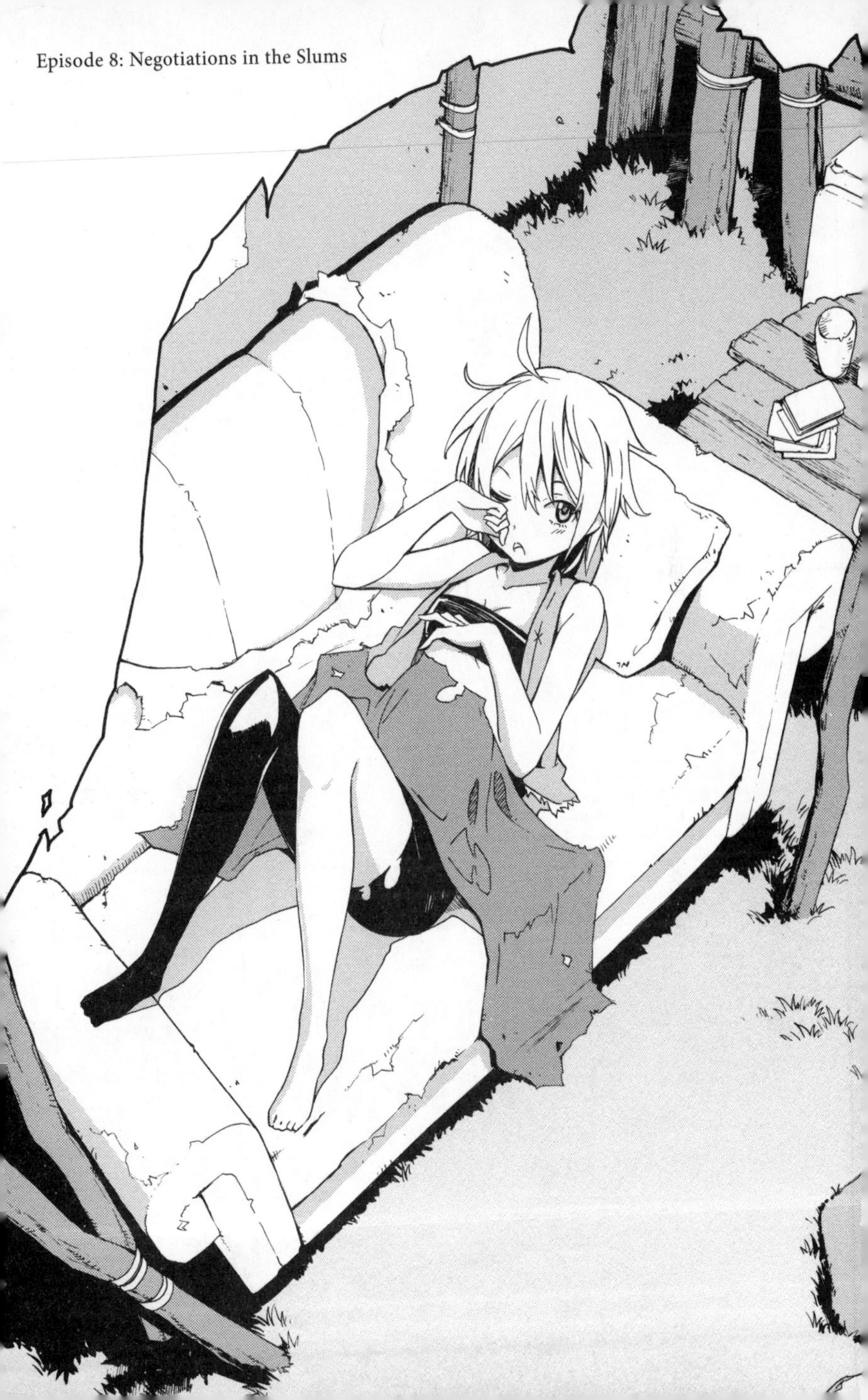

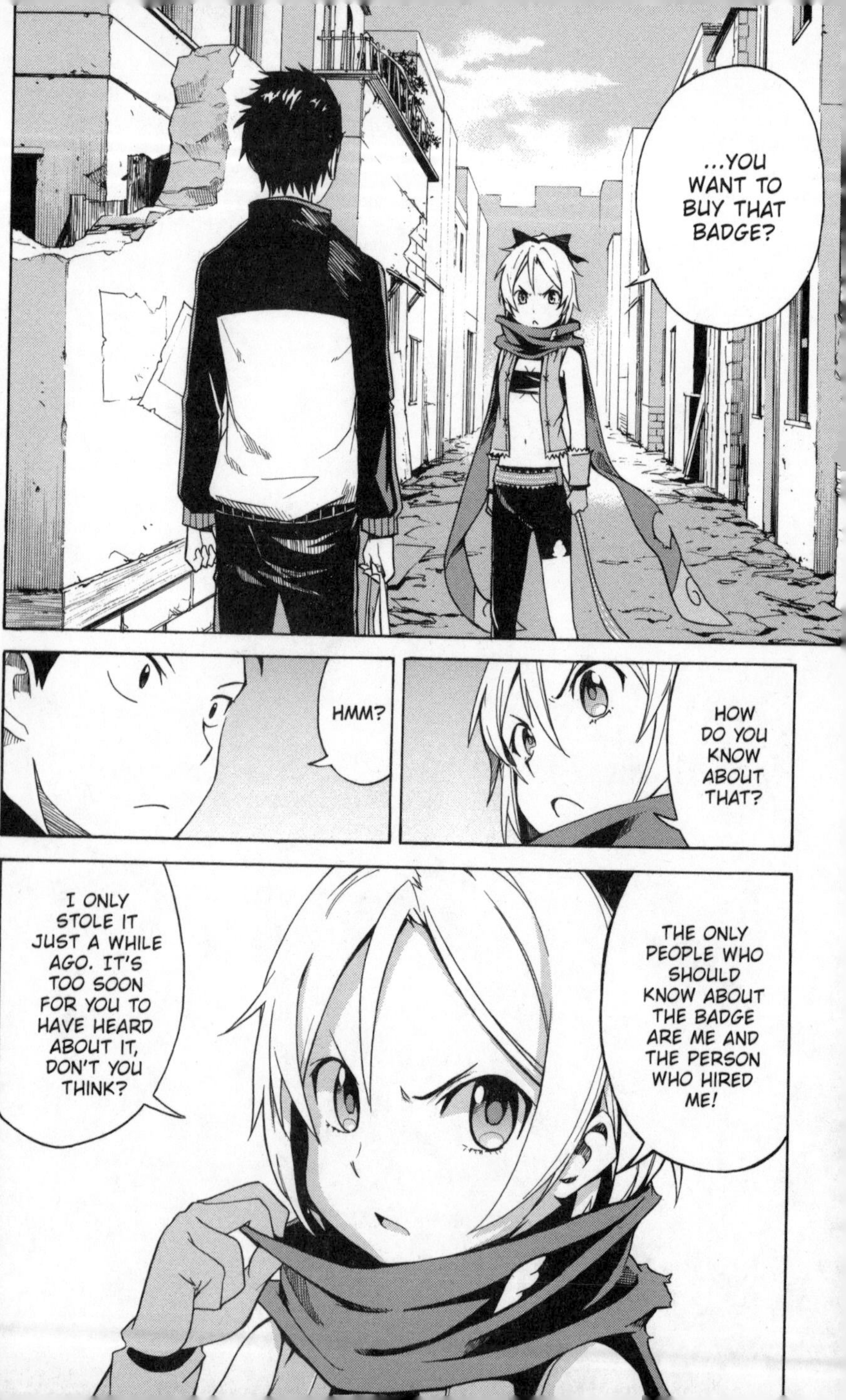
...YOU WANT TO BUY THAT BADGE?
HOW DO YOU KNOW ABOUT THAT?
HMM?
THE ONLY PEOPLE WHO SHOULD KNOW ABOUT THE BADGE ARE ME AND THE PERSON WHO HIRED ME!
I ONLY STOLE IT JUST A WHILE AGO. IT'S TOO SOON FOR YOU TO HAVE HEARD ABOUT IT, DON'T YOU THINK?

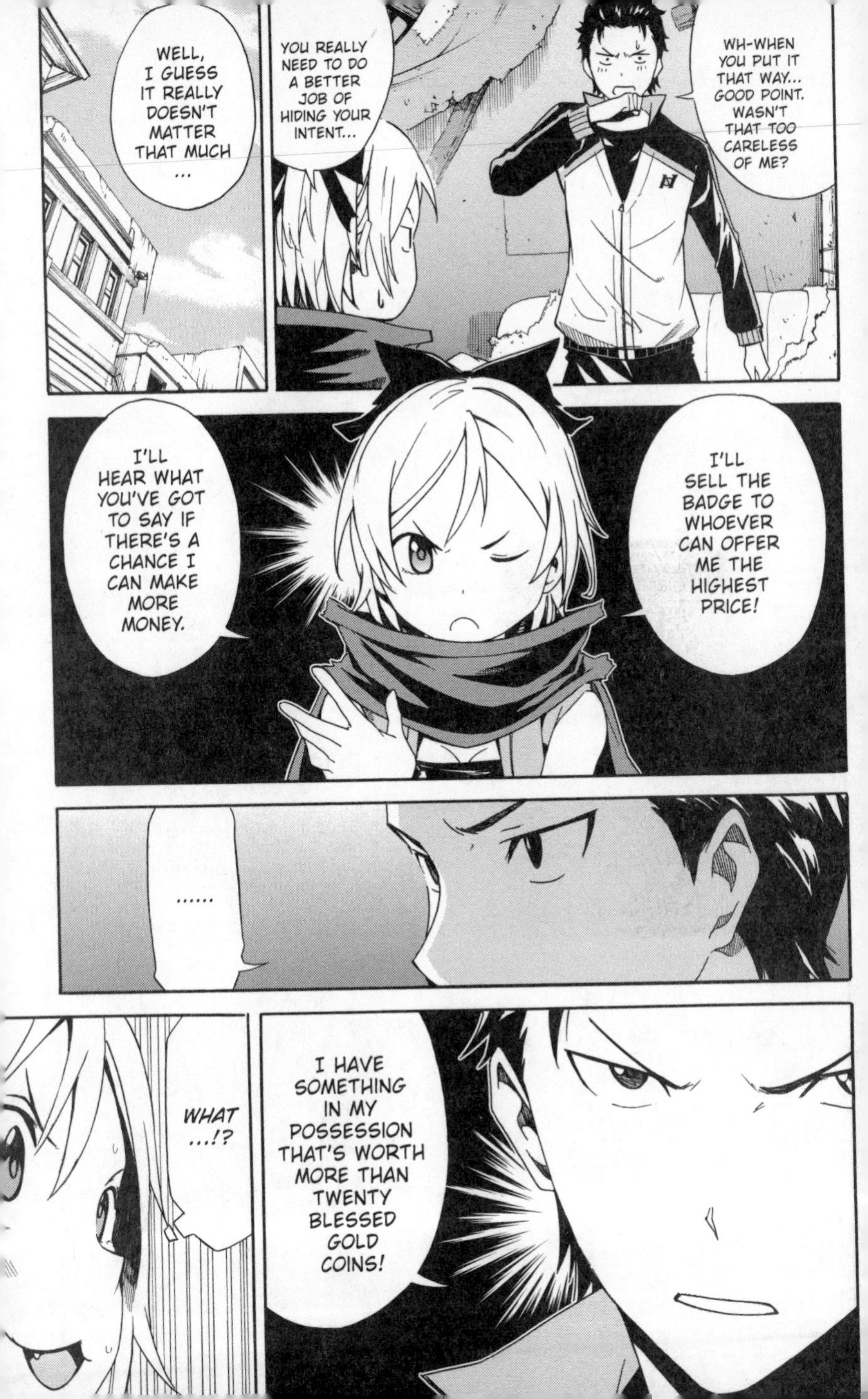
WH-WHEN YOU PUT IT THAT WAY... GOOD POINT. WASN'T THAT TOO CARELESS OF ME?
YOU REALLY NEED TO DO A BETTER JOB OF HIDING YOUR INTENT...
WELL, I GUESS IT REALLY DOESN'T MATTER THAT MUCH ...
I'LL SELL THE BADGE TO WHOEVER CAN OFFER ME THE HIGHEST PRICE!
I'LL HEAR WHAT YOU'VE GOT TO SAY IF THERE'S A CHANCE I CAN MAKE MORE MONEY.
......
I HAVE SOMETHING IN MY POSSESSION THAT'S WORTH MORE THAN TWENTY BLESSED GOLD COINS!
WHAT ...!?

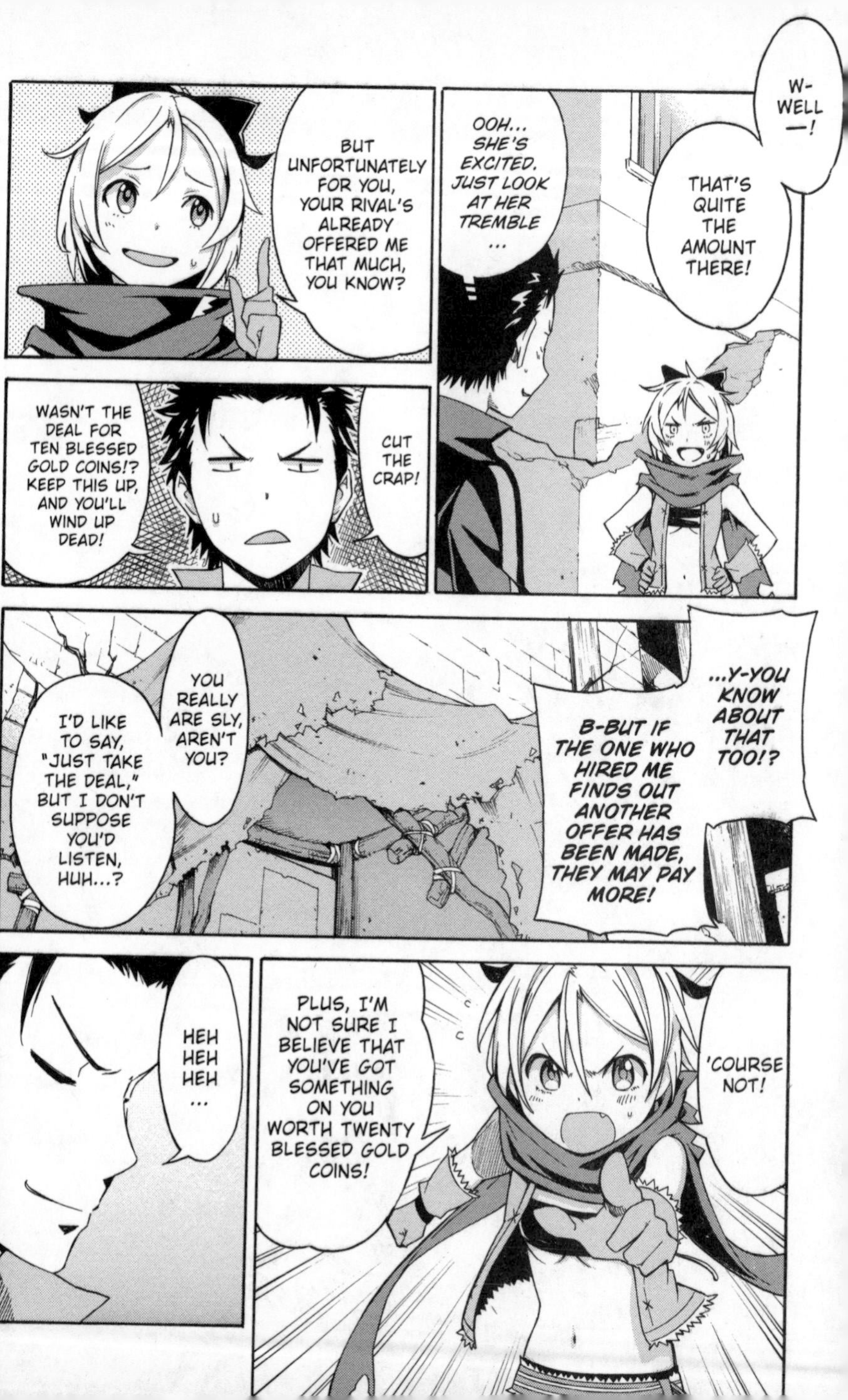
W-WELL—!
THAT'S QUITE THE AMOUNT THERE!
OOH... SHE'S EXCITED. JUST LOOK AT HER TREMBLE...
BUT UNFORTUNATELY FOR YOU, YOUR RIVAL'S ALREADY OFFERED ME THAT MUCH, YOU KNOW?
CUT THE CRAP!
WASN'T THE DEAL FOR TEN BLESSED GOLD COINS!? KEEP THIS UP, AND YOU'LL WIND UP DEAD!
...Y-YOU KNOW ABOUT THAT TOO!?
B-BUT IF THE ONE WHO HIRED ME FINDS OUT ANOTHER OFFER HAS BEEN MADE, THEY MAY PAY MORE!
YOU REALLY ARE SLY, AREN'T YOU?
I'D LIKE TO SAY, "JUST TAKE THE DEAL," BUT I DON'T SUPPOSE YOU'D LISTEN, HUH...?
'COURSE NOT!
PLUS, I'M NOT SURE I BELIEVE THAT YOU'VE GOT SOMETHING ON YOU WORTH TWENTY BLESSED GOLD COINS!
HEH HEH HEH...

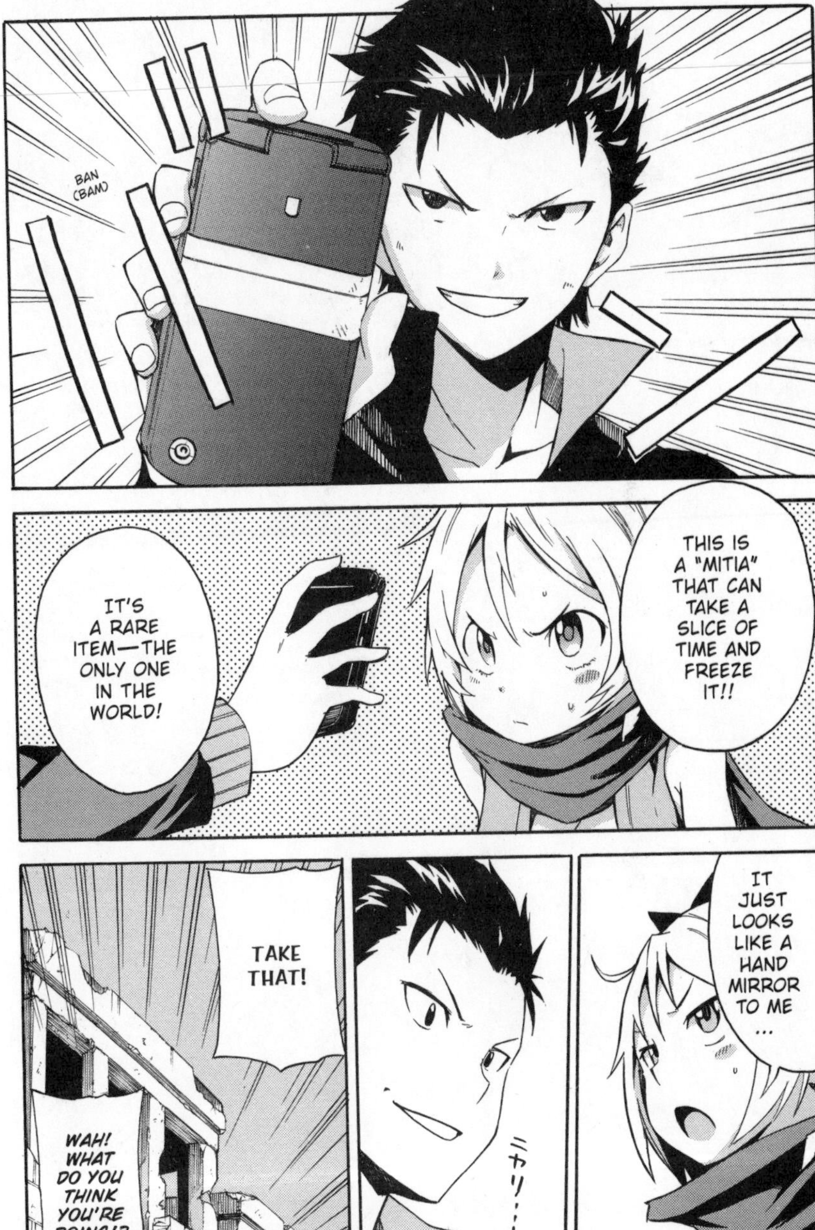
BAN (BAM)
THIS IS A "MITIA" THAT CAN TAKE A SLICE OF TIME AND FREEZE IT!!
IT'S A RARE ITEM—THE ONLY ONE IN THE WORLD!
IT JUST LOOKS LIKE A HAND MIRROR TO ME ...
ニヤリ・・・
NIYARI (SMIRK)
TAKE THAT!
WAH! WHAT DO YOU THINK YOU'RE DOING!?

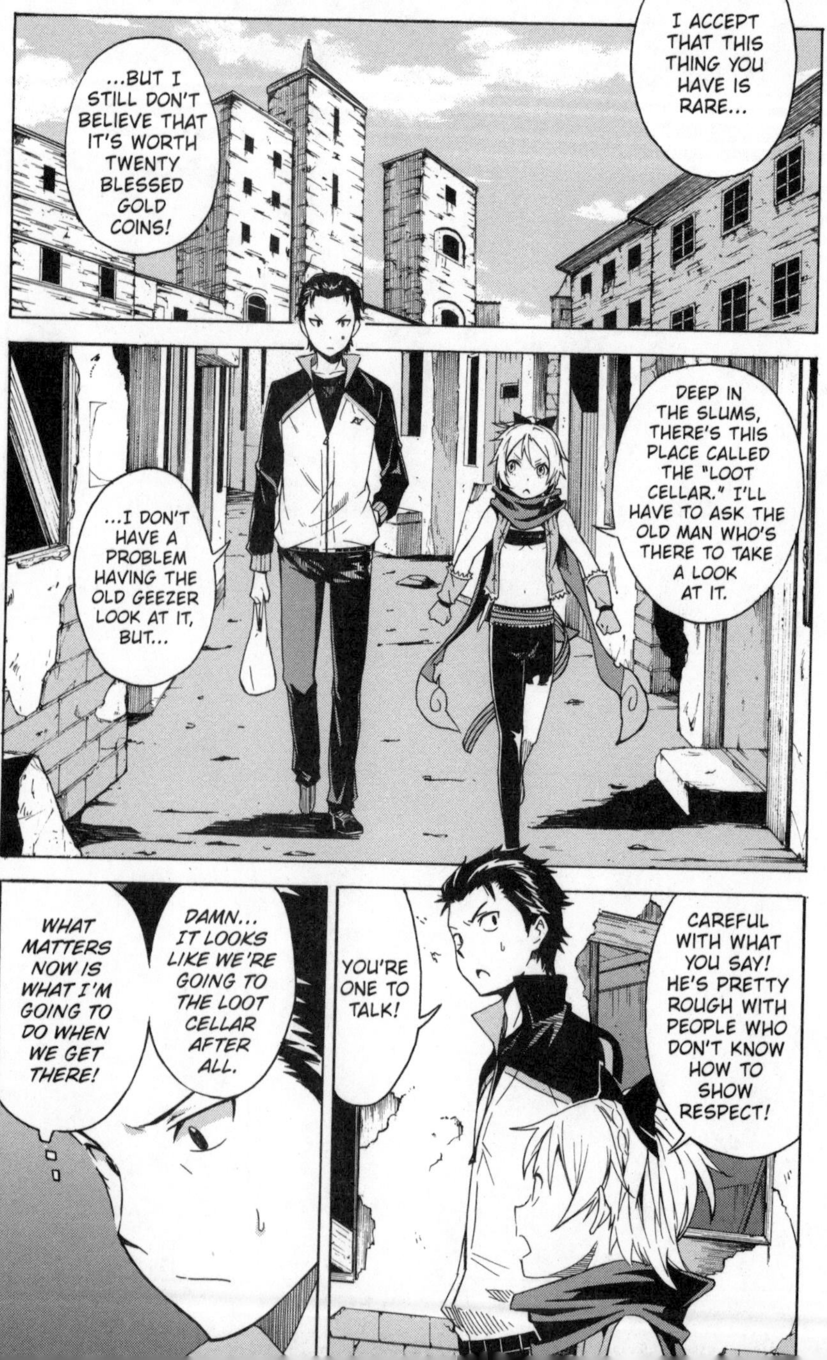
I ACCEPT THAT THIS THING YOU HAVE IS RARE...
...BUT I STILL DON'T BELIEVE THAT IT'S WORTH TWENTY BLESSED GOLD COINS!
DEEP IN THE SLUMS, THERE'S THIS PLACE CALLED THE "LOOT CELLAR." I'LL HAVE TO ASK THE OLD MAN WHO'S THERE TO TAKE A LOOK AT IT.
...I DON'T HAVE A PROBLEM HAVING THE OLD GEEZER LOOK AT IT, BUT...
CAREFUL WITH WHAT YOU SAY! HE'S PRETTY ROUGH WITH PEOPLE WHO DON'T KNOW HOW TO SHOW RESPECT!
YOU'RE ONE TO TALK!
DAMN... IT LOOKS LIKE WE'RE GOING TO THE LOOT CELLAR AFTER ALL.
WHAT MATTERS NOW IS WHAT I'M GOING TO DO WHEN WE GET THERE!

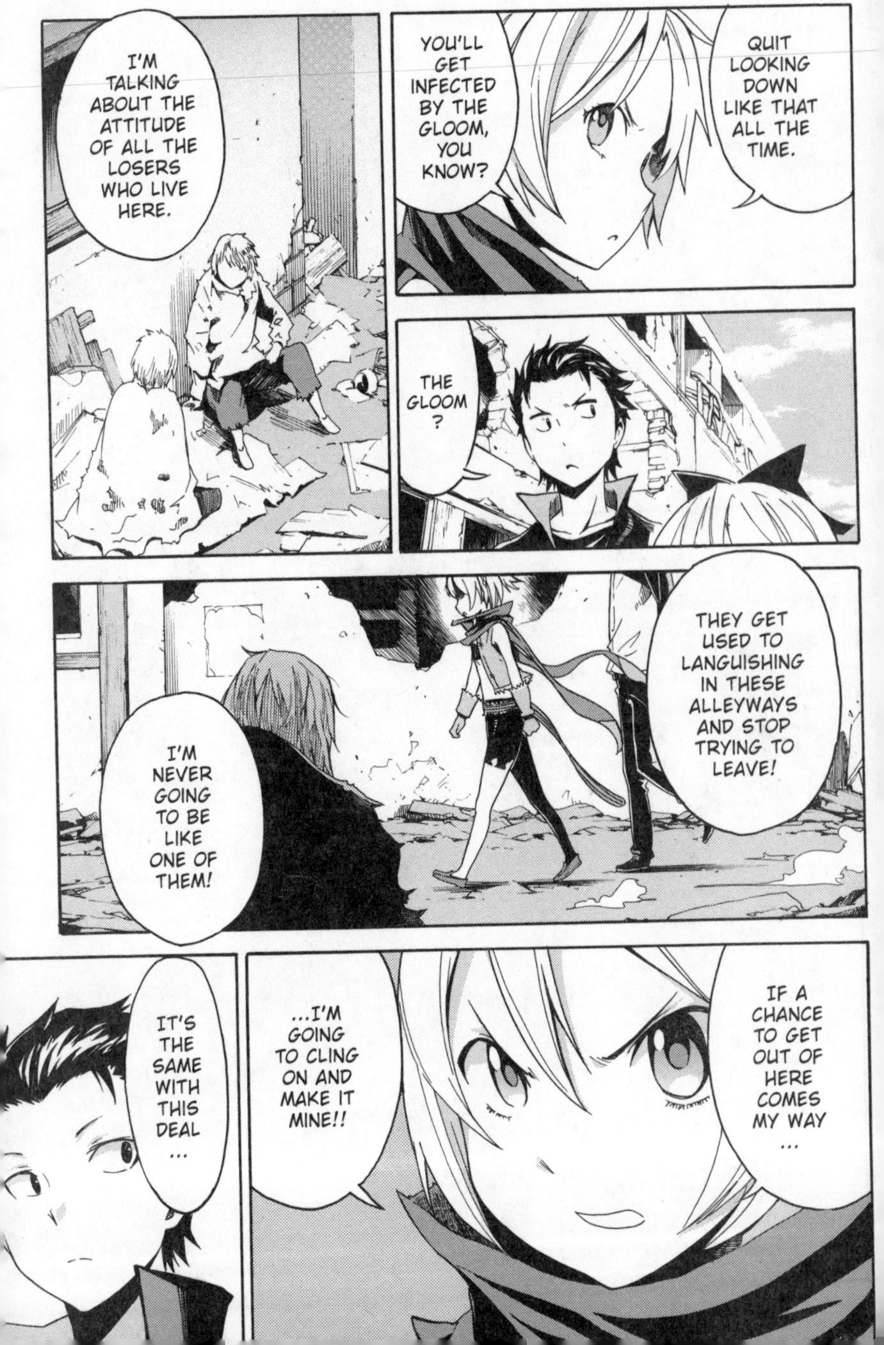
QUIT LOOKING DOWN LIKE THAT ALL THE TIME.
YOU'LL GET INFECTED BY THE GLOOM, YOU KNOW?
THE GLOOM?
I'M TALKING ABOUT THE ATTITUDE OF ALL THE LOSERS WHO LIVE HERE.
THEY GET USED TO LANGUISHING IN THESE ALLEYWAYS AND STOP TRYING TO LEAVE!
I'M NEVER GOING TO BE LIKE ONE OF THEM!
IF A CHANCE TO GET OUT OF HERE COMES MY WAY ...
...I'M GOING TO CLING ON AND MAKE IT MINE!!
IT'S THE SAME WITH THIS DEAL ...

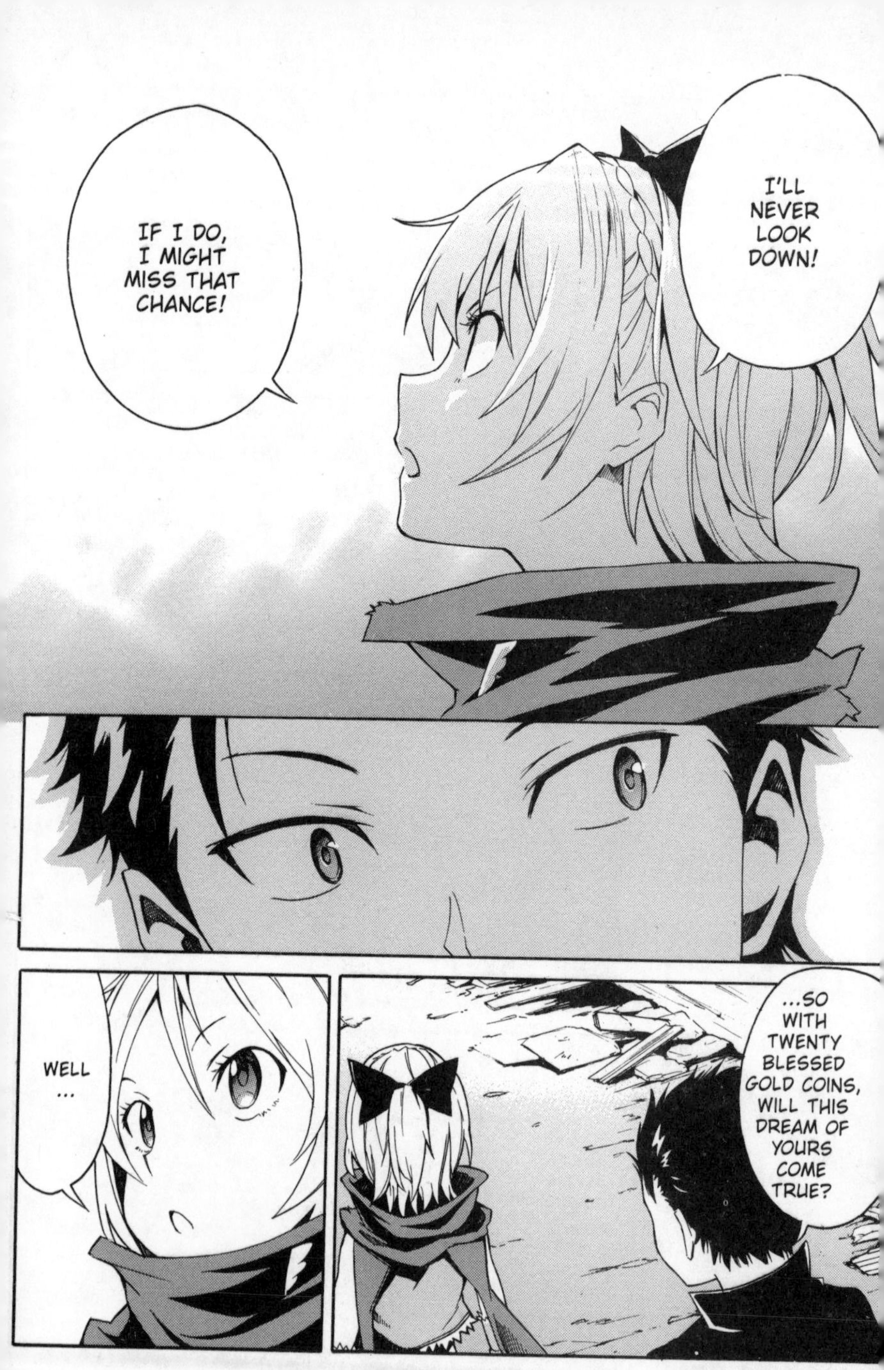
I'LL NEVER LOOK DOWN!
IF I DO, I MIGHT MISS THAT CHANCE!
...SO WITH TWENTY BLESSED GOLD COINS, WILL THIS DREAM OF YOURS COME TRUE?
WELL ...

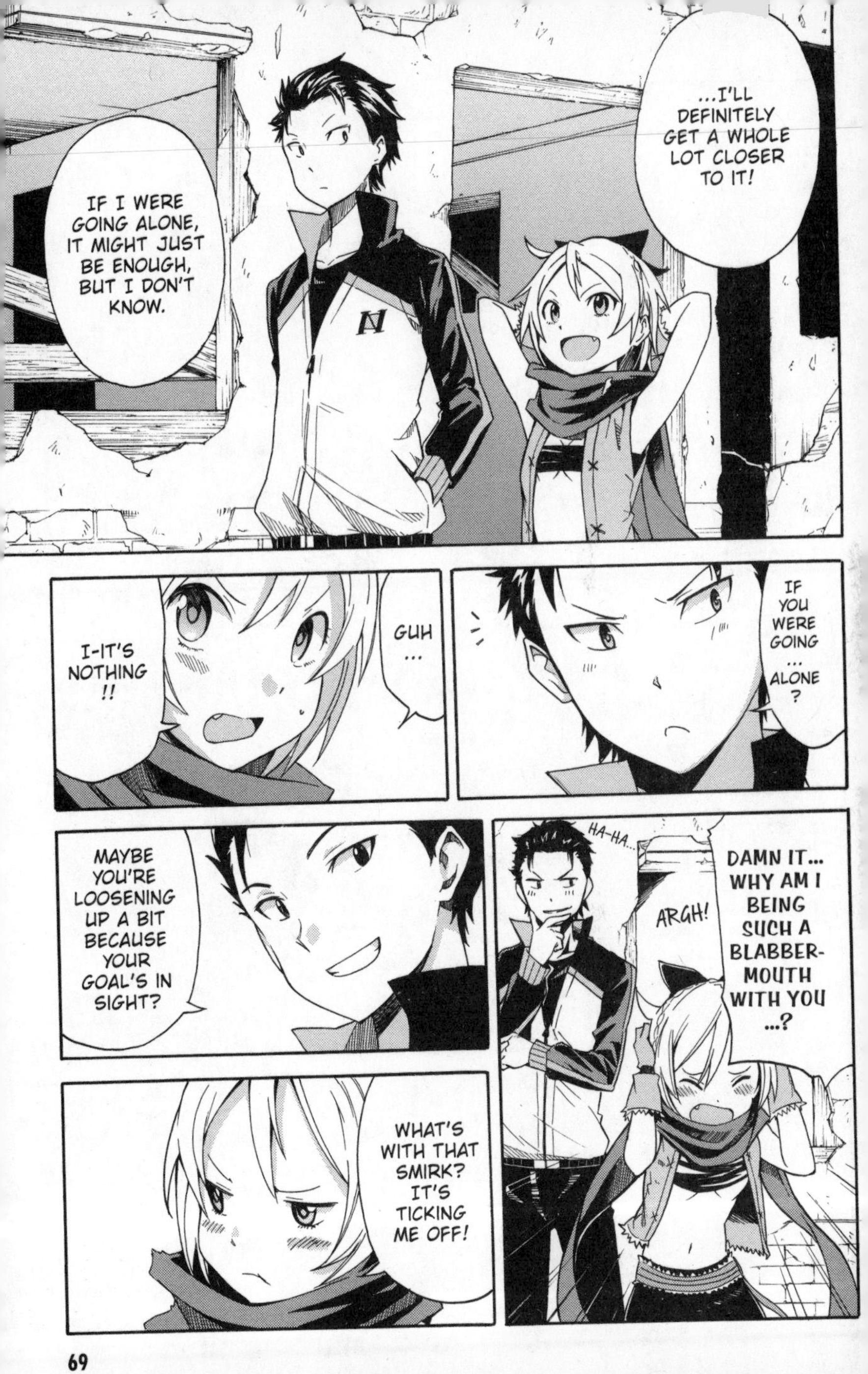
...I'LL DEFINITELY GET A WHOLE LOT CLOSER TO IT!
IF I WERE GOING ALONE, IT MIGHT JUST BE ENOUGH, BUT I DON'T KNOW.
IF YOU WERE GOING ... ALONE?
GUH ...
I-IT'S NOTHING !!
DAMN IT... WHY AM I BEING SUCH A BLABBER-MOUTH WITH YOU ...?
HA-HA...
ARGH!
MAYBE YOU'RE LOOSENING UP A BIT BECAUSE YOUR GOAL'S IN SIGHT?
WHAT'S WITH THAT SMIRK? IT'S TICKING ME OFF!

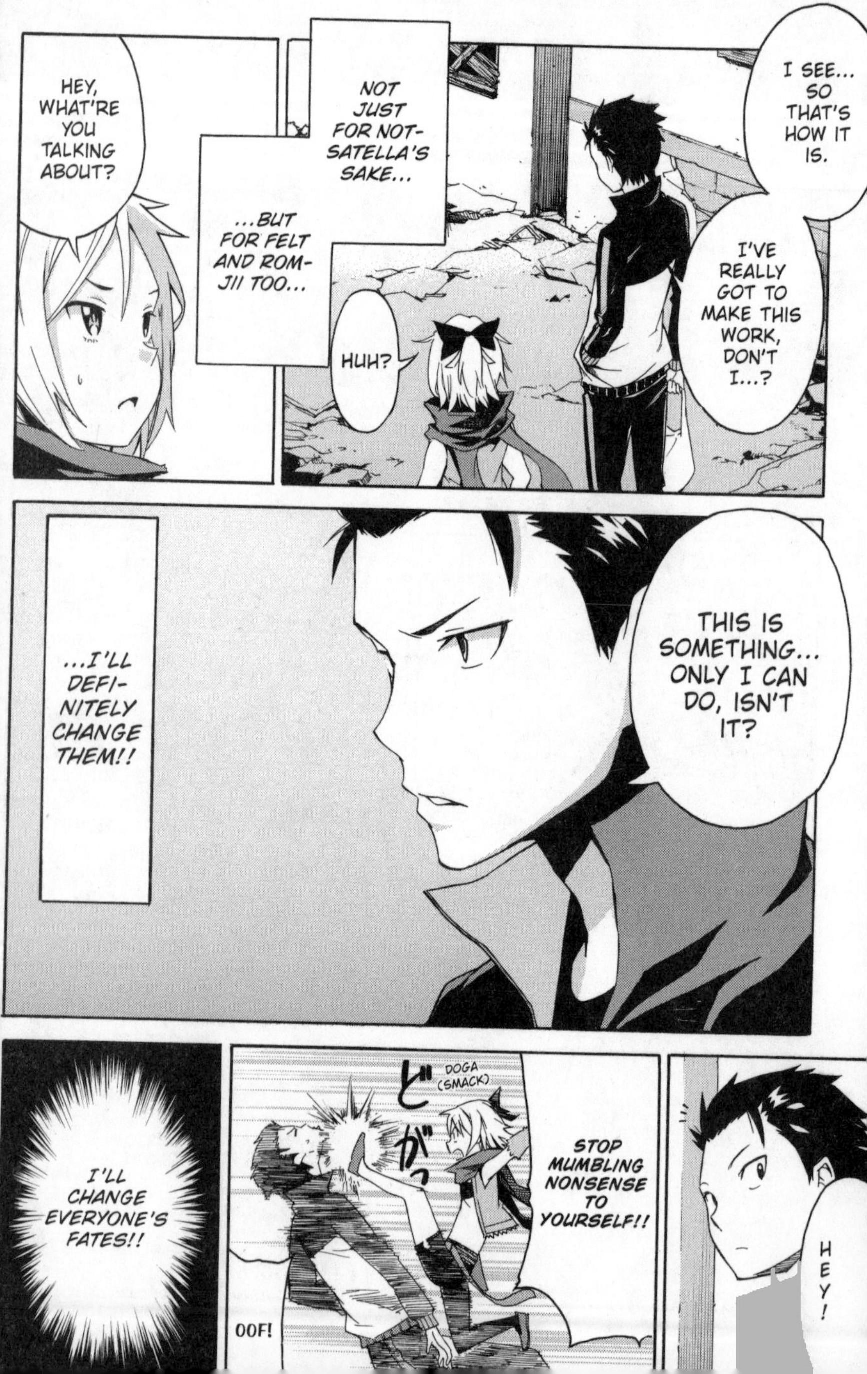
I SEE... SO THAT'S HOW IT IS.
I'VE REALLY GOT TO MAKE THIS WORK, DON'T I...?
HUH?
NOT JUST FOR NOT-SATELLA'S SAKE...
...BUT FOR FELT AND ROM-JII TOO...
HEY, WHAT'RE YOU TALKING ABOUT?
THIS IS SOMETHING... ONLY I CAN DO, ISN'T IT?
...I'LL DEFINITELY CHANGE THEM!!
HEY!
どがっ
DOGA (SMACK)
STOP MUMBLING NONSENSE TO YOURSELF!!
OOF!
I'LL CHANGE EVERYONE'S FATES!!

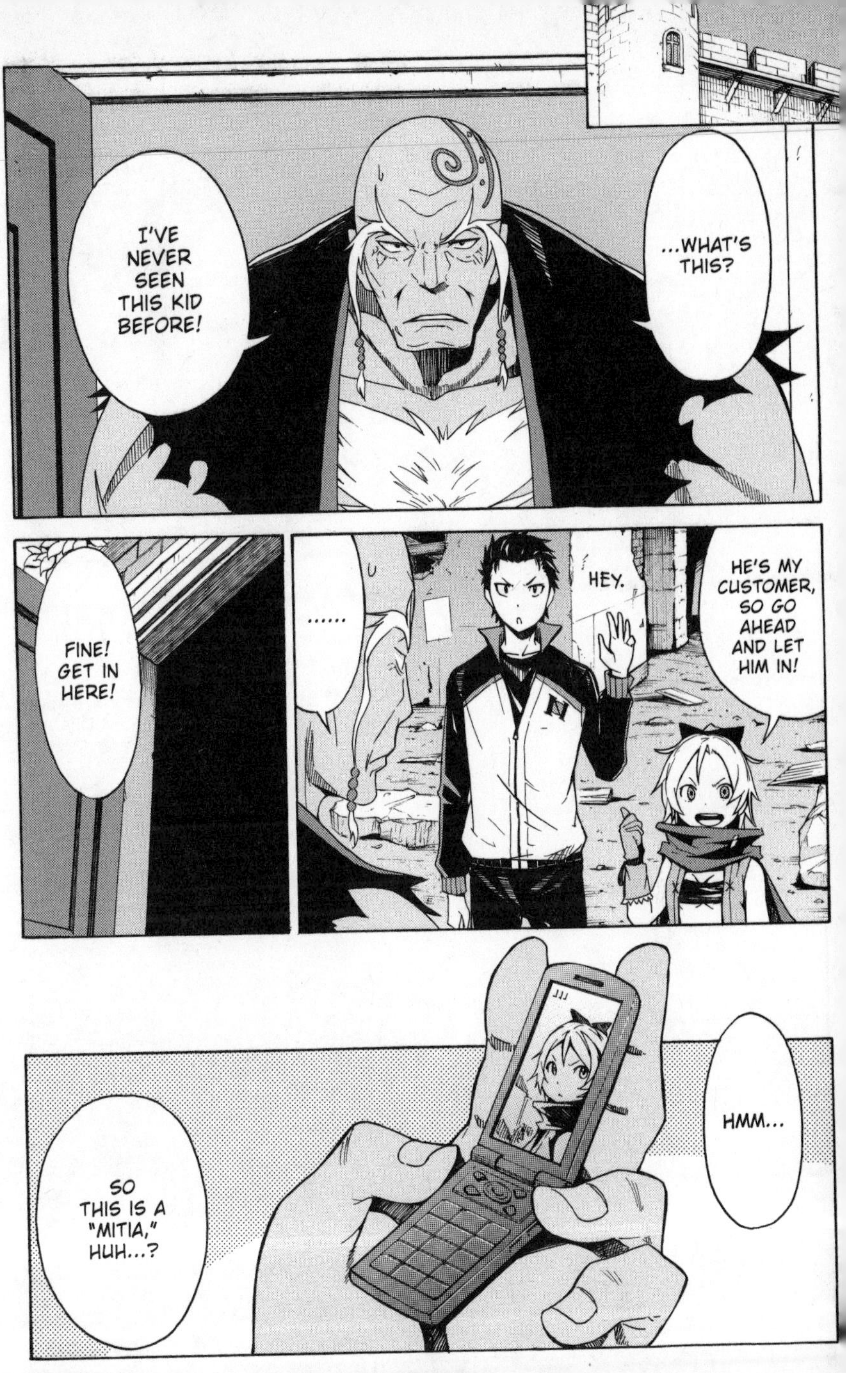
...WHAT'S THIS?
I'VE NEVER SEEN THIS KID BEFORE!
HE'S MY CUSTOMER, SO GO AHEAD AND LET HIM IN!
HEY.
......
FINE! GET IN HERE!
HMM...
SO THIS IS A "MITIA," HUH...?

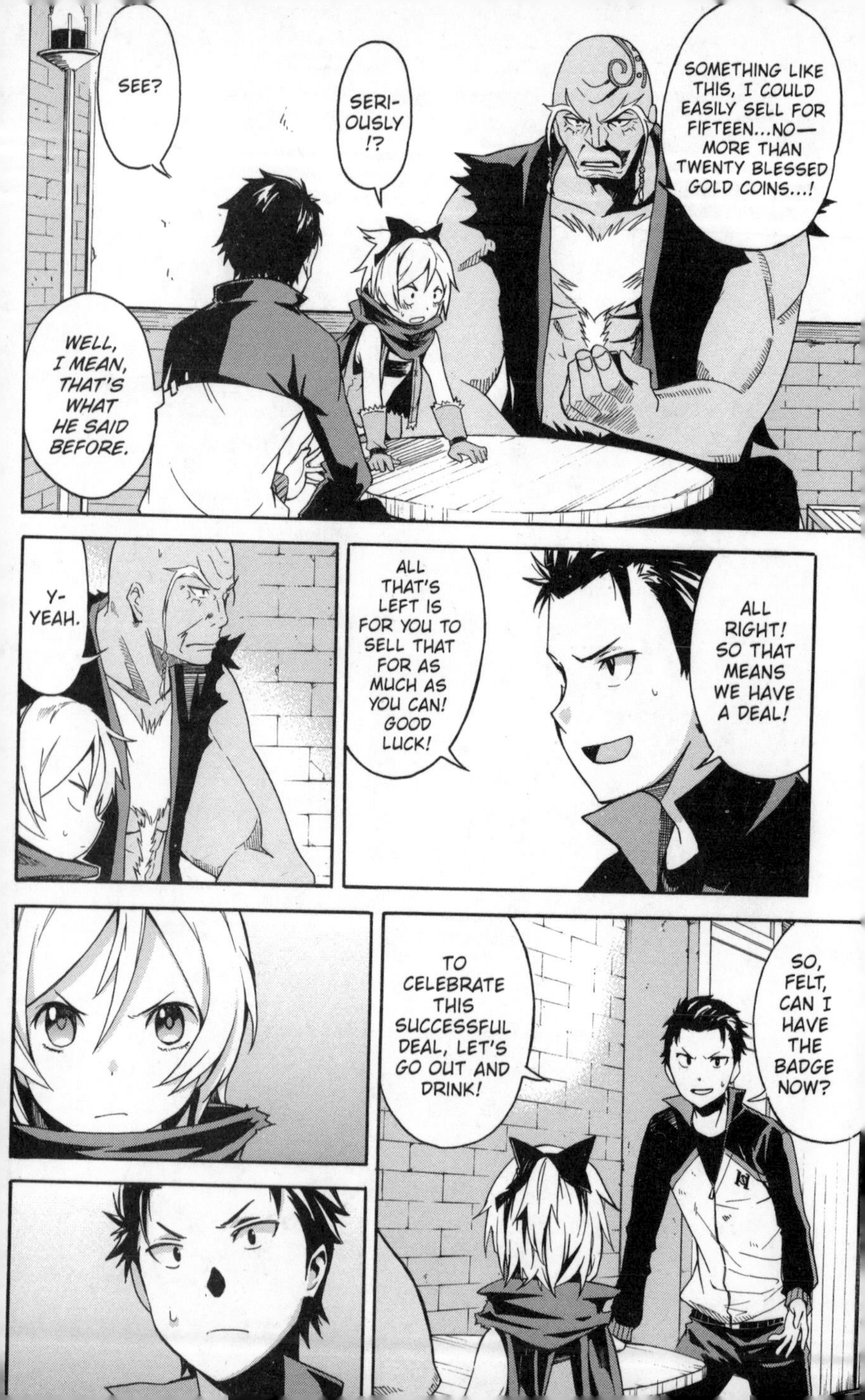
SOMETHING LIKE THIS, I COULD EASILY SELL FOR FIFTEEN...NO—MORE THAN TWENTY BLESSED GOLD COINS...!
SERI-OUSLY!?
SEE?
WELL, I MEAN, THAT'S WHAT HE SAID BEFORE.
ALL RIGHT! SO THAT MEANS WE HAVE A DEAL!
ALL THAT'S LEFT IS FOR YOU TO SELL THAT FOR AS MUCH AS YOU CAN! GOOD LUCK!
Y-YEAH.
SO, FELT, CAN I HAVE THE BADGE NOW?
TO CELEBRATE THIS SUCCESSFUL DEAL, LET'S GO OUT AND DRINK!

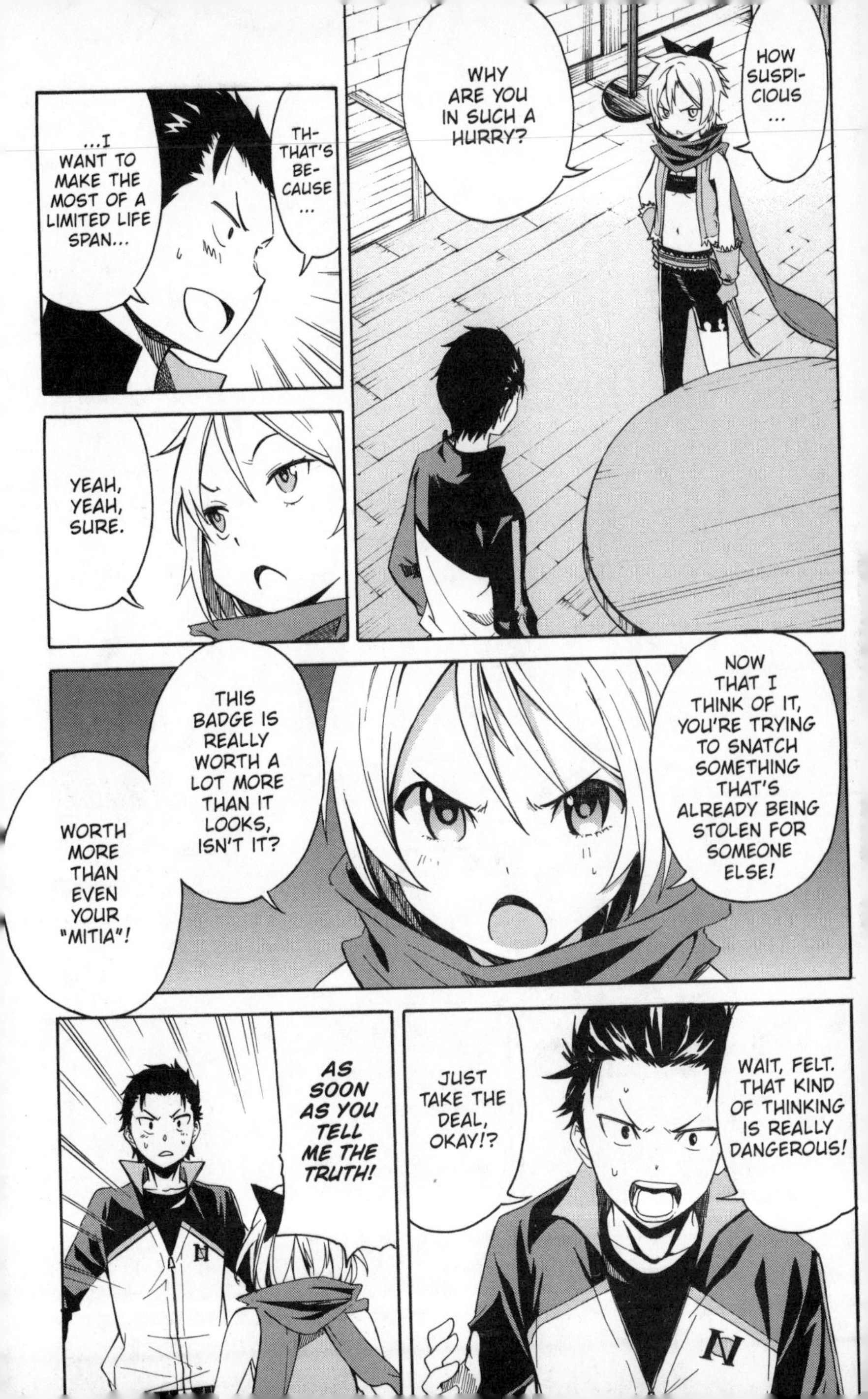
HOW SUSPICIOUS...
WHY ARE YOU IN SUCH A HURRY?
TH-THAT'S BECAUSE...
...I WANT TO MAKE THE MOST OF A LIMITED LIFE SPAN...
YEAH, YEAH, SURE.
NOW THAT I THINK OF IT, YOU'RE TRYING TO SNATCH SOMETHING THAT'S ALREADY BEING STOLEN FOR SOMEONE ELSE!
THIS BADGE IS REALLY WORTH A LOT MORE THAN IT LOOKS, ISN'T IT?
WORTH MORE THAN EVEN YOUR "MITIA"!
WAIT, FELT. THAT KIND OF THINKING IS REALLY DANGEROUS!
JUST TAKE THE DEAL, OKAY!?
AS SOON AS YOU TELL ME THE TRUTH!

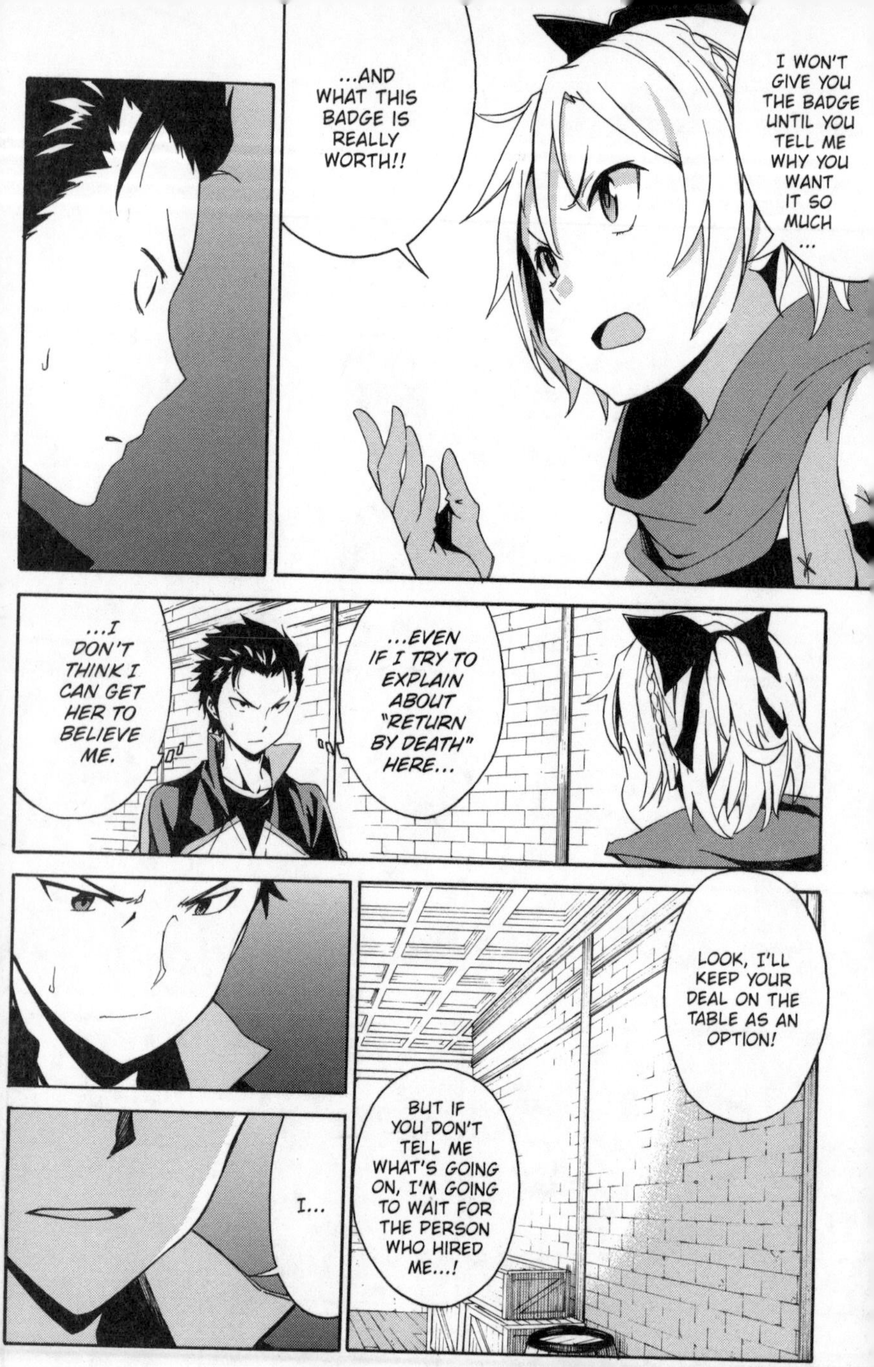
I WON'T GIVE YOU THE BADGE UNTIL YOU TELL ME WHY YOU WANT IT SO MUCH...
...AND WHAT THIS BADGE IS REALLY WORTH!!
...EVEN IF I TRY TO EXPLAIN ABOUT "RETURN BY DEATH" HERE...
...I DON'T THINK I CAN GET HER TO BELIEVE ME.
LOOK, I'LL KEEP YOUR DEAL ON THE TABLE AS AN OPTION!
BUT IF YOU DON'T TELL ME WHAT'S GOING ON, I'M GOING TO WAIT FOR THE PERSON WHO HIRED ME...!
I...

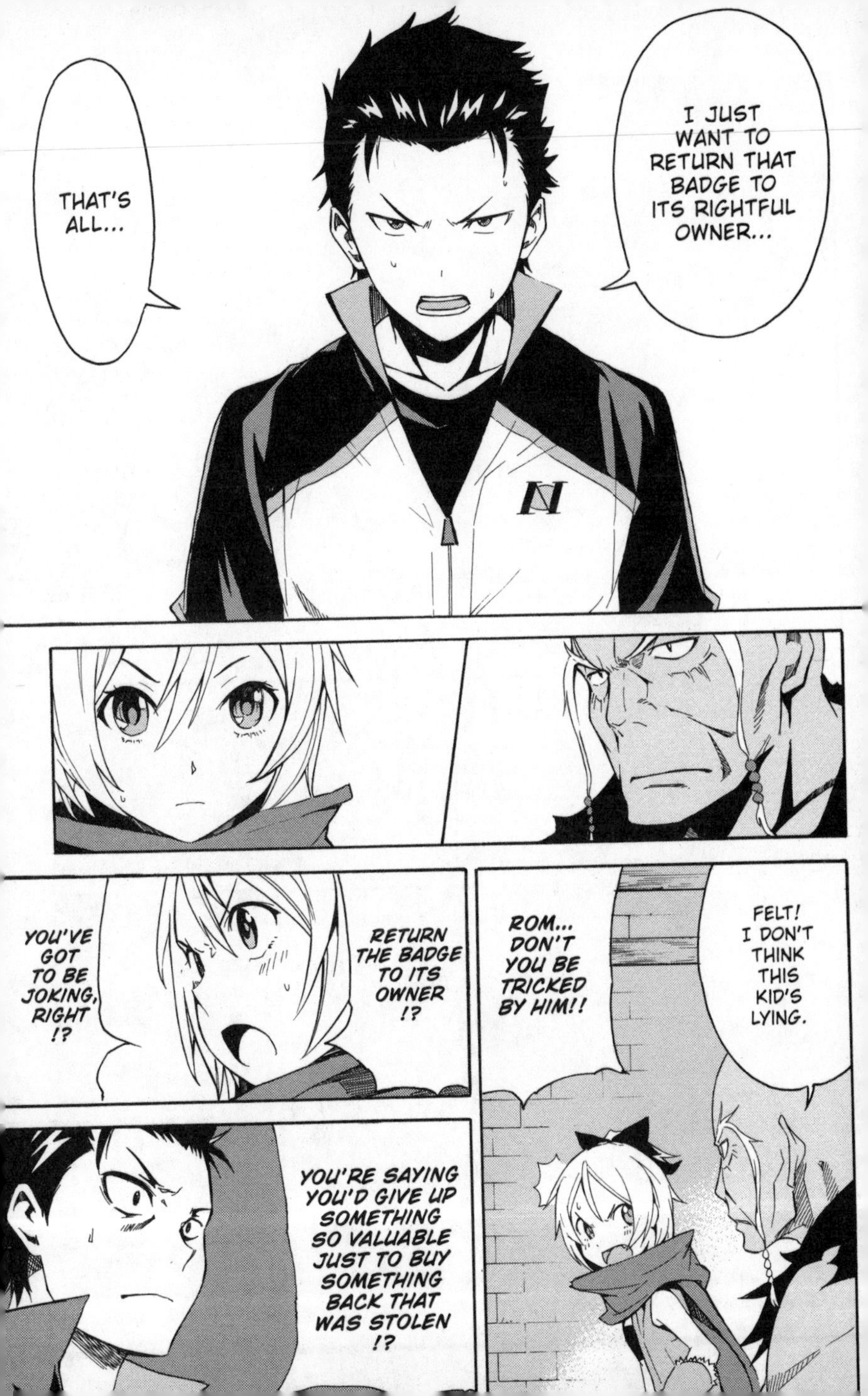
I JUST WANT TO RETURN THAT BADGE TO ITS RIGHTFUL OWNER...
THAT'S ALL...
FELT! I DON'T THINK THIS KID'S LYING.
ROM... DON'T YOU BE TRICKED BY HIM!!
RETURN THE BADGE TO ITS OWNER !?
YOU'VE GOT TO BE JOKING, RIGHT !?
YOU'RE SAYING YOU'D GIVE UP SOMETHING SO VALUABLE JUST TO BUY SOMETHING BACK THAT WAS STOLEN !?

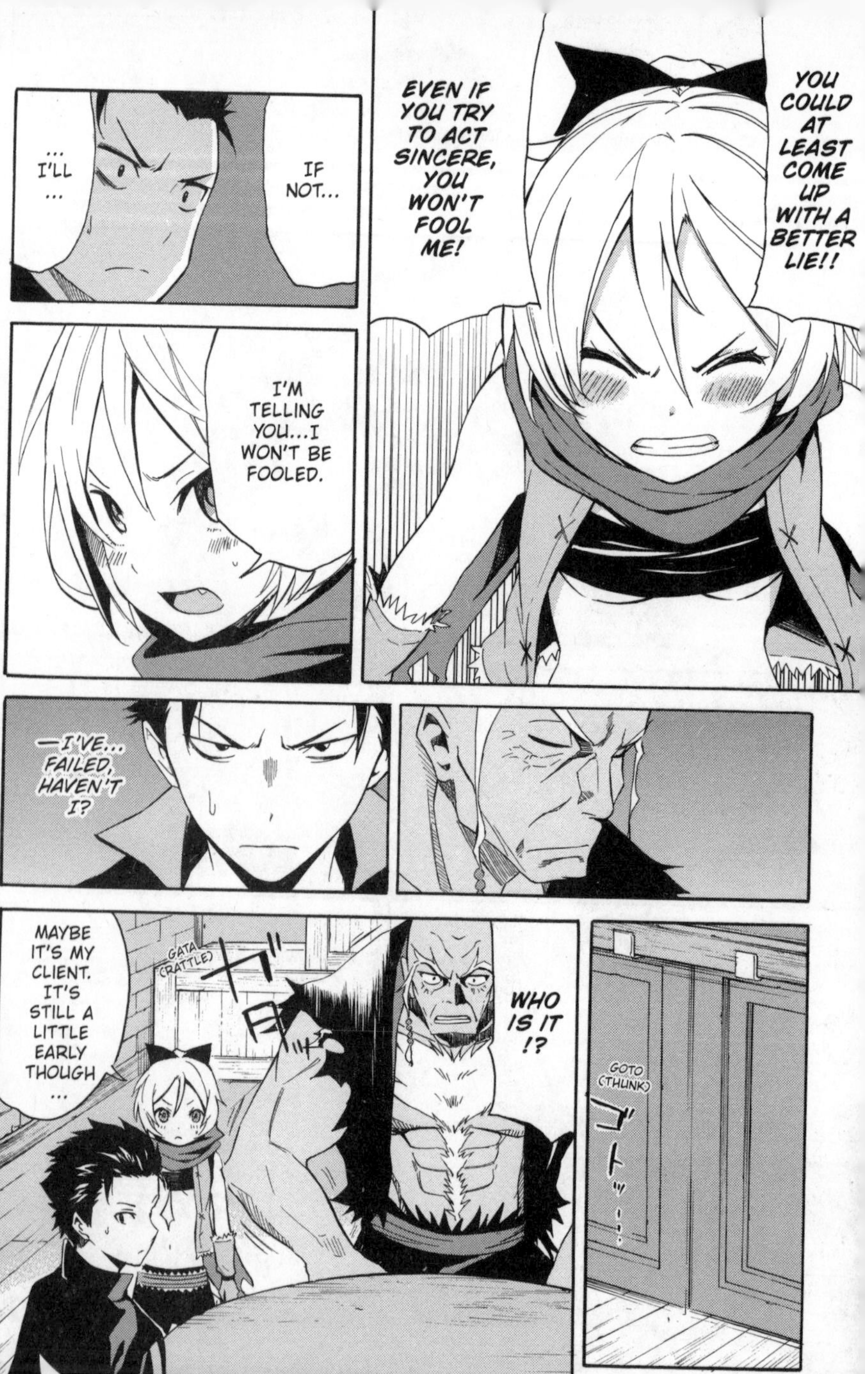
YOU COULD AT LEAST COME UP WITH A BETTER LIE!!
EVEN IF YOU TRY TO ACT SINCERE, YOU WON'T FOOL ME!
IF NOT...
...I'LL...
I'M TELLING YOU...I WON'T BE FOOLED.
—I'VE... FAILED, HAVEN'T I?
GOTO (THUNK)
WHO IS IT!?
GATA (RATTLE)
MAYBE IT'S MY CLIENT. IT'S STILL A LITTLE EARLY THOUGH...

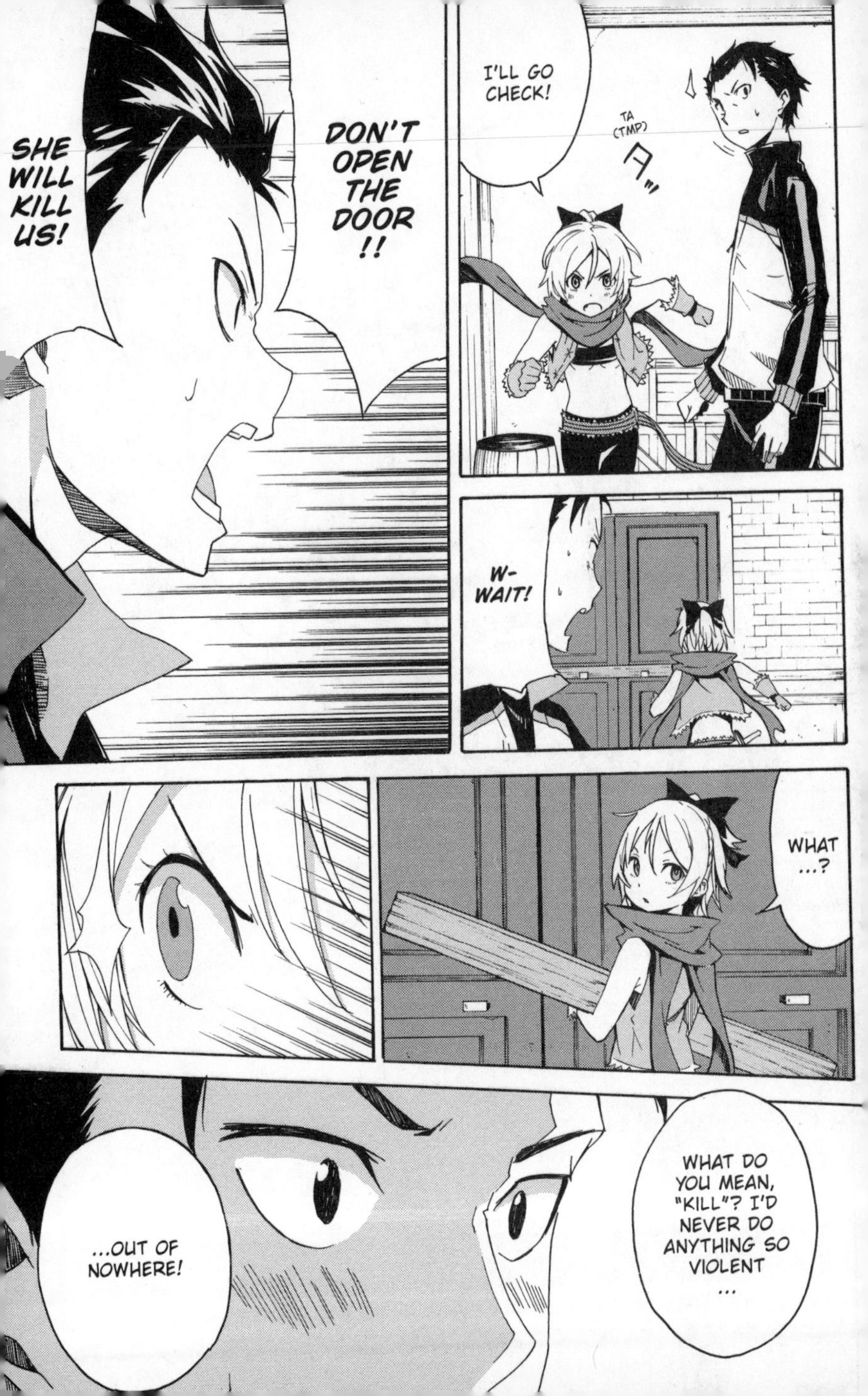
I'LL GO CHECK!
TA (TMP)
W-WAIT!
DON'T OPEN THE DOOR!!
SHE WILL KILL US!
WHAT ...?
WHAT DO YOU MEAN, "KILL"? I'D NEVER DO ANYTHING SO VIOLENT ...
...OUT OF NOWHERE!

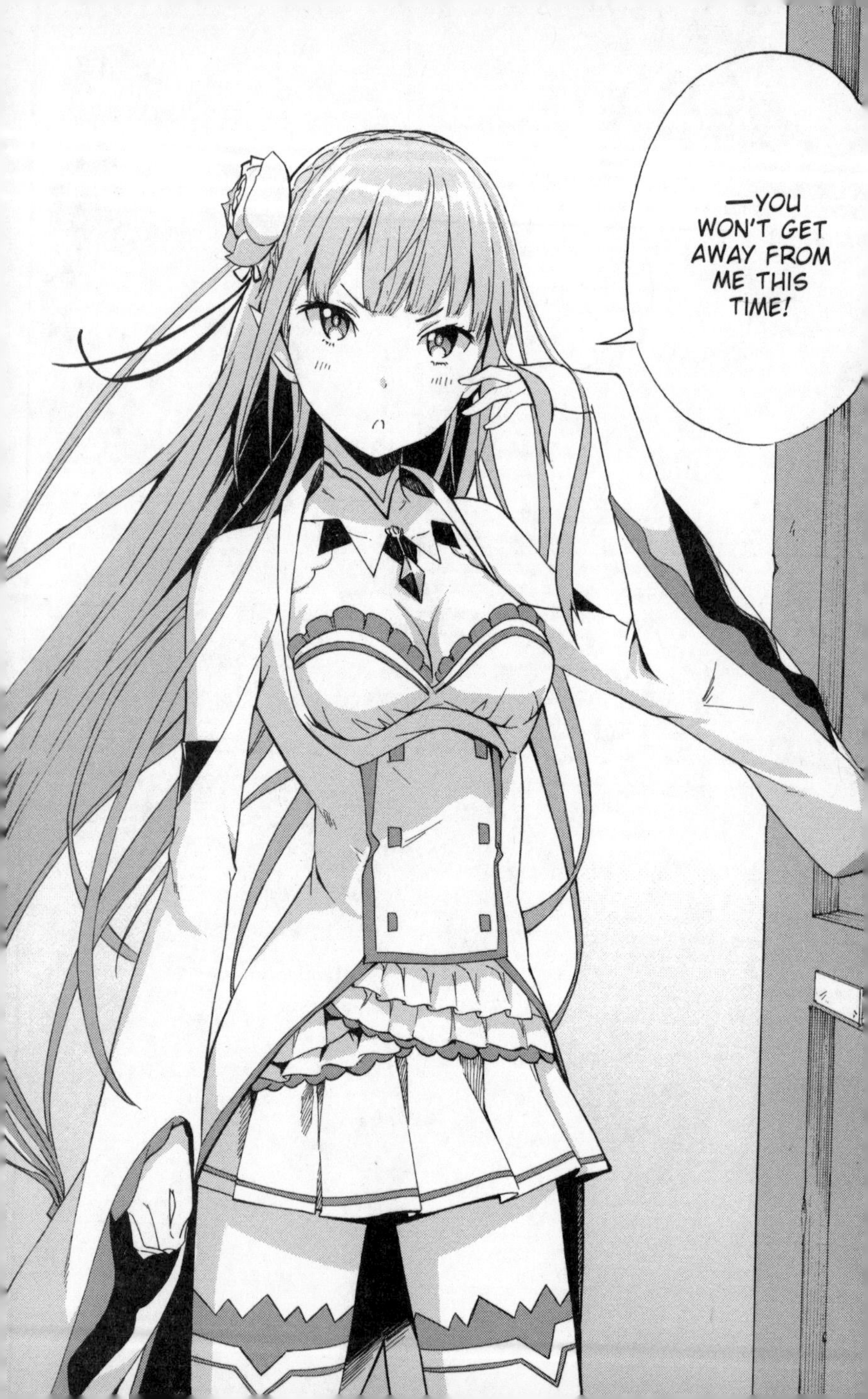
—YOU WON'T GET AWAY FROM ME THIS TIME!

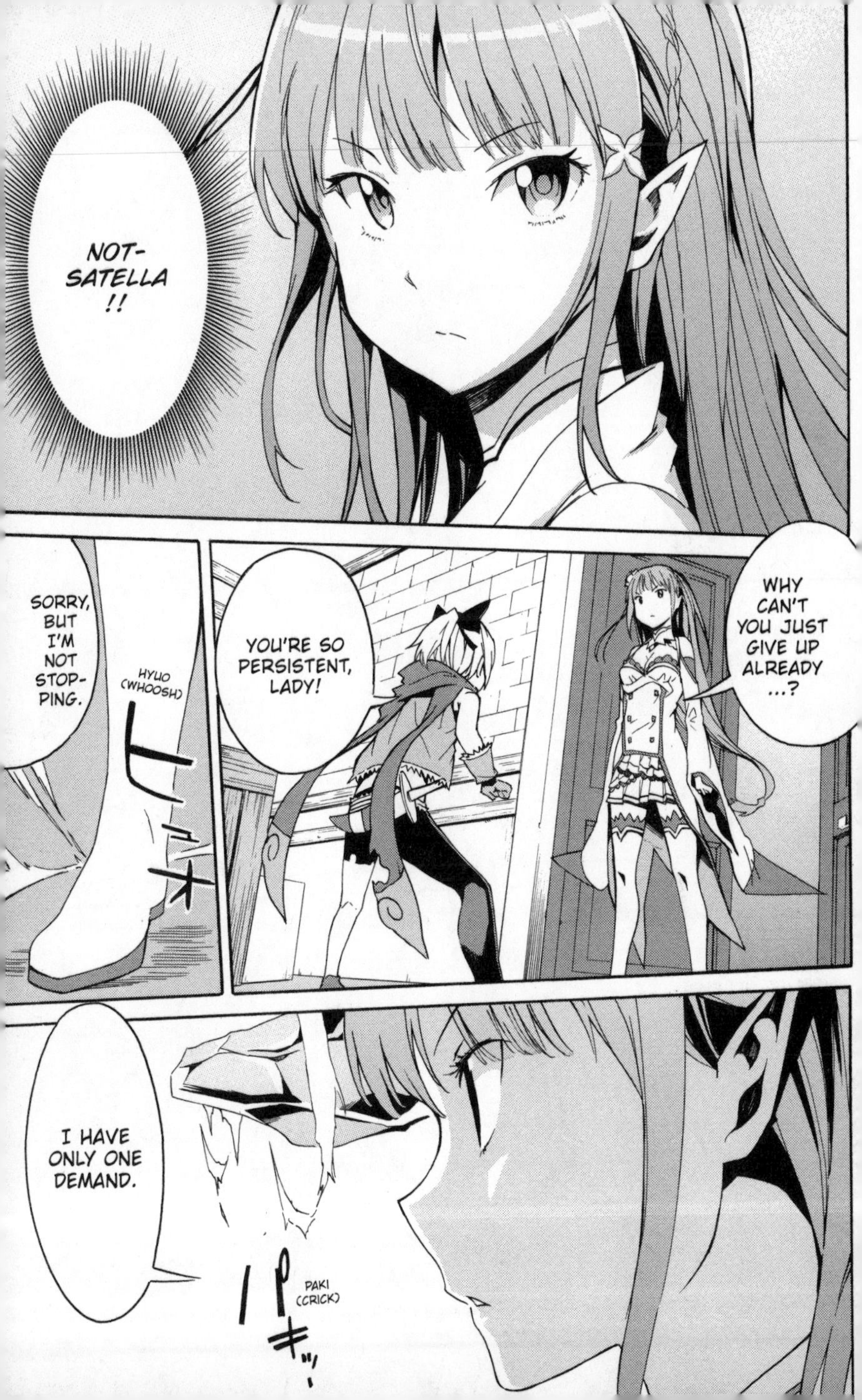
NOT-SATELLA!!
WHY CAN'T YOU JUST GIVE UP ALREADY ...?
YOU'RE SO PERSISTENT, LADY!
SORRY, BUT I'M NOT STOP-PING.
HYUO (WHOOSH)
I HAVE ONLY ONE DEMAND.
PAKI (CRICK)

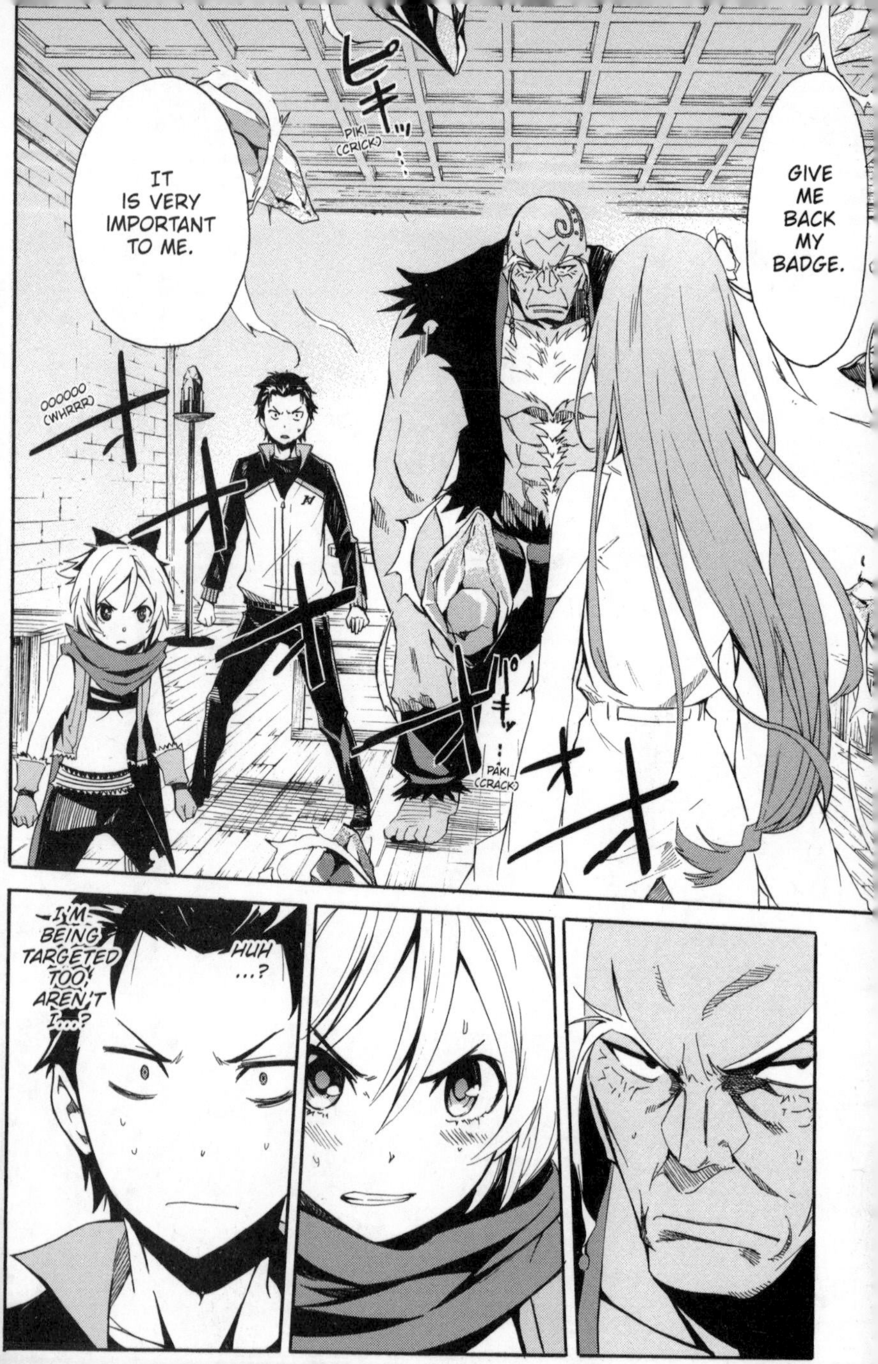
GIVE ME BACK MY BADGE.
ピキッ…
PIKI (CRICK)
IT IS VERY IMPORTANT TO ME.
OOOOOO (WHRRR)
PAKI (CRACK)
HUH ...?
I'M BEING TARGETED TOO, AREN'T I...?

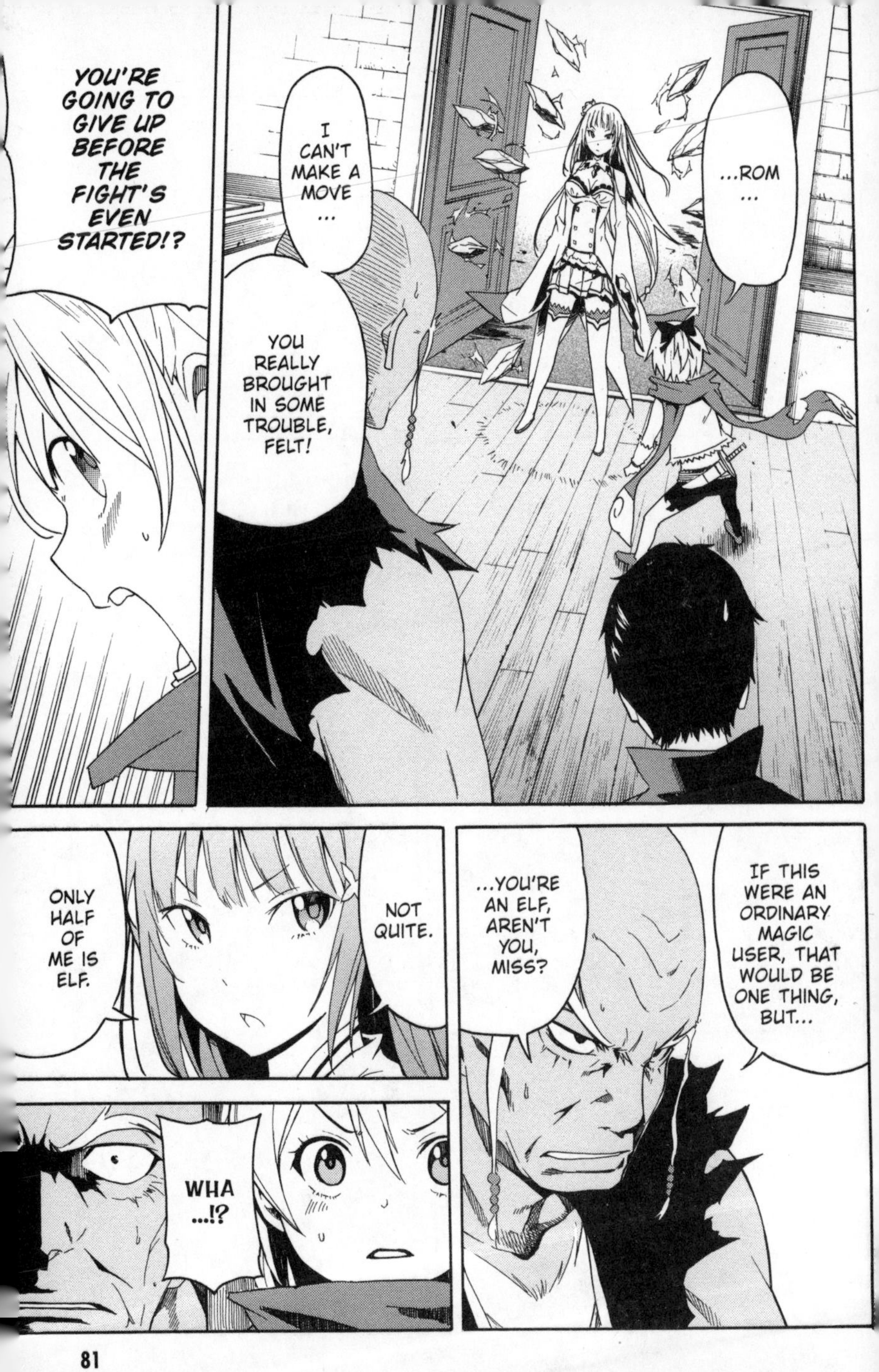
...ROM ...
I CAN'T MAKE A MOVE ...
YOU REALLY BROUGHT IN SOME TROUBLE, FELT!
YOU'RE GOING TO GIVE UP BEFORE THE FIGHT'S EVEN STARTED!?
IF THIS WERE AN ORDINARY MAGIC USER, THAT WOULD BE ONE THING, BUT...
...YOU'RE AN ELF, AREN'T YOU, MISS?
NOT QUITE.
ONLY HALF OF ME IS ELF.
WHA ...!?

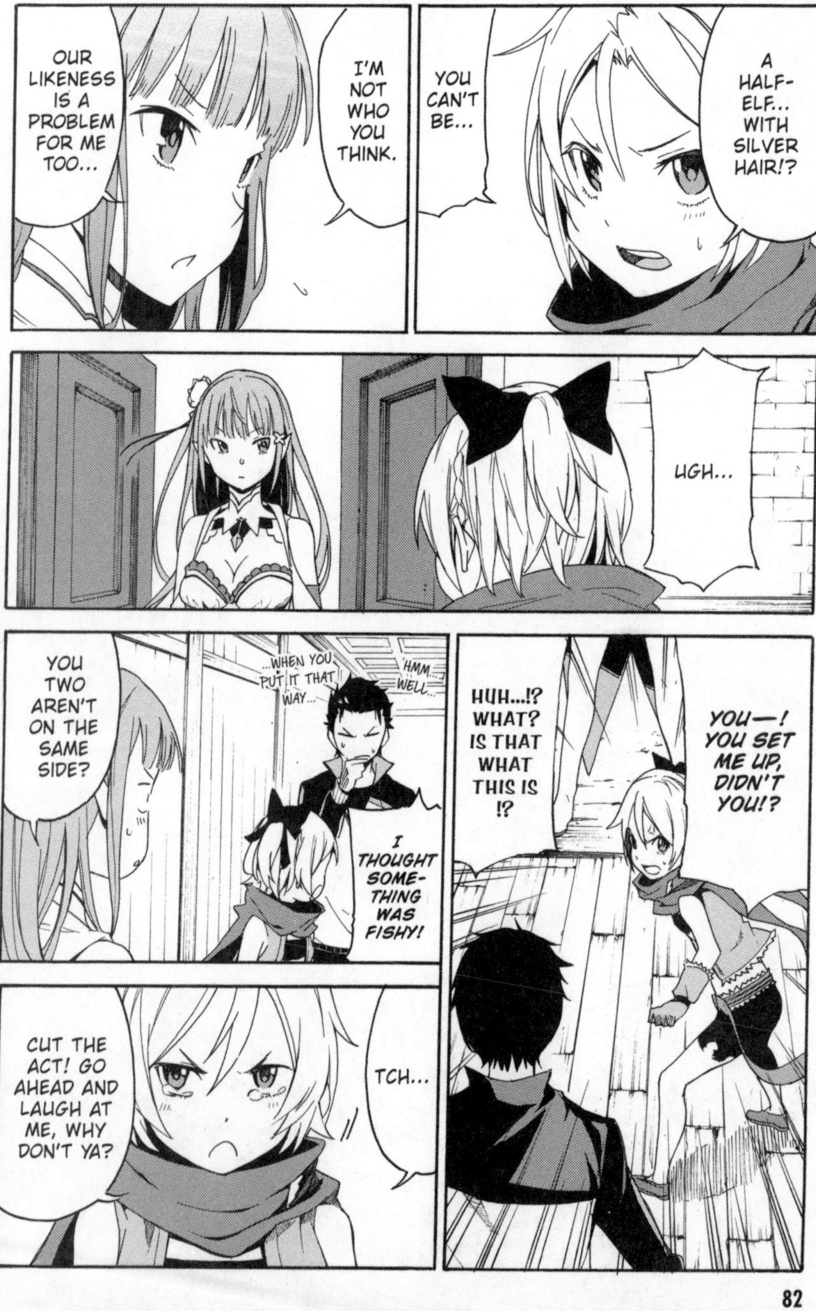
A HALF-ELF... WITH SILVER HAIR!?
YOU CAN'T BE...
I'M NOT WHO YOU THINK.
OUR LIKENESS IS A PROBLEM FOR ME TOO...
UGH...
YOU—! YOU SET ME UP, DIDN'T YOU!?
HUH...!? WHAT? IS THAT WHAT THIS IS !?
I THOUGHT SOMETHING WAS FISHY!
HMM... WELL...
...WHEN YOU PUT IT THAT WAY...
YOU TWO AREN'T ON THE SAME SIDE?
TCH...
CUT THE ACT! GO AHEAD AND LAUGH AT ME, WHY DON'T YA?

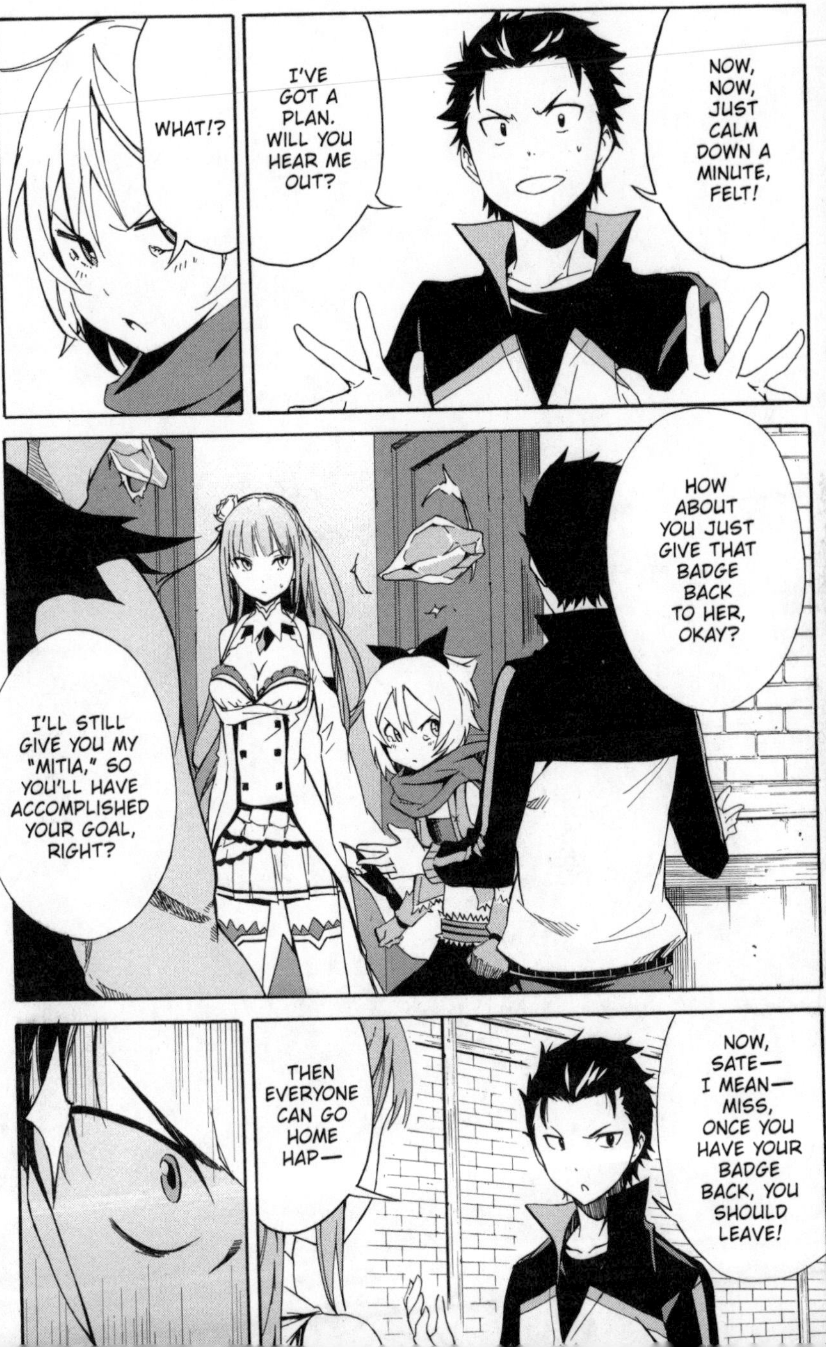
NOW, NOW, JUST CALM DOWN A MINUTE, FELT!
I'VE GOT A PLAN. WILL YOU HEAR ME OUT?
WHAT!?
HOW ABOUT YOU JUST GIVE THAT BADGE BACK TO HER, OKAY?
I'LL STILL GIVE YOU MY "MITIA," SO YOU'LL HAVE ACCOMPLISHED YOUR GOAL, RIGHT?
NOW, SATE— I MEAN— MISS, ONCE YOU HAVE YOUR BADGE BACK, YOU SHOULD LEAVE!
THEN EVERYONE CAN GO HOME HAP—

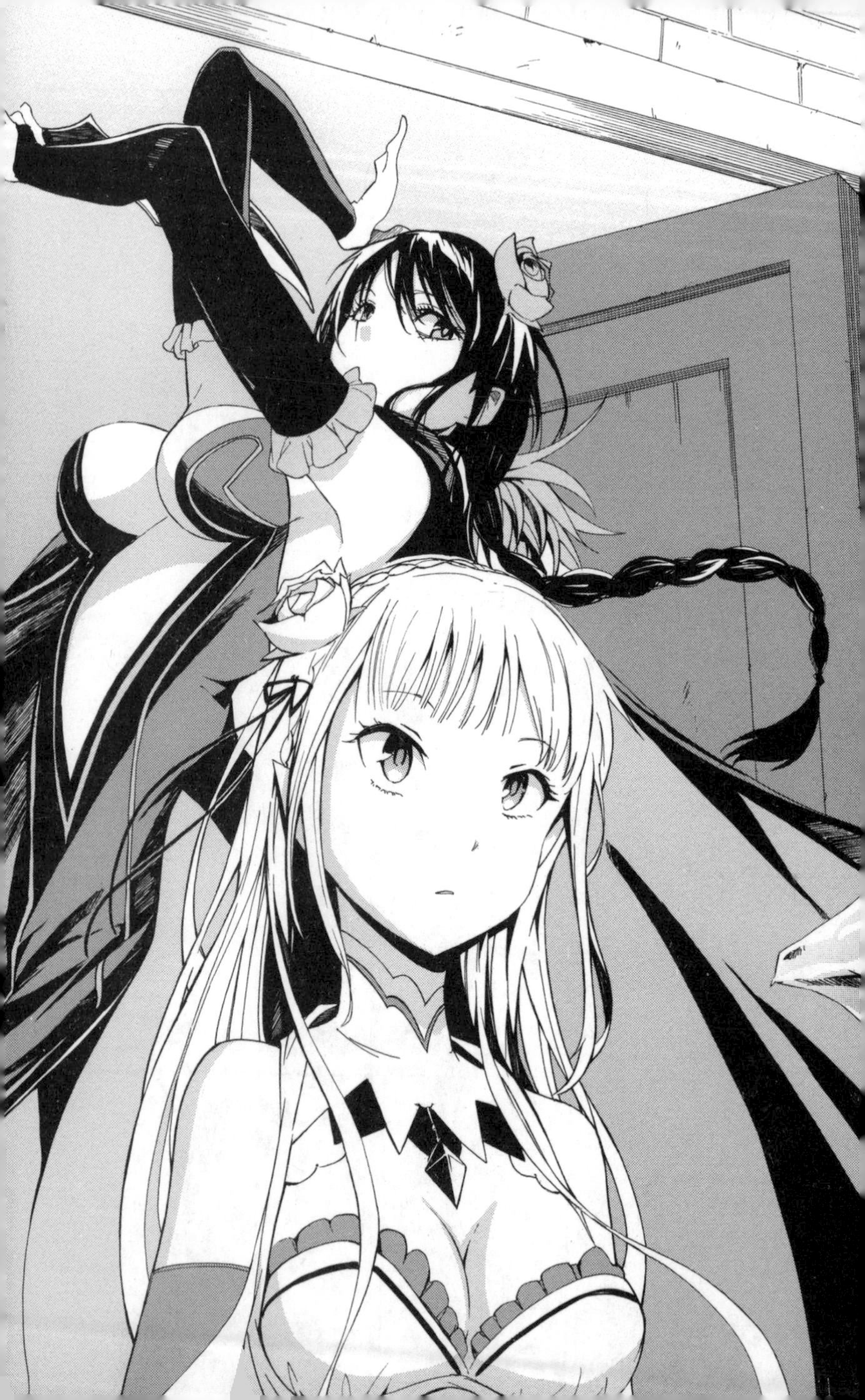

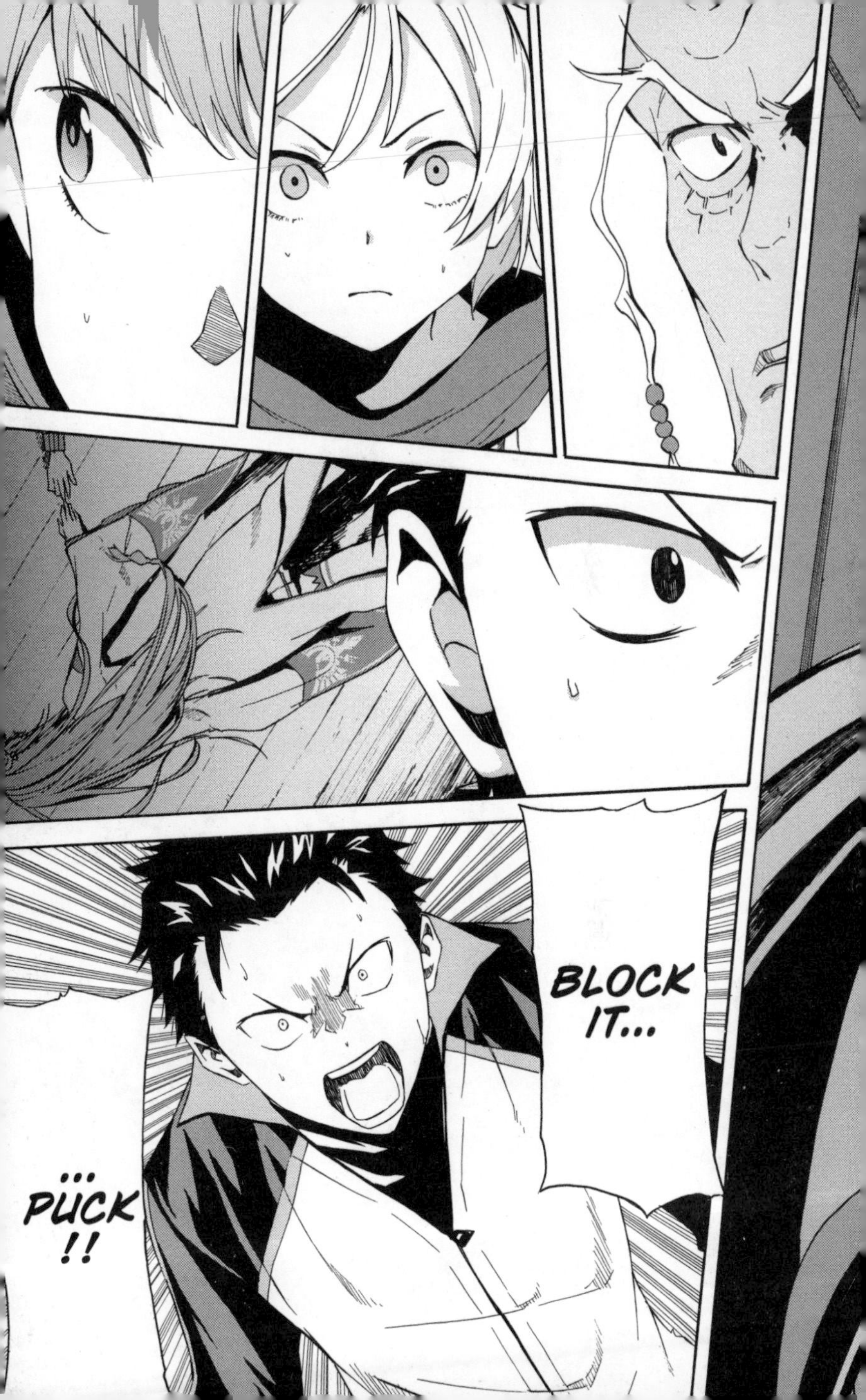
BLOCK IT...
... PÜCK !!

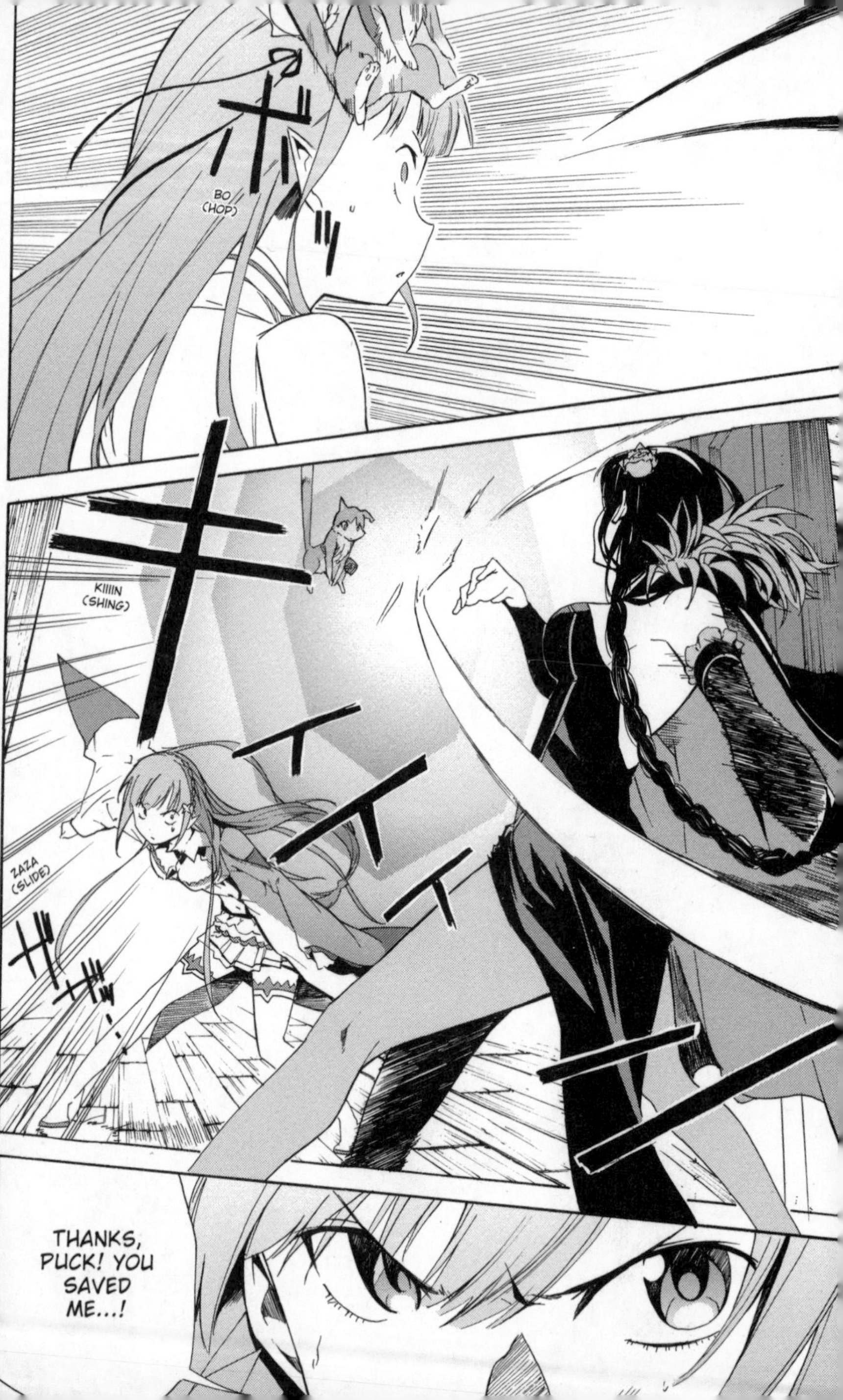
BO
(HOP)
KIIIN
(SHING)
ZAZA
(SLIDE)
THANKS, PUCK! YOU SAVED ME...!

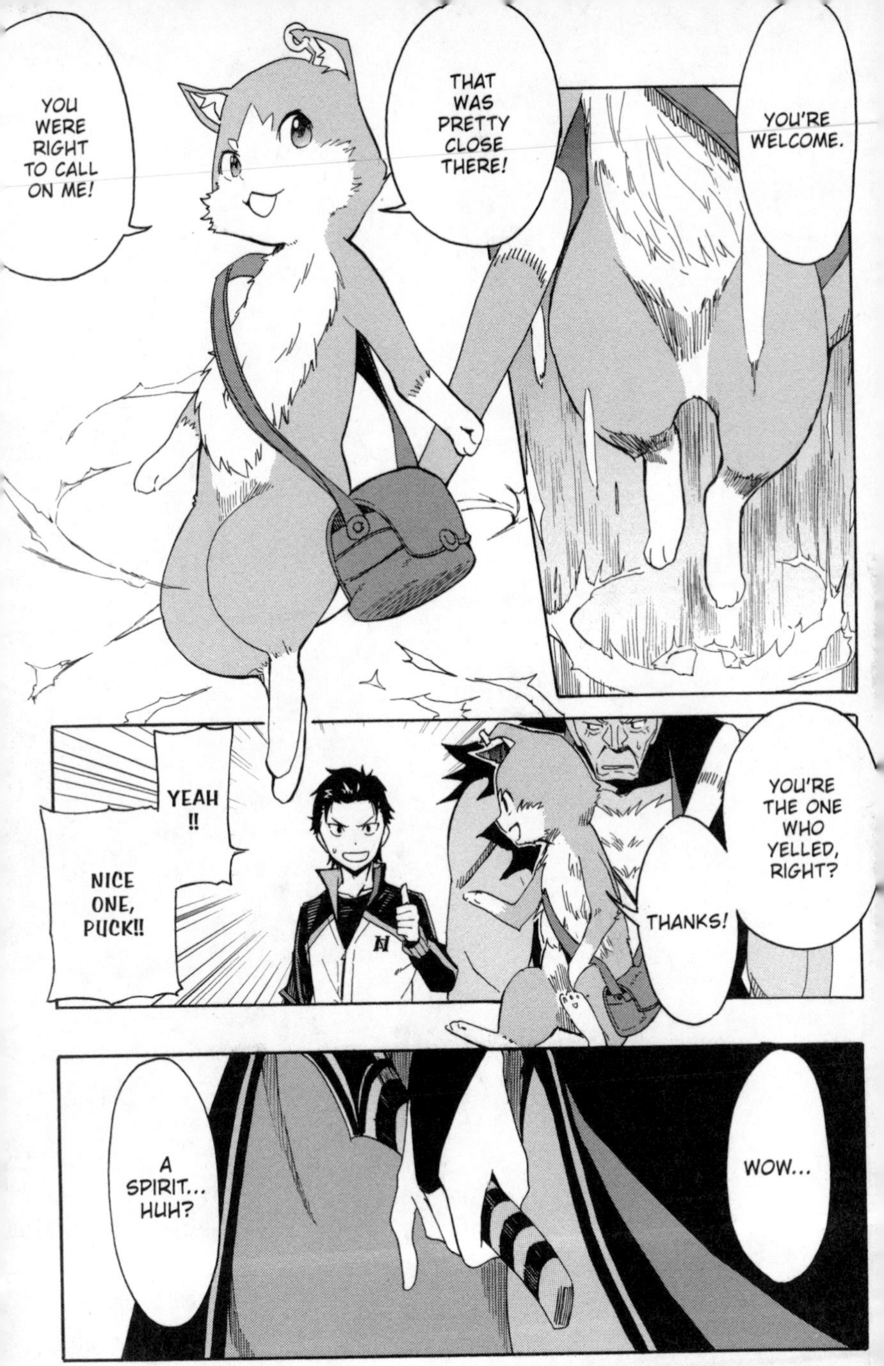
YOU'RE WELCOME.
THAT WAS PRETTY CLOSE THERE!
YOU WERE RIGHT TO CALL ON ME!
YOU'RE THE ONE WHO YELLED, RIGHT?
THANKS!
YEAH!!
NICE ONE, PUCK!!
WOW...
A SPIRIT... HUH?

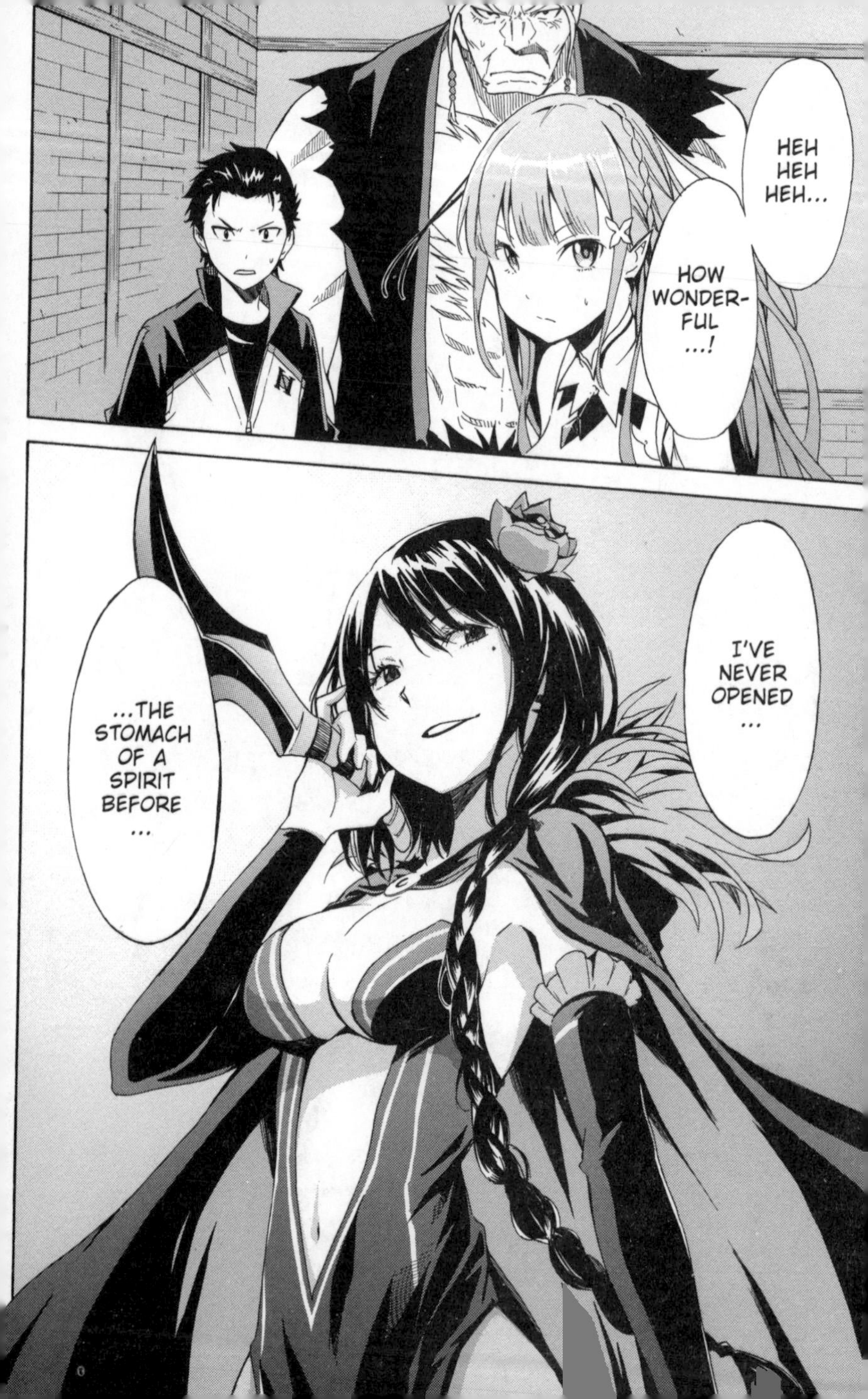
HEH HEH HEH...
HOW WONDERFUL...!
I'VE NEVER OPENED...
...THE STOMACH OF A SPIRIT BEFORE...

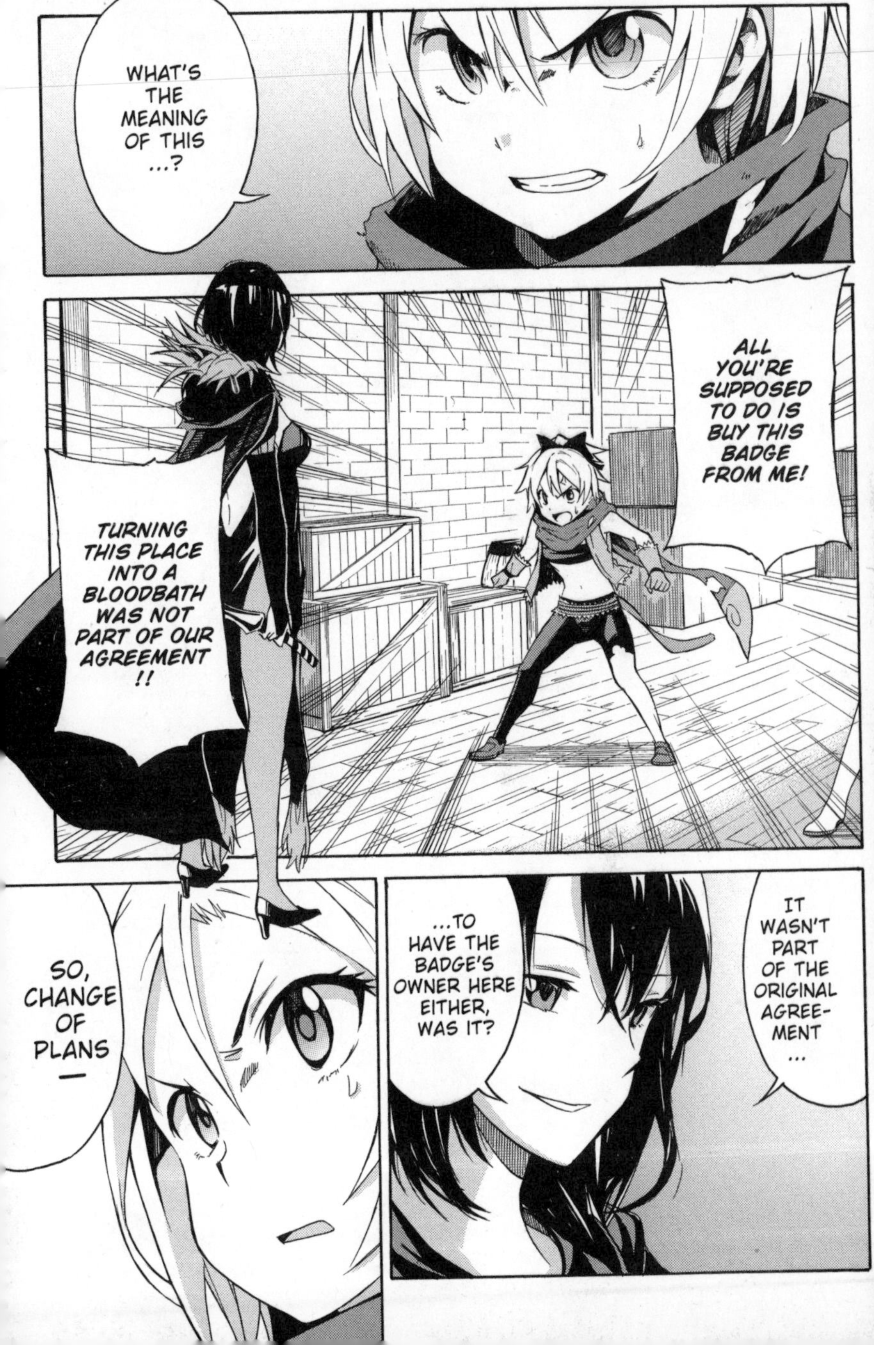
WHAT'S THE MEANING OF THIS ...?
ALL YOU'RE SUPPOSED TO DO IS BUY THIS BADGE FROM ME!
TURNING THIS PLACE INTO A BLOODBATH WAS NOT PART OF OUR AGREEMENT !!
IT WASN'T PART OF THE ORIGINAL AGREE-MENT ...
...TO HAVE THE BADGE'S OWNER HERE EITHER, WAS IT?
SO, CHANGE OF PLANS —

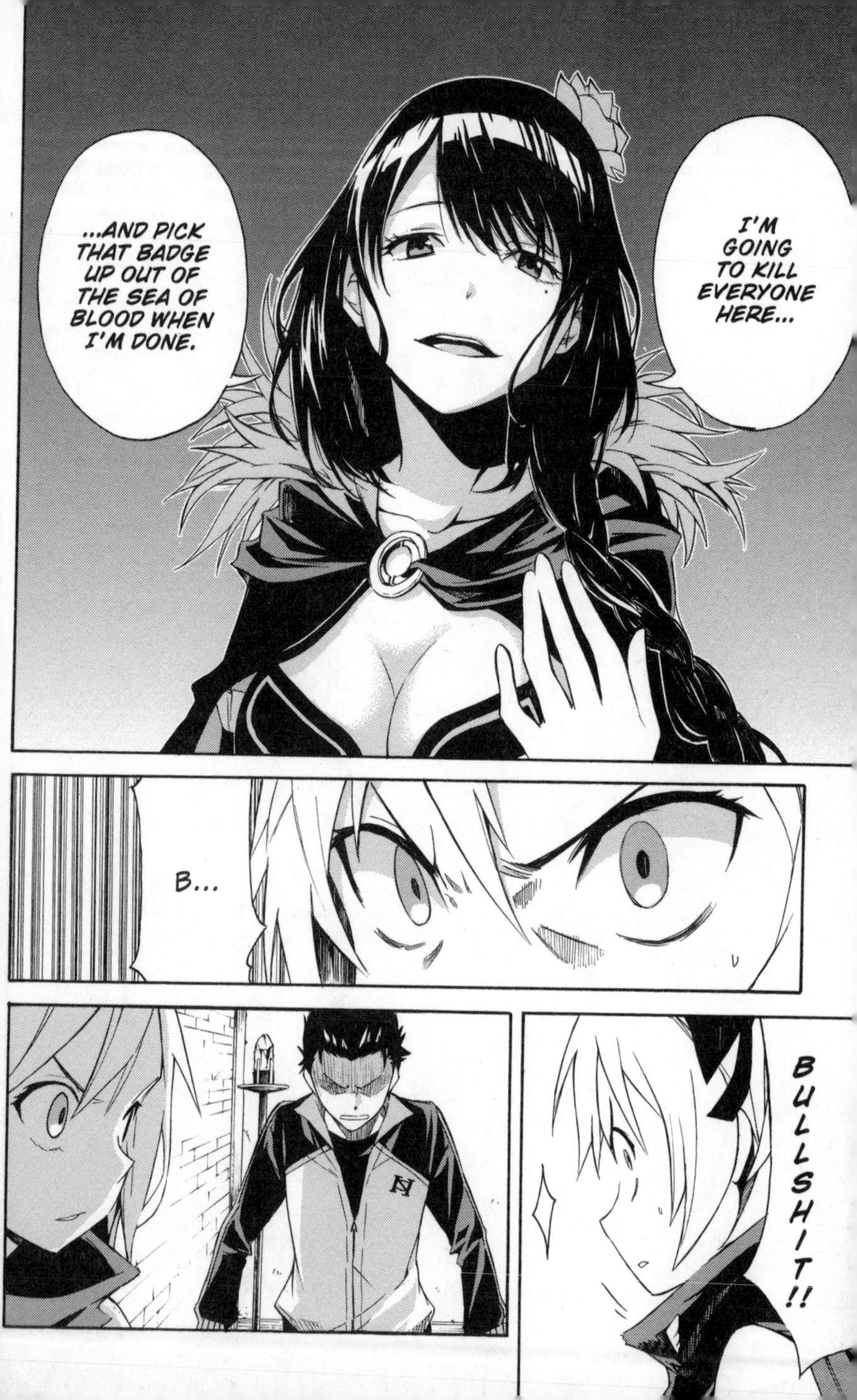
I'M GOING TO KILL EVERYONE HERE...
...AND PICK THAT BADGE UP OUT OF THE SEA OF BLOOD WHEN I'M DONE.
B...
BULLSHIT!!

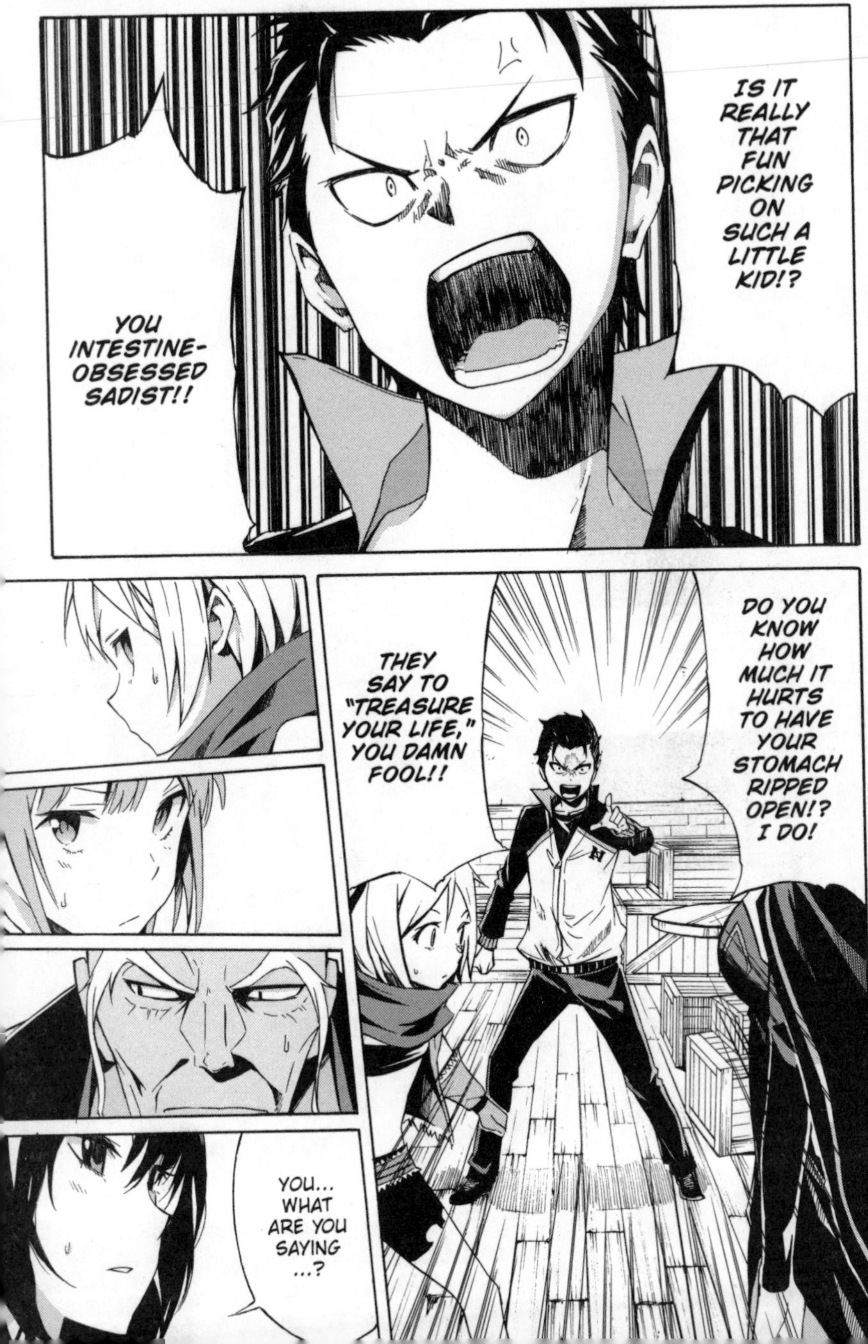
IS IT REALLY THAT FUN PICKING ON SUCH A LITTLE KID!?
YOU INTESTINE-OBSESSED SADIST!!
DO YOU KNOW HOW MUCH IT HURTS TO HAVE YOUR STOMACH RIPPED OPEN!? I DO!
THEY SAY TO "TREASURE YOUR LIFE," YOU DAMN FOOL!!
YOU... WHAT ARE YOU SAYING ...?

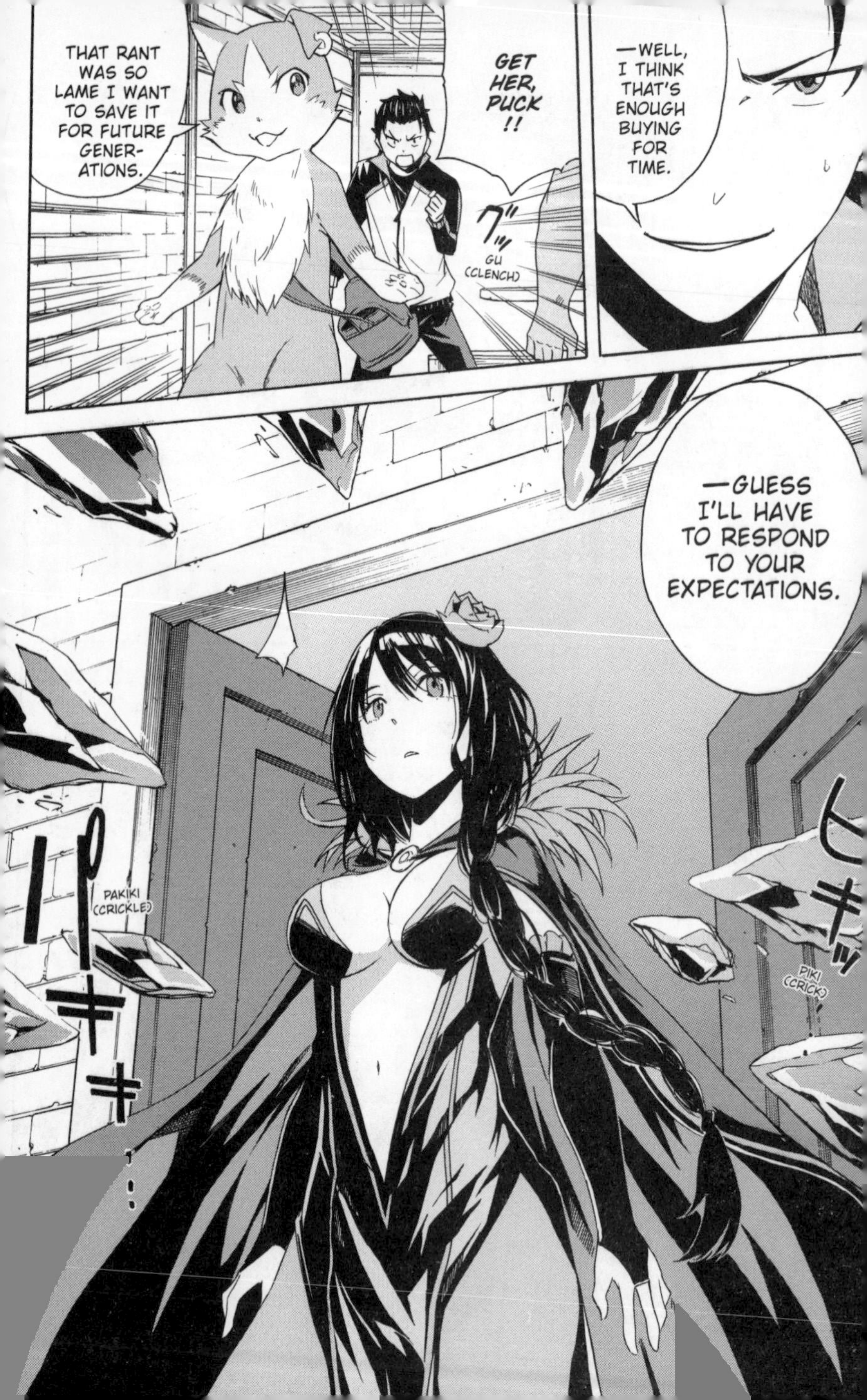
—WELL, I THINK THAT'S ENOUGH BUYING FOR TIME.
GET HER, PUCK!!
THAT RANT WAS SO LAME I WANT TO SAVE IT FOR FUTURE GENERATIONS.
GU (CLENCH)
—GUESS I'LL HAVE TO RESPOND TO YOUR EXPECTATIONS.
PIKI (CRICK)
PAKIKI (CRICKLE)
...

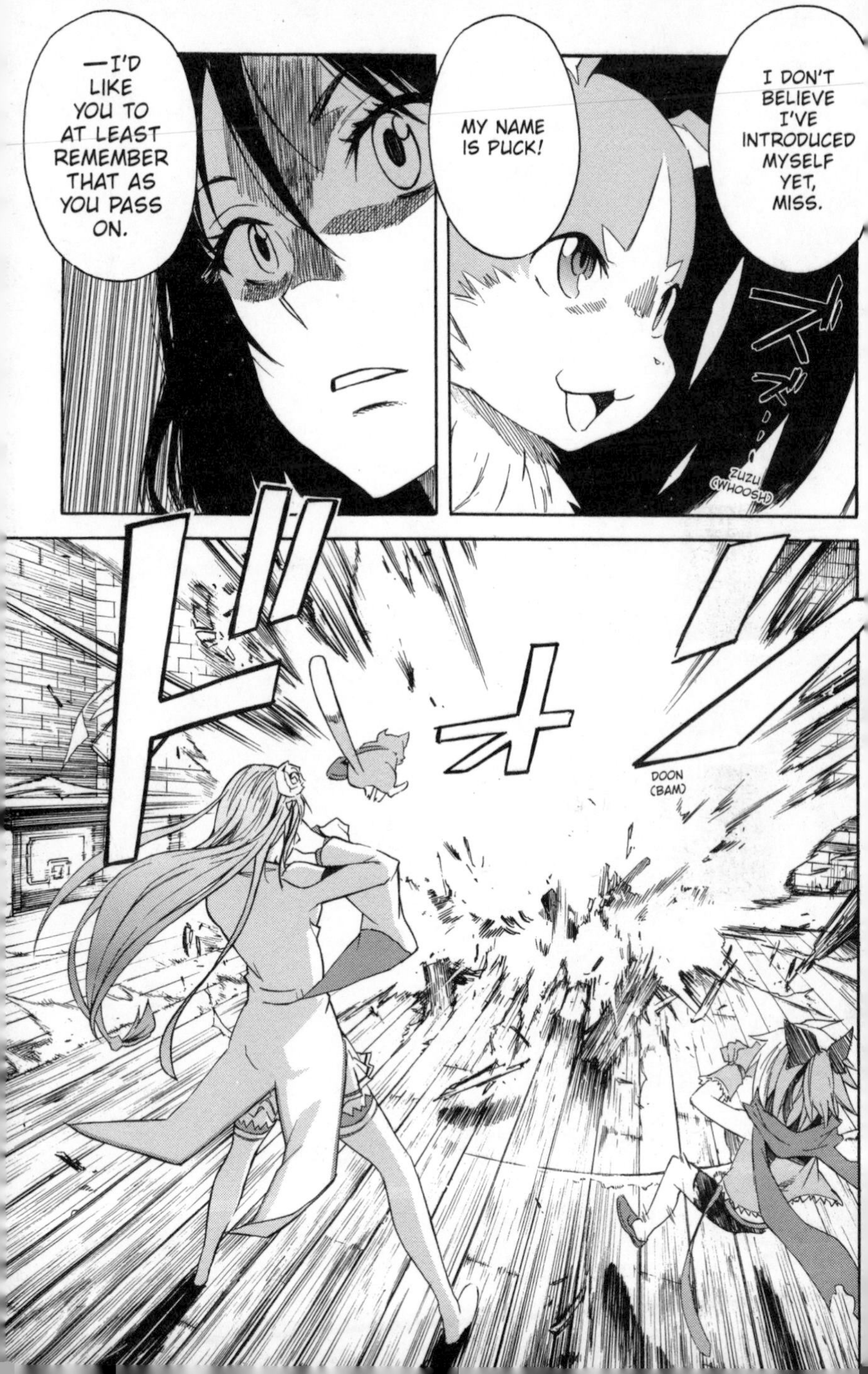
I DON'T BELIEVE I'VE INTRODUCED MYSELF YET, MISS.
MY NAME IS PUCK!
ZUZU (WHOOSH)
—I'D LIKE YOU TO AT LEAST REMEMBER THAT AS YOU PASS ON.
DOON (BAM)

Episode 9: Battle in the Loot Cellar

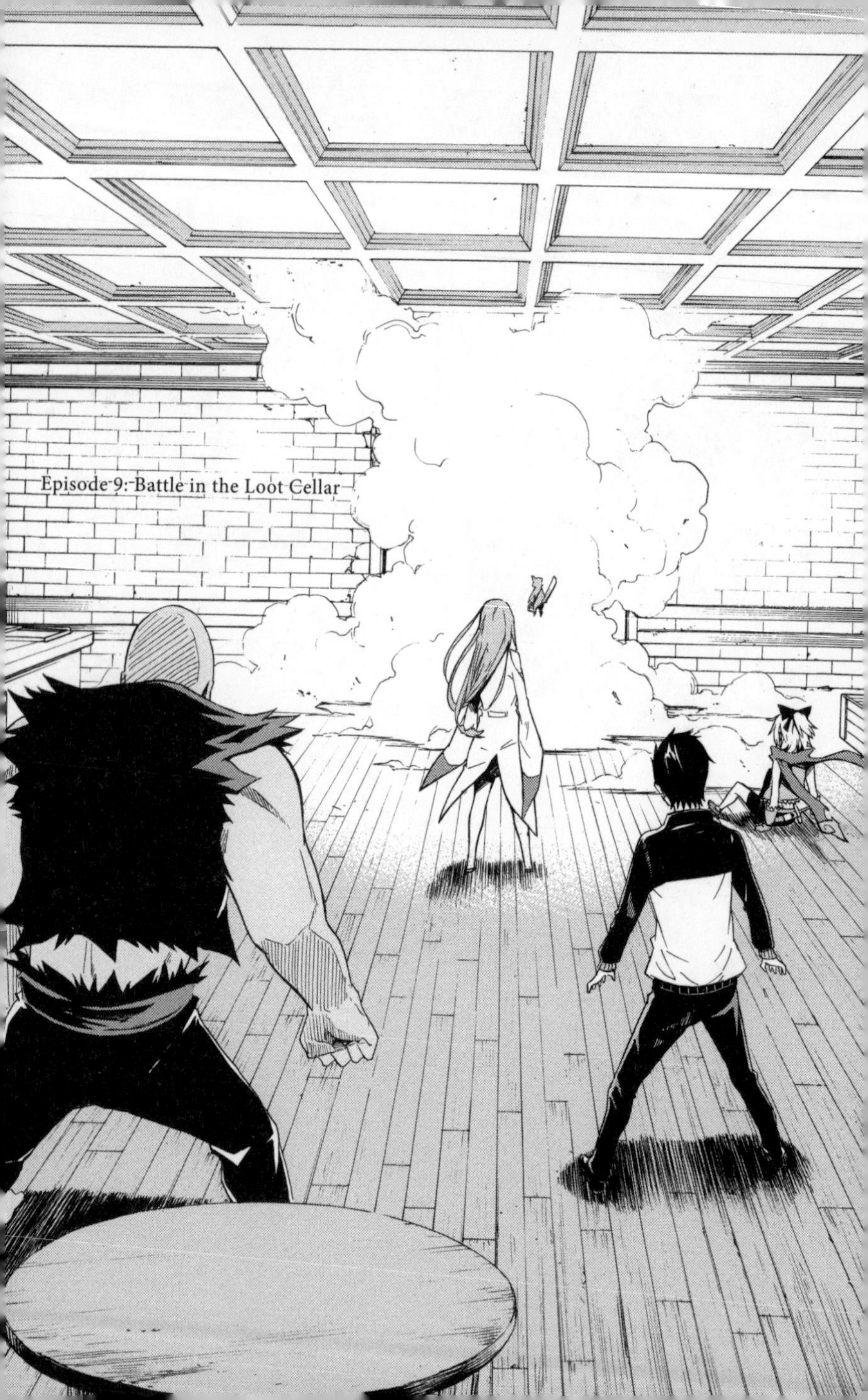

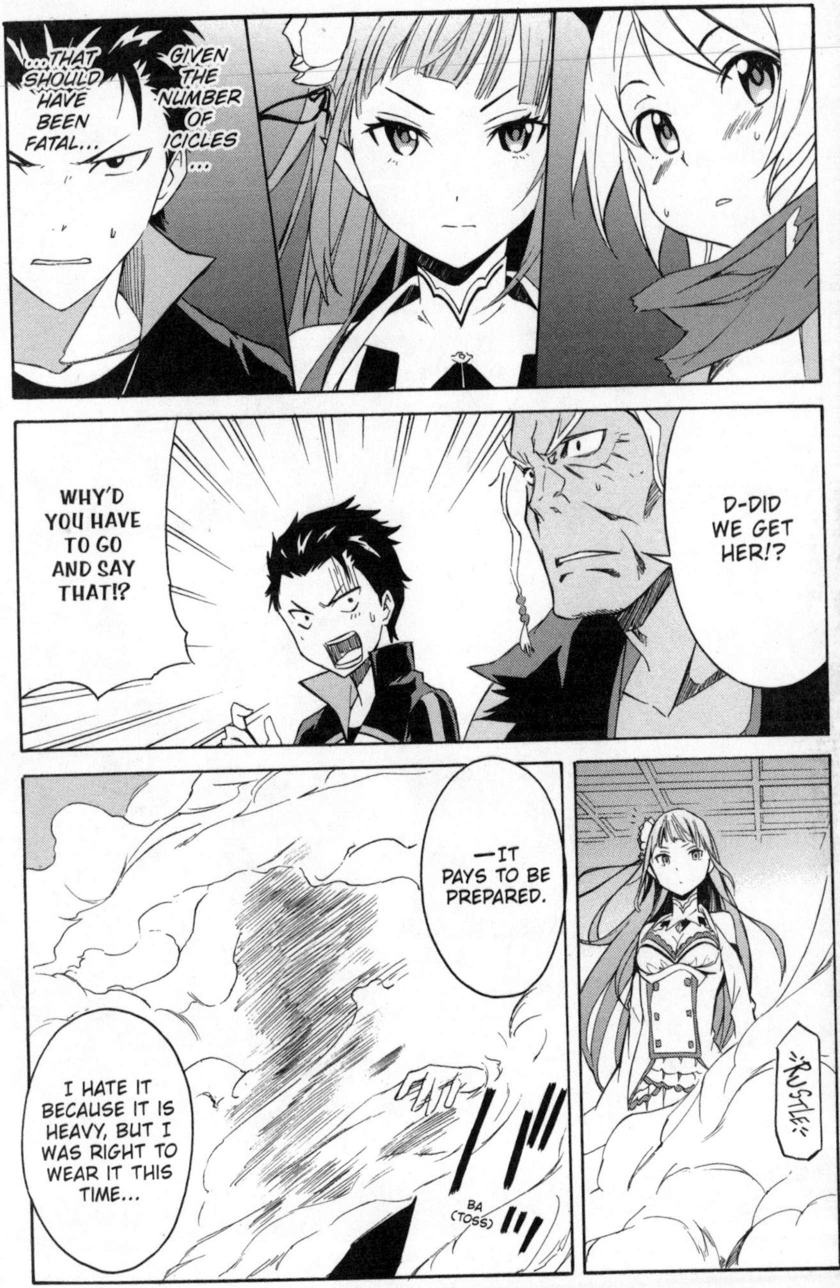
GIVEN THE NUMBER OF ICICLES...
...THAT SHOULD HAVE BEEN FATAL...
D-DID WE GET HER!?
WHY'D YOU HAVE TO GO AND SAY THAT!?
RUSTLE
—IT PAYS TO BE PREPARED.
I HATE IT BECAUSE IT IS HEAVY, BUT I WAS RIGHT TO WEAR IT THIS TIME...
BA (TOSS)

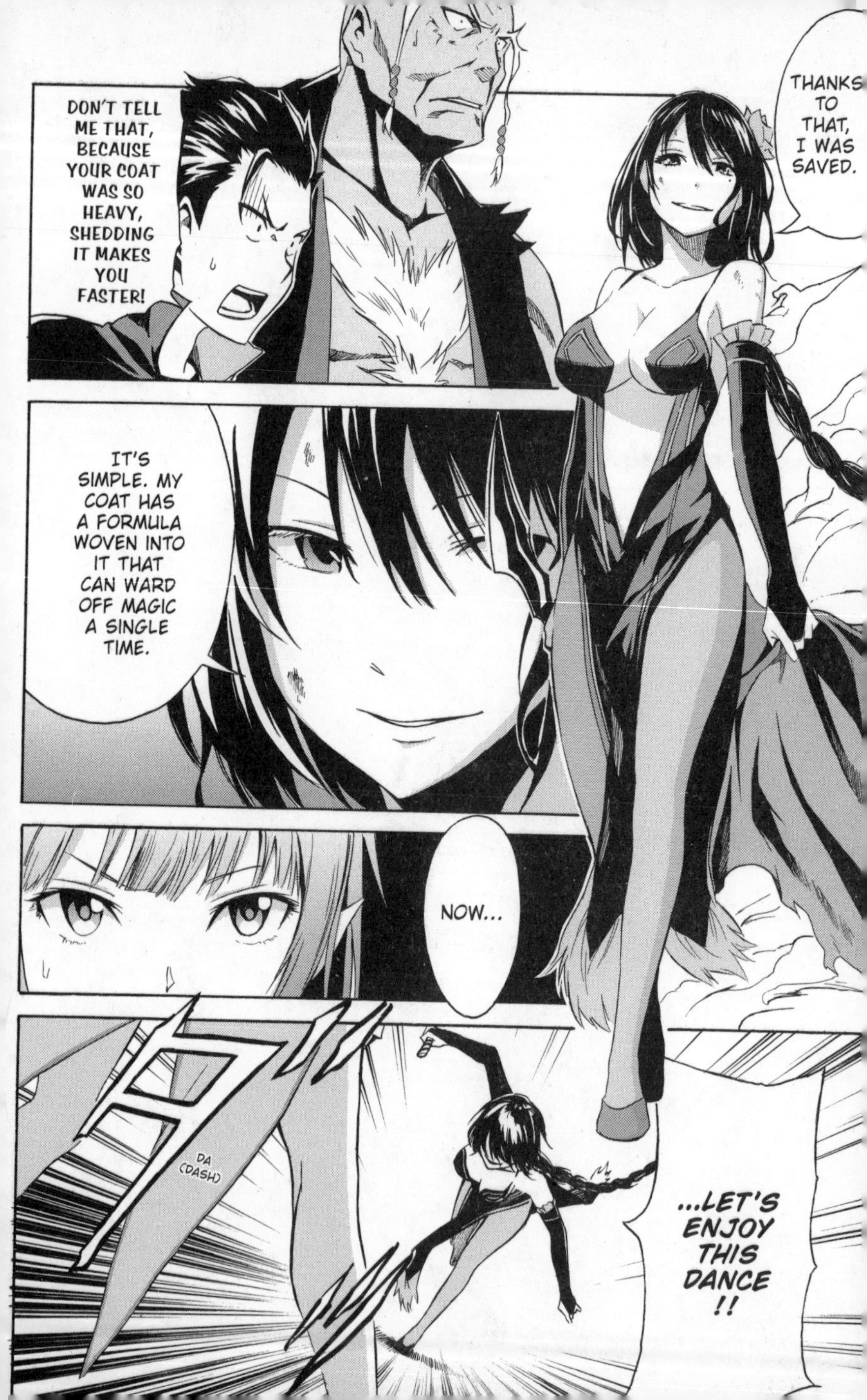
THANKS TO THAT, I WAS SAVED.
DON'T TELL ME THAT, BECAUSE YOUR COAT WAS SO HEAVY, SHEDDING IT MAKES YOU FASTER!
IT'S SIMPLE. MY COAT HAS A FORMULA WOVEN INTO IT THAT CAN WARD OFF MAGIC A SINGLE TIME.
NOW...
...LET'S ENJOY THIS DANCE!!
DA (DASH)

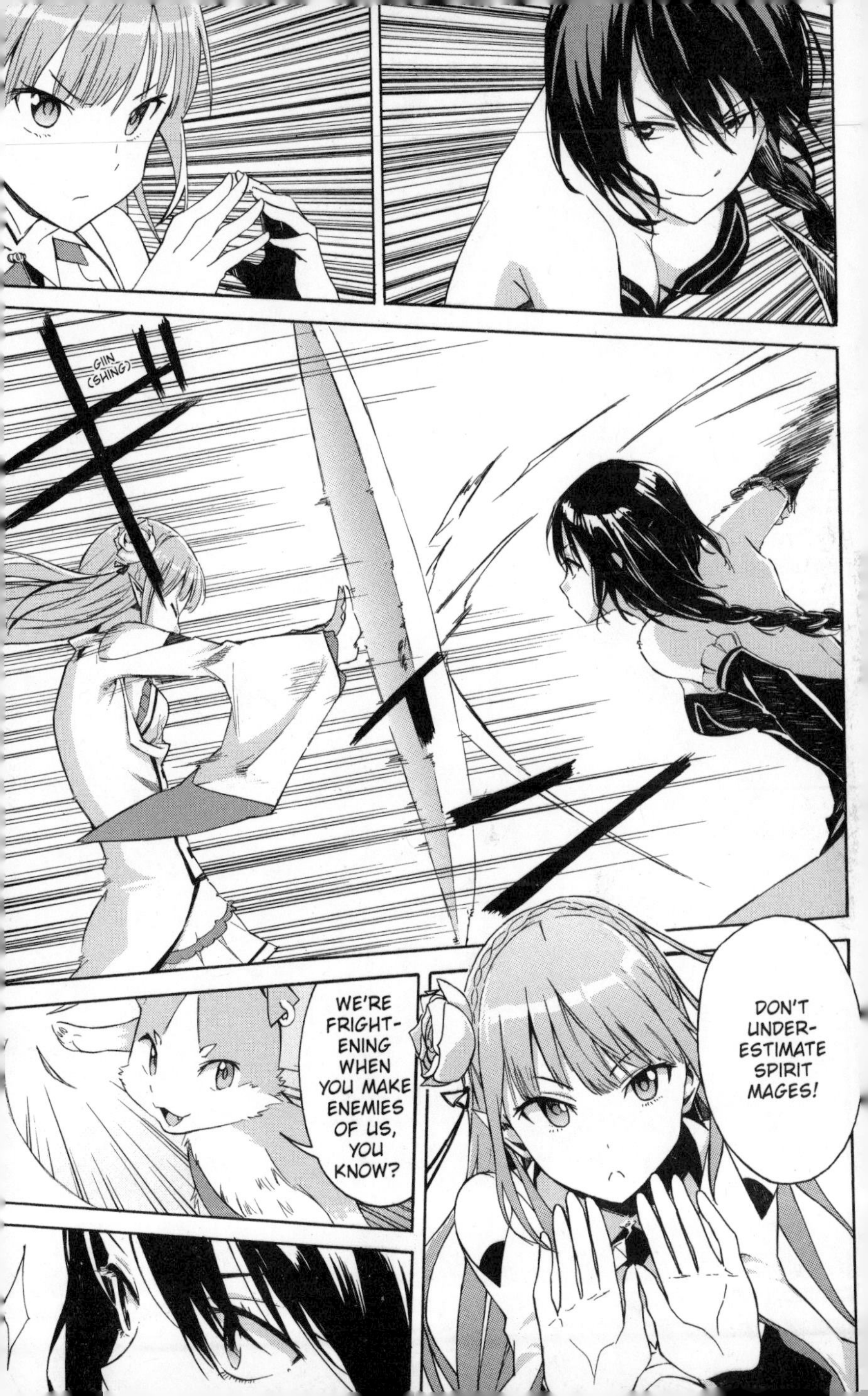
GIIN (SHING)
DON'T UNDER-ESTIMATE SPIRIT MAGES!
WE'RE FRIGHT-ENING WHEN YOU MAKE ENEMIES OF US, YOU KNOW?

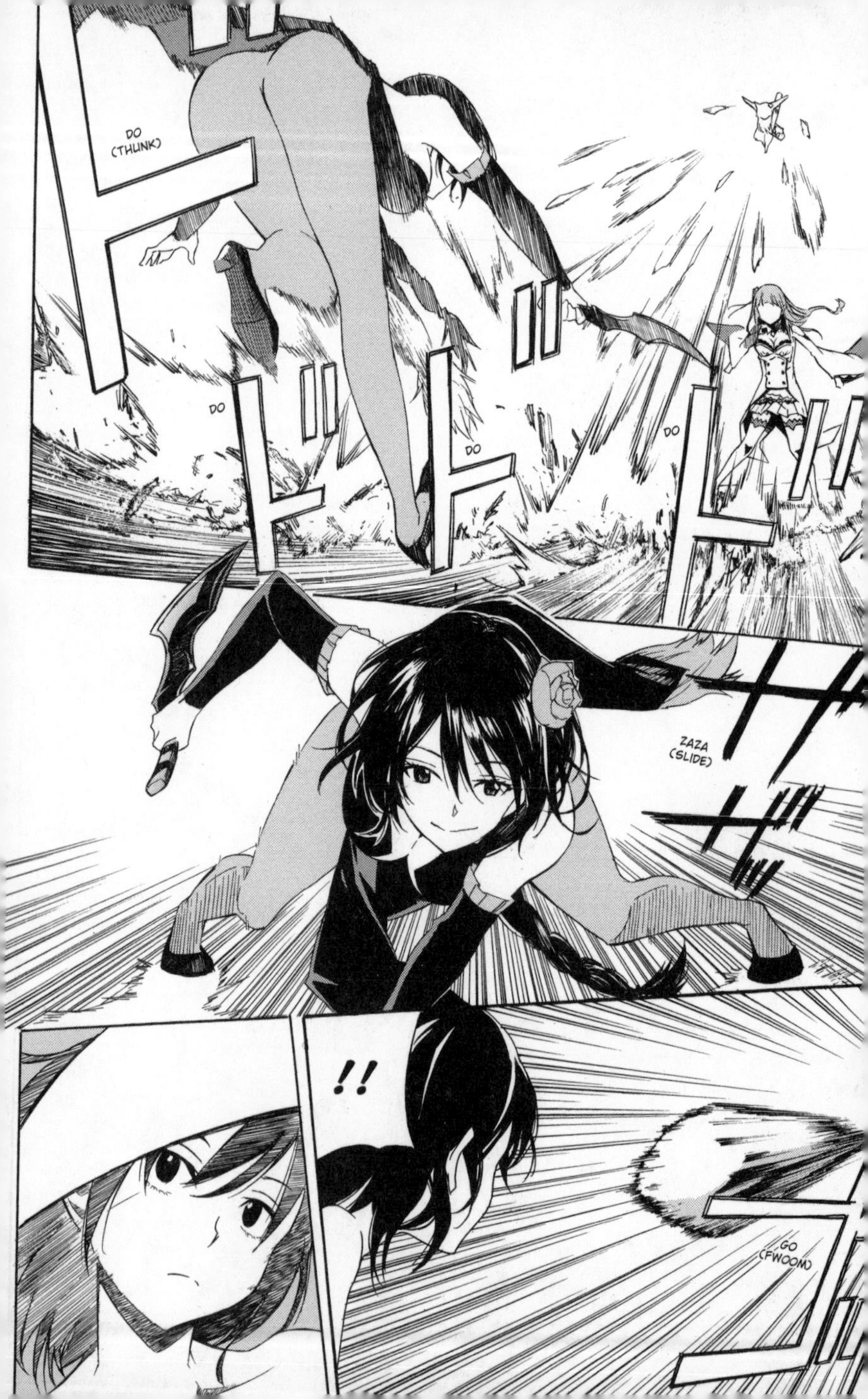
DO
(THUNK)
DO
DO
DO
ZAZA
(SLIDE)
!!
GO
(FWOOM)

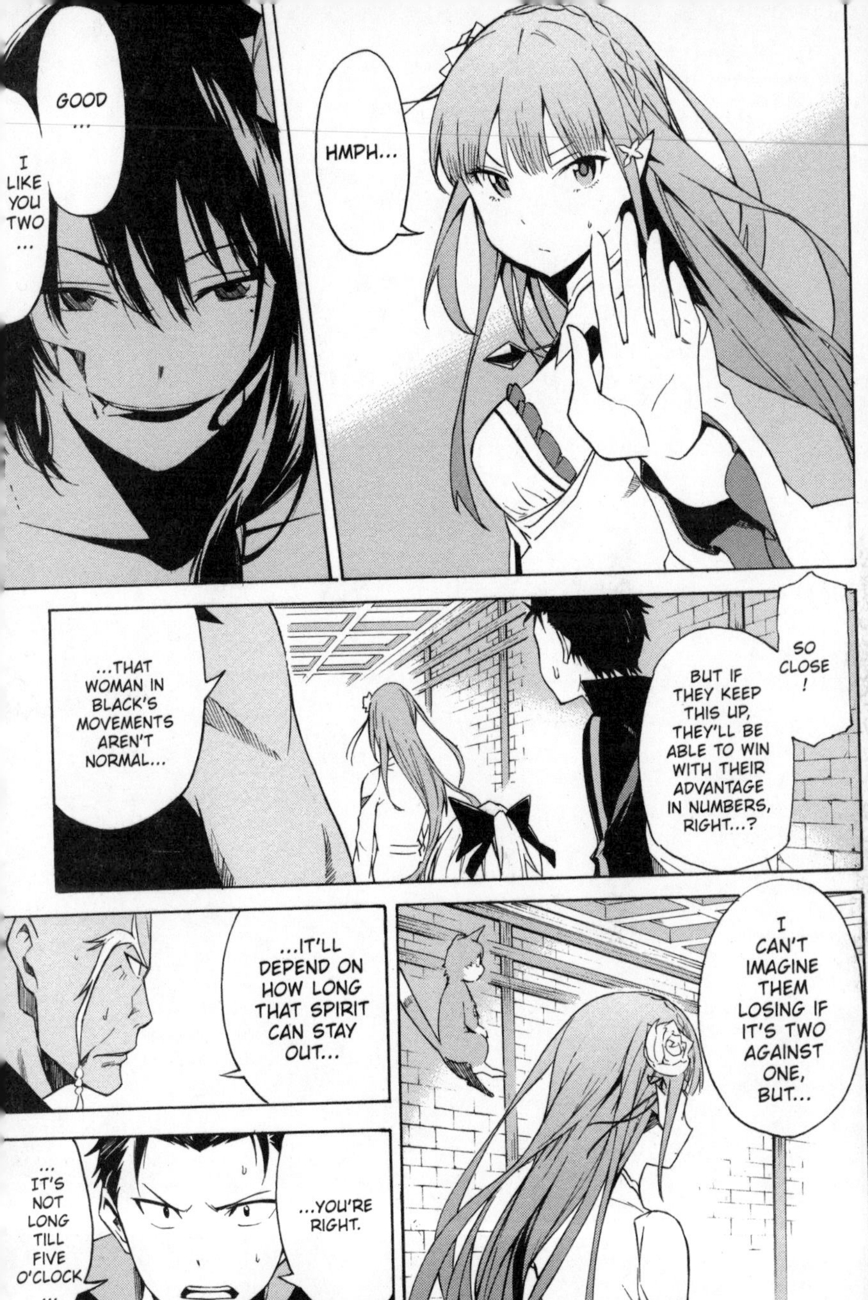
HMPH...
GOOD... I LIKE YOU TWO...
SO CLOSE!
BUT IF THEY KEEP THIS UP, THEY'LL BE ABLE TO WIN WITH THEIR ADVANTAGE IN NUMBERS, RIGHT...?
...THAT WOMAN IN BLACK'S MOVEMENTS AREN'T NORMAL...
I CAN'T IMAGINE THEM LOSING IF IT'S TWO AGAINST ONE, BUT...
...IT'LL DEPEND ON HOW LONG THAT SPIRIT CAN STAY OUT...
...YOU'RE RIGHT.
...IT'S NOT LONG TILL FIVE O'CLOCK...

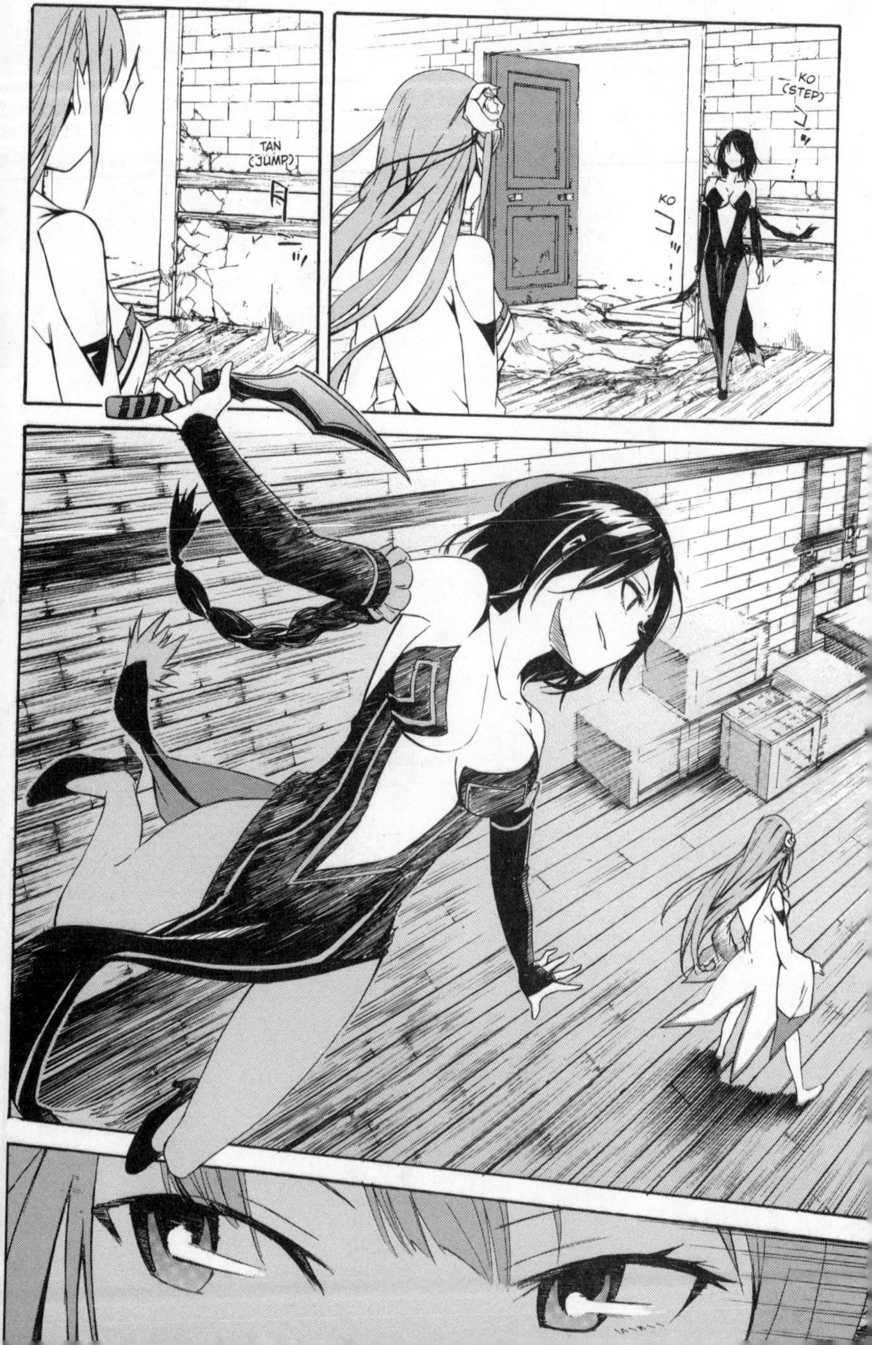
KO (STEP)
KO
TAN (JUMP)

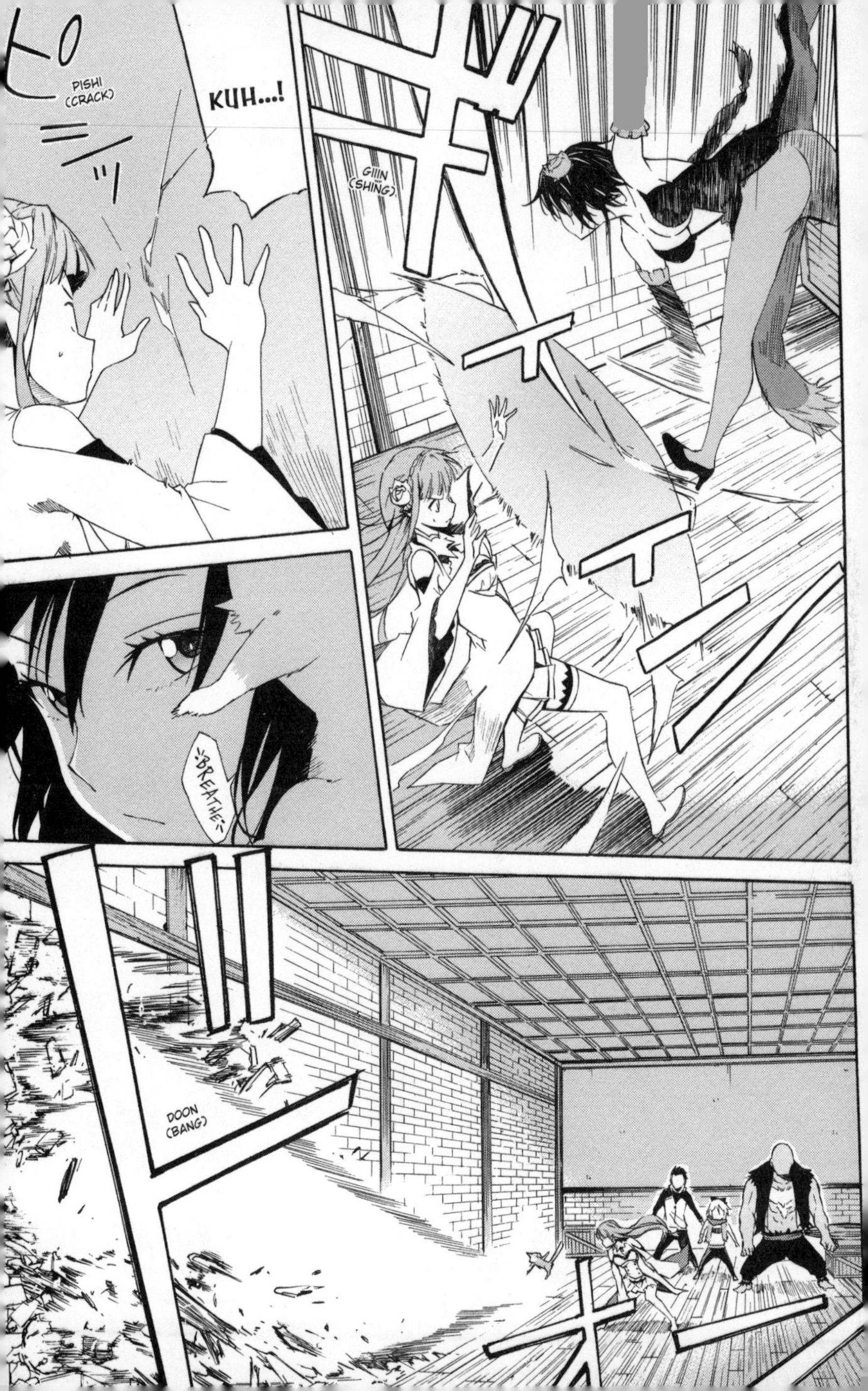
GIIIN (SHING)
KUH...!
PISHI (CRACK)
...BREATHE...
DOON (BANG)

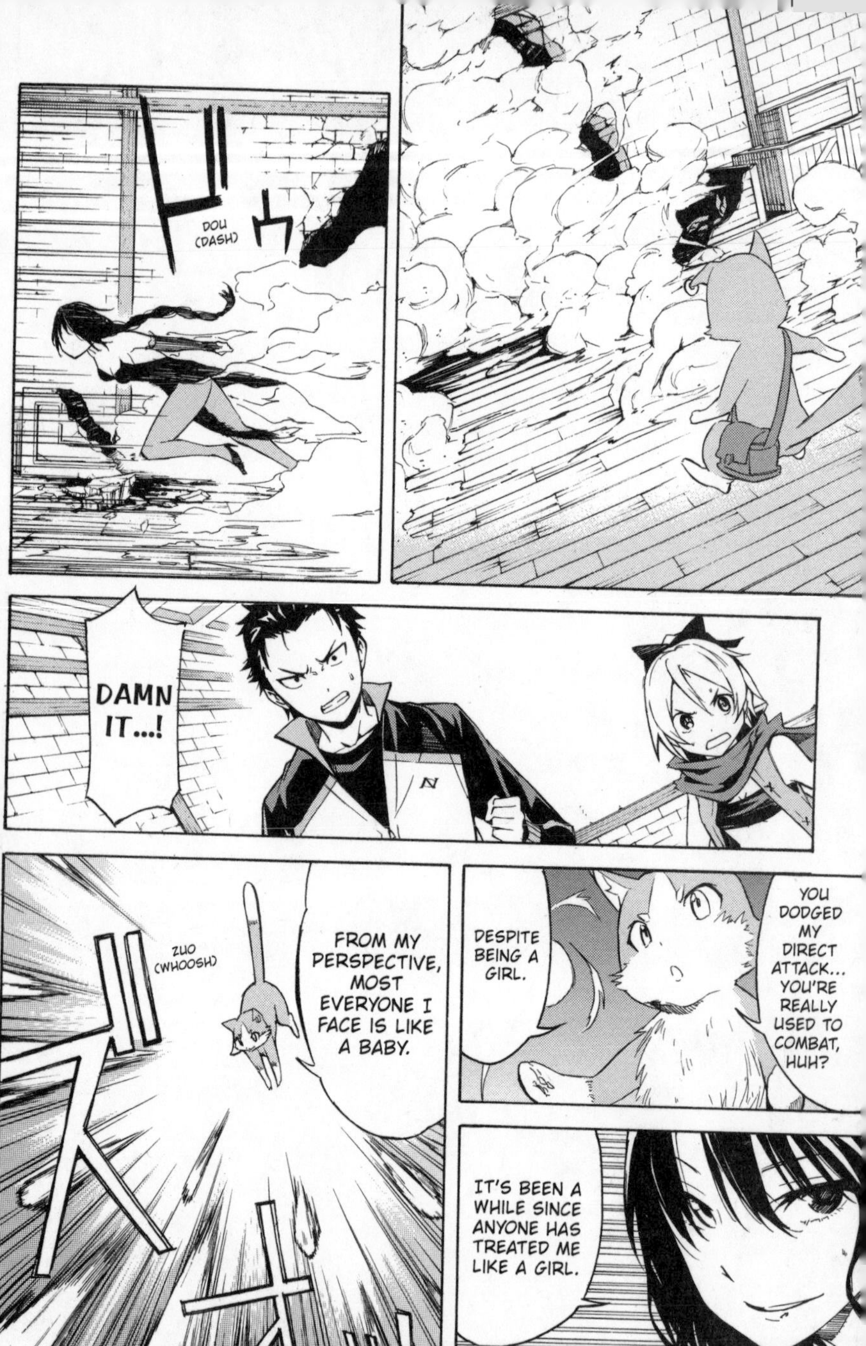
DOU (DASH)
DAMN IT...!
YOU DODGED MY DIRECT ATTACK... YOU'RE REALLY USED TO COMBAT, HUH?
DESPITE BEING A GIRL.
IT'S BEEN A WHILE SINCE ANYONE HAS TREATED ME LIKE A GIRL.
FROM MY PERSPECTIVE, MOST EVERYONE I FACE IS LIKE A BABY.
ZUO (WHOOSH)

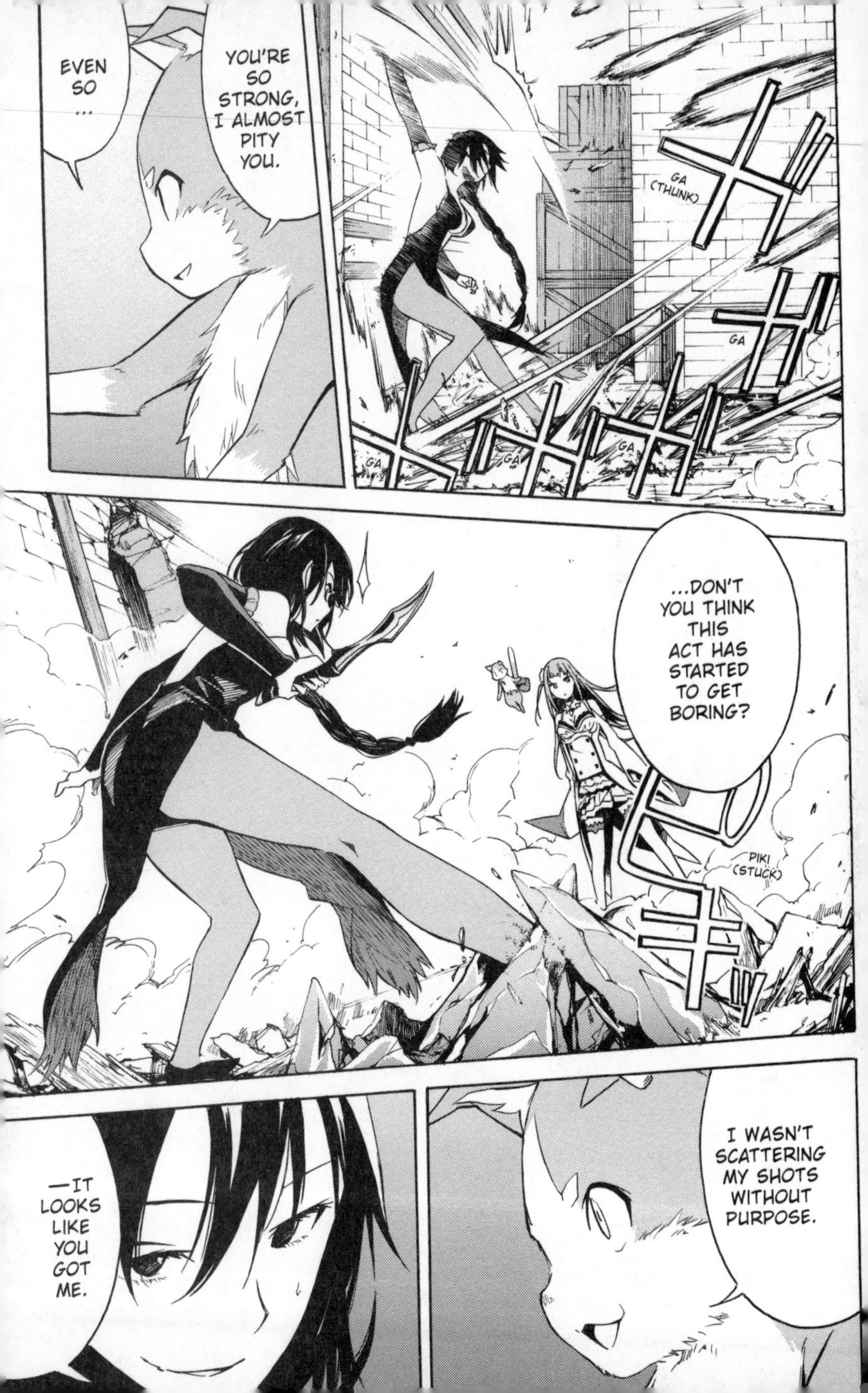
GA (THUNK)
GA
GA
GA
GA
YOU'RE SO STRONG, I ALMOST PITY YOU.
EVEN SO ...
...DON'T YOU THINK THIS ACT HAS STARTED TO GET BORING?
PIKI (STUCK)
I WASN'T SCATTERING MY SHOTS WITHOUT PURPOSE.
—IT LOOKS LIKE YOU GOT ME.

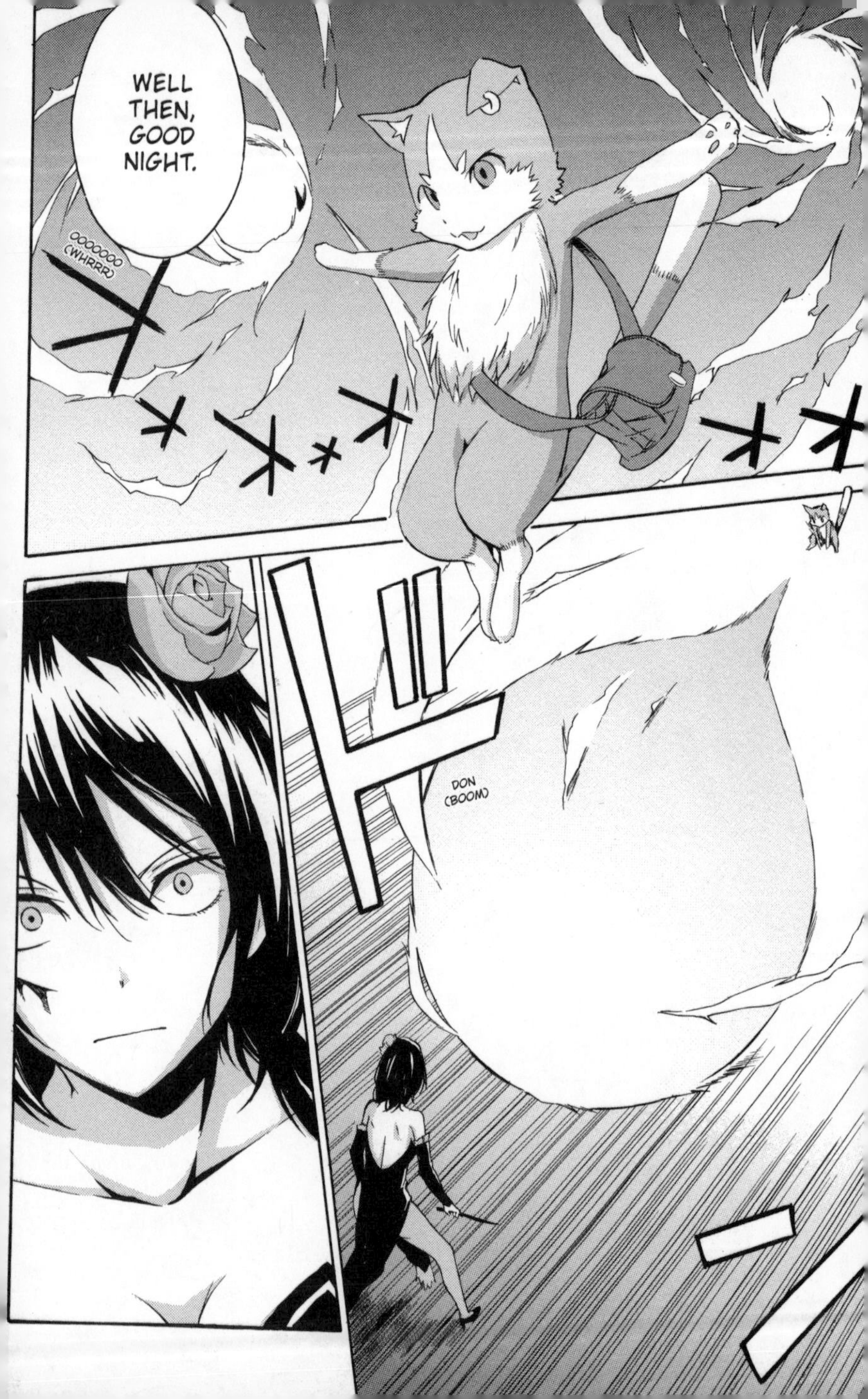
WELL THEN, GOOD NIGHT.
OOOOOOO (WHRRR)
DON (BOOM)

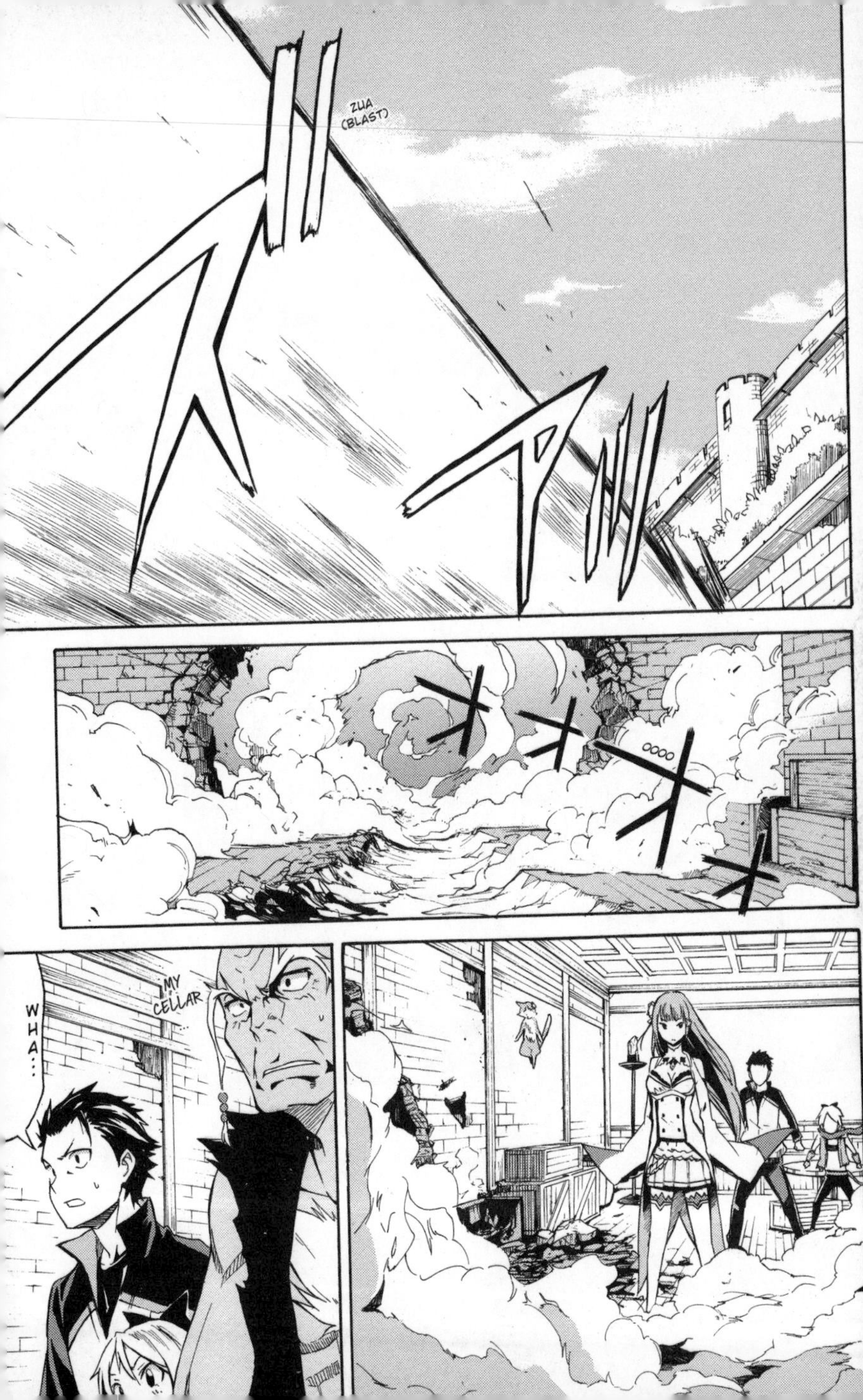
ZUA
(BLAST)
oooo
MY CELLAR...
WHA...

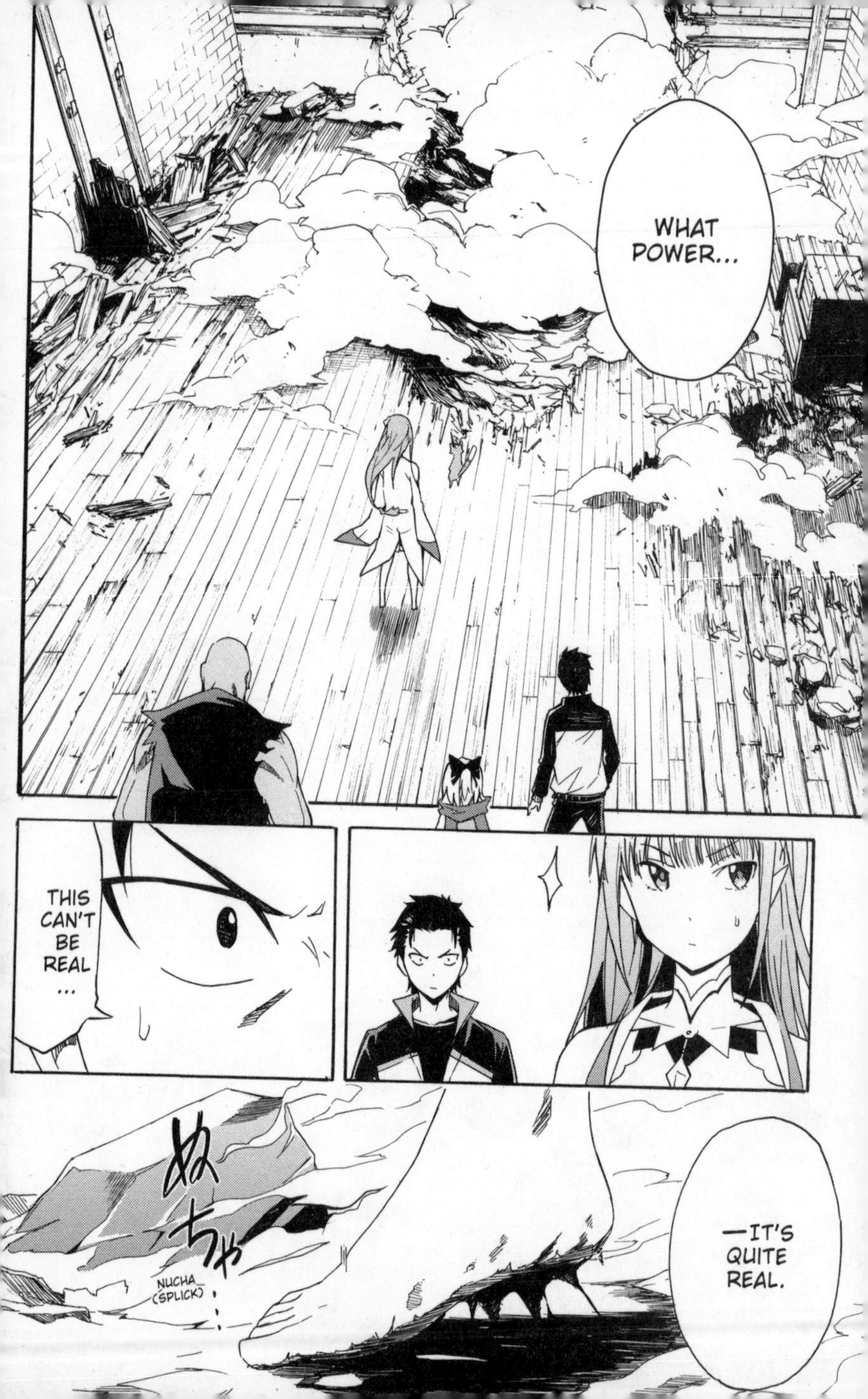

WHAT POWER...
THIS CAN'T BE REAL...
—IT'S QUITE REAL.
ぬちゃ
NUCHA (SPLICK)

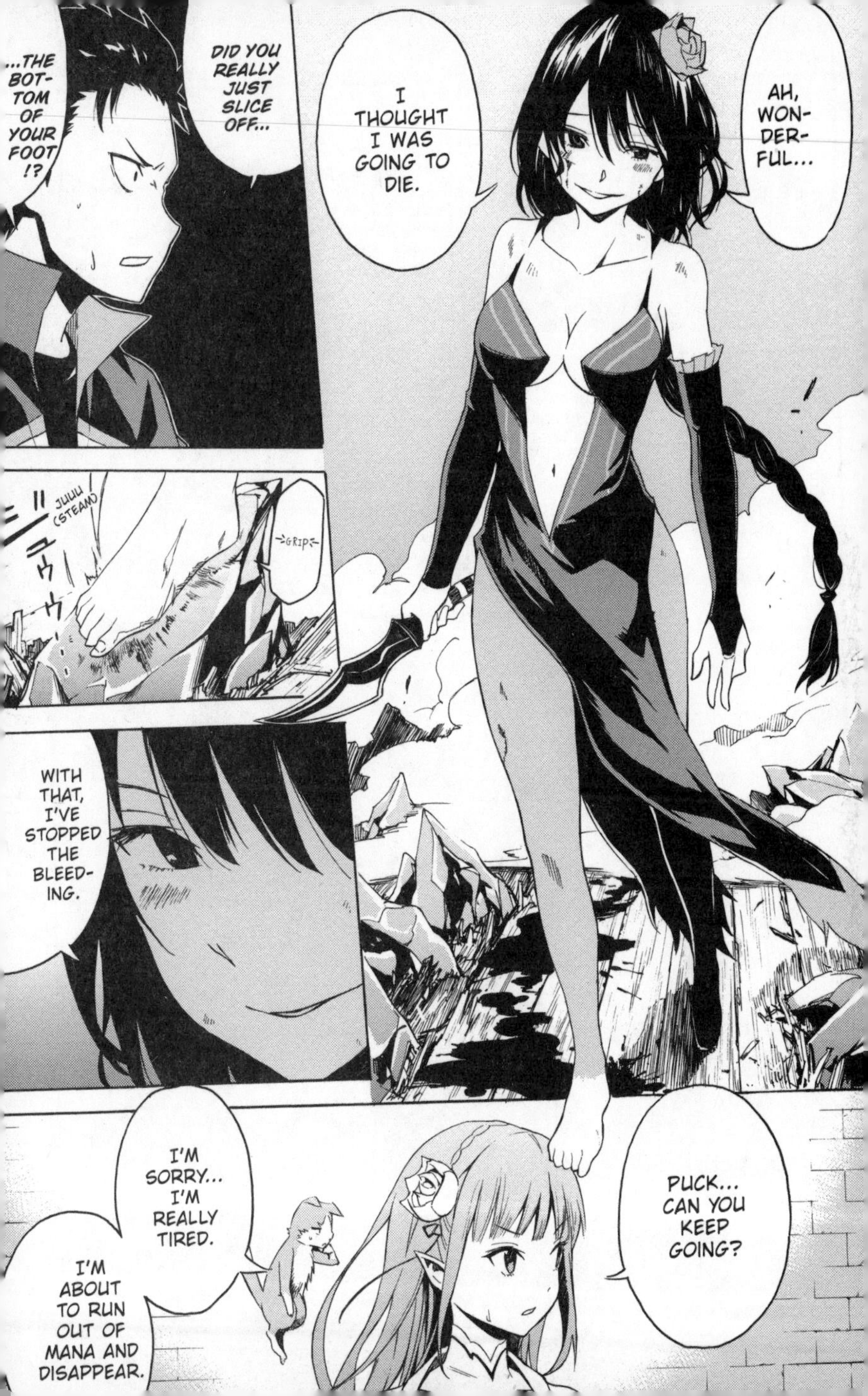
AH, WONDERFUL...
I THOUGHT I WAS GOING TO DIE.
DID YOU REALLY JUST SLICE OFF...
...THE BOTTOM OF YOUR FOOT!?
GRIP
JUUU (STEAM)
WITH THAT, I'VE STOPPED THE BLEEDING.
PUCK... CAN YOU KEEP GOING?
I'M SORRY... I'M REALLY TIRED.
I'M ABOUT TO RUN OUT OF MANA AND DISAPPEAR.

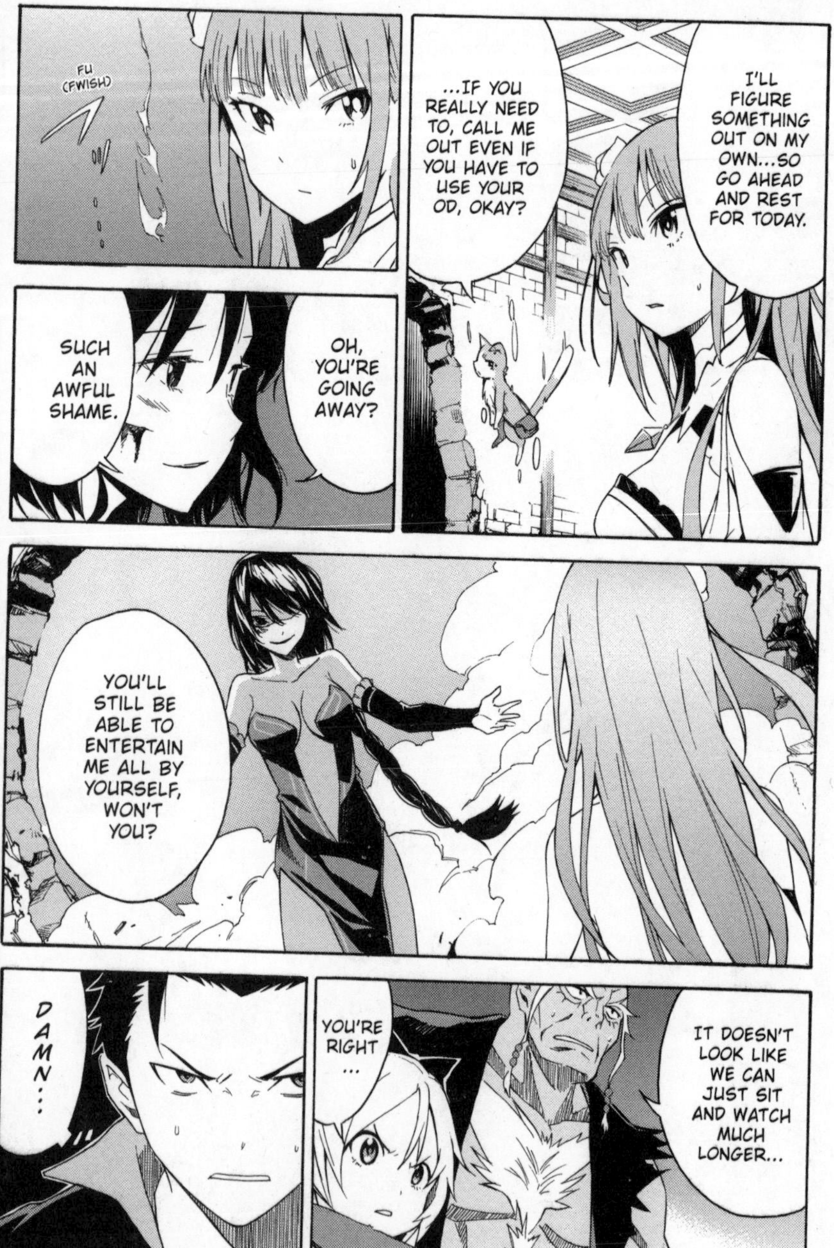
I'LL FIGURE SOMETHING OUT ON MY OWN...SO GO AHEAD AND REST FOR TODAY.
...IF YOU REALLY NEED TO, CALL ME OUT EVEN IF YOU HAVE TO USE YOUR OD, OKAY?
FU (FWISH)
OH, YOU'RE GOING AWAY?
SUCH AN AWFUL SHAME.
YOU'LL STILL BE ABLE TO ENTERTAIN ME ALL BY YOURSELF, WON'T YOU?
IT DOESN'T LOOK LIKE WE CAN JUST SIT AND WATCH MUCH LONGER...
YOU'RE RIGHT...
DAMN...

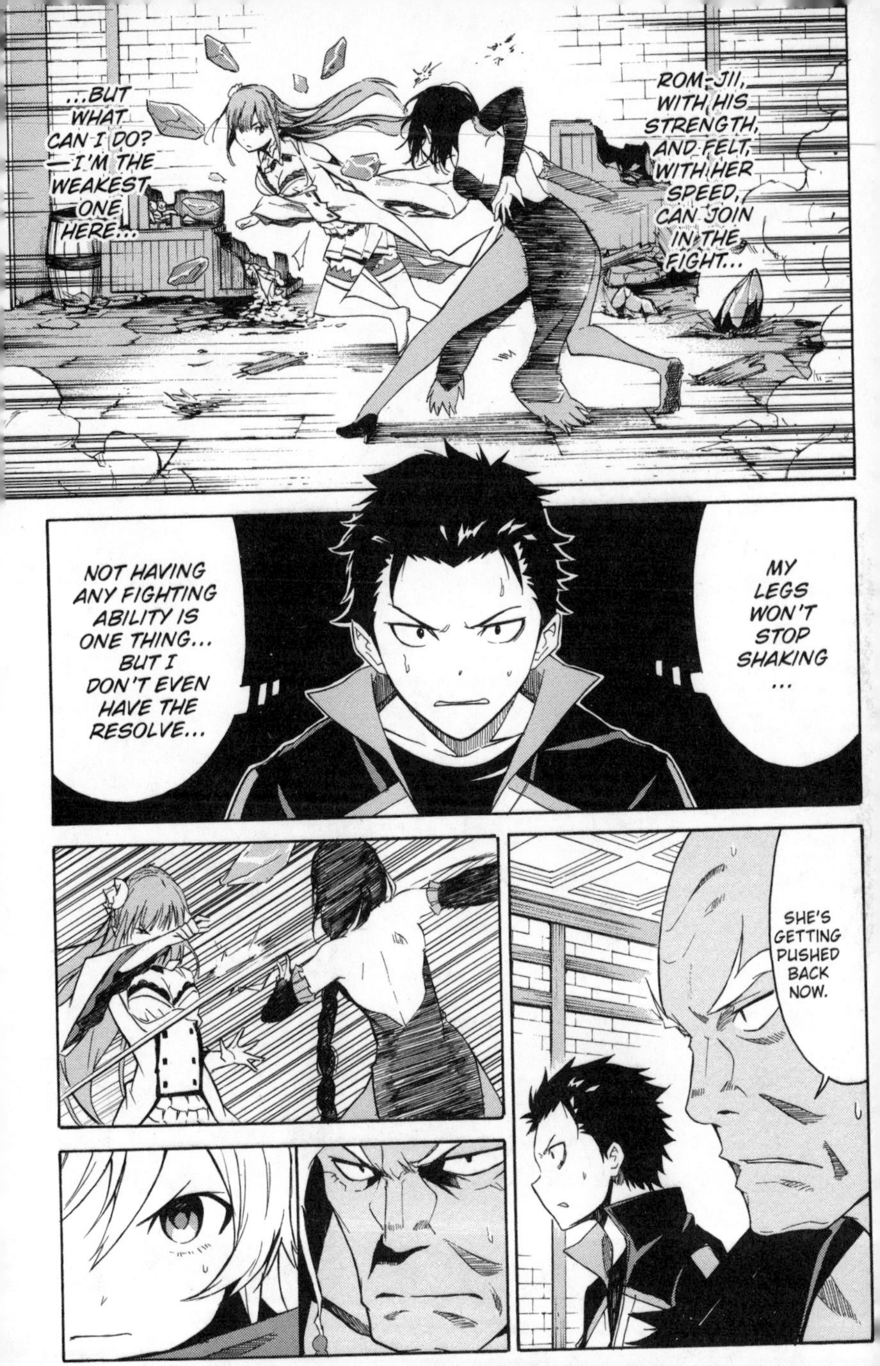
ROM-JII, WITH HIS STRENGTH, AND FELT, WITH HER SPEED, CAN JOIN IN THE FIGHT...
...BUT WHAT CAN I DO? —I'M THE WEAKEST ONE HERE...
MY LEGS WON'T STOP SHAKING...
NOT HAVING ANY FIGHTING ABILITY IS ONE THING... BUT I DON'T EVEN HAVE THE RESOLVE...
SHE'S GETTING PUSHED BACK NOW.

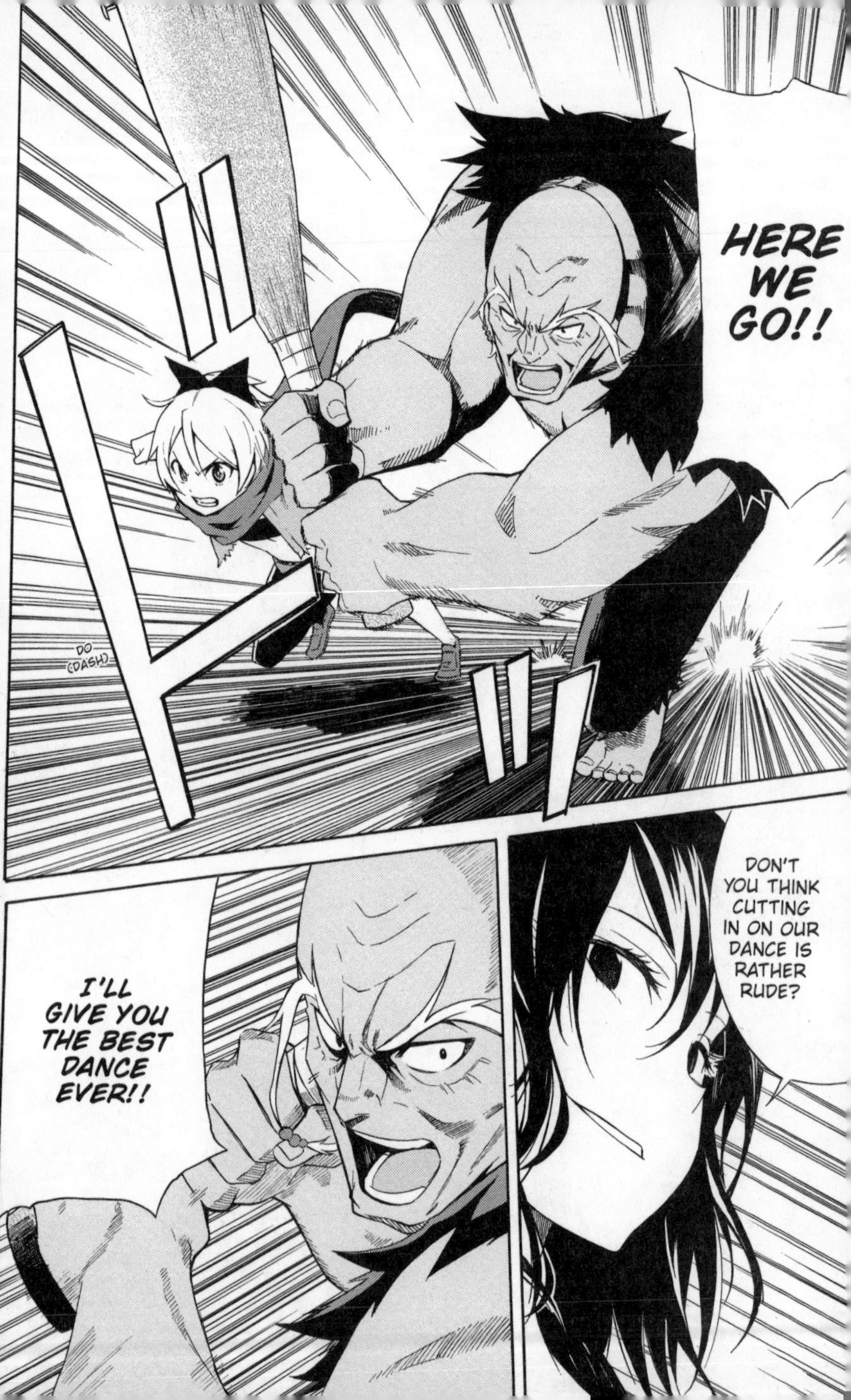
HERE WE GO!!
DO (DASH)
DON'T YOU THINK CUTTING IN ON OUR DANCE IS RATHER RUDE?
I'LL GIVE YOU THE BEST DANCE EVER!!

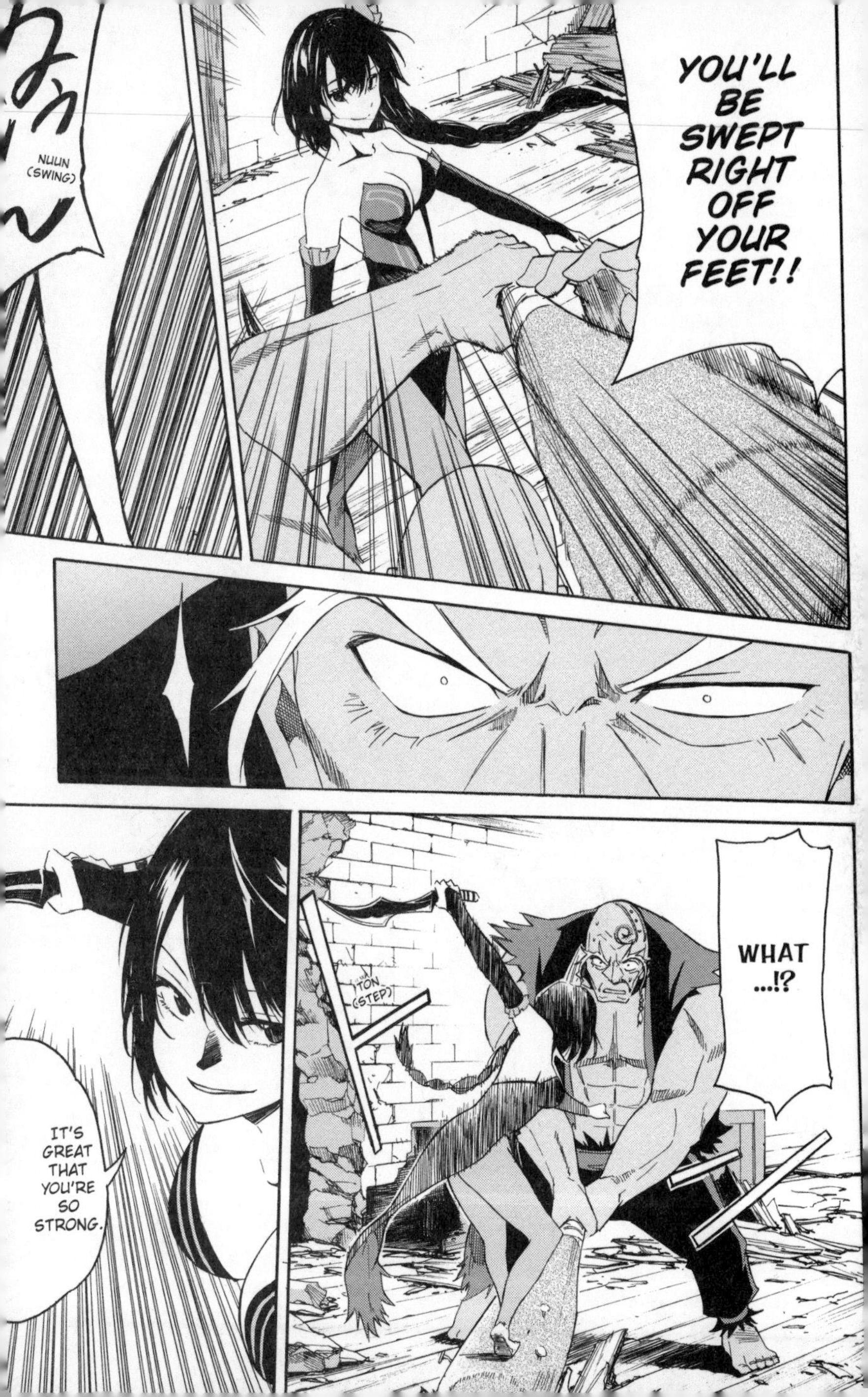
YOU'LL BE SWEPT RIGHT OFF YOUR FEET!!
NUUN (SWING)
WHAT ...!?
TON (STEP)
IT'S GREAT THAT YOU'RE SO STRONG.

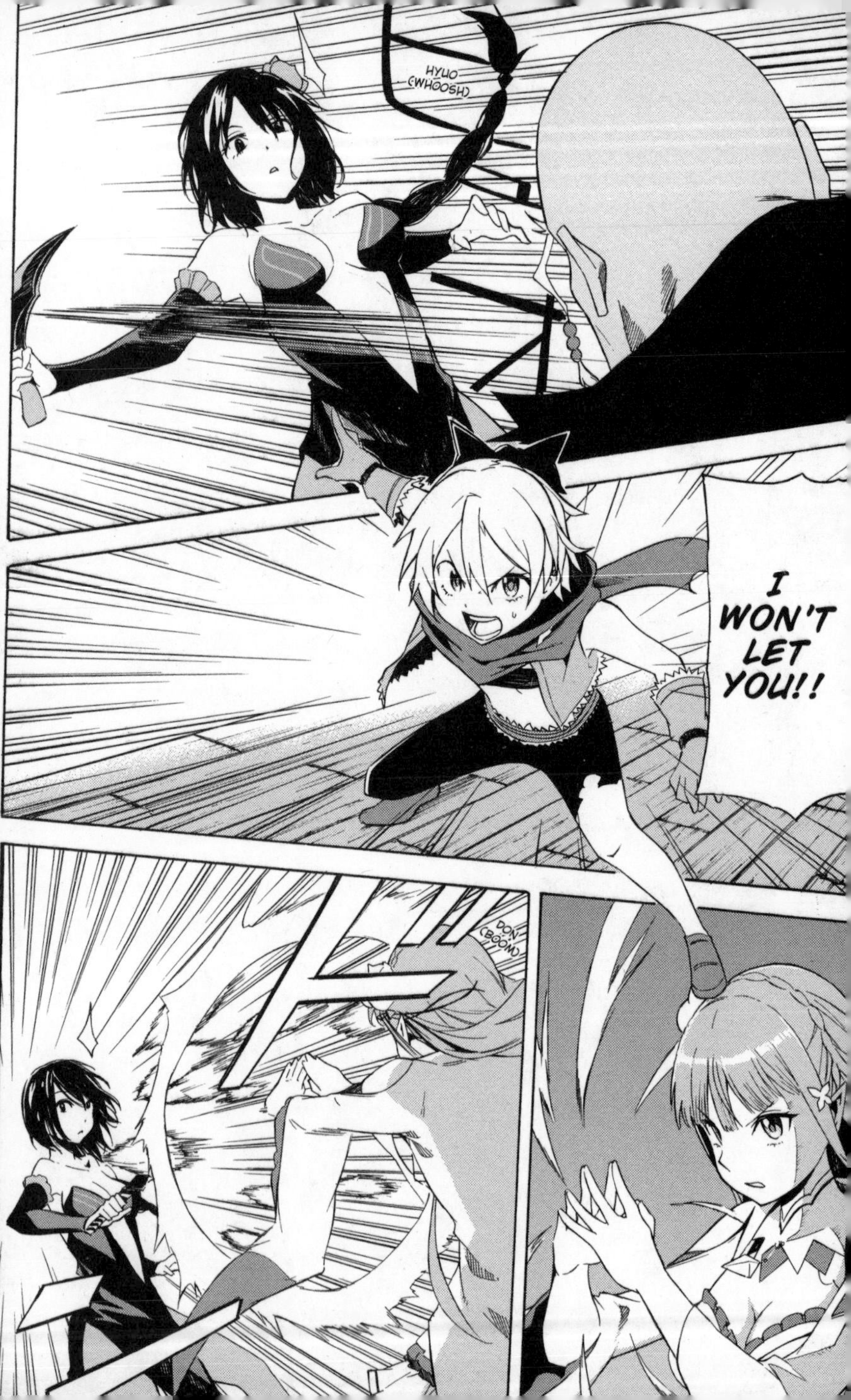
HYUO (WHOOSH)
I WON'T LET YOU!!
DON (BOOM)

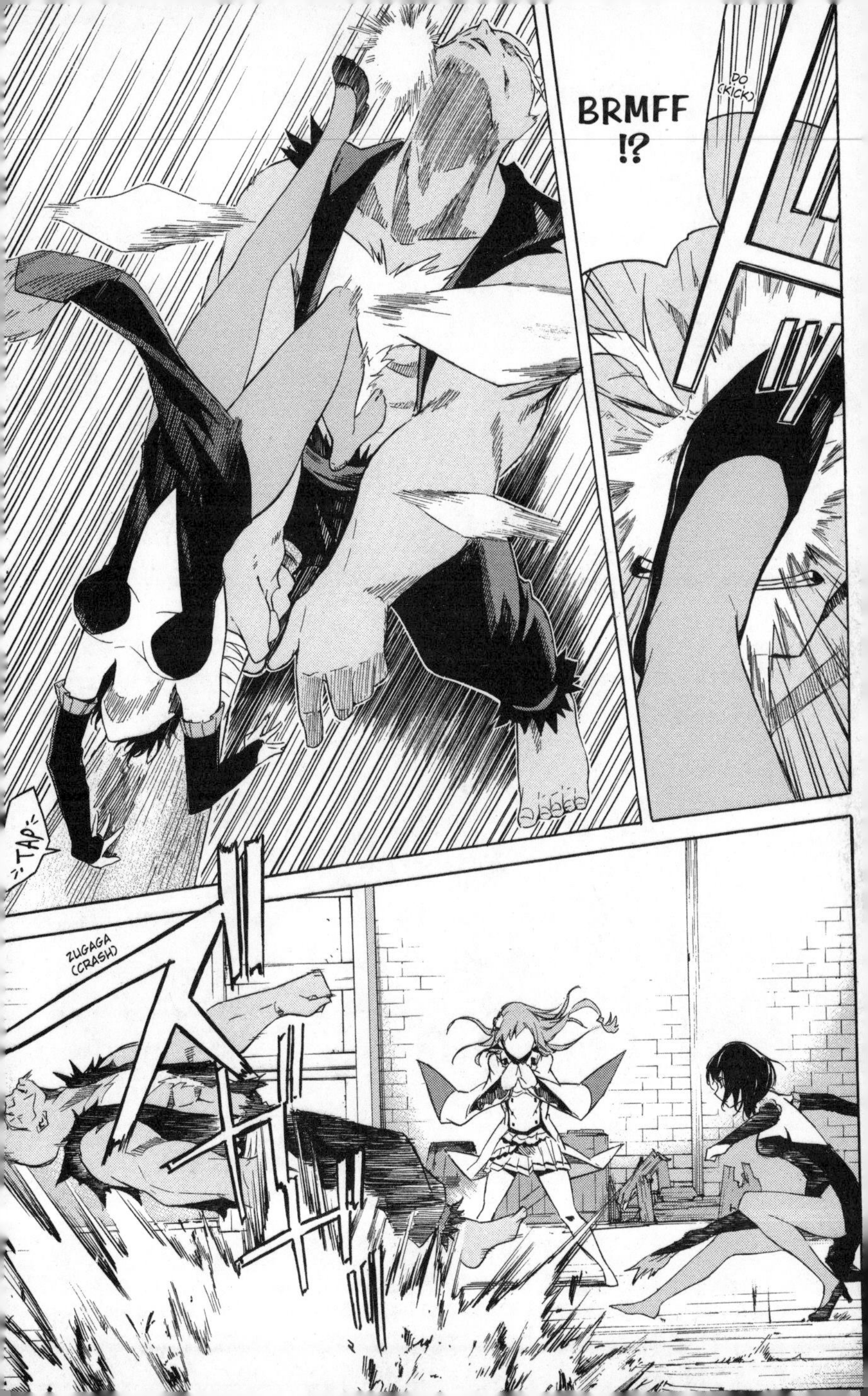
DO (KICK)
BRMFF !?
TAP
ZUGAGA (CRASH)

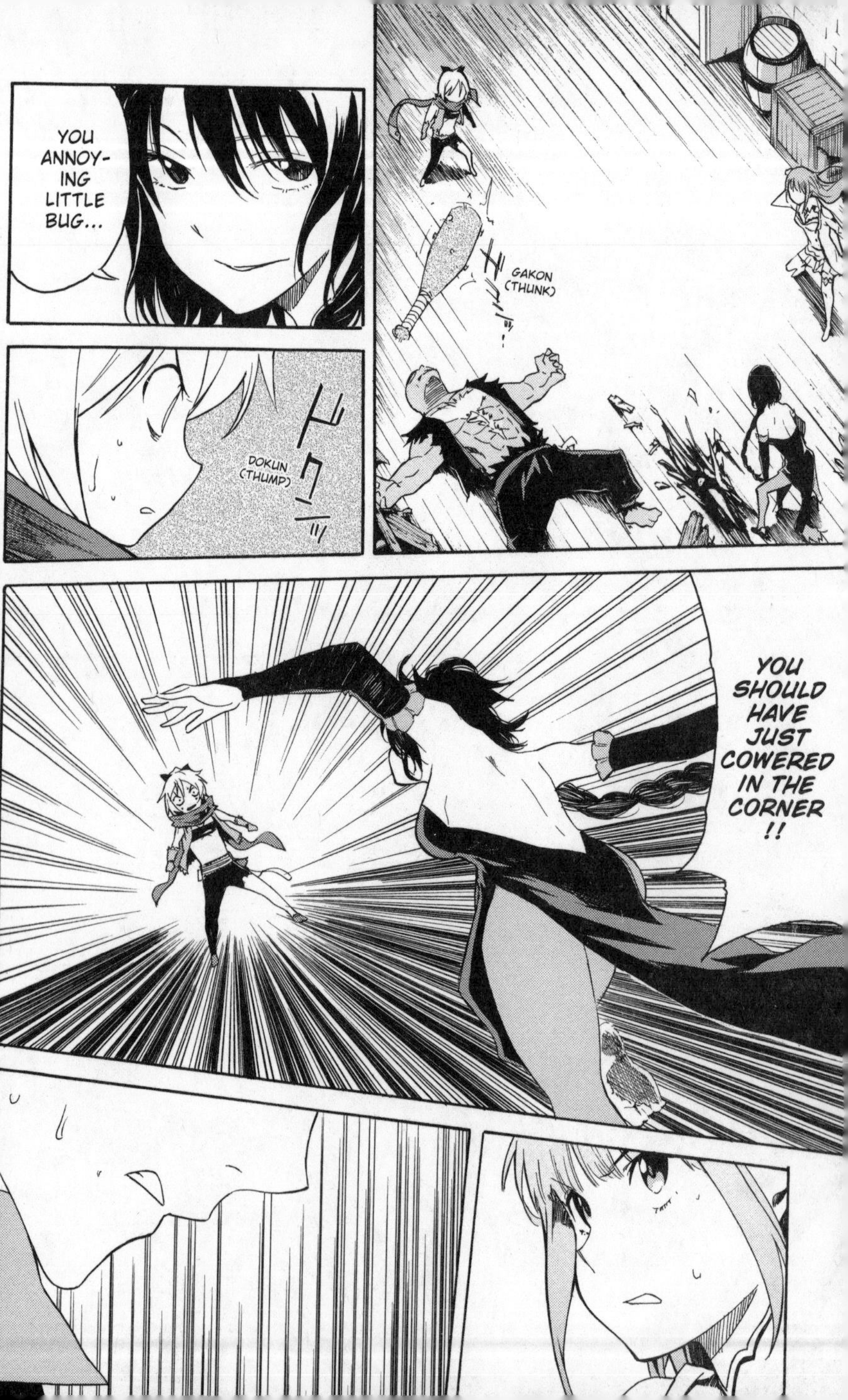
GAKON (THUNK)
YOU ANNOY-ING LITTLE BUG...
DOKUN (THUMP)
YOU SHOULD HAVE JUST COWERED IN THE CORNER !!

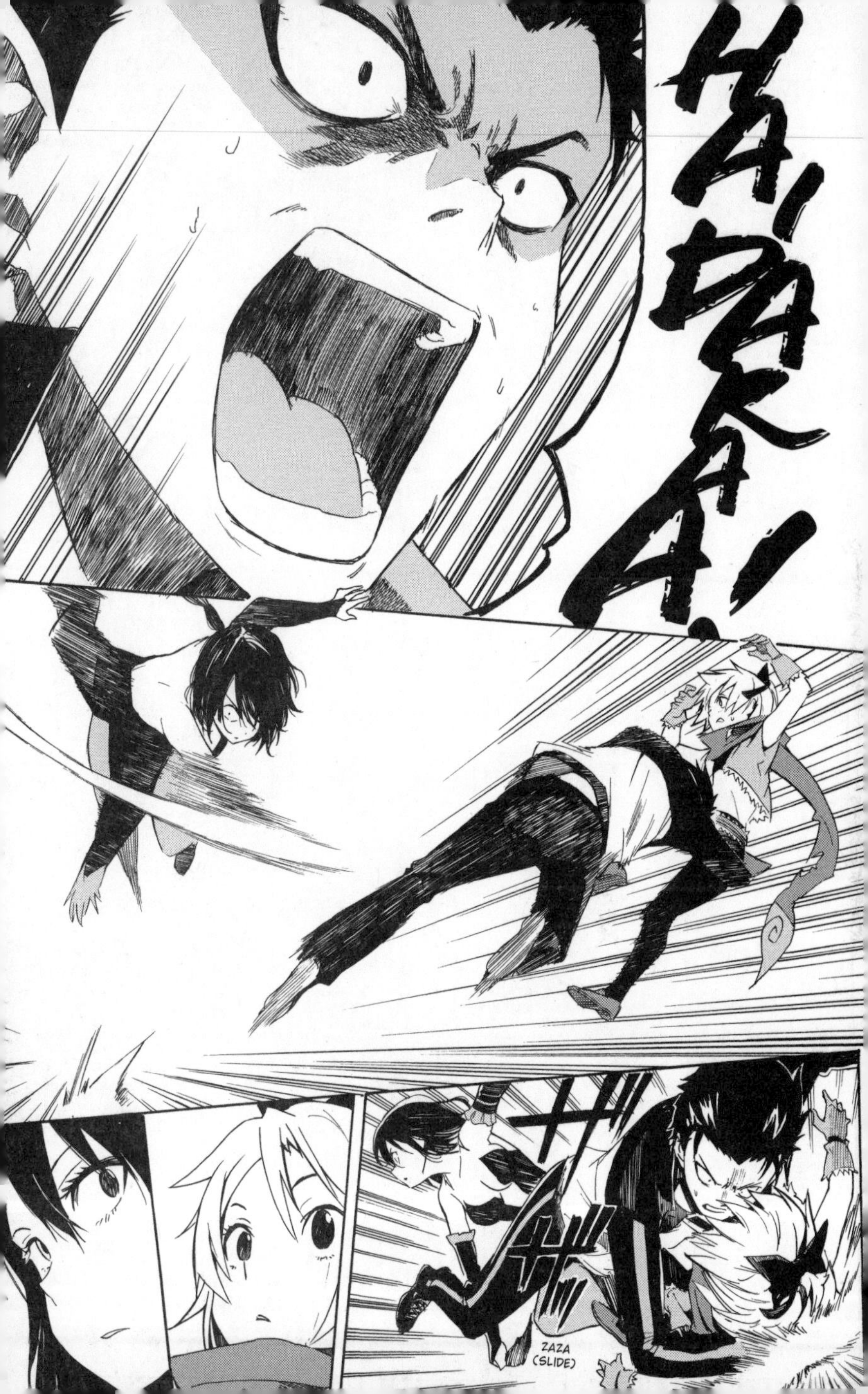
ZAZA
(SLIDE)

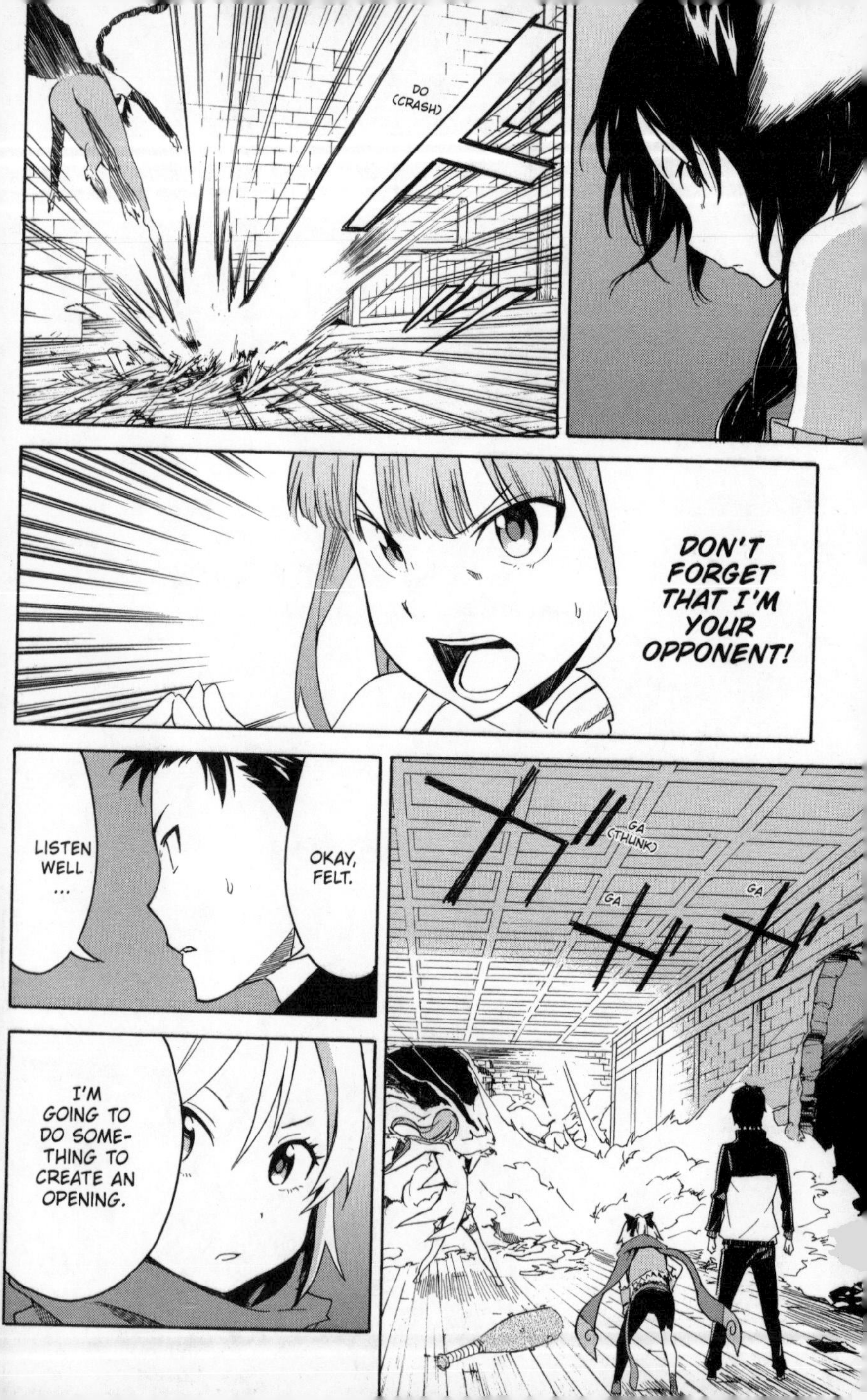
DO
(CRASH)
DON'T FORGET THAT I'M YOUR OPPONENT!
GA
(THUNK)
GA
GA
OKAY, FELT.
LISTEN WELL ...
I'M GOING TO DO SOME-THING TO CREATE AN OPENING.

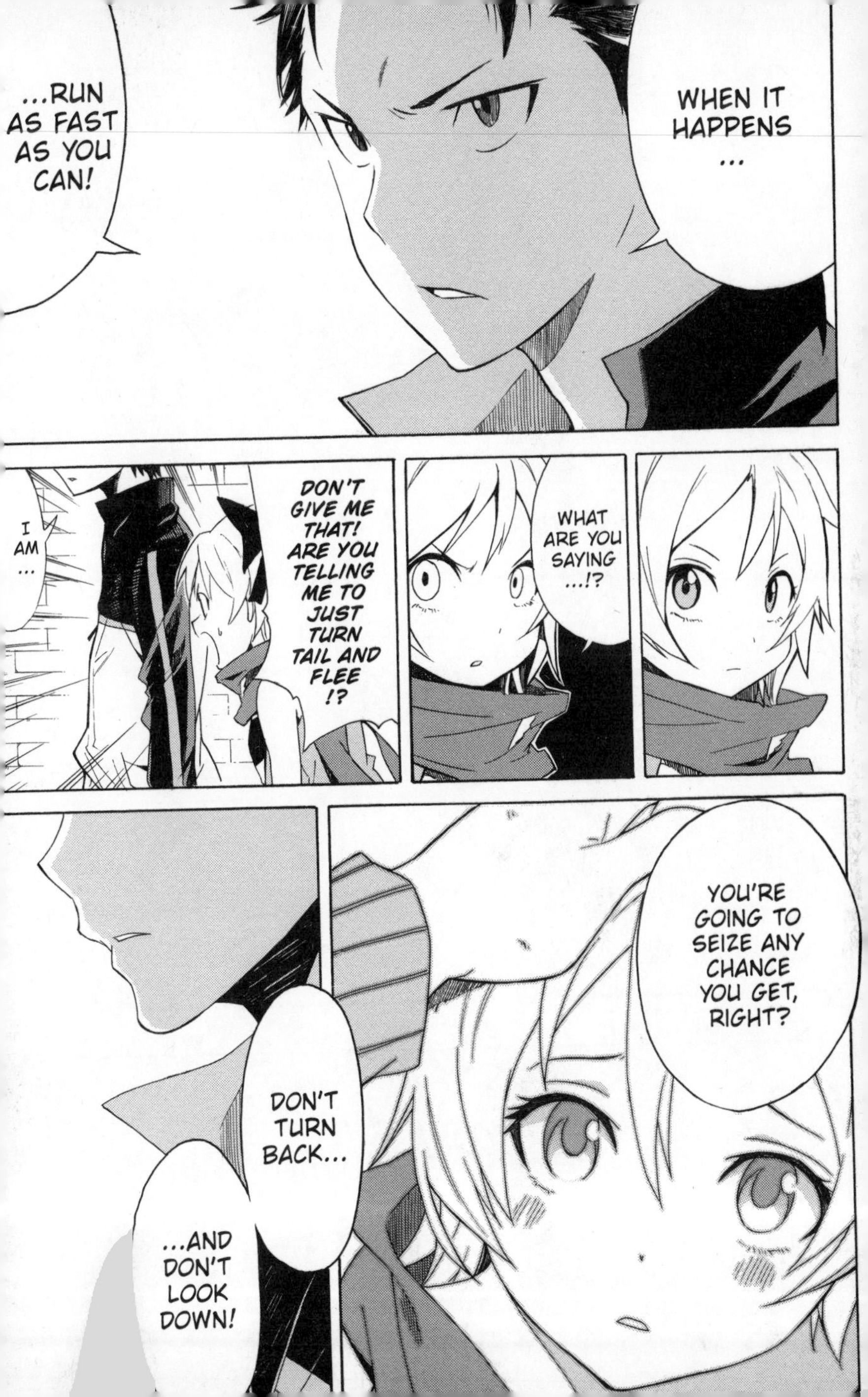
WHEN IT HAPPENS...
...RUN AS FAST AS YOU CAN!
WHAT ARE YOU SAYING...!?
DON'T GIVE ME THAT! ARE YOU TELLING ME TO JUST TURN TAIL AND FLEE!?
I AM...
YOU'RE GOING TO SEIZE ANY CHANCE YOU GET, RIGHT?
DON'T TURN BACK...
...AND DON'T LOOK DOWN!

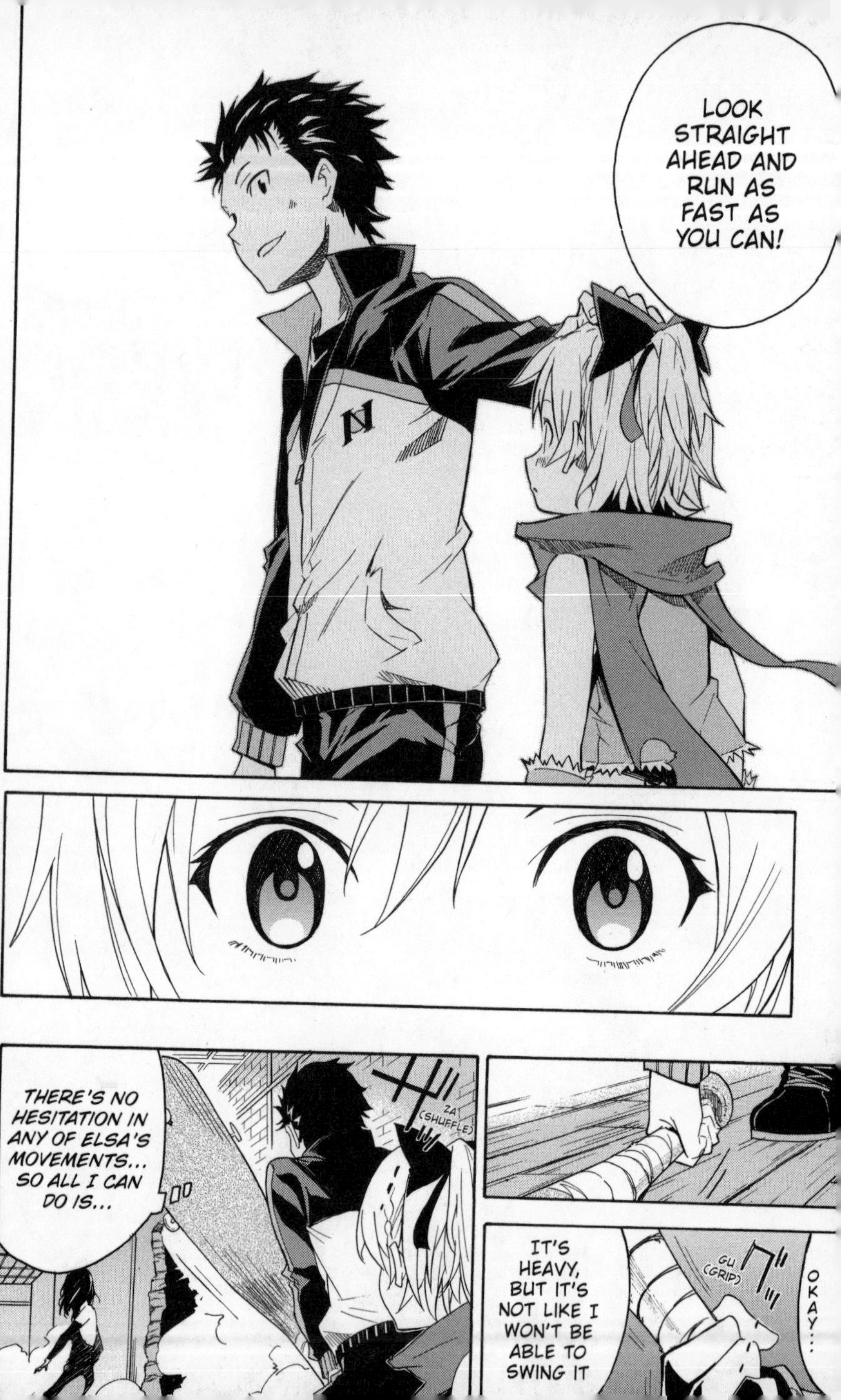
LOOK STRAIGHT AHEAD AND RUN AS FAST AS YOU CAN!
OKAY...
GU (GRIP)
IT'S HEAVY, BUT IT'S NOT LIKE I WON'T BE ABLE TO SWING IT
ZA (SHUFFLE)
THERE'S NO HESITATION IN ANY OF ELSA'S MOVEMENTS... SO ALL I CAN DO IS...

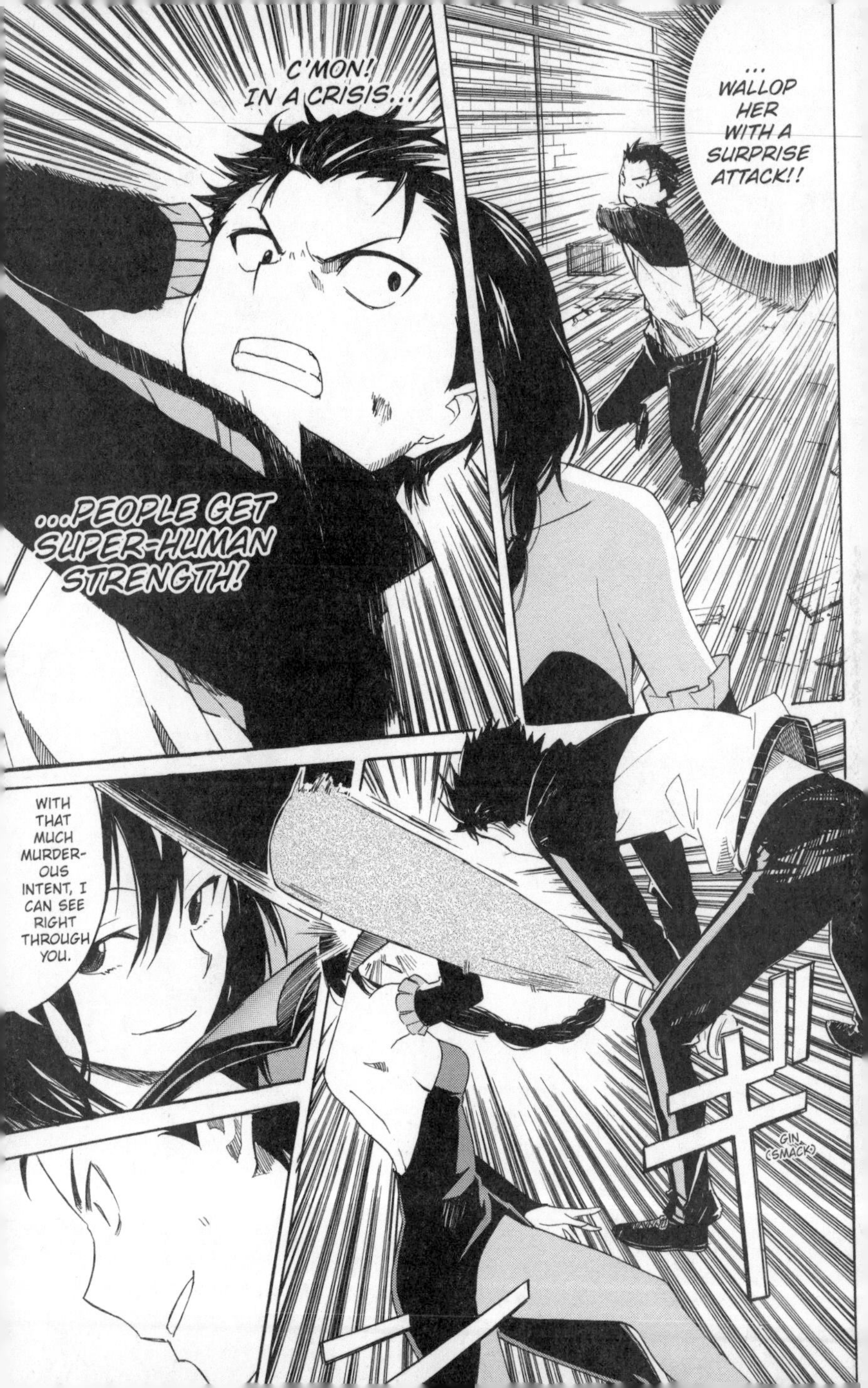
...WALLOP HER WITH A SURPRISE ATTACK!!
C'MON! IN A CRISIS...
...PEOPLE GET SUPER-HUMAN STRENGTH!
WITH THAT MUCH MURDER-OUS INTENT, I CAN SEE RIGHT THROUGH YOU.
GIN (SMACK)

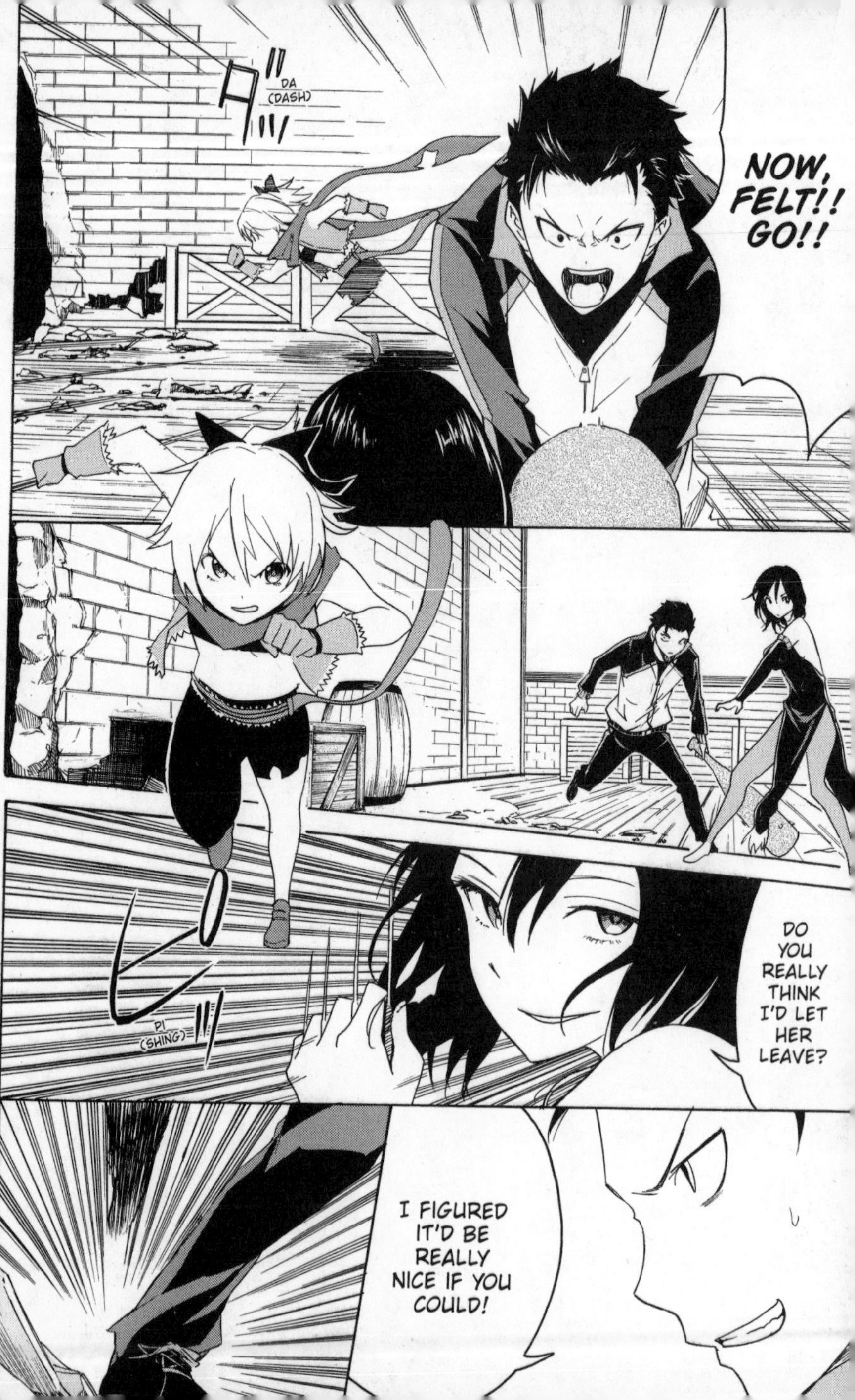
NOW, FELT!! GO!!
DA (DASH)
PI (SHING)
DO YOU REALLY THINK I'D LET HER LEAVE?
I FIGURED IT'D BE REALLY NICE IF YOU COULD!

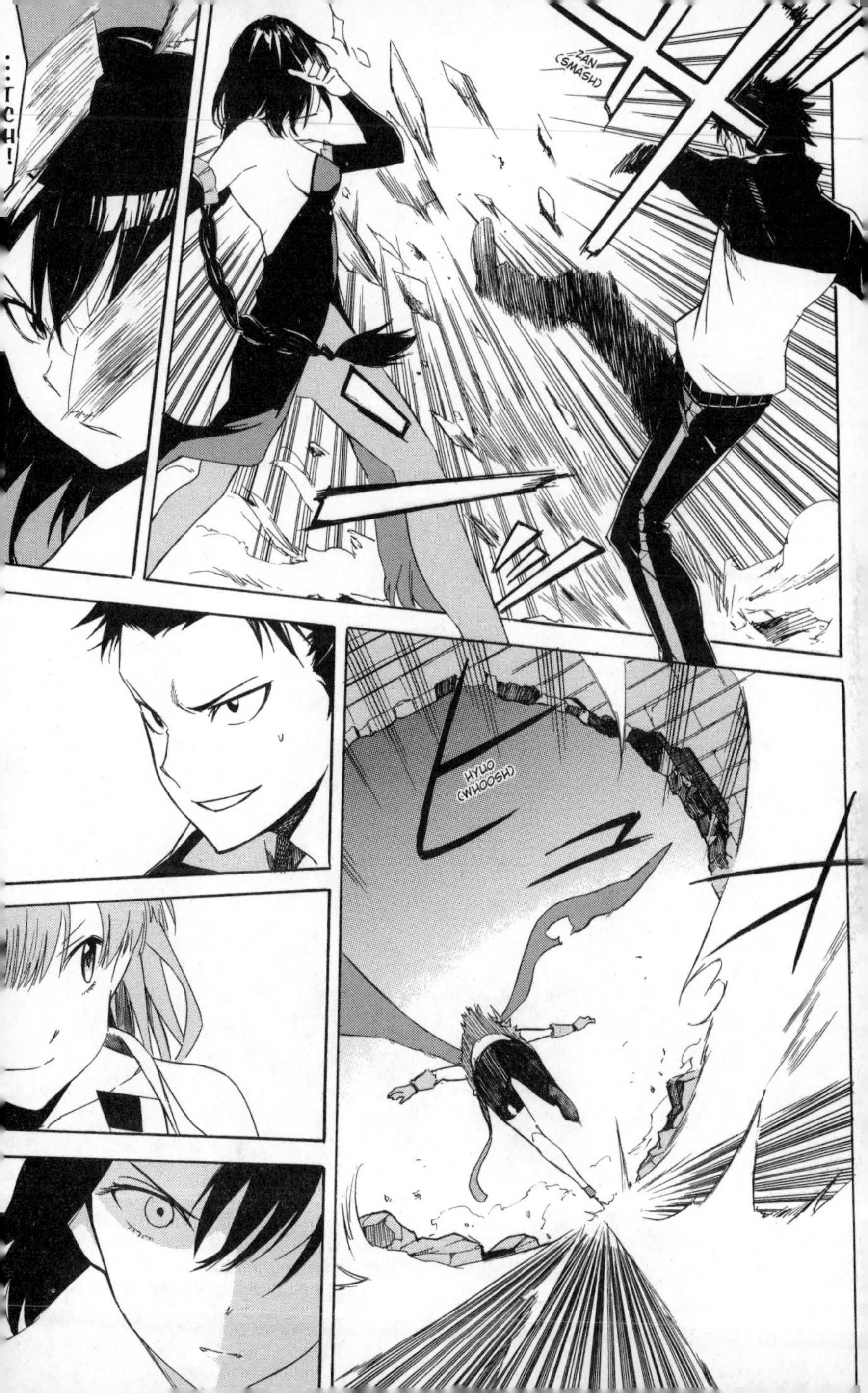
ZAN
(SMASH)
...TCH!
HYUO
(WHOOSH)

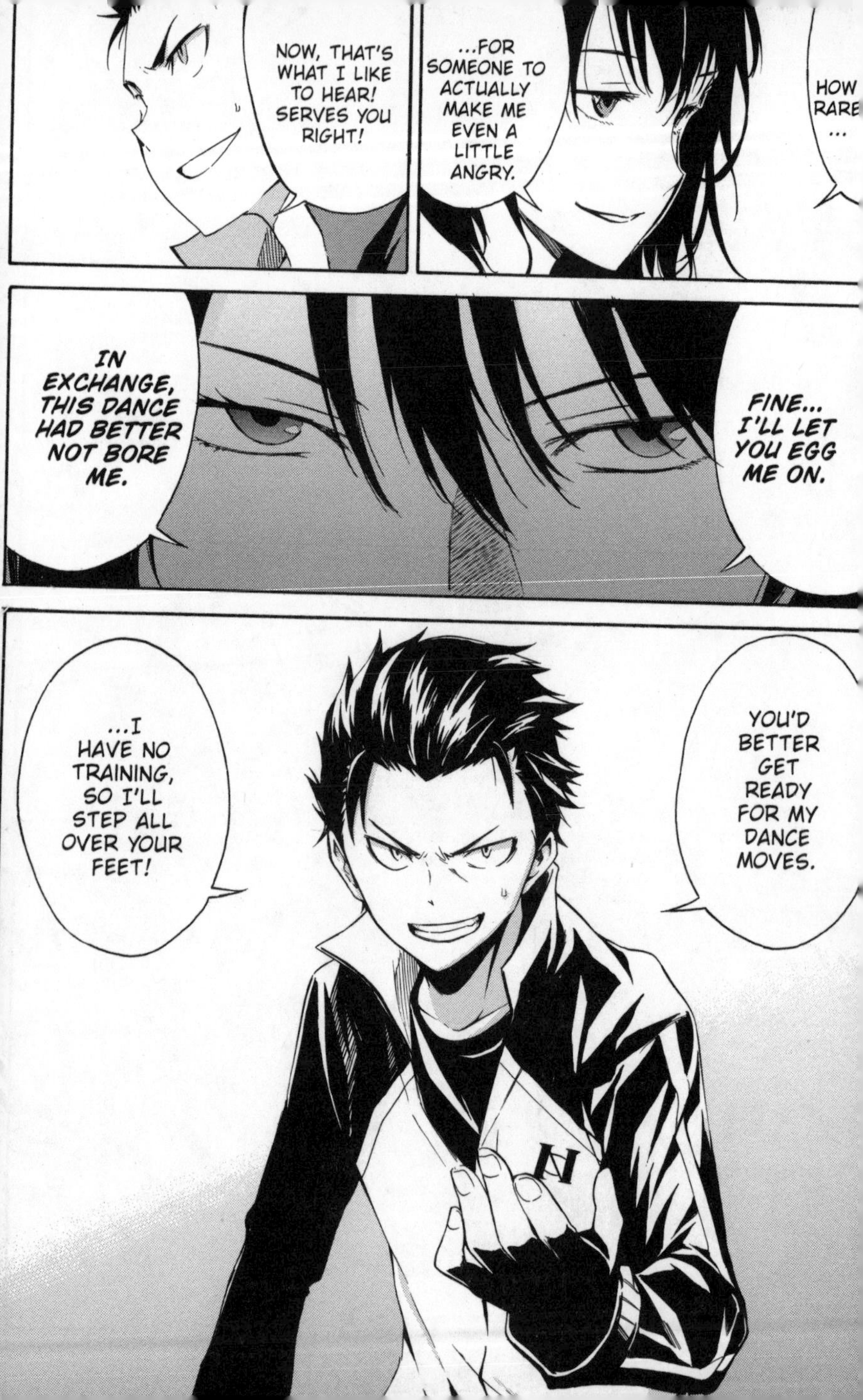
HOW RARE...
...FOR SOMEONE TO ACTUALLY MAKE ME EVEN A LITTLE ANGRY.
NOW, THAT'S WHAT I LIKE TO HEAR! SERVES YOU RIGHT!
FINE... I'LL LET YOU EGG ME ON.
IN EXCHANGE, THIS DANCE HAD BETTER NOT BORE ME.
YOU'D BETTER GET READY FOR MY DANCE MOVES.
...I HAVE NO TRAINING, SO I'LL STEP ALL OVER YOUR FEET!

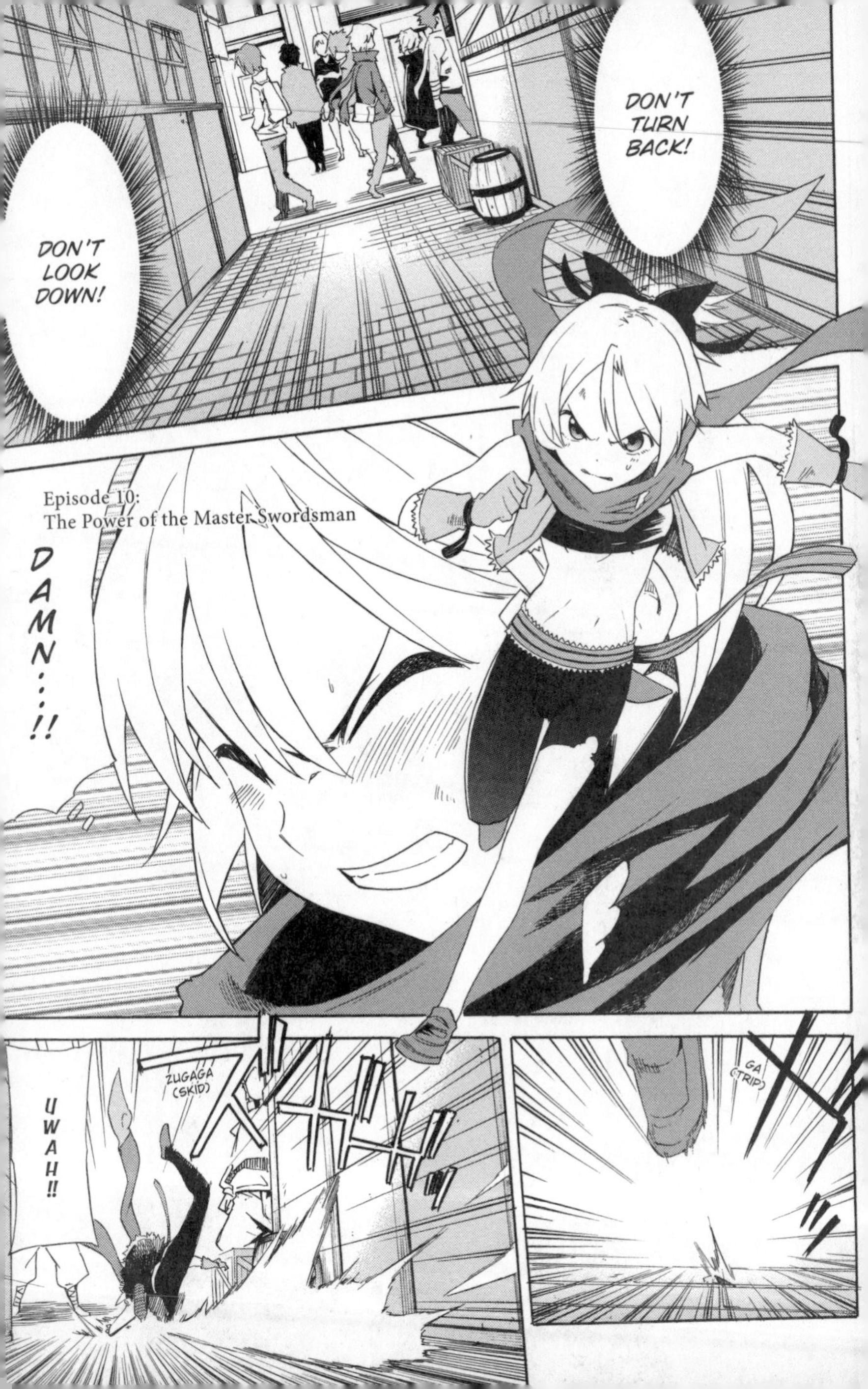
DON'T TURN BACK!
DON'T LOOK DOWN!
Episode 10:
The Power of the Master Swordsman
DAMN...!!
GA (TRIP)
ZUGAGA (SKID)
UWAH!!

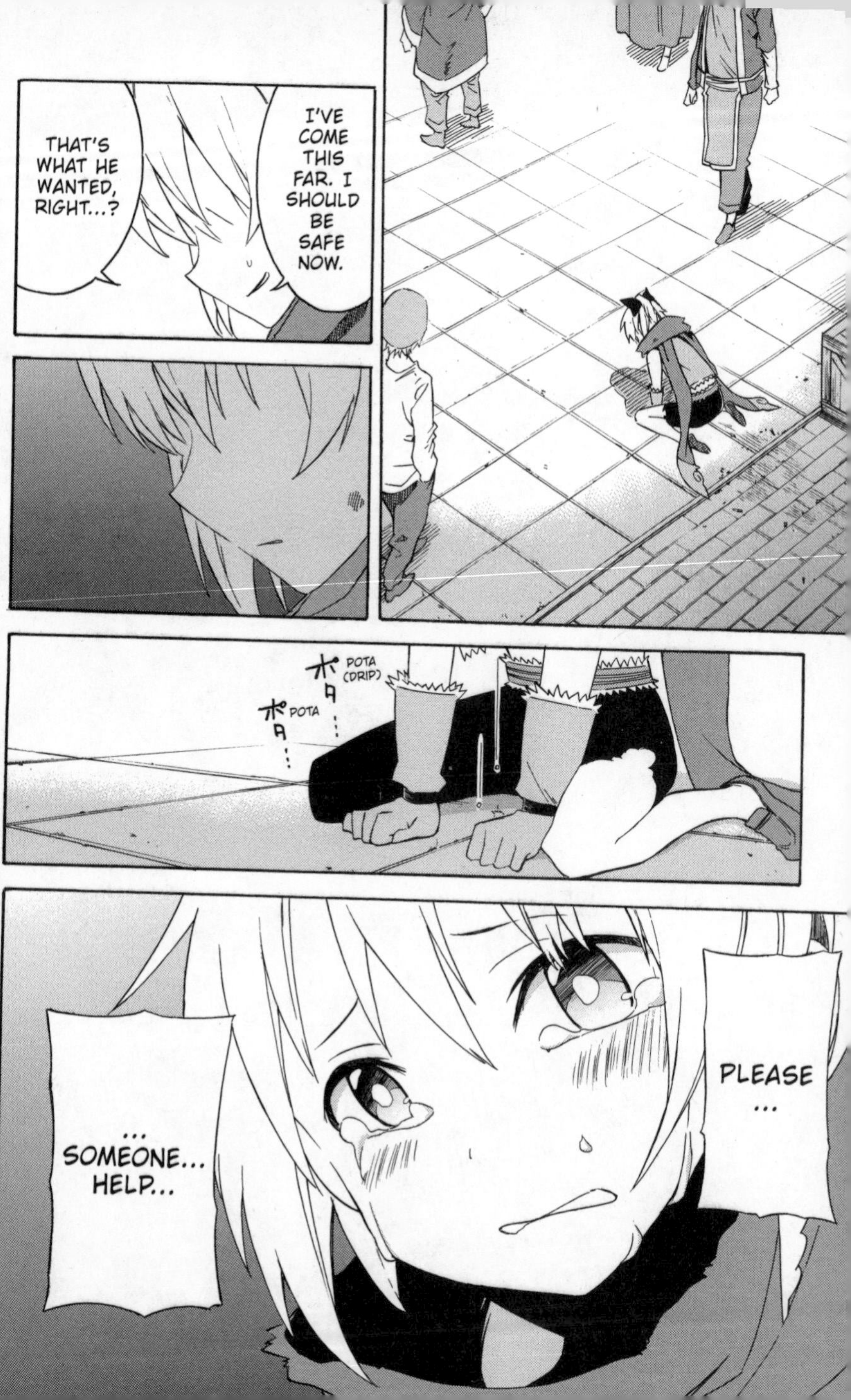
I'VE COME THIS FAR. I SHOULD BE SAFE NOW.
THAT'S WHAT HE WANTED, RIGHT...?
ポタ... POTA (DRIP)
ポタ... POTA
PLEASE ...
... SOMEONE... HELP...

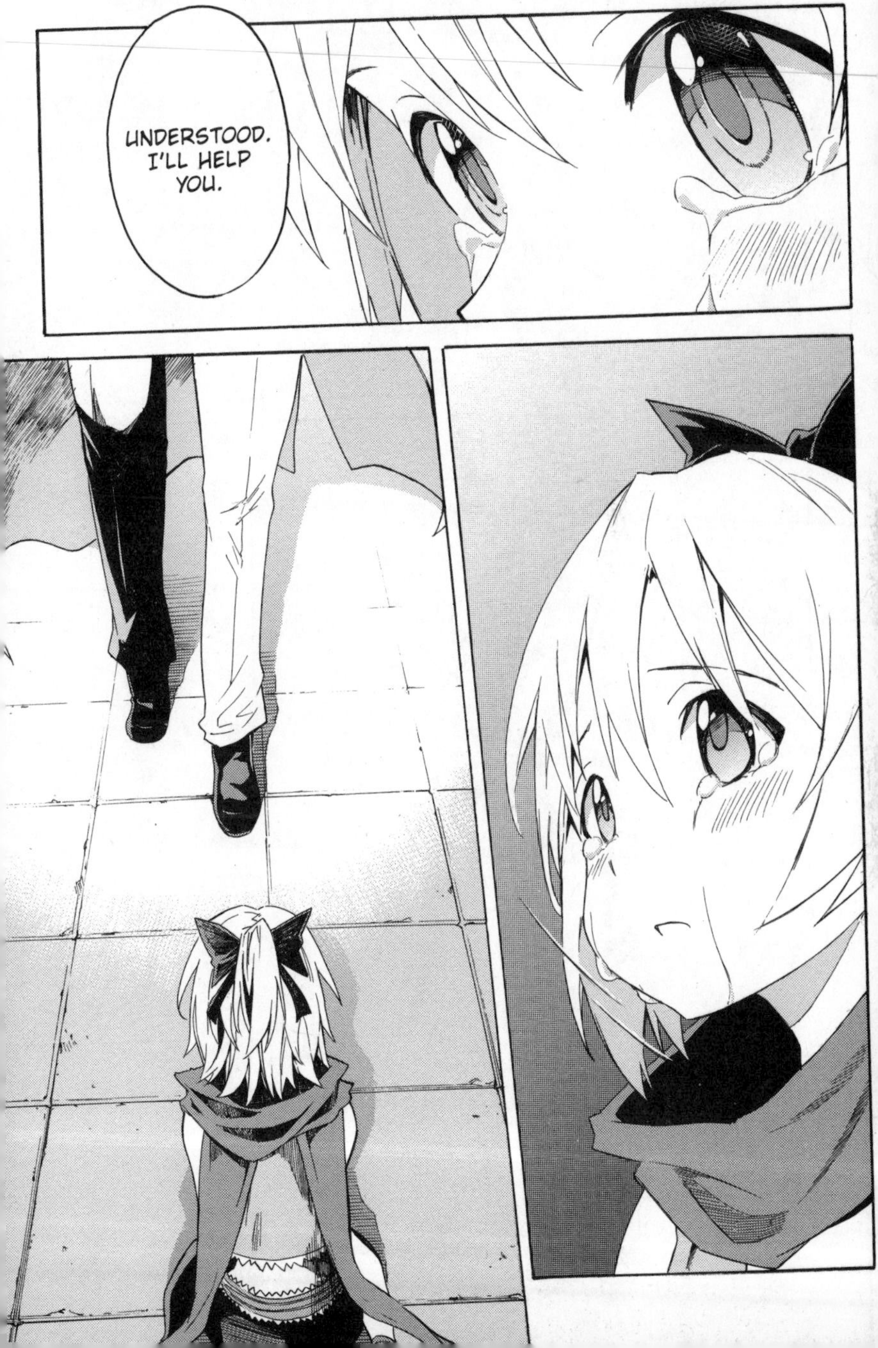
UNDERSTOOD. I'LL HELP YOU.

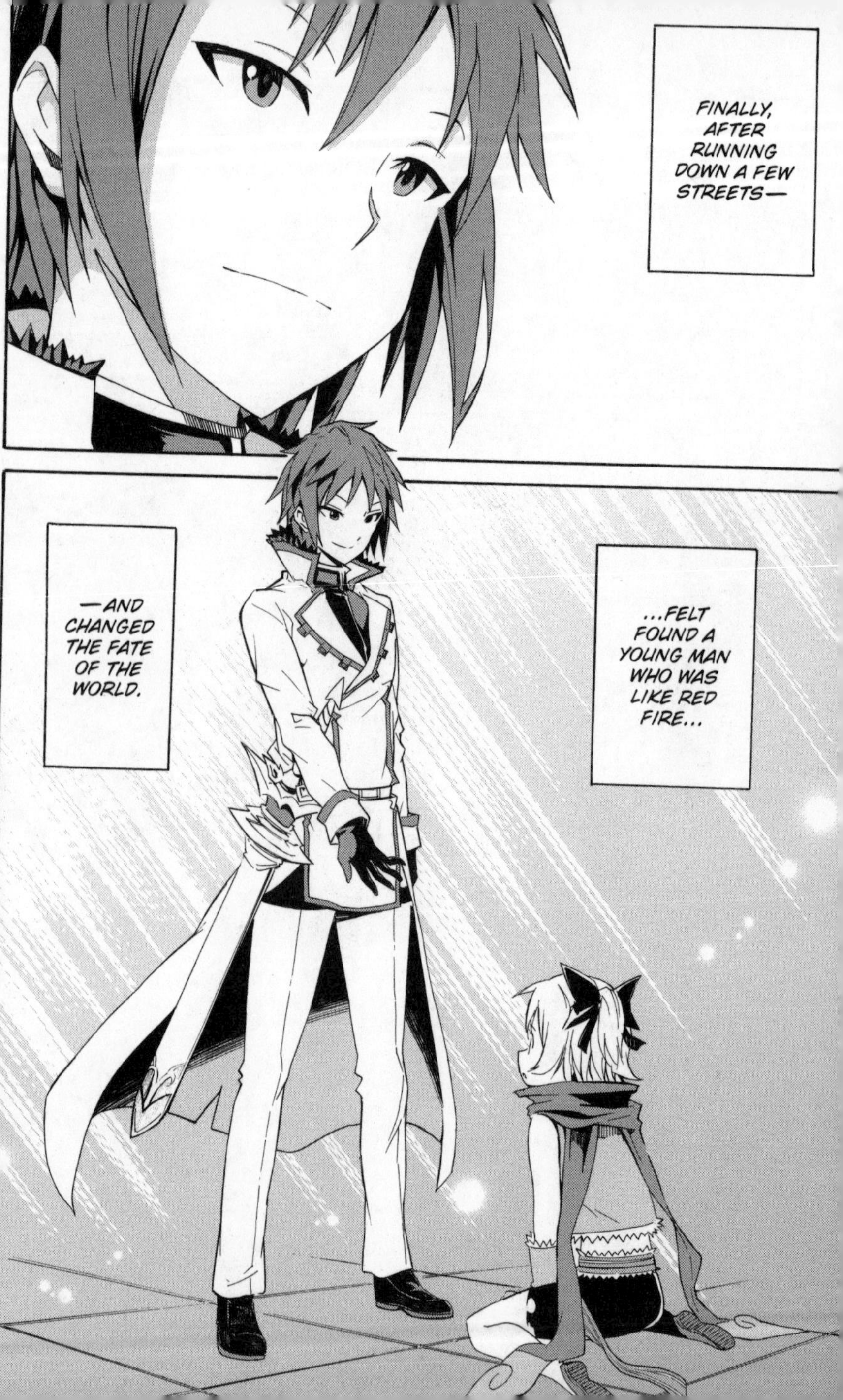
FINALLY, AFTER RUNNING DOWN A FEW STREETS—
...FELT FOUND A YOUNG MAN WHO WAS LIKE RED FIRE...
—AND CHANGED THE FATE OF THE WORLD.

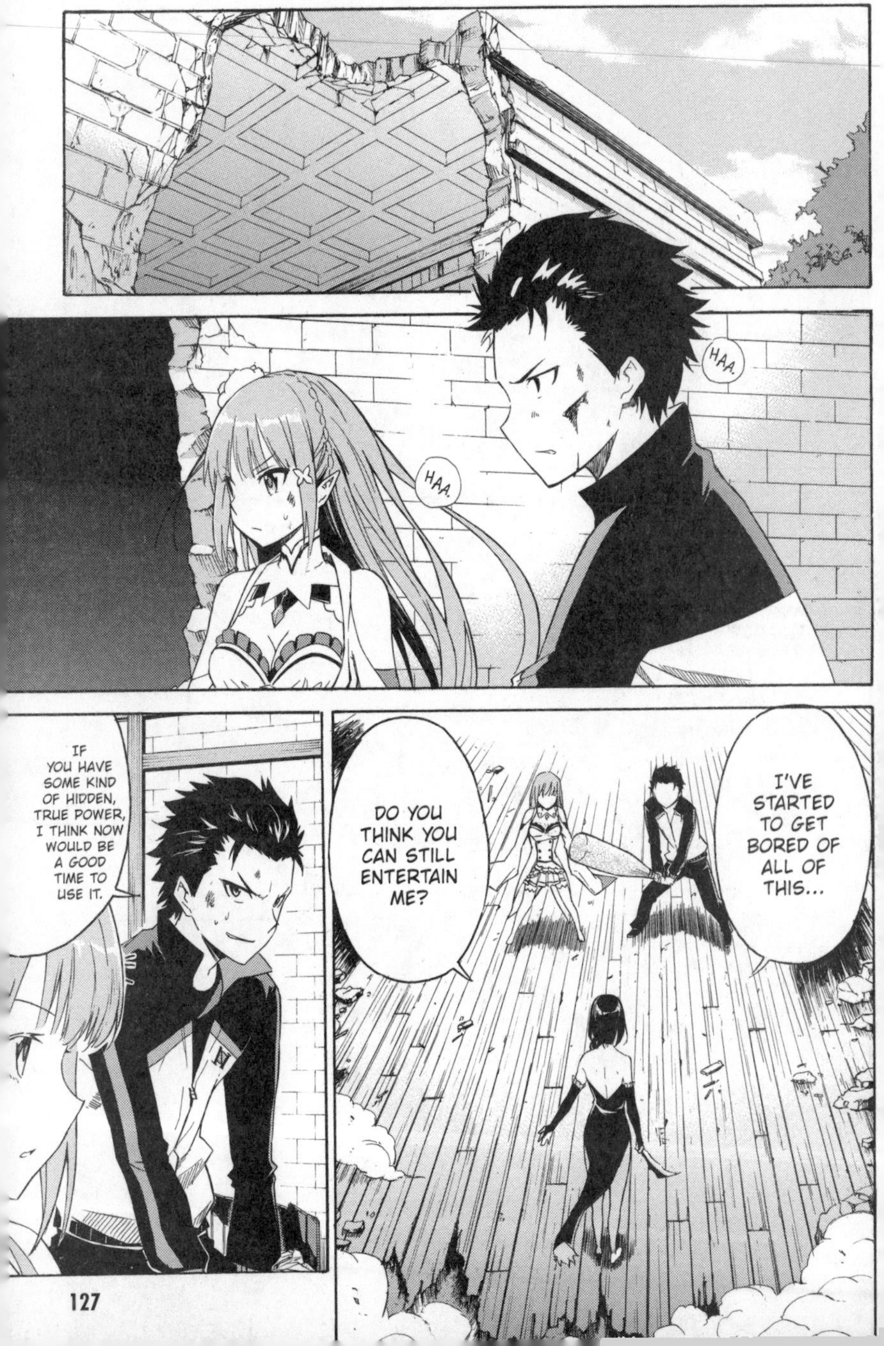
HAA.
HAA.
I'VE STARTED TO GET BORED OF ALL OF THIS...
DO YOU THINK YOU CAN STILL ENTERTAIN ME?
IF YOU HAVE SOME KIND OF HIDDEN, TRUE POWER, I THINK NOW WOULD BE A GOOD TIME TO USE IT.

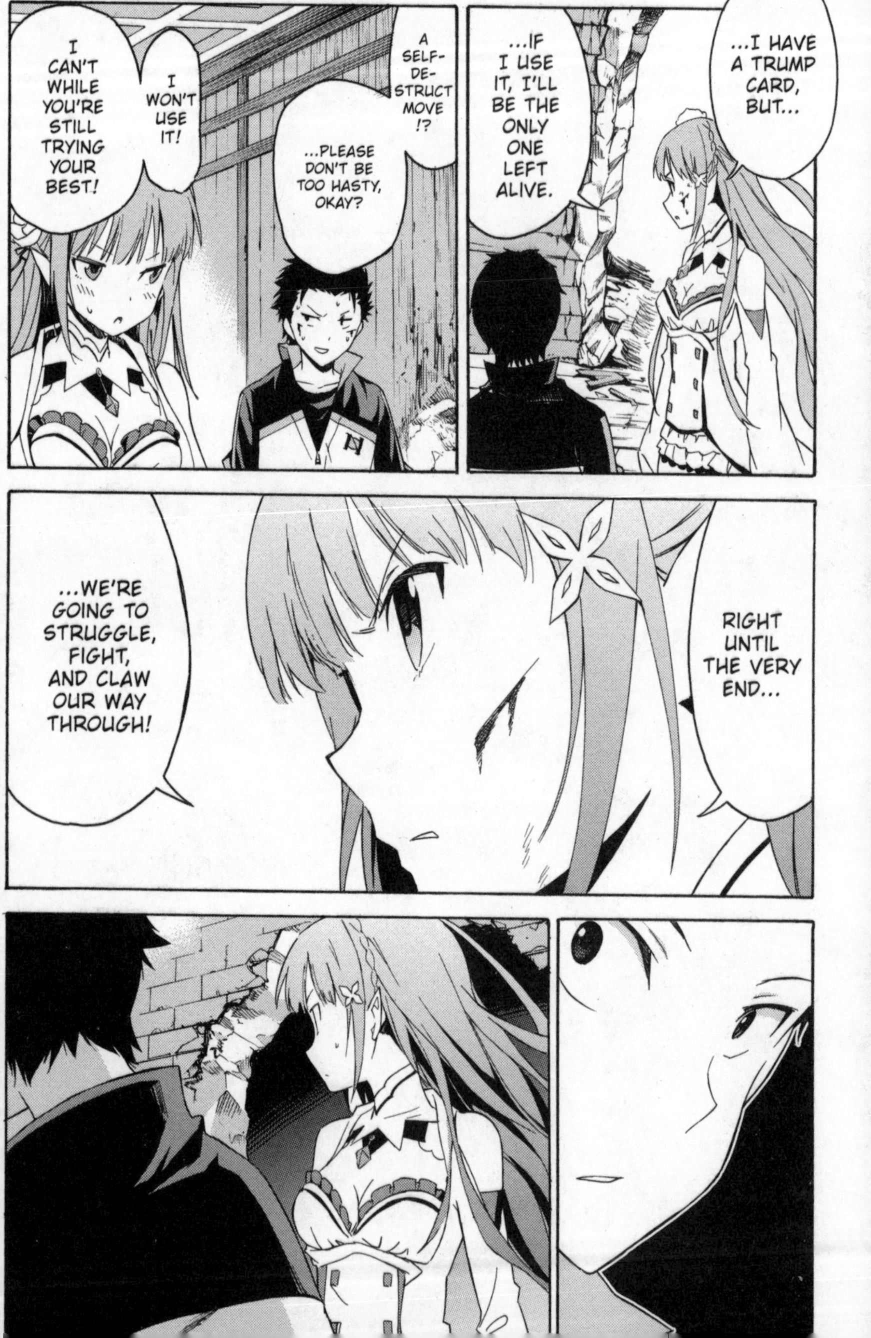
...I HAVE A TRUMP CARD, BUT...
...IF I USE IT, I'LL BE THE ONLY ONE LEFT ALIVE.
A SELF-DESTRUCT MOVE!?
...PLEASE DON'T BE TOO HASTY, OKAY?
I WON'T USE IT!
I CAN'T WHILE YOU'RE STILL TRYING YOUR BEST!
RIGHT UNTIL THE VERY END...
...WE'RE GOING TO STRUGGLE, FIGHT, AND CLAW OUR WAY THROUGH!

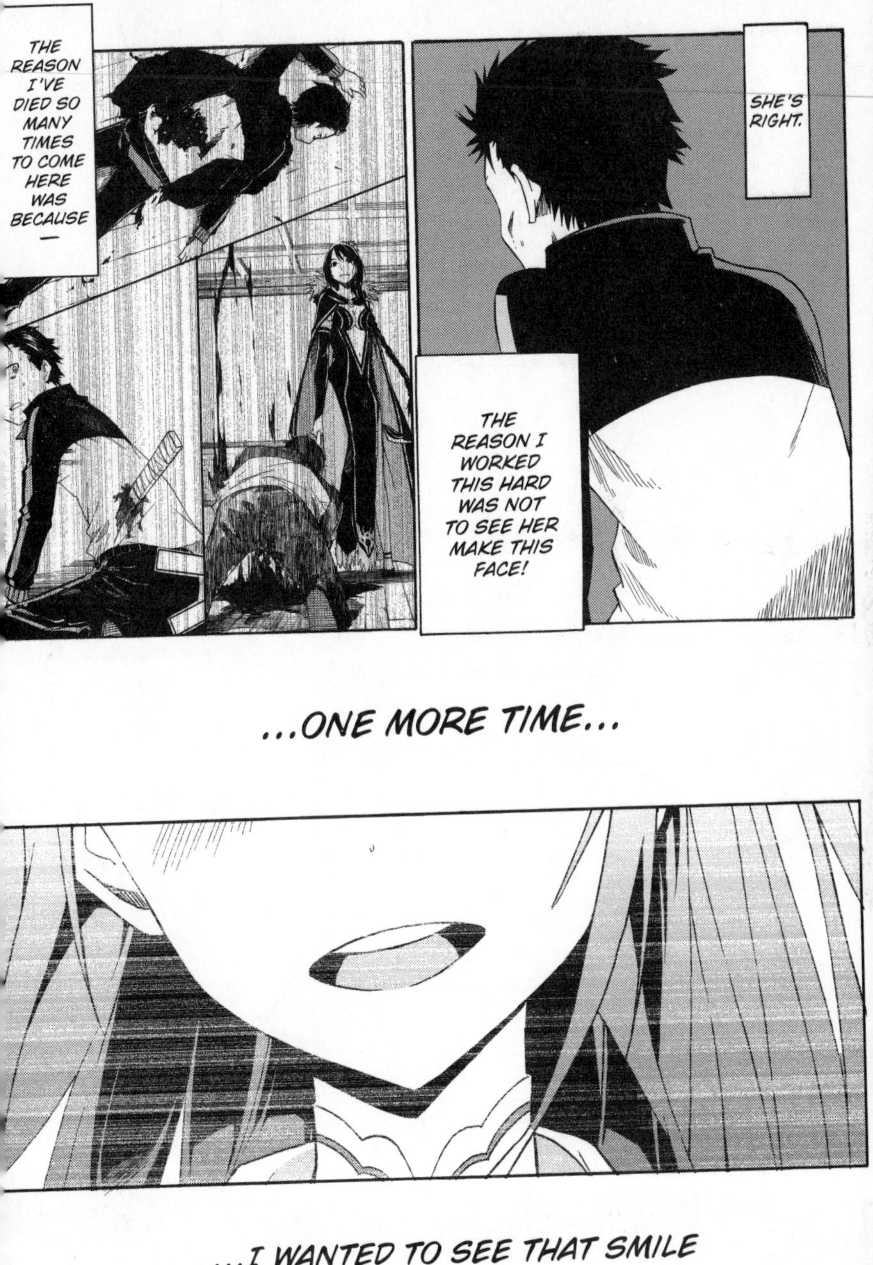
SHE'S RIGHT.
THE REASON I WORKED THIS HARD WAS NOT TO SEE HER MAKE THIS FACE!
THE REASON I'VE DIED SO MANY TIMES TO COME HERE WAS BECAUSE—
...ONE MORE TIME...
...I WANTED TO SEE THAT SMILE ON HER FACE!

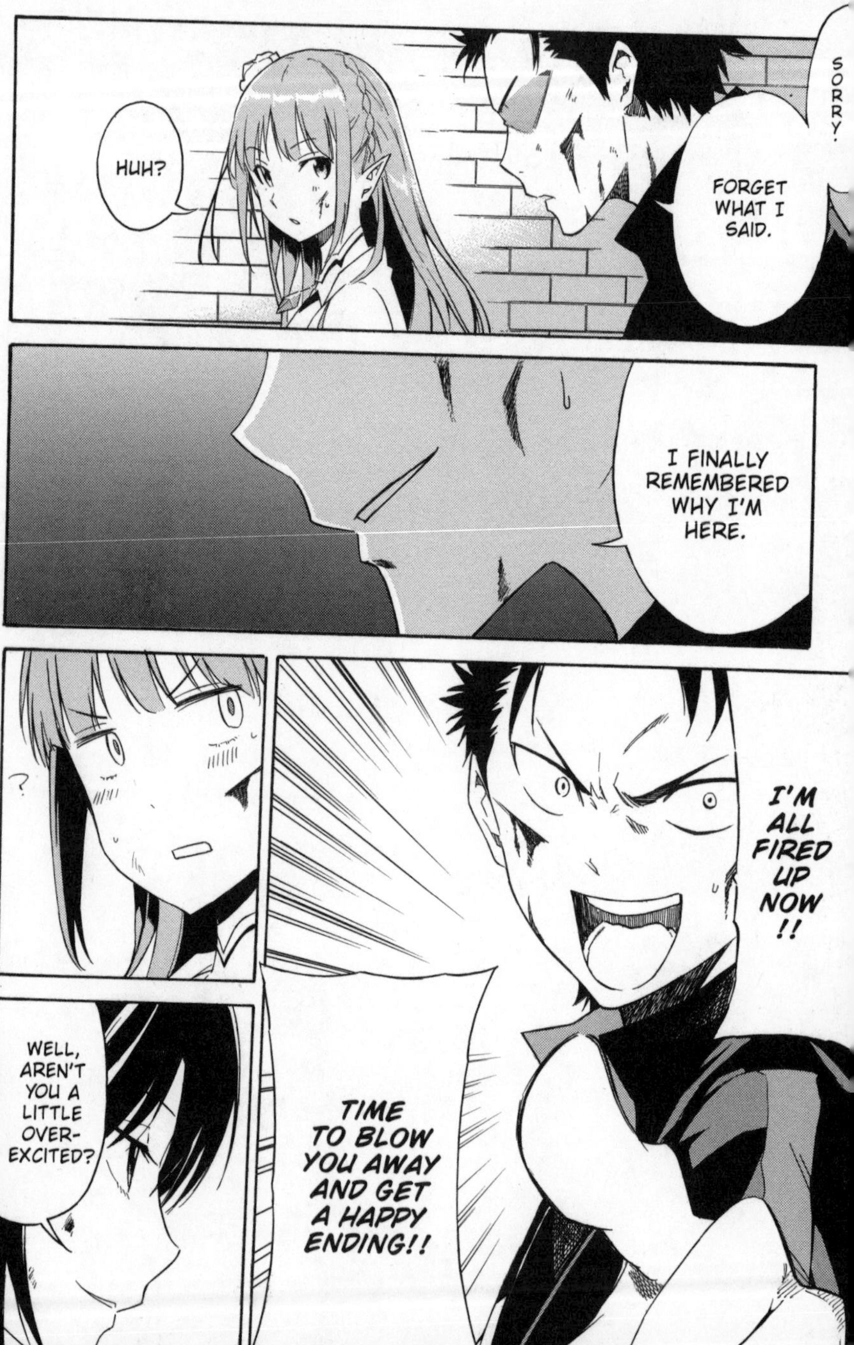
SORRY.
FORGET WHAT I SAID.
HUH?
I FINALLY REMEMBERED WHY I'M HERE.
I'M ALL FIRED UP NOW!!
TIME TO BLOW YOU AWAY AND GET A HAPPY ENDING!!
?
WELL, AREN'T YOU A LITTLE OVER-EXCITED?

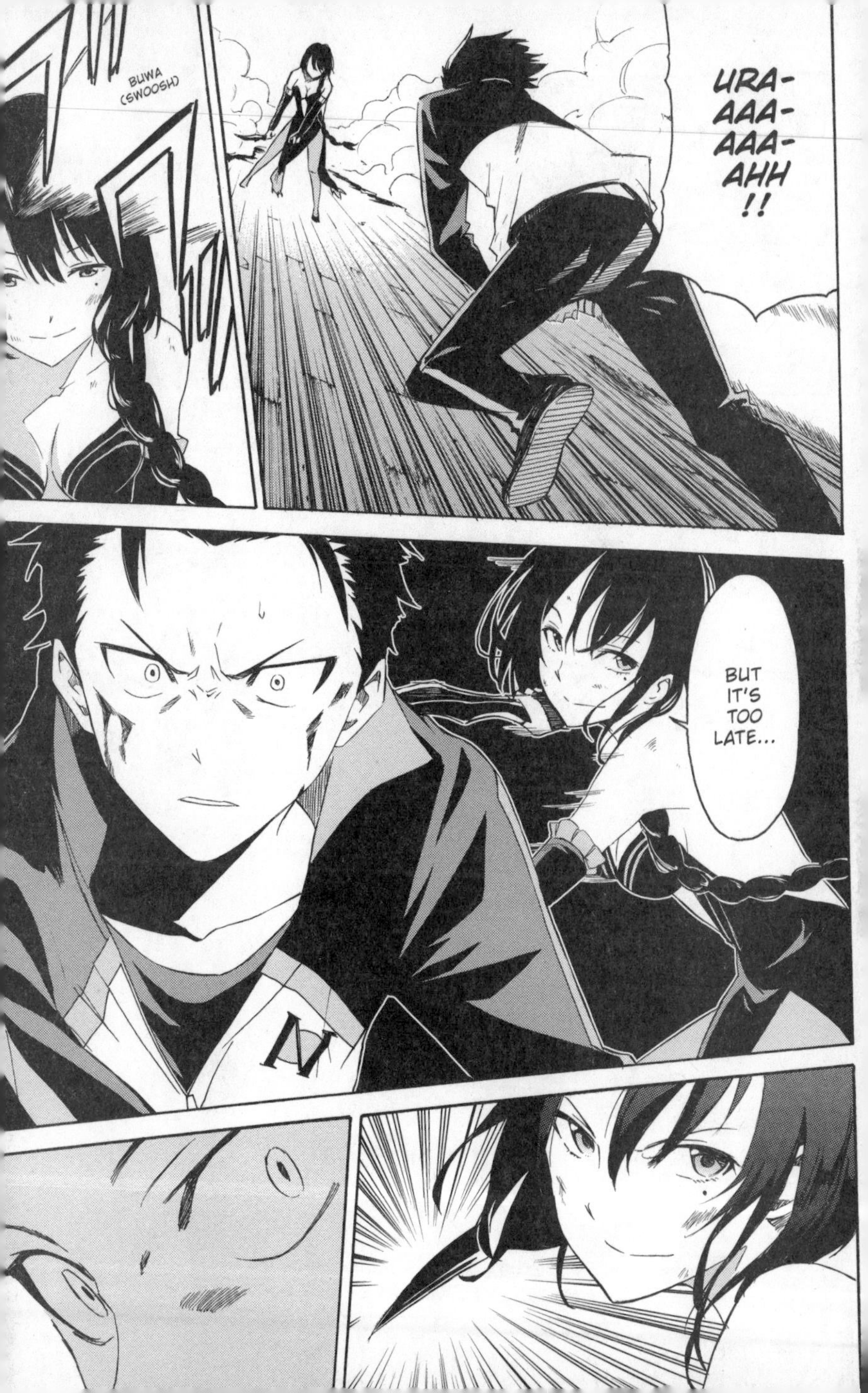
URA-AAA-AAA-AHH!!
BUWA (SWOOSH)
BUT IT'S TOO LATE...

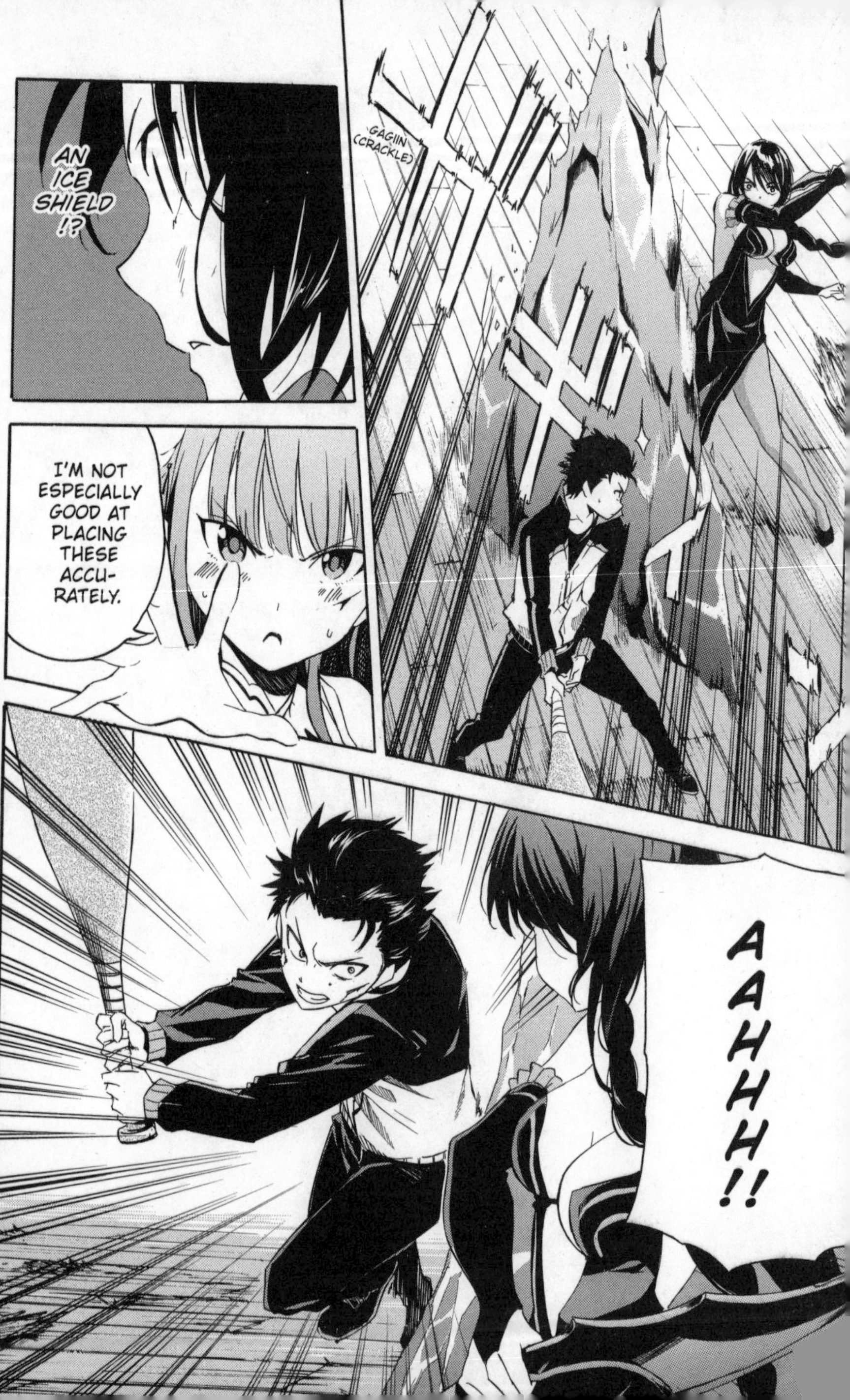
GAGIIN (CRACKLE)
AN ICE SHIELD !?
I'M NOT ESPECIALLY GOOD AT PLACING THESE ACCURATELY.
AAHHH!!

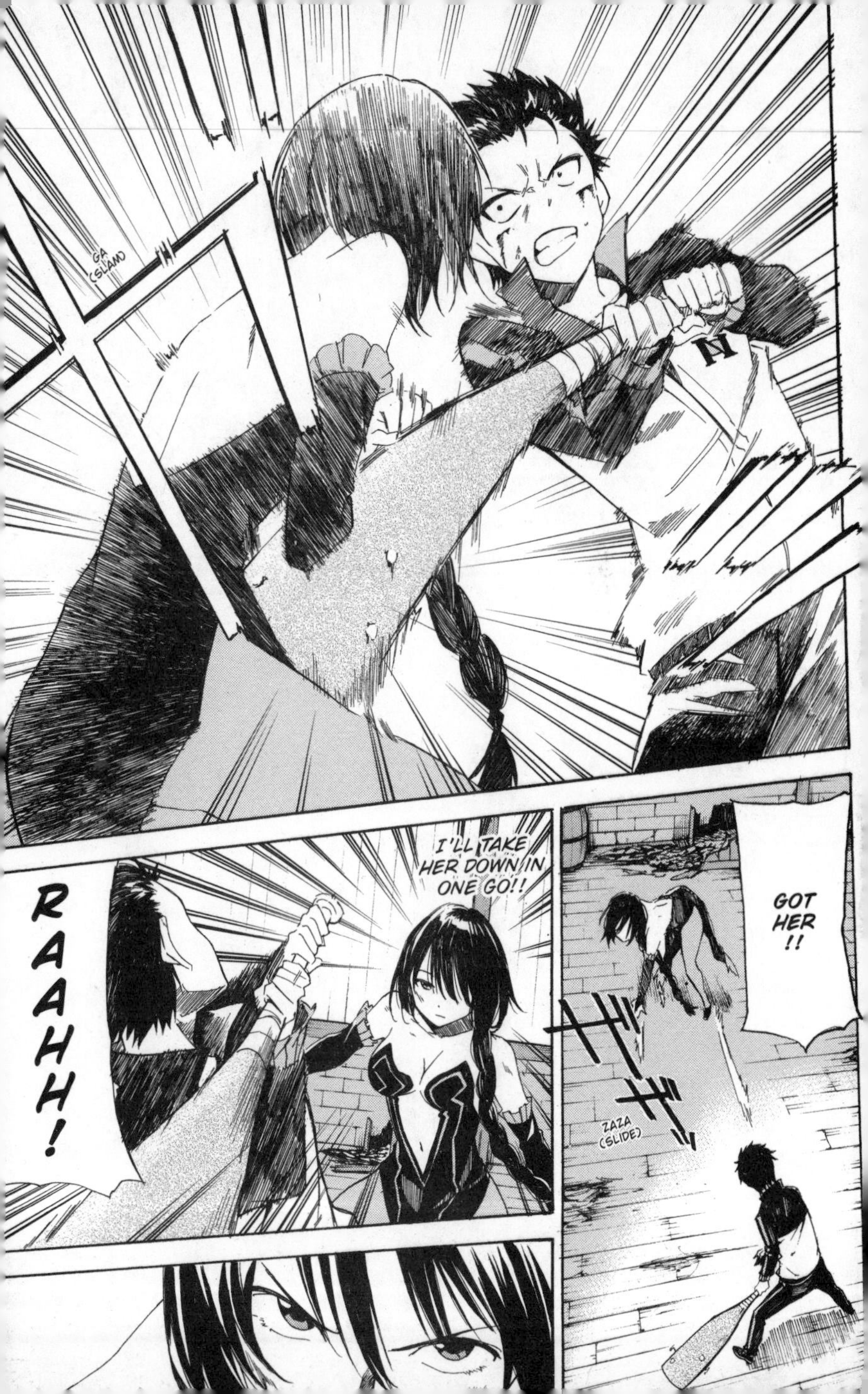
GA
(SLAM)
GOT HER!!
ZAZA
(SLIDE)
I'LL TAKE HER DOWN IN ONE GO!!
RAAHH!

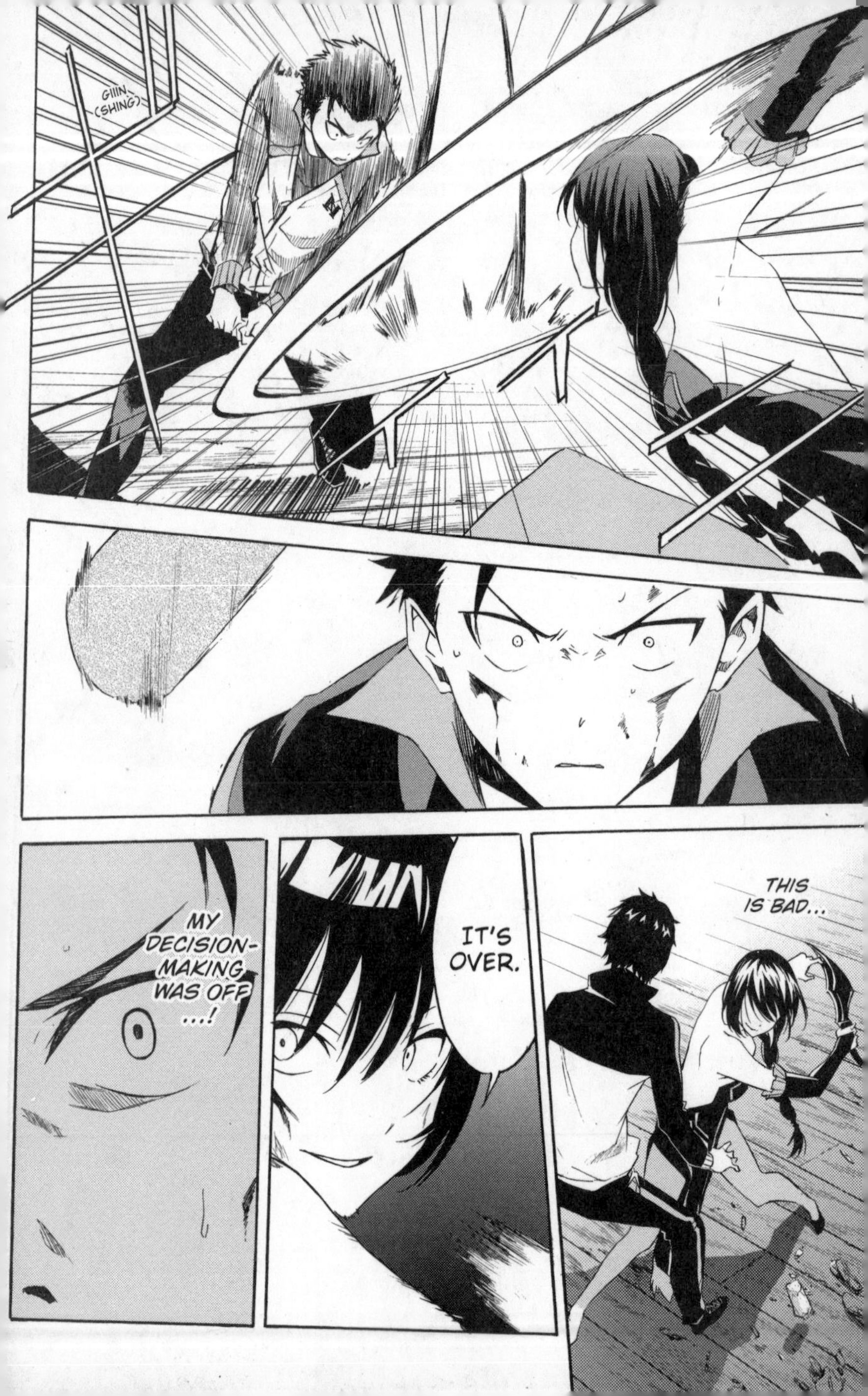
GIIIN (SHING)
THIS IS BAD...
IT'S OVER.
MY DECISION-MAKING WAS OFF ...!

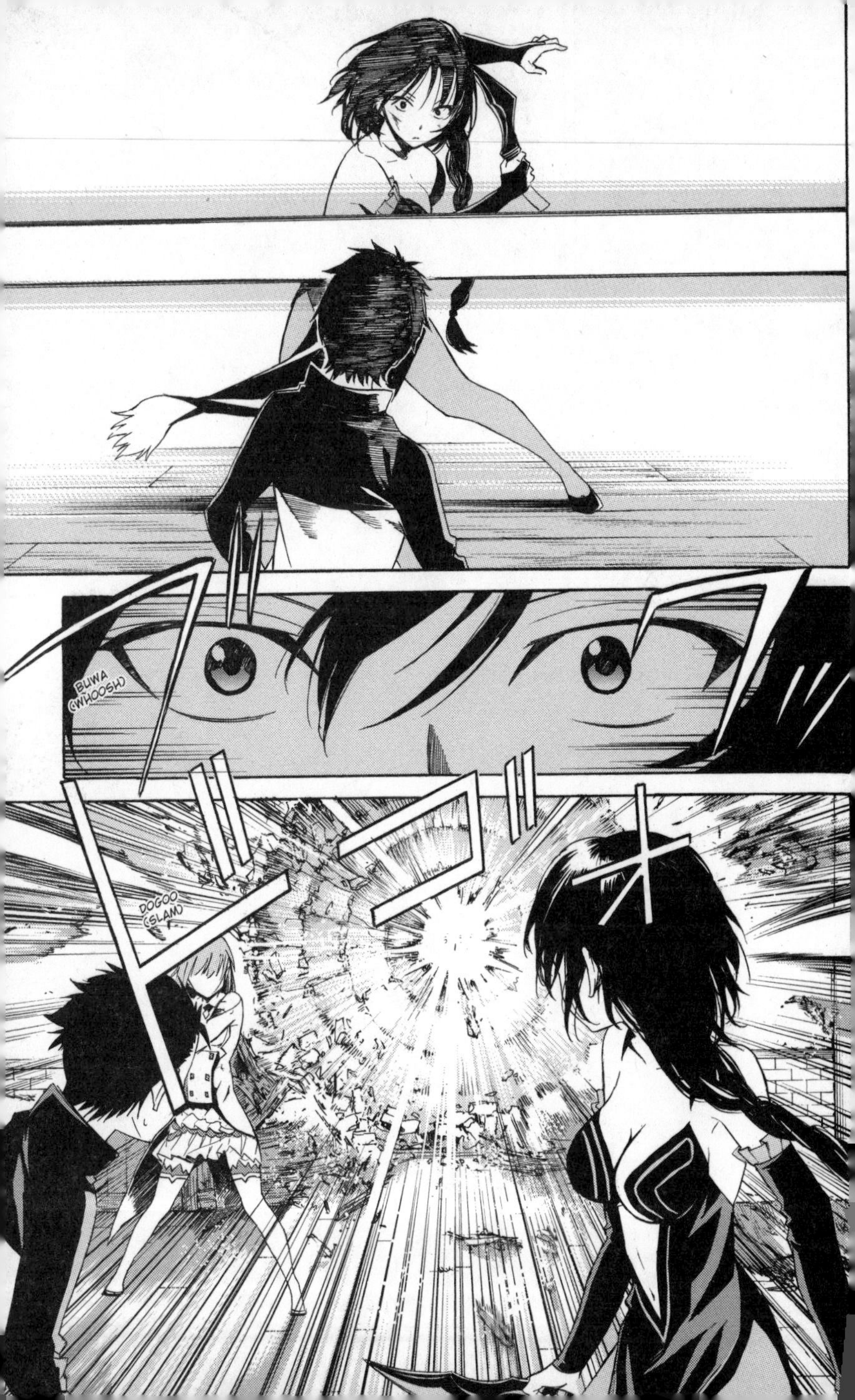
BUWA (WHOOSH)
DOGOO (SLAM)

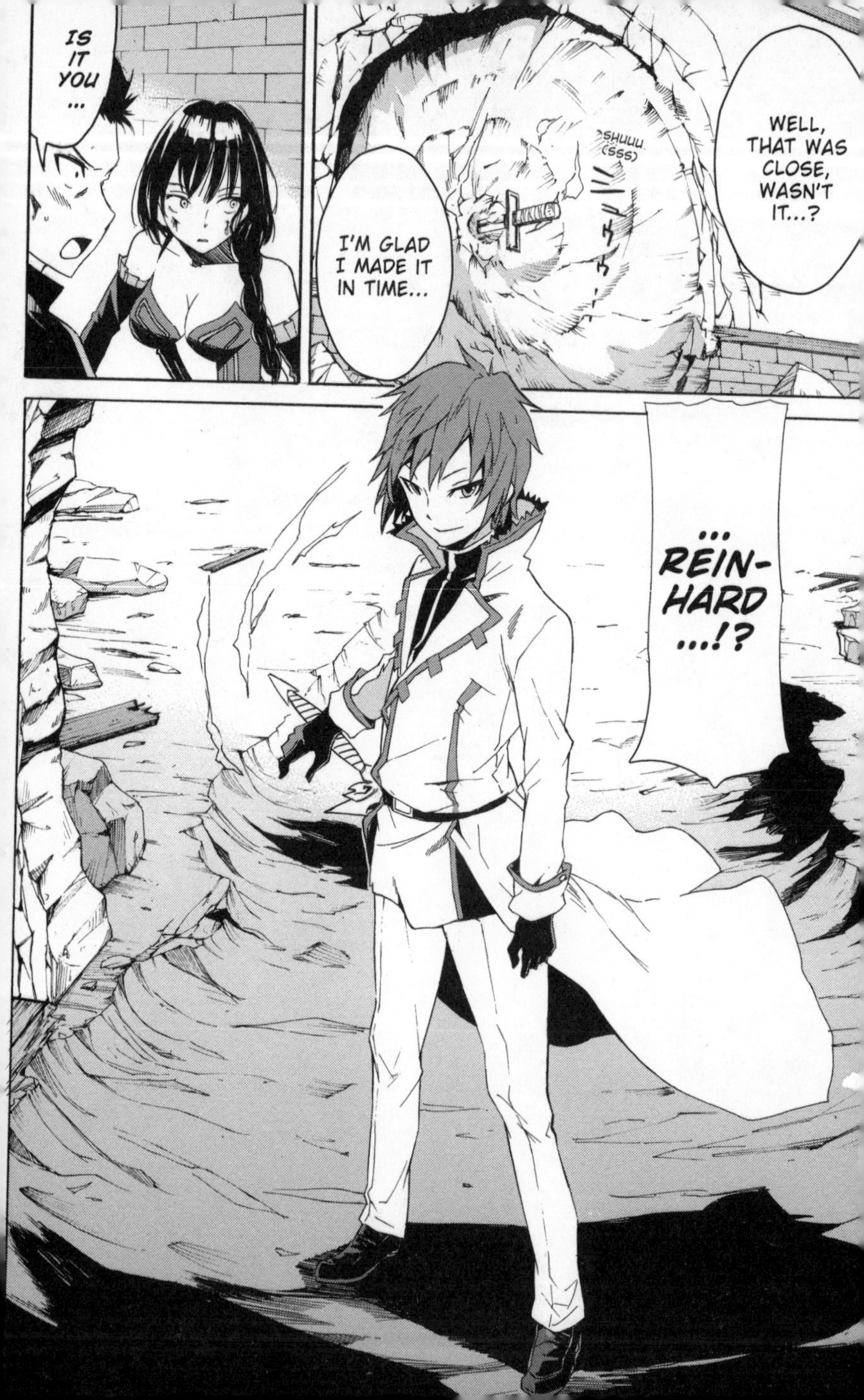
WELL, THAT WAS CLOSE, WASN'T IT...?
SHUUU (SSS)
I'M GLAD I MADE IT IN TIME...
IS IT YOU ...
...REIN-HARD ...!?

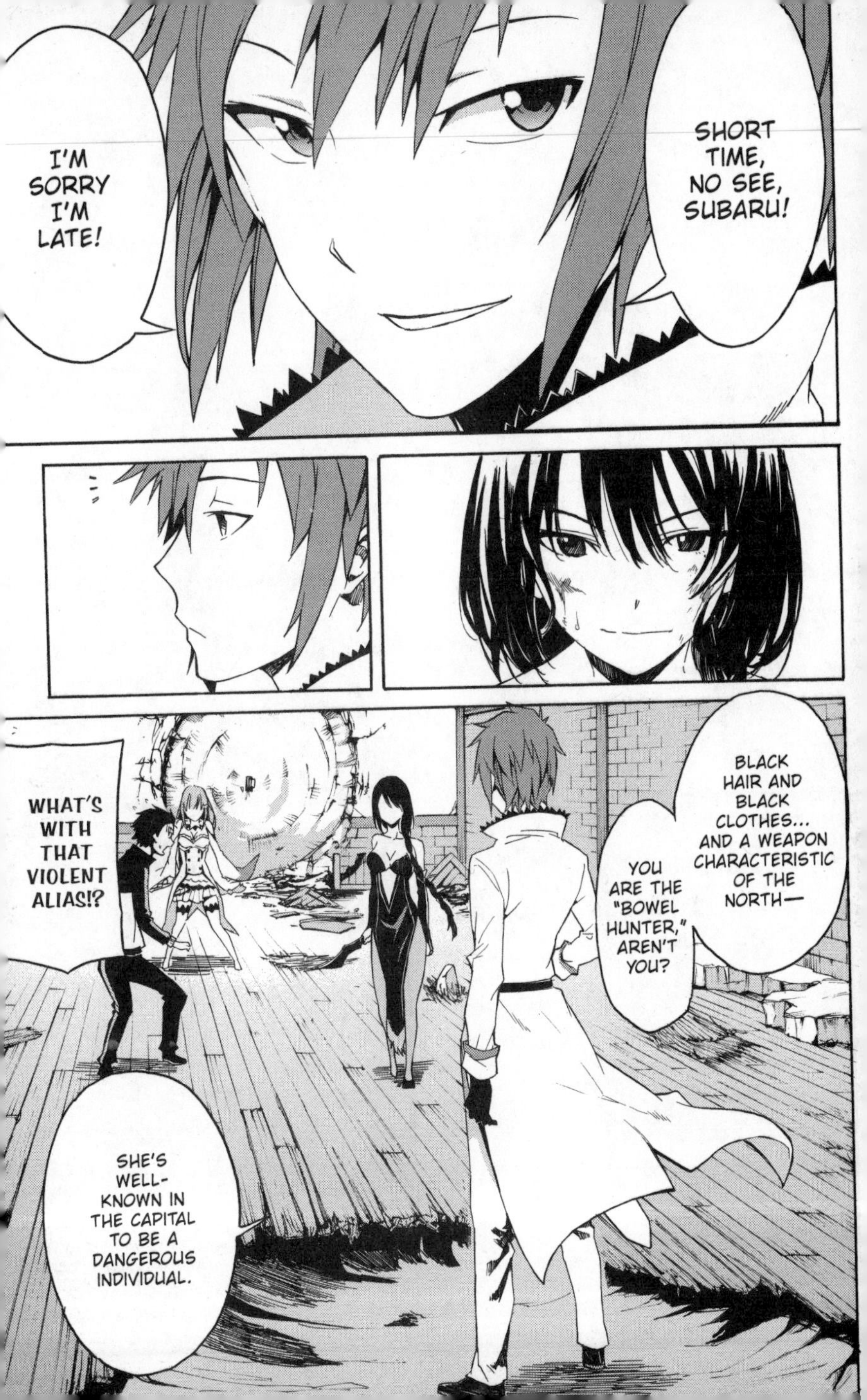
SHORT TIME, NO SEE, SUBARU!
I'M SORRY I'M LATE!
BLACK HAIR AND BLACK CLOTHES... AND A WEAPON CHARACTERISTIC OF THE NORTH—
YOU ARE THE "BOWEL HUNTER," AREN'T YOU?
WHAT'S WITH THAT VIOLENT ALIAS!?
SHE'S WELL-KNOWN IN THE CAPITAL TO BE A DANGEROUS INDIVIDUAL.

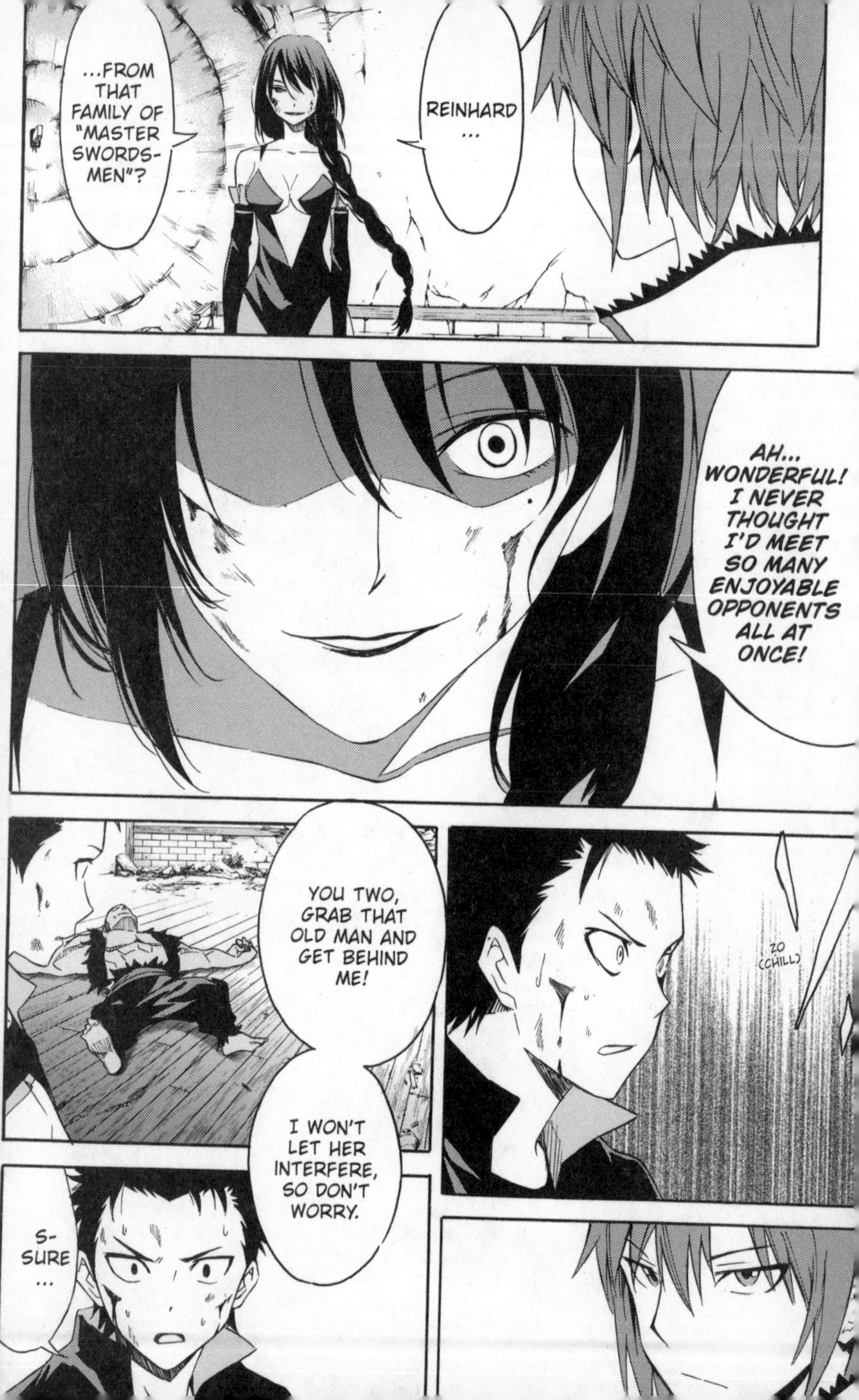
REINHARD ...
...FROM THAT FAMILY OF "MASTER SWORDS-MEN"?
AH... WONDERFUL! I NEVER THOUGHT I'D MEET SO MANY ENJOYABLE OPPONENTS ALL AT ONCE!
ZO (CHILL)
YOU TWO, GRAB THAT OLD MAN AND GET BEHIND ME!
I WON'T LET HER INTERFERE, SO DON'T WORRY.
S-SURE ...

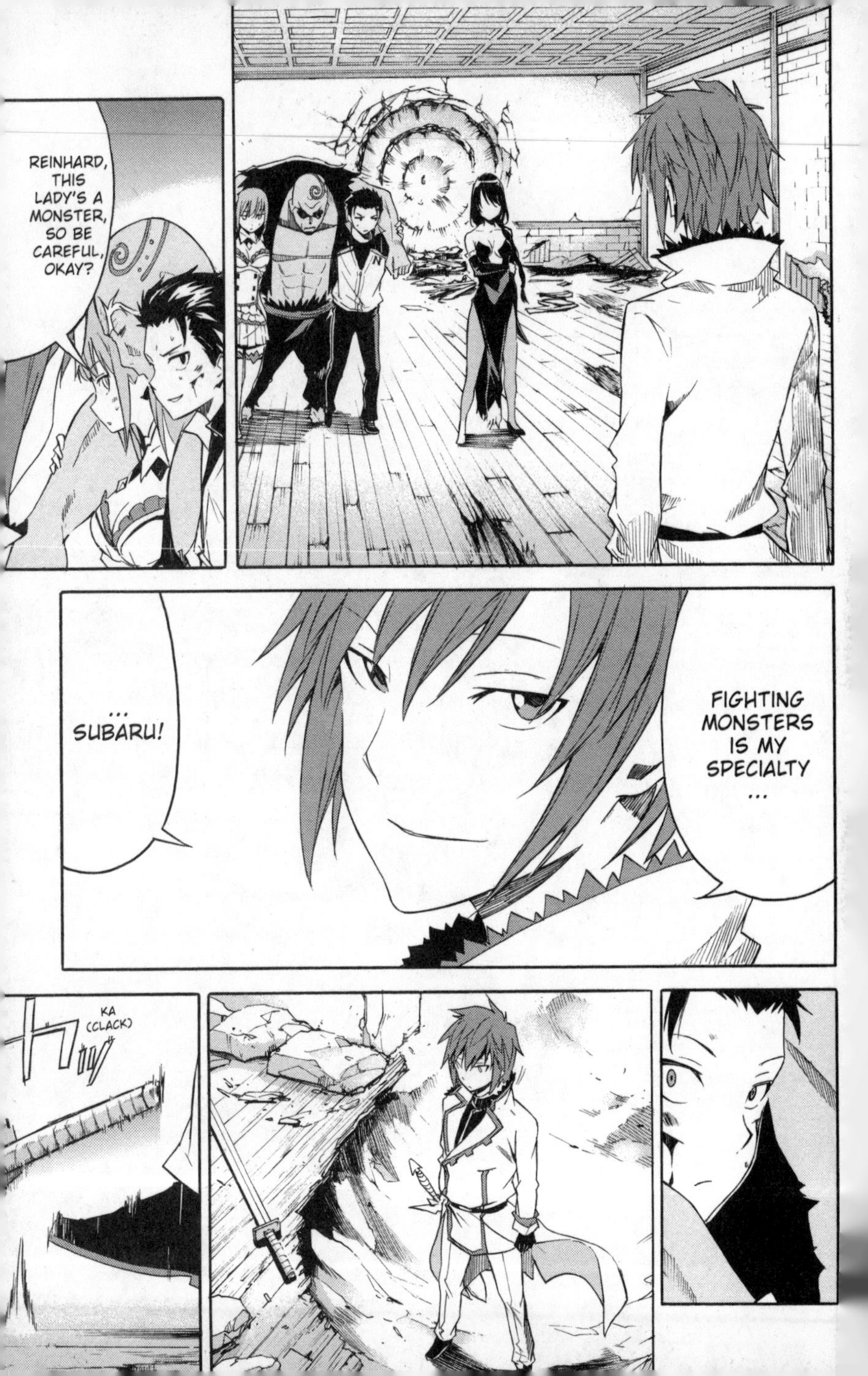
REINHARD, THIS LADY'S A MONSTER, SO BE CAREFUL, OKAY?
FIGHTING MONSTERS IS MY SPECIALTY...
... SUBARU!
カッ
KA (CLACK)

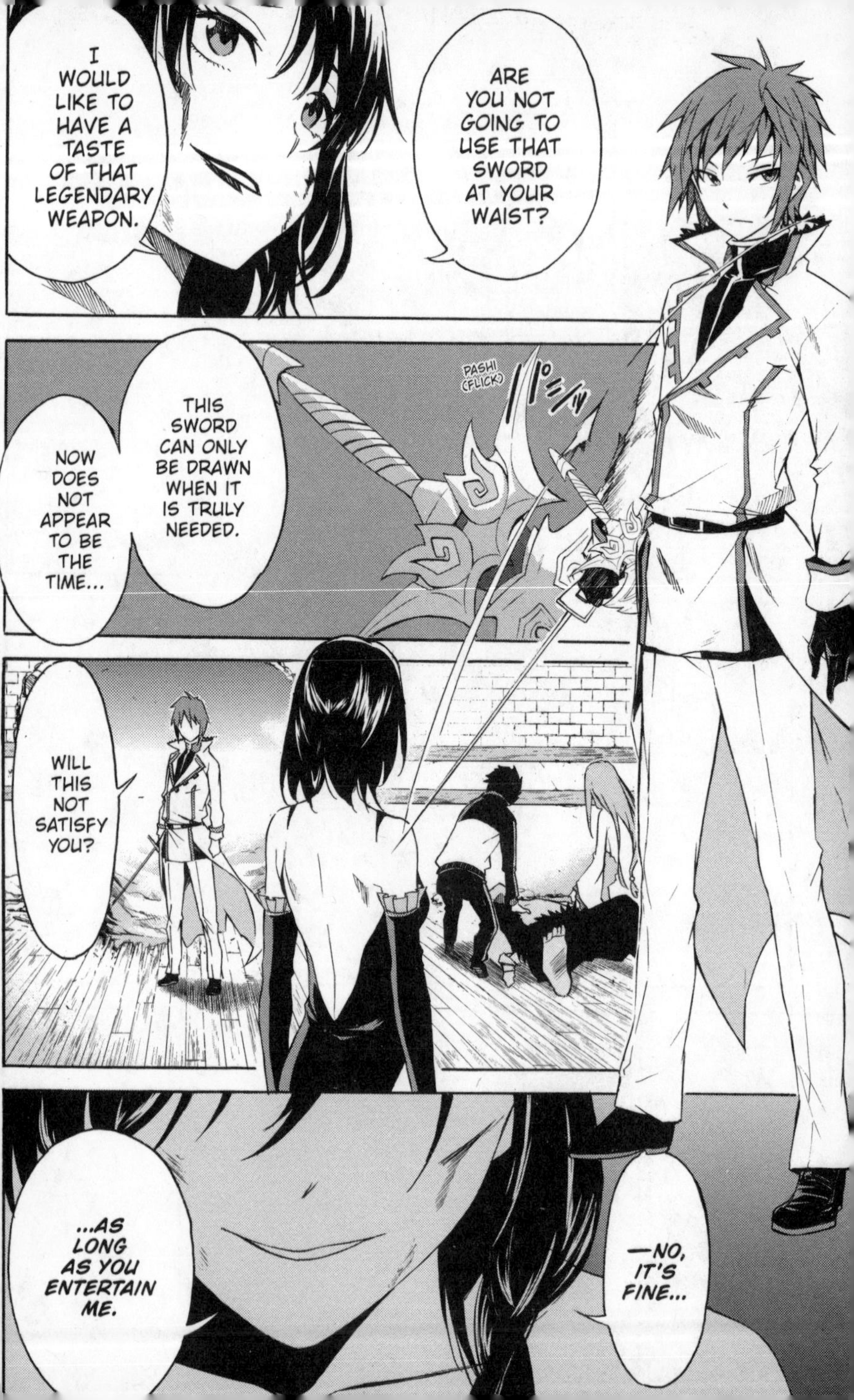
ARE YOU NOT GOING TO USE THAT SWORD AT YOUR WAIST?
I WOULD LIKE TO HAVE A TASTE OF THAT LEGENDARY WEAPON.
PASHI (FLICK)
THIS SWORD CAN ONLY BE DRAWN WHEN IT IS TRULY NEEDED.
NOW DOES NOT APPEAR TO BE THE TIME...
WILL THIS NOT SATISFY YOU?
—NO, IT'S FINE...
...AS LONG AS YOU ENTERTAIN ME.

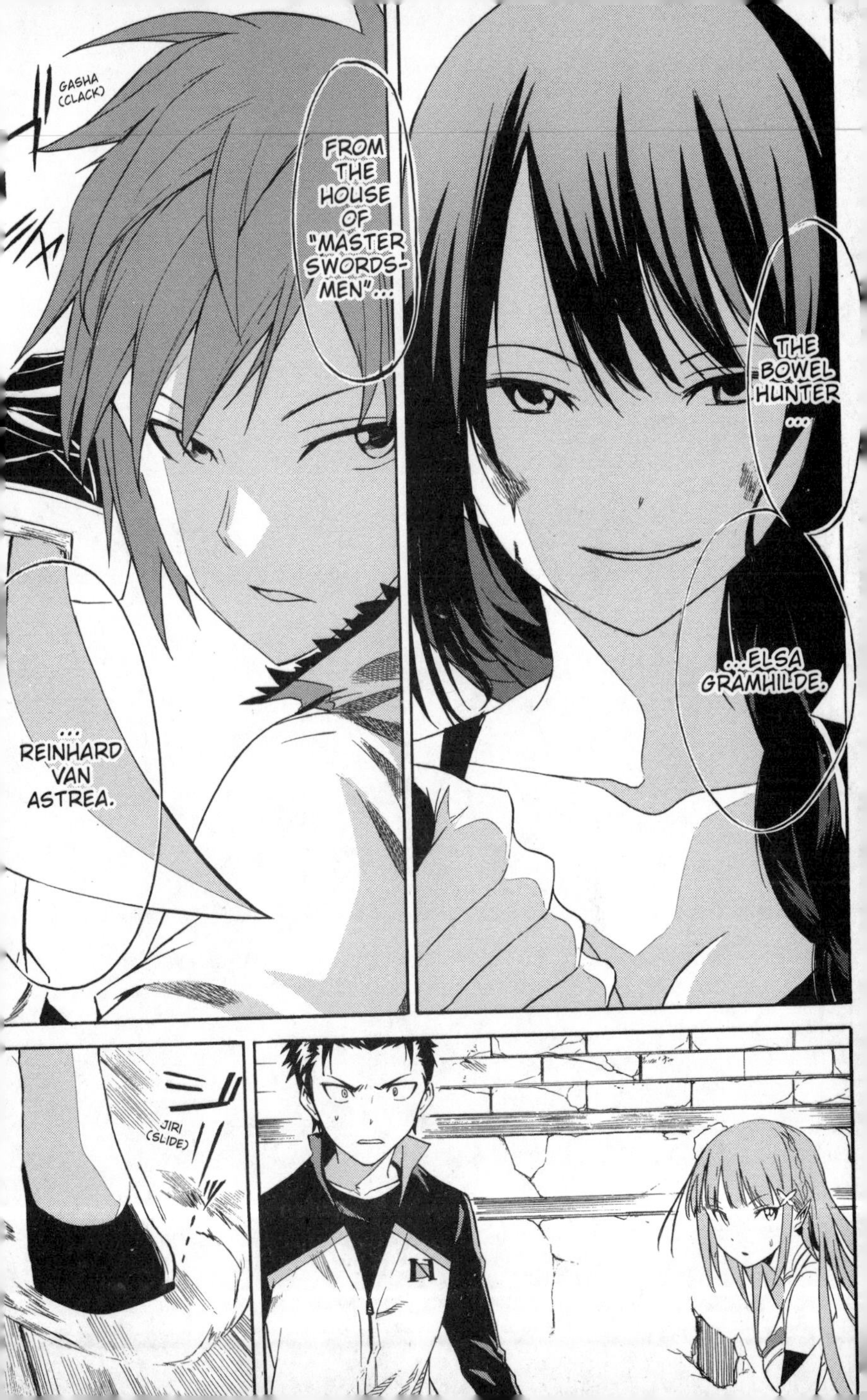
THE BOWEL HUNTER ...
...ELSA GRAMHILDE.
GASHA (CLACK)
FROM THE HOUSE OF "MASTER SWORDS-MEN"...
... REINHARD VAN ASTREA.
JIRI (SLIDE)

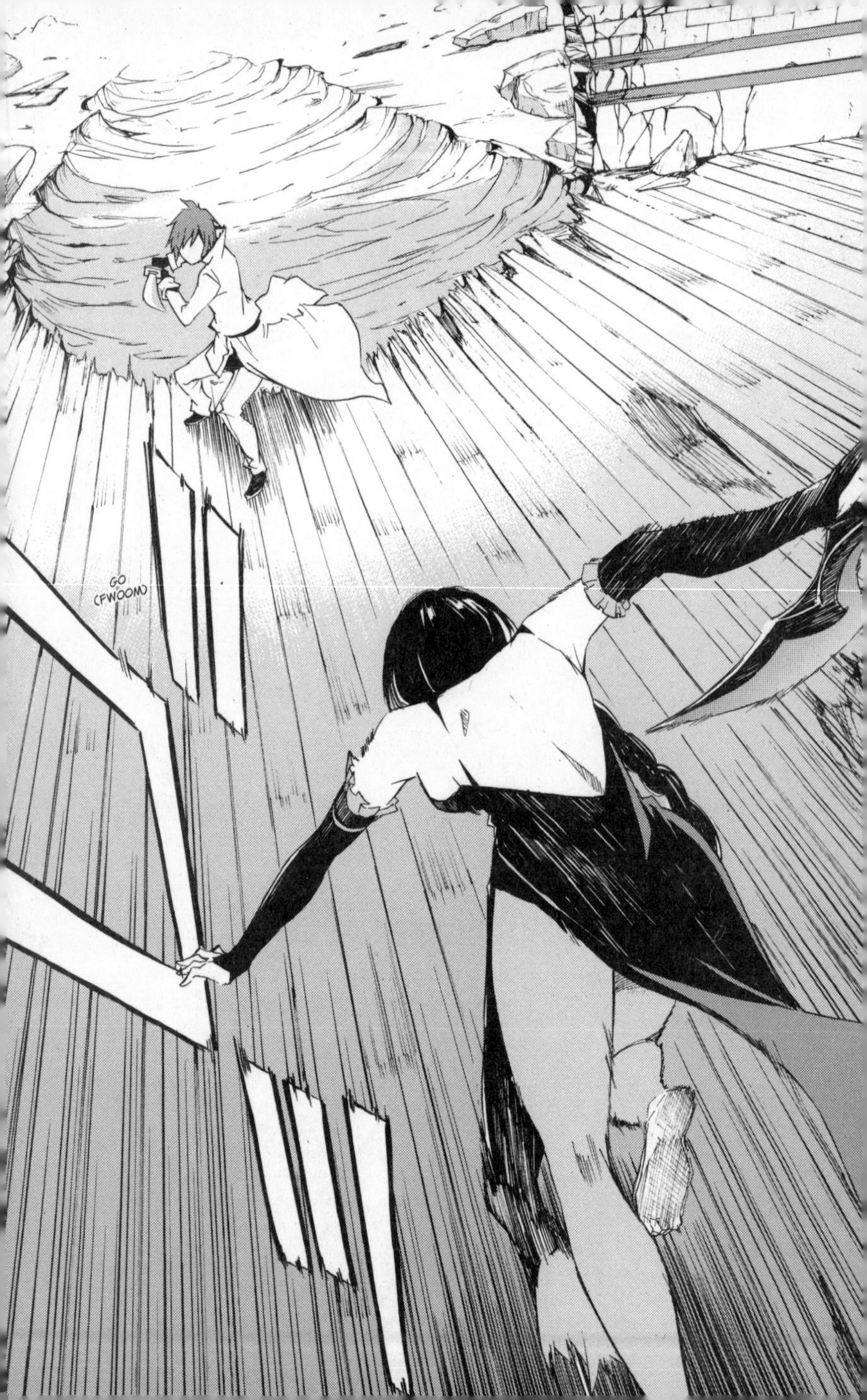
GO
(FWOOM)

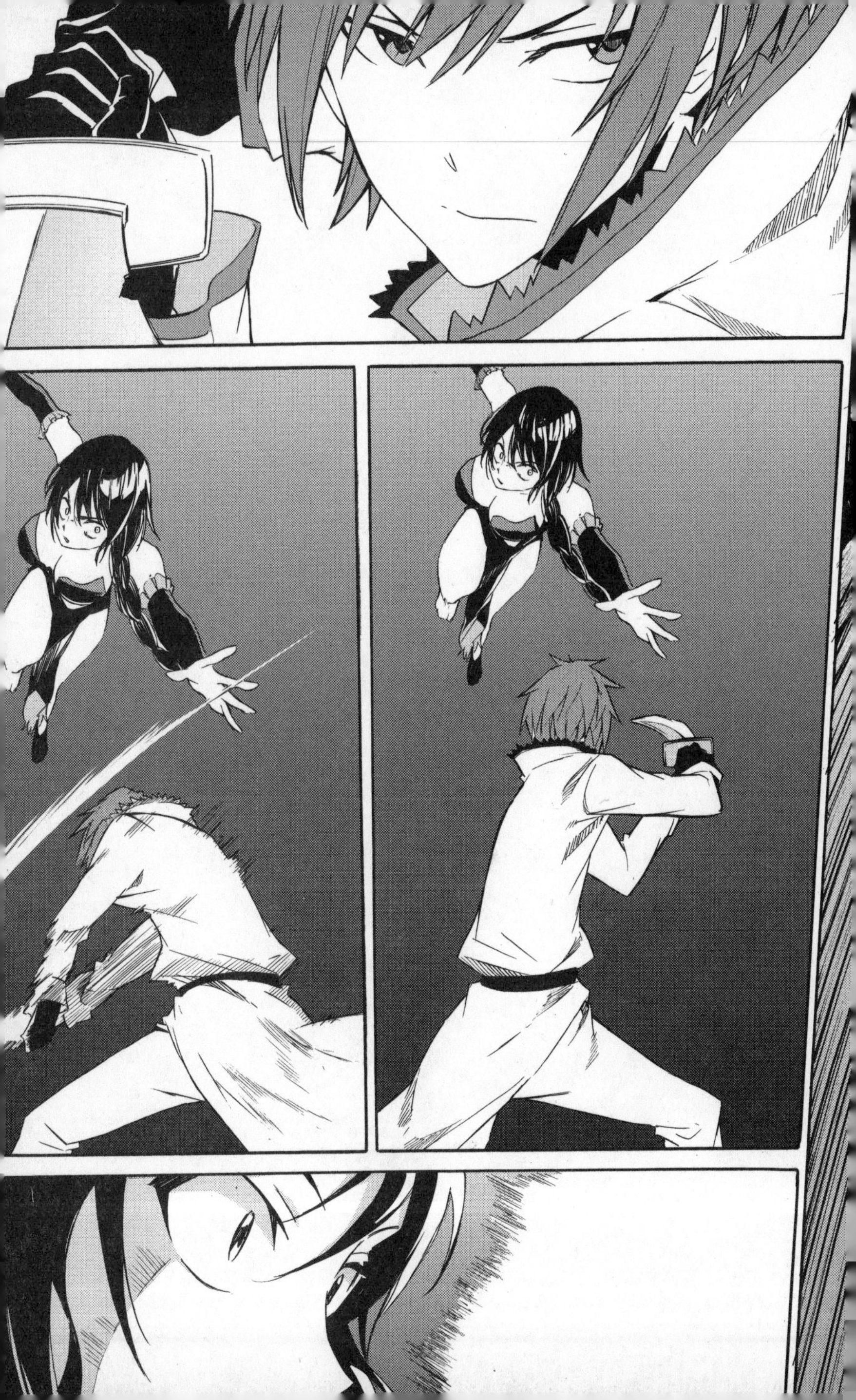

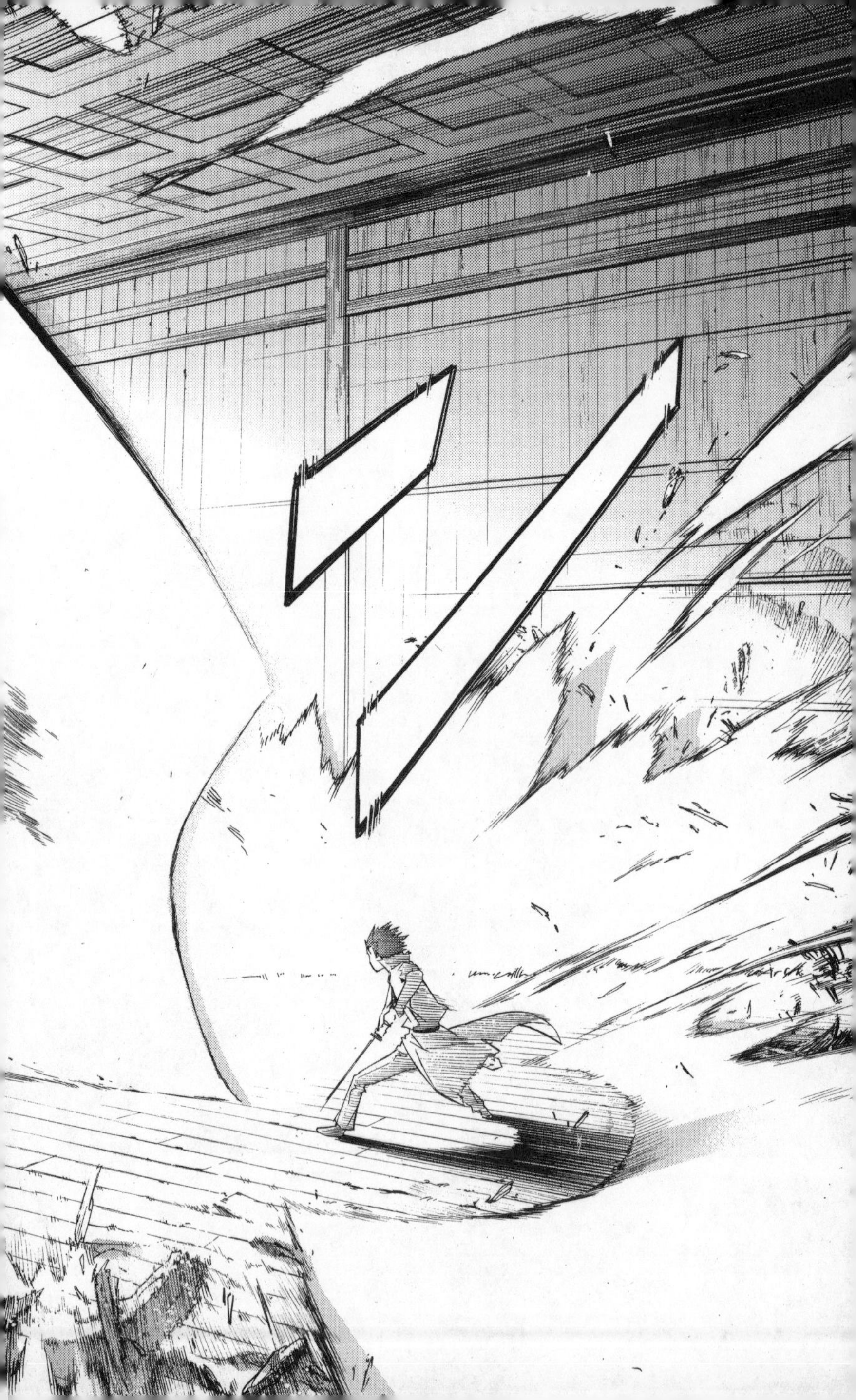

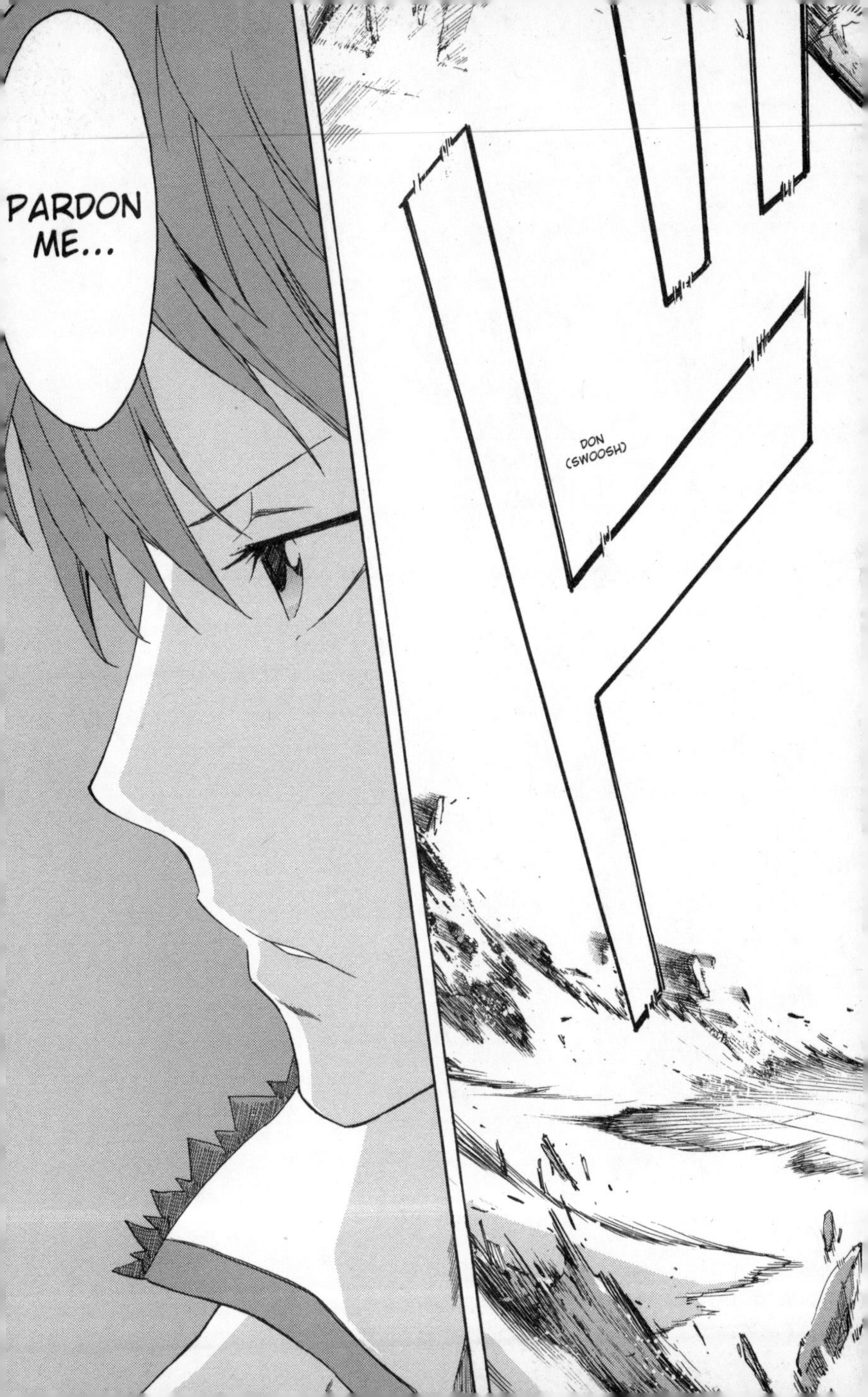
DON (SWOOSH)
PARDON ME...

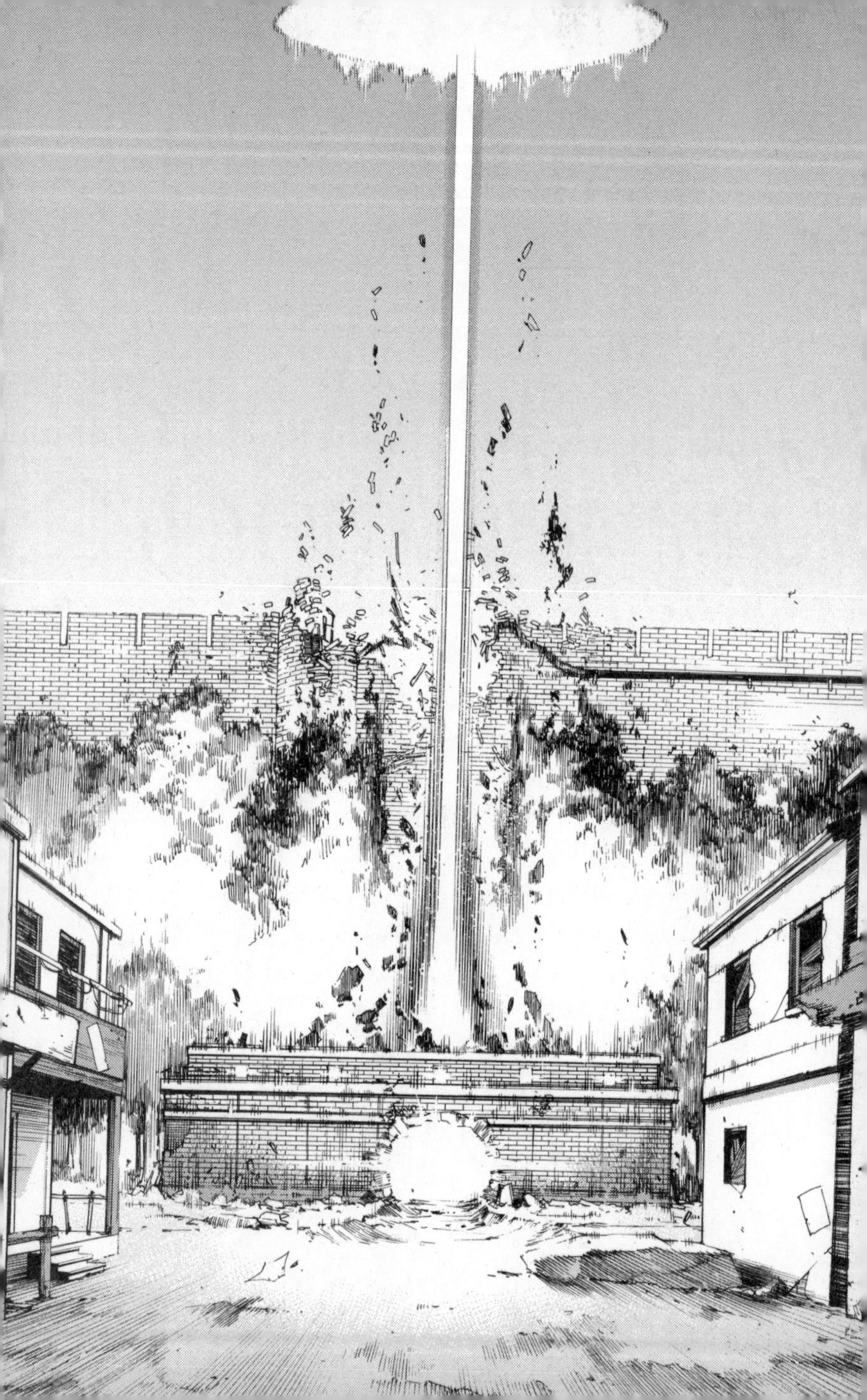

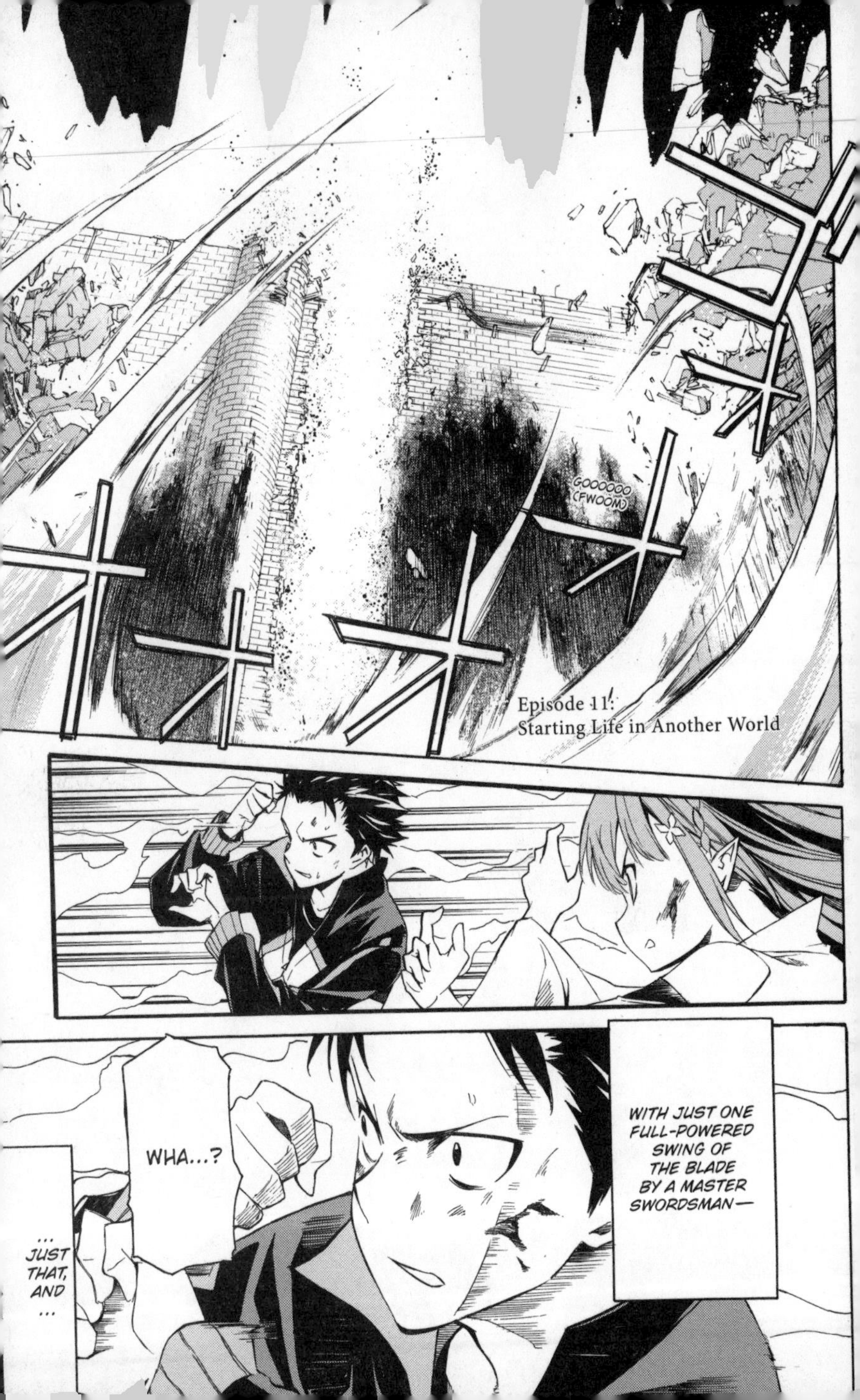
GOOOOOO (FWOOM)
Episode 11: Starting Life in Another World
WITH JUST ONE FULL-POWERED SWING OF THE BLADE BY A MASTER SWORDSMAN—
WHA...?
...JUST THAT, AND ...

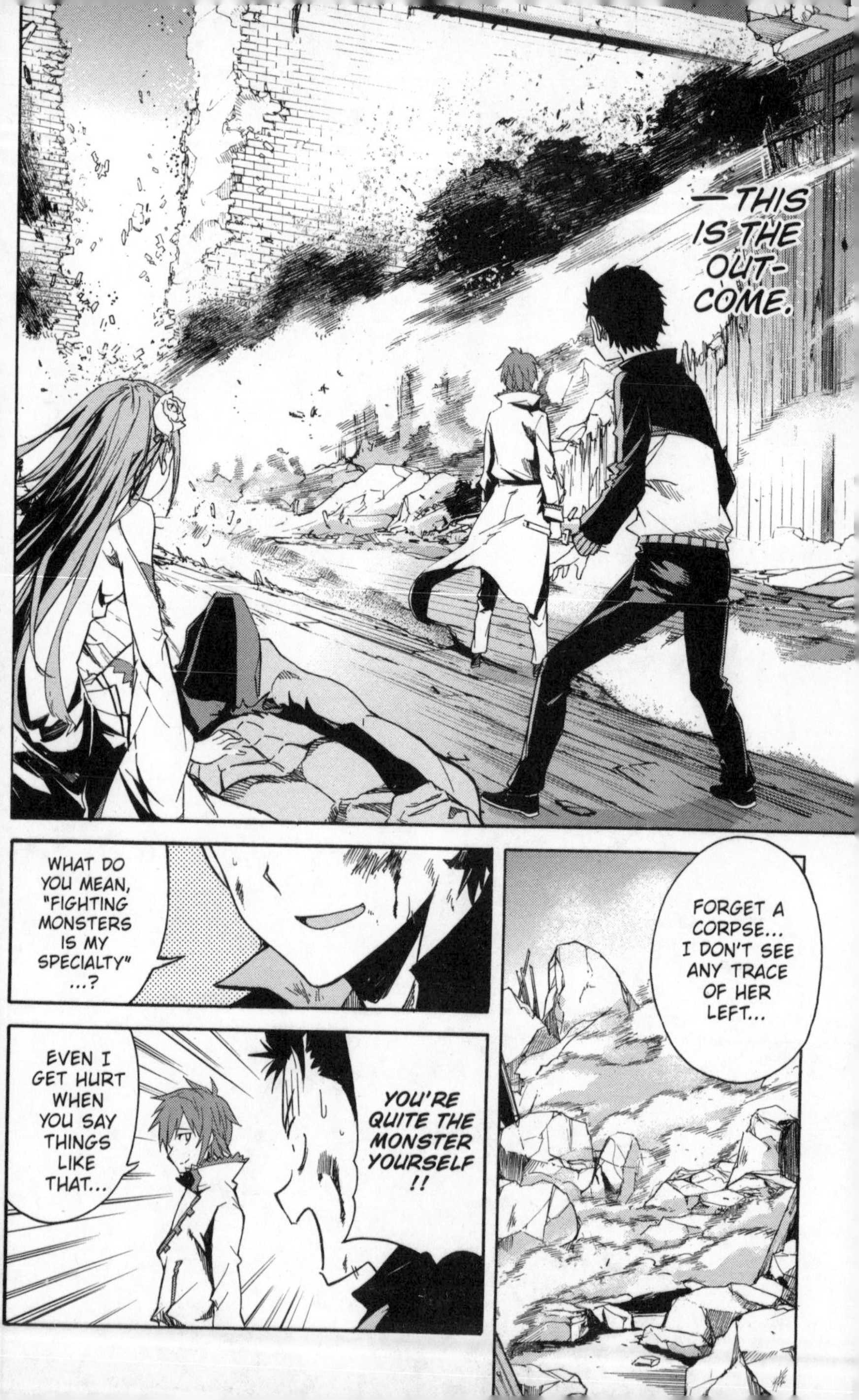
—THIS IS THE OUT-COME.
FORGET A CORPSE... I DON'T SEE ANY TRACE OF HER LEFT...
WHAT DO YOU MEAN, "FIGHTING MONSTERS IS MY SPECIALTY" ...?
YOU'RE QUITE THE MONSTER YOURSELF !!
EVEN I GET HURT WHEN YOU SAY THINGS LIKE THAT...

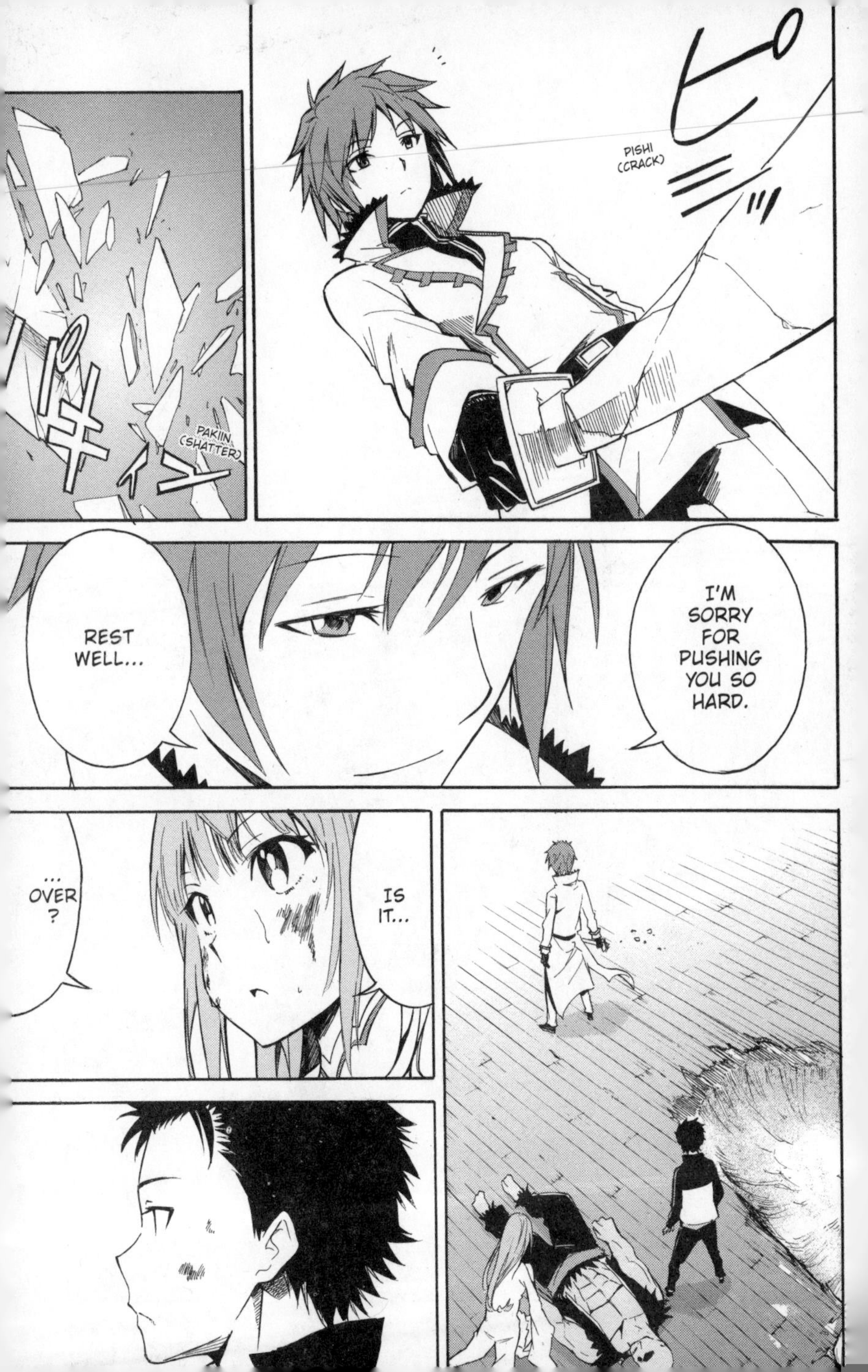
PISHI (CRACK)
PAKIIN (SHATTER)
I'M SORRY FOR PUSHING YOU SO HARD.
REST WELL...
IS IT...
... OVER?

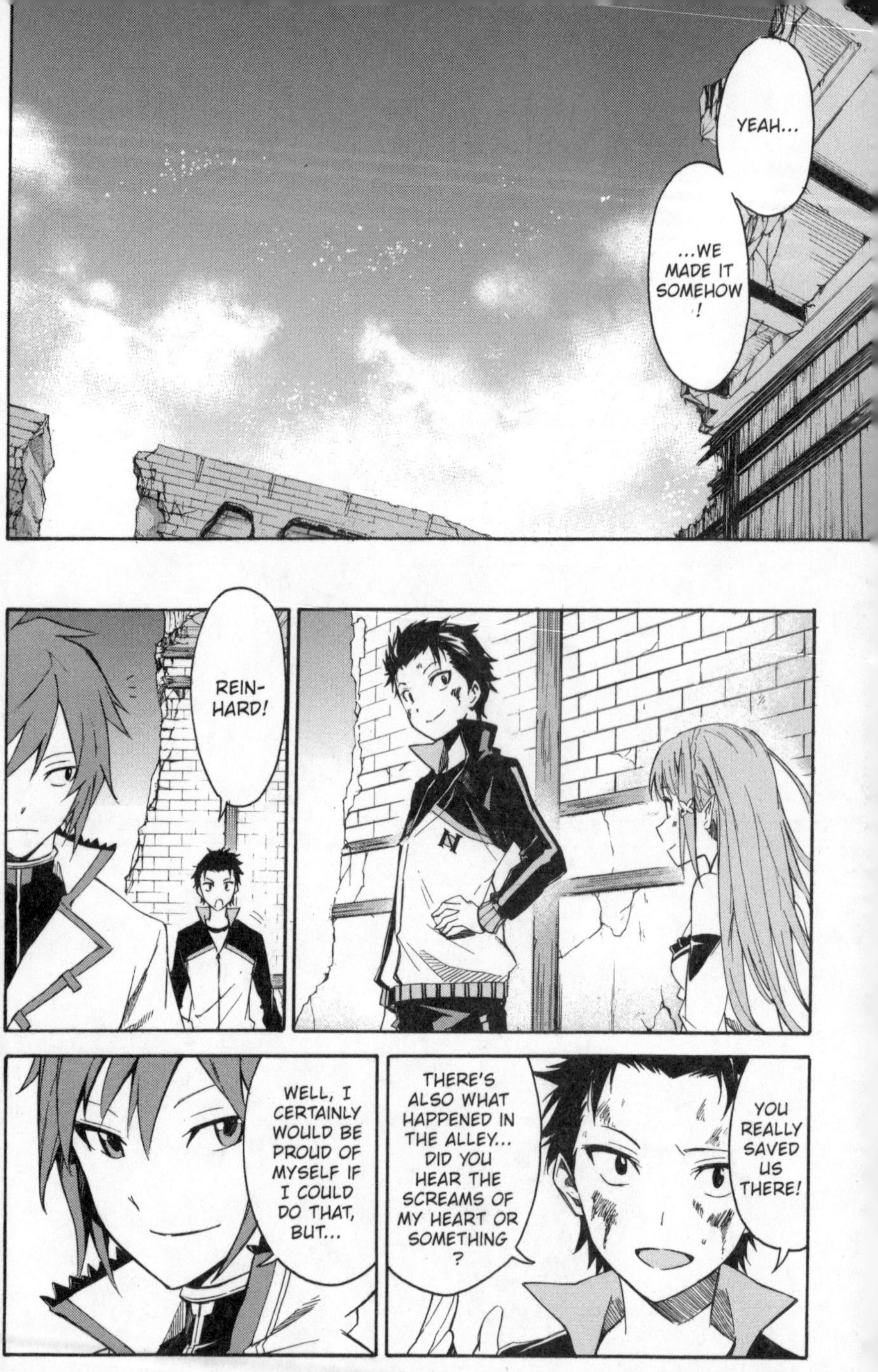
YEAH...
...WE MADE IT SOMEHOW!
REIN-HARD!
YOU REALLY SAVED US THERE!
THERE'S ALSO WHAT HAPPENED IN THE ALLEY... DID YOU HEAR THE SCREAMS OF MY HEART OR SOMETHING?
WELL, I CERTAINLY WOULD BE PROUD OF MYSELF IF I COULD DO THAT, BUT...

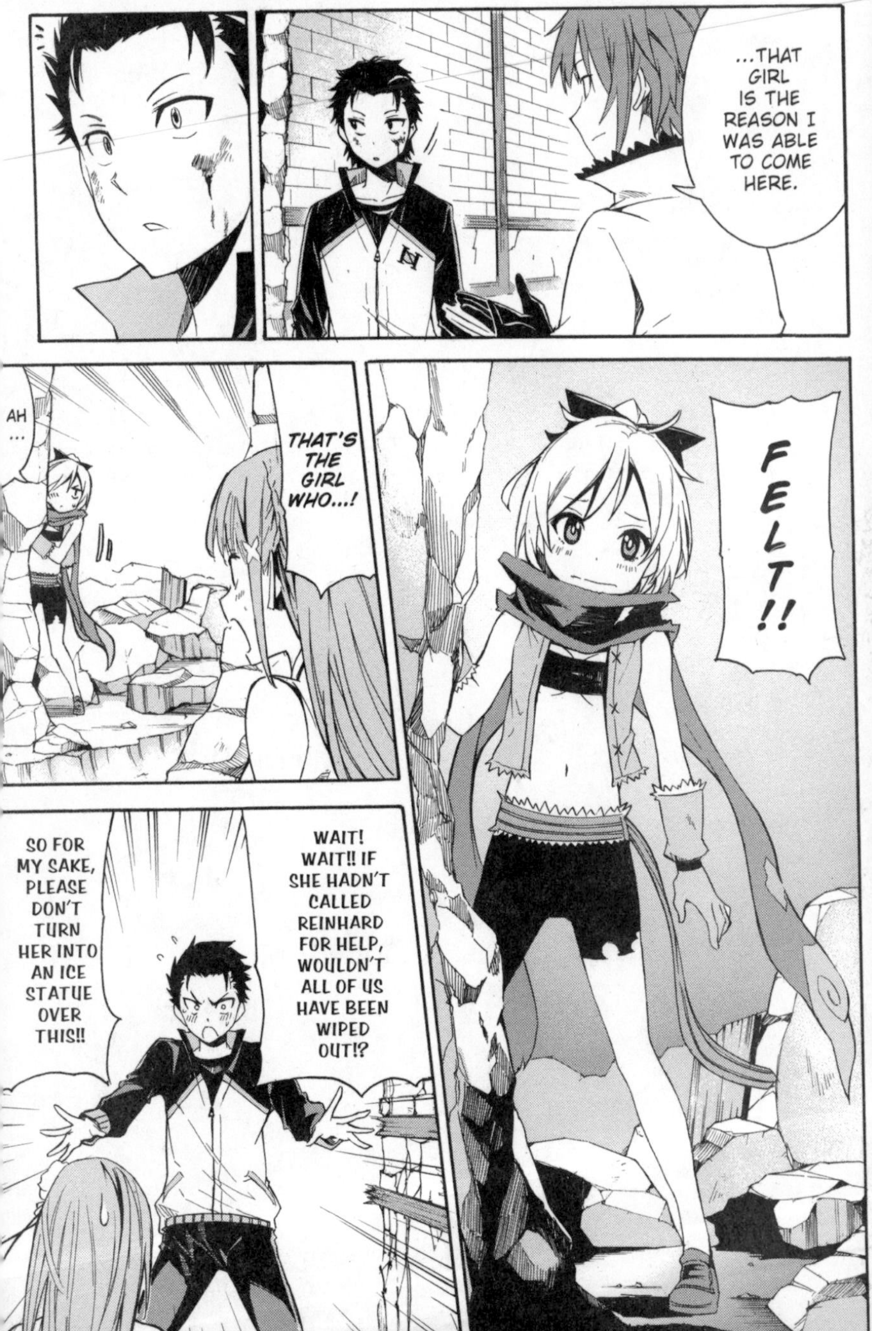
...THAT GIRL IS THE REASON I WAS ABLE TO COME HERE.
FELT!!
THAT'S THE GIRL WHO...!
AH ...
WAIT! WAIT!! IF SHE HADN'T CALLED REINHARD FOR HELP, WOULDN'T ALL OF US HAVE BEEN WIPED OUT!?
SO FOR MY SAKE, PLEASE DON'T TURN HER INTO AN ICE STATUE OVER THIS!!

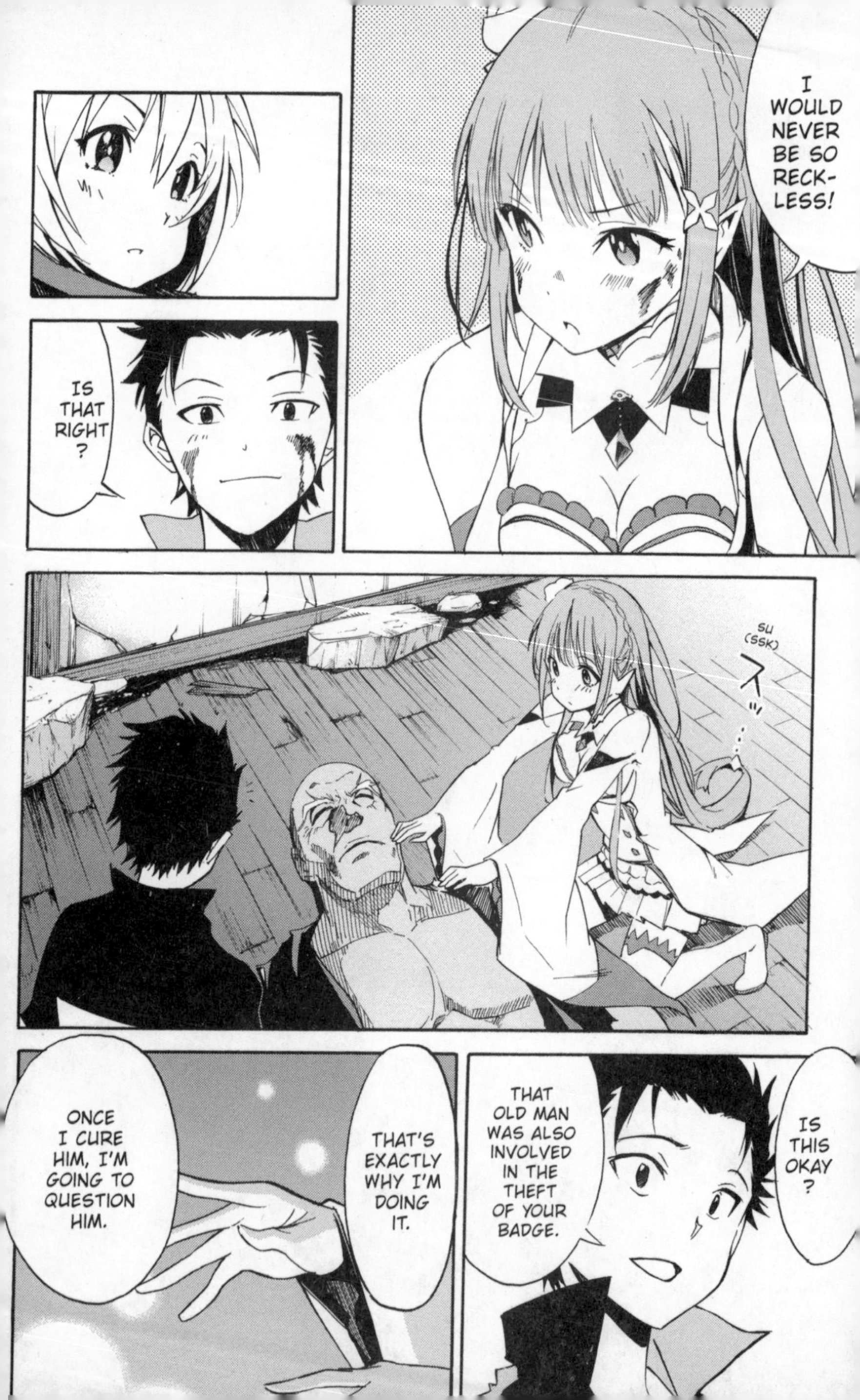
I WOULD NEVER BE SO RECK-LESS!
IS THAT RIGHT?
SU (SSK)
IS THIS OKAY?
THAT OLD MAN WAS ALSO INVOLVED IN THE THEFT OF YOUR BADGE.
THAT'S EXACTLY WHY I'M DOING IT.
ONCE I CURE HIM, I'M GOING TO QUESTION HIM.

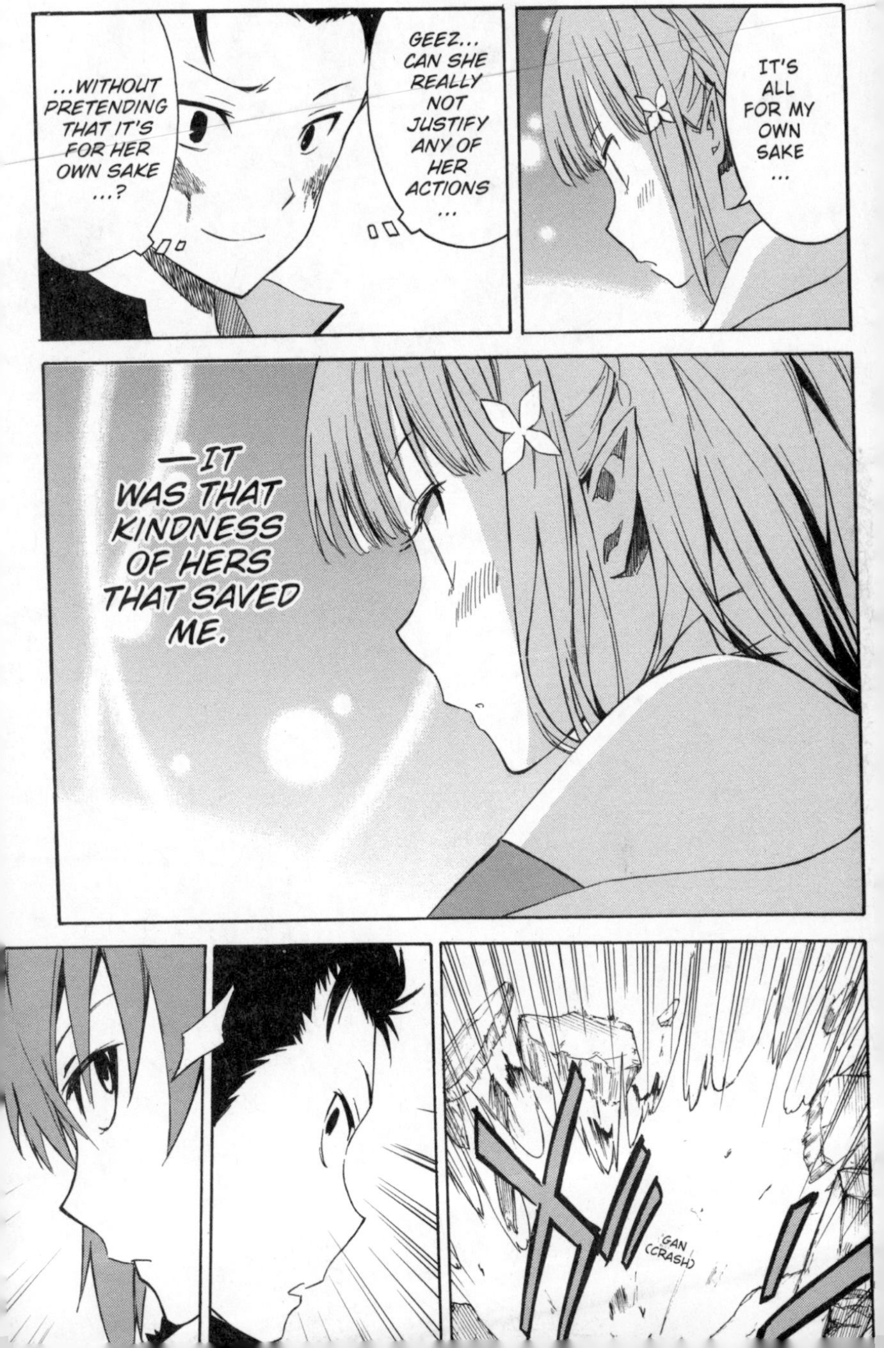
IT'S ALL FOR MY OWN SAKE ...
GEEZ... CAN SHE REALLY NOT JUSTIFY ANY OF HER ACTIONS ...
...WITHOUT PRETENDING THAT IT'S FOR HER OWN SAKE ...?
—IT WAS THAT KINDNESS OF HERS THAT SAVED ME.
GAN (CRASH)

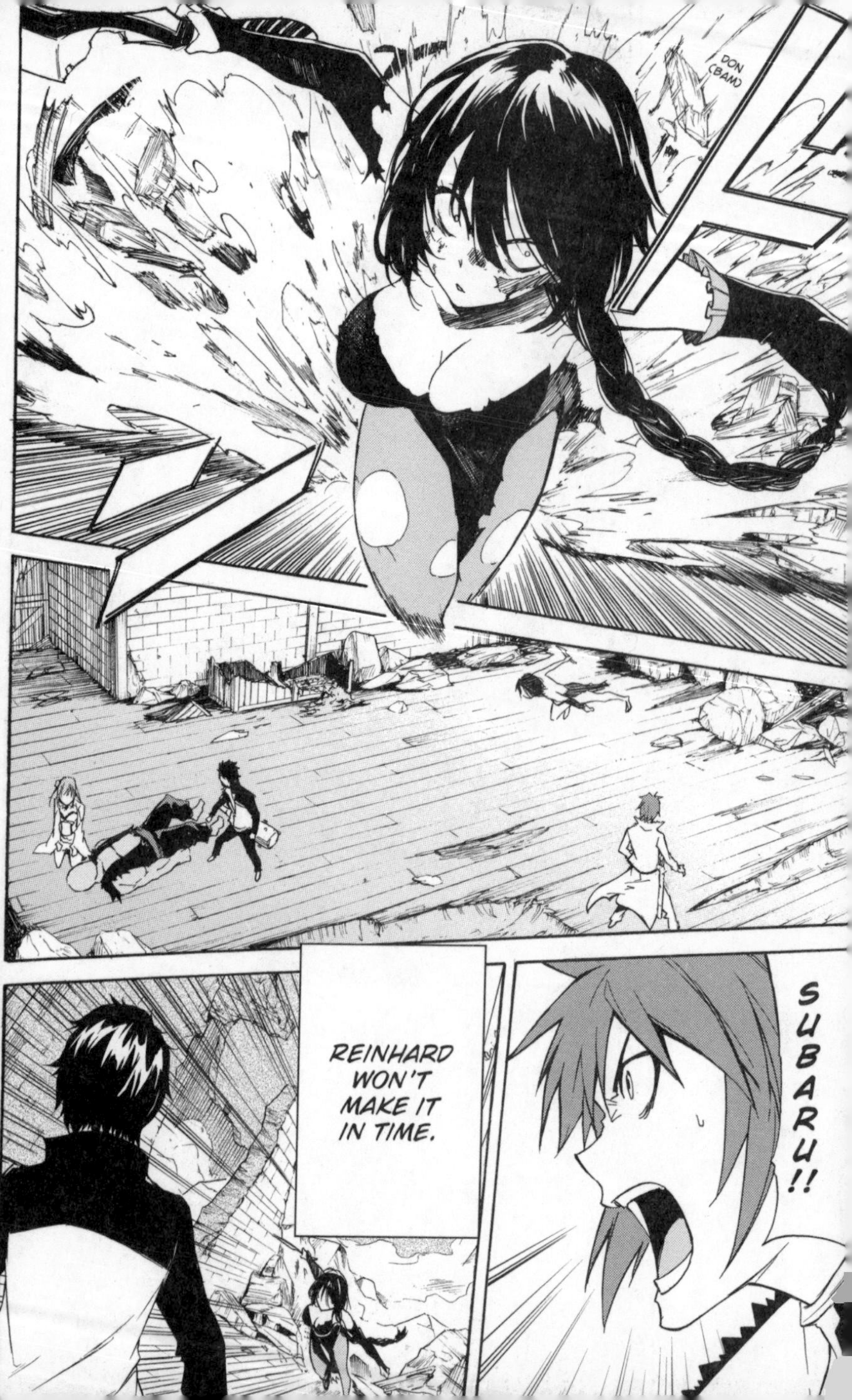
DON (BAM)
SUBARU!!
REINHARD WON'T MAKE IT IN TIME.

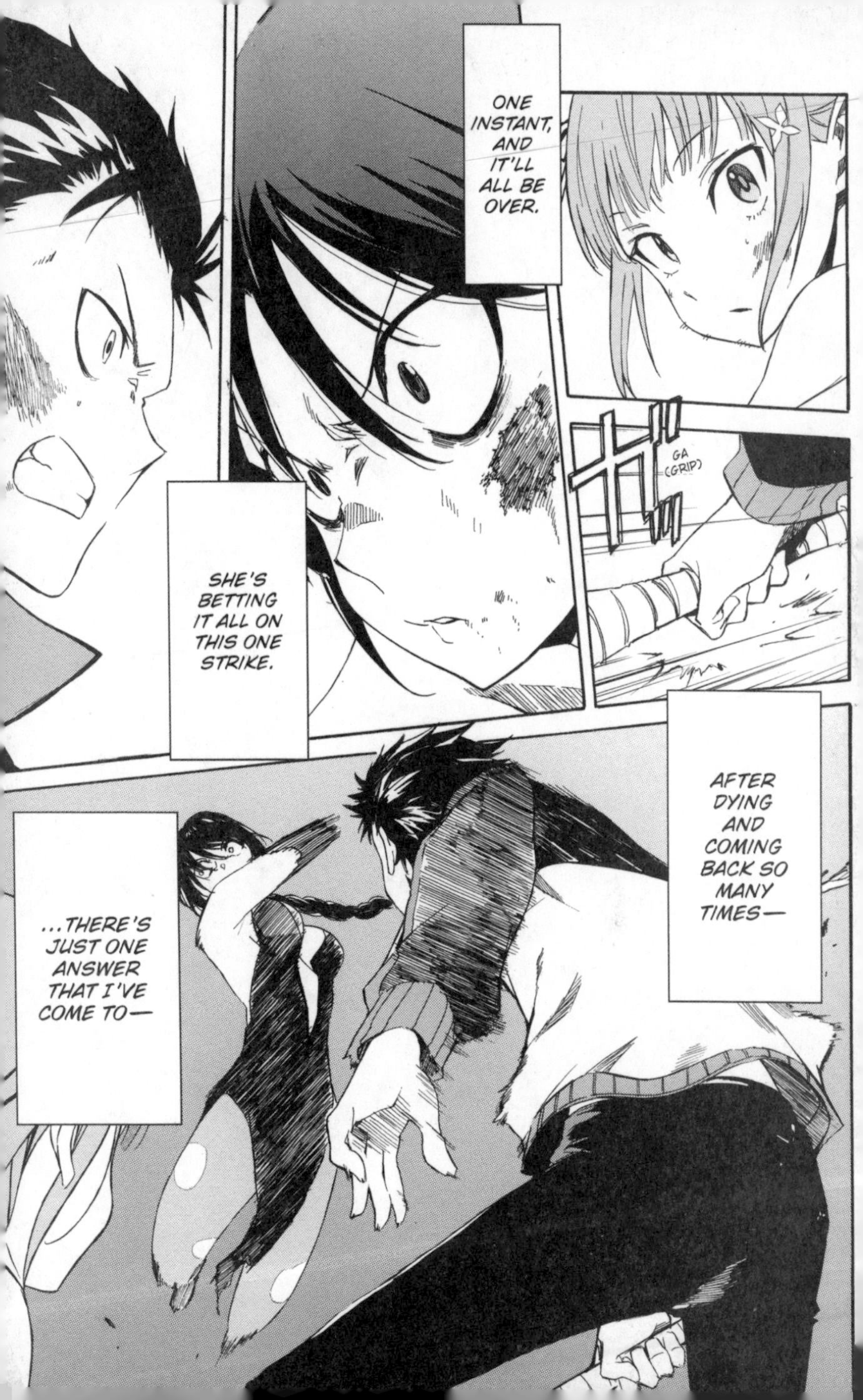
ONE INSTANT, AND IT'LL ALL BE OVER.
SHE'S BETTING IT ALL ON THIS ONE STRIKE.
GA (GRIP)
AFTER DYING AND COMING BACK SO MANY TIMES—
...THERE'S JUST ONE ANSWER THAT I'VE COME TO—

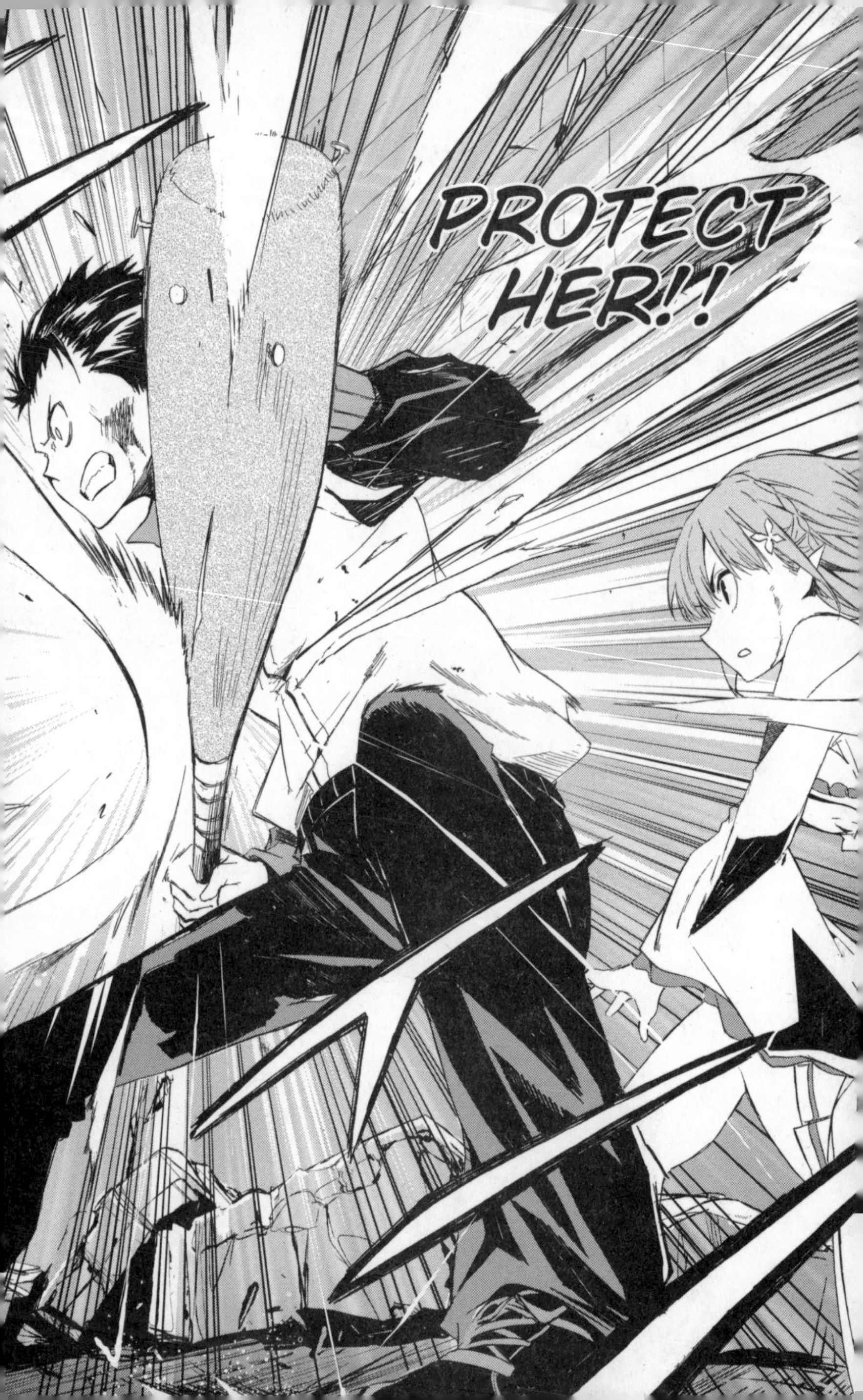
PROTECT HER!!

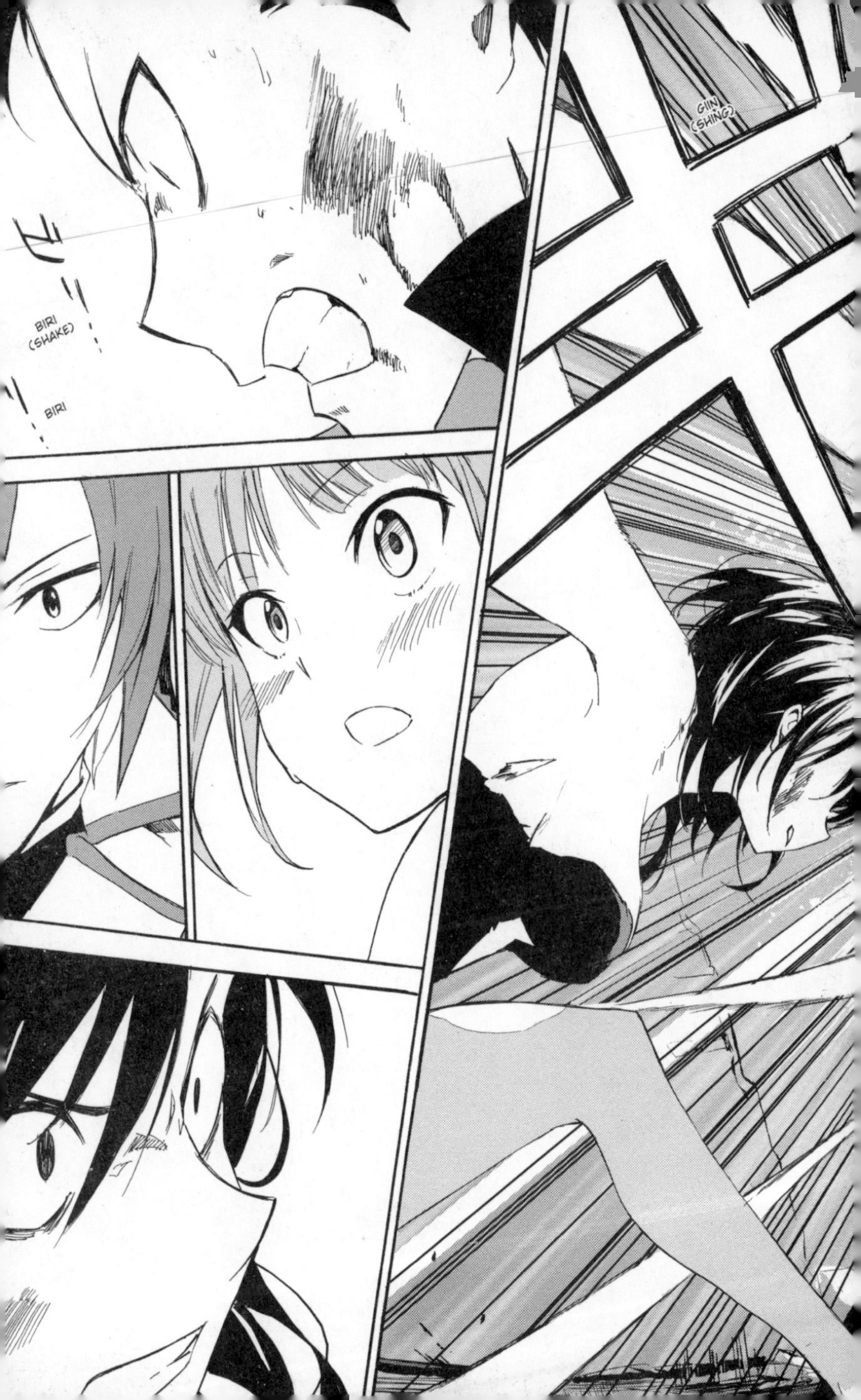
GIIN (SHING)
BIRI (SHAKE)
BIRI

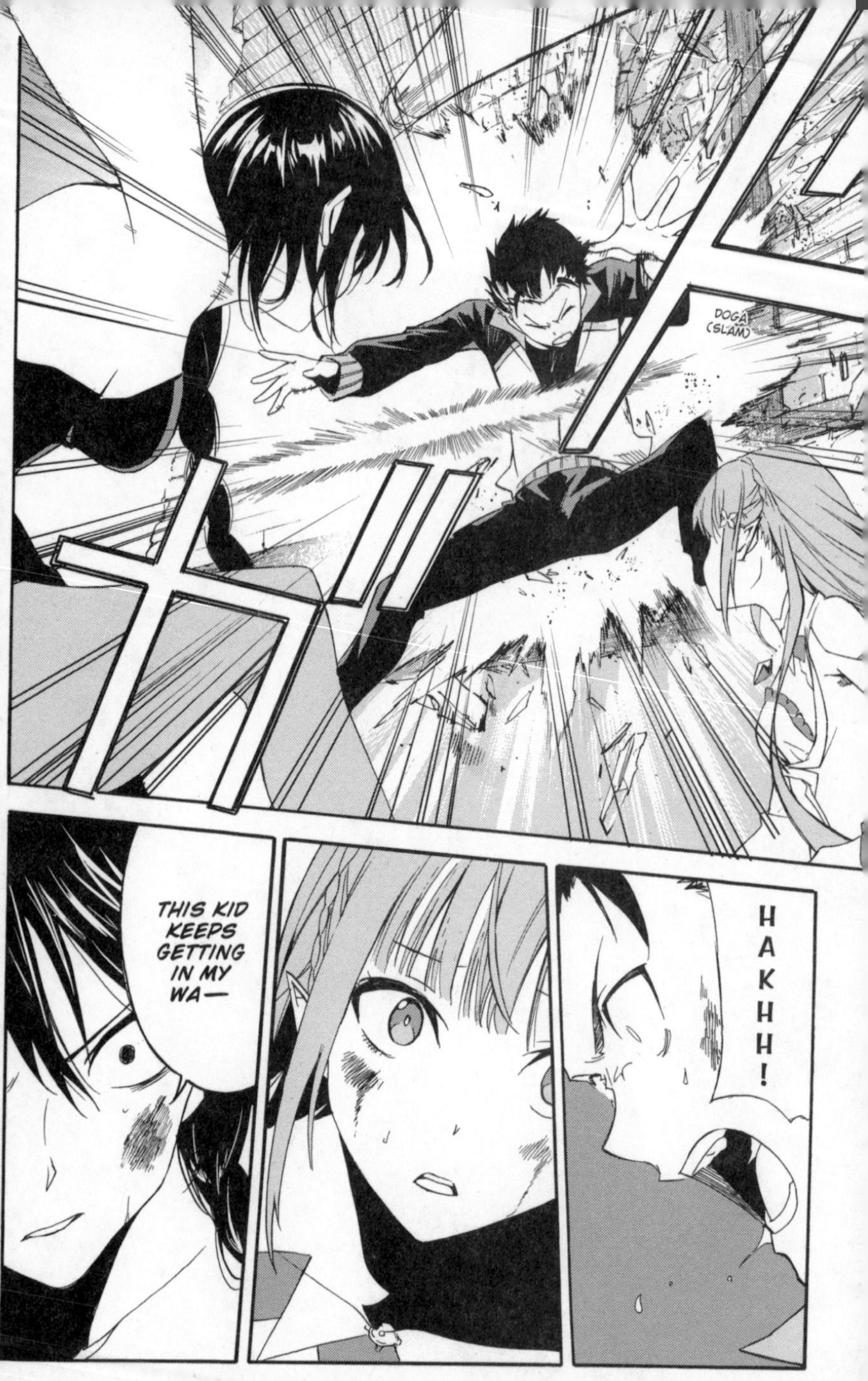
DOGA (SLAM)
HAKHHH!
THIS KID KEEPS GETTING IN MY WA—

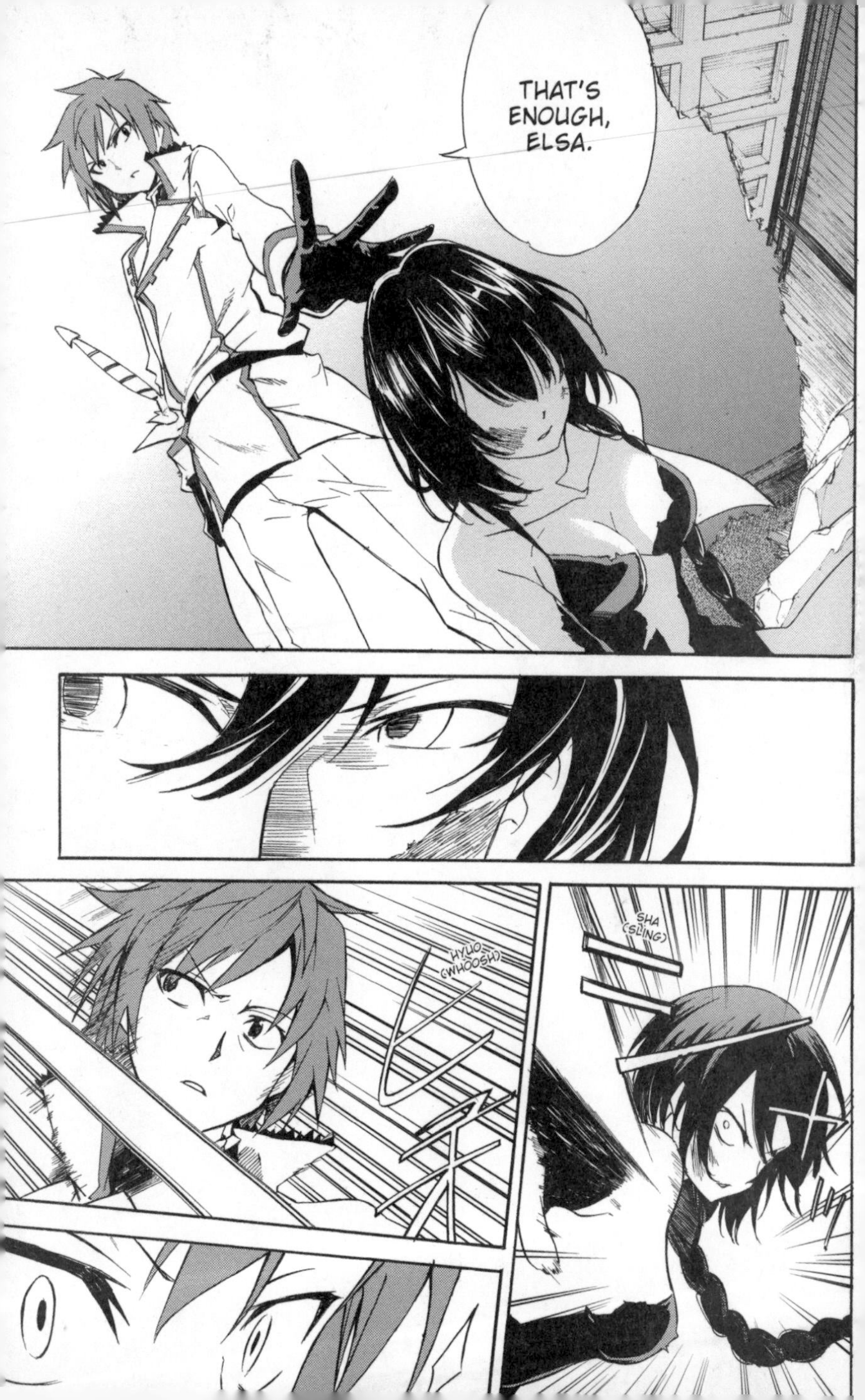
THAT'S ENOUGH, ELSA.
SHA (SLING)
HYUO (WHOOSH)

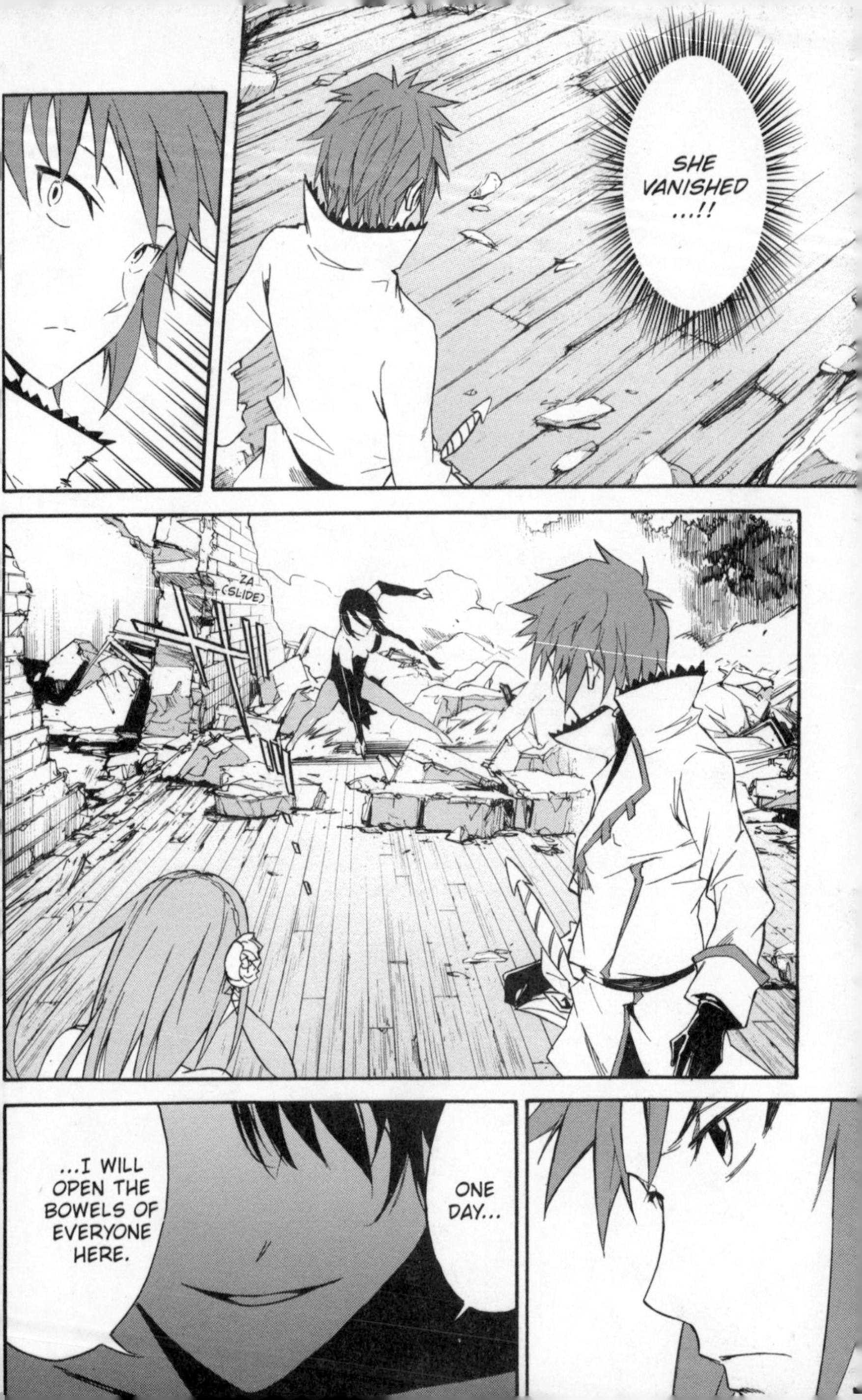
SHE VANISHED ...!!
ZA (SLIDE)
ONE DAY...
...I WILL OPEN THE BOWELS OF EVERYONE HERE.

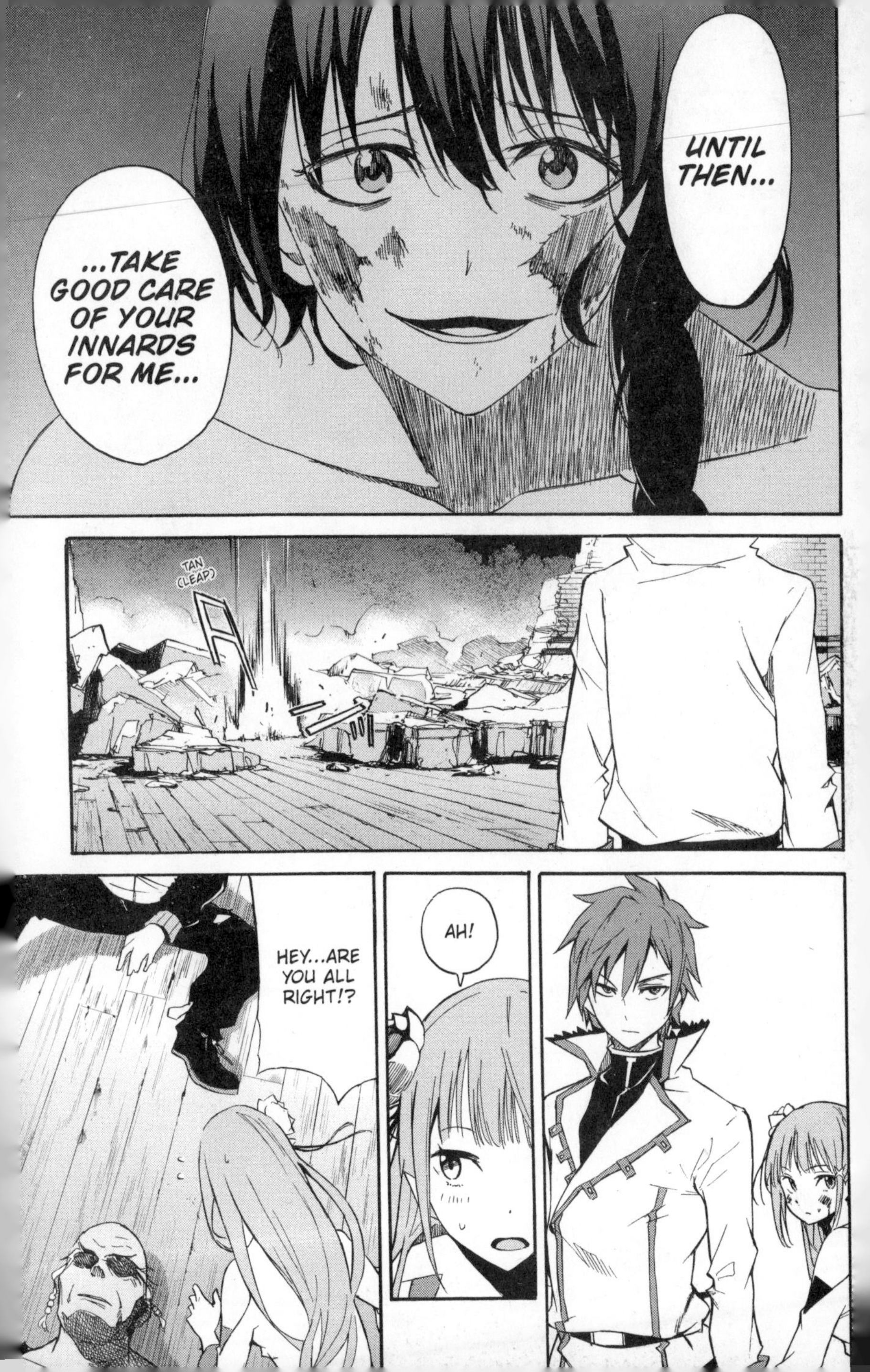
UNTIL THEN...
...TAKE GOOD CARE OF YOUR INNARDS FOR ME...
TAN (LEAP)
AH!
HEY...ARE YOU ALL RIGHT!?

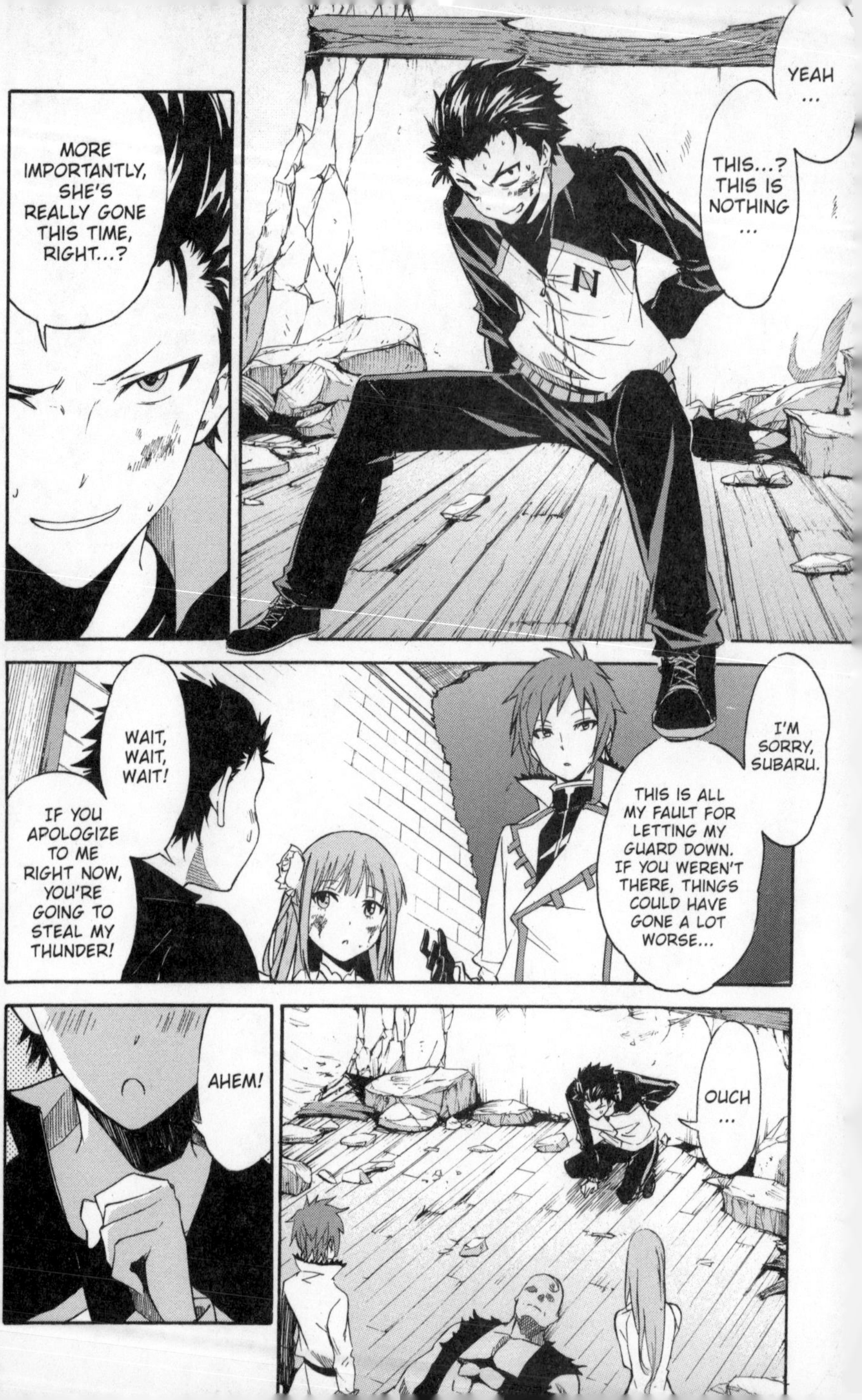
YEAH...
THIS...? THIS IS NOTHING...
MORE IMPORTANTLY, SHE'S REALLY GONE THIS TIME, RIGHT...?
I'M SORRY, SUBARU.
THIS IS ALL MY FAULT FOR LETTING MY GUARD DOWN. IF YOU WEREN'T THERE, THINGS COULD HAVE GONE A LOT WORSE...
WAIT, WAIT, WAIT!
IF YOU APOLOGIZE TO ME RIGHT NOW, YOU'RE GOING TO STEAL MY THUNDER!
OUCH...
AHEM!

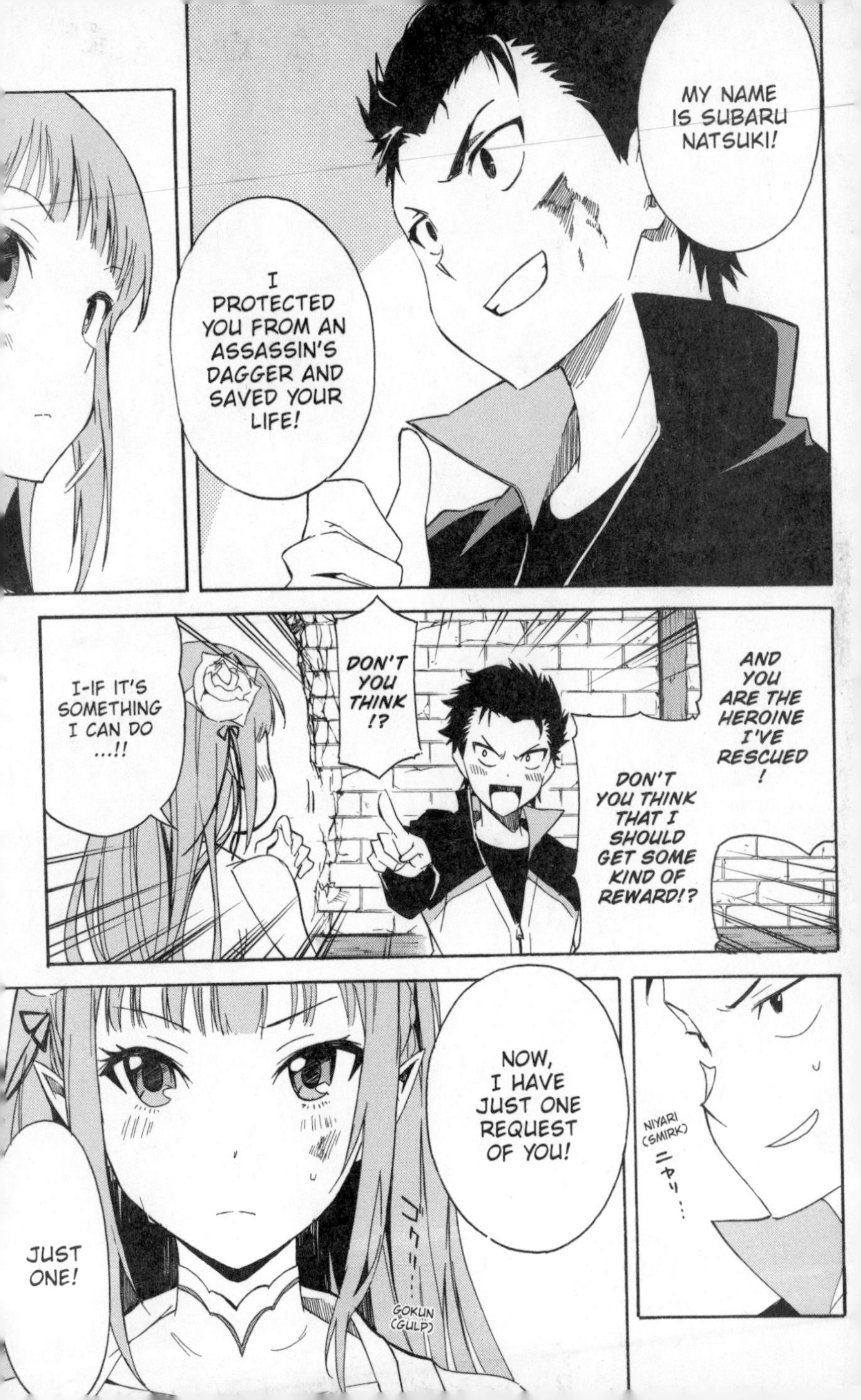
MY NAME IS SUBARU NATSUKI!
I PROTECTED YOU FROM AN ASSASSIN'S DAGGER AND SAVED YOUR LIFE!
AND YOU ARE THE HEROINE I'VE RESCUED!
DON'T YOU THINK THAT I SHOULD GET SOME KIND OF REWARD!?
DON'T YOU THINK!?
I-IF IT'S SOMETHING I CAN DO ...!!
NIYARI (SMIRK)
ニヤリ…
NOW, I HAVE JUST ONE REQUEST OF YOU!
JUST ONE!
GOKUN (GULP)

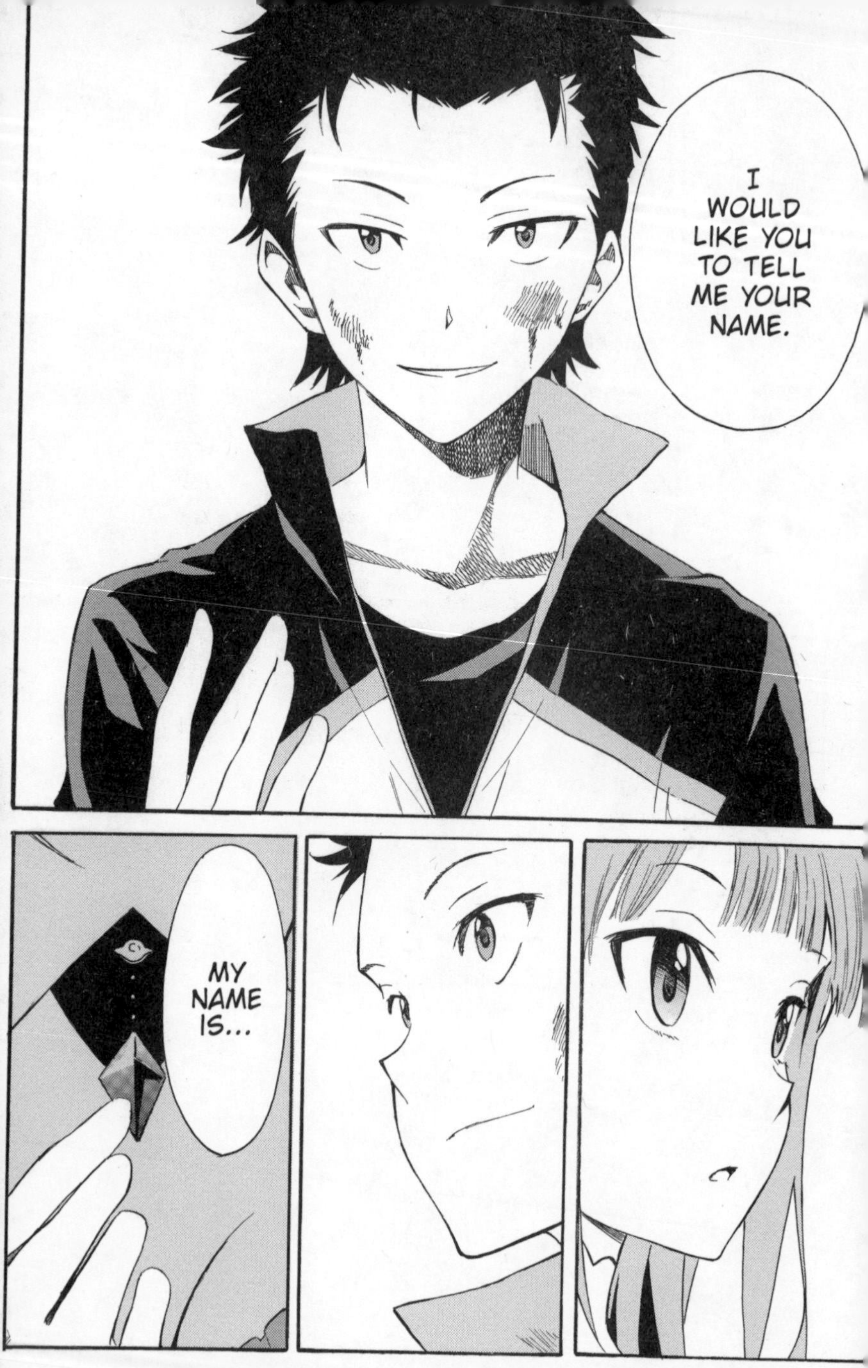
I WOULD LIKE YOU TO TELL ME YOUR NAME.
MY NAME IS...

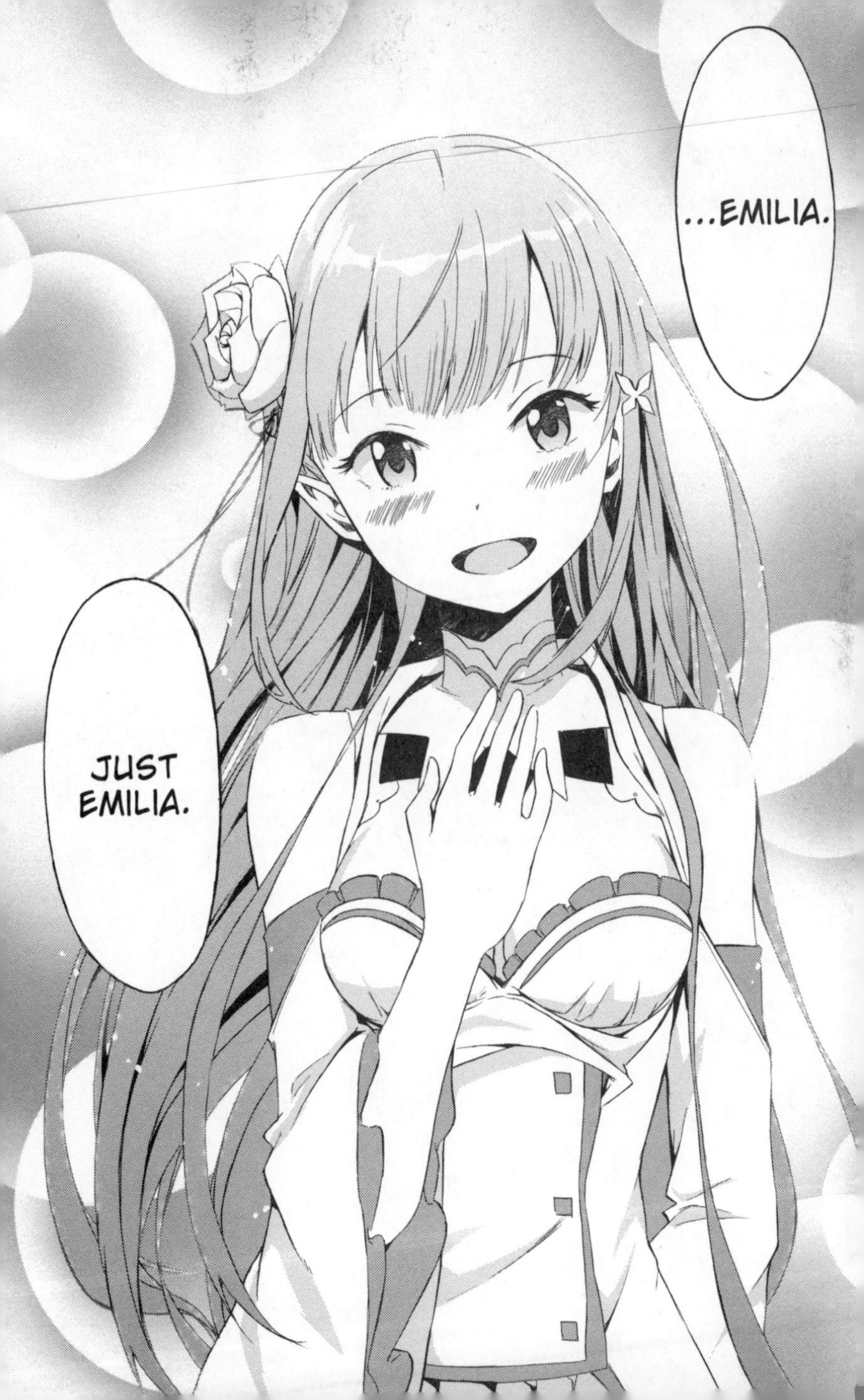
...EMILIA.
JUST EMILIA.

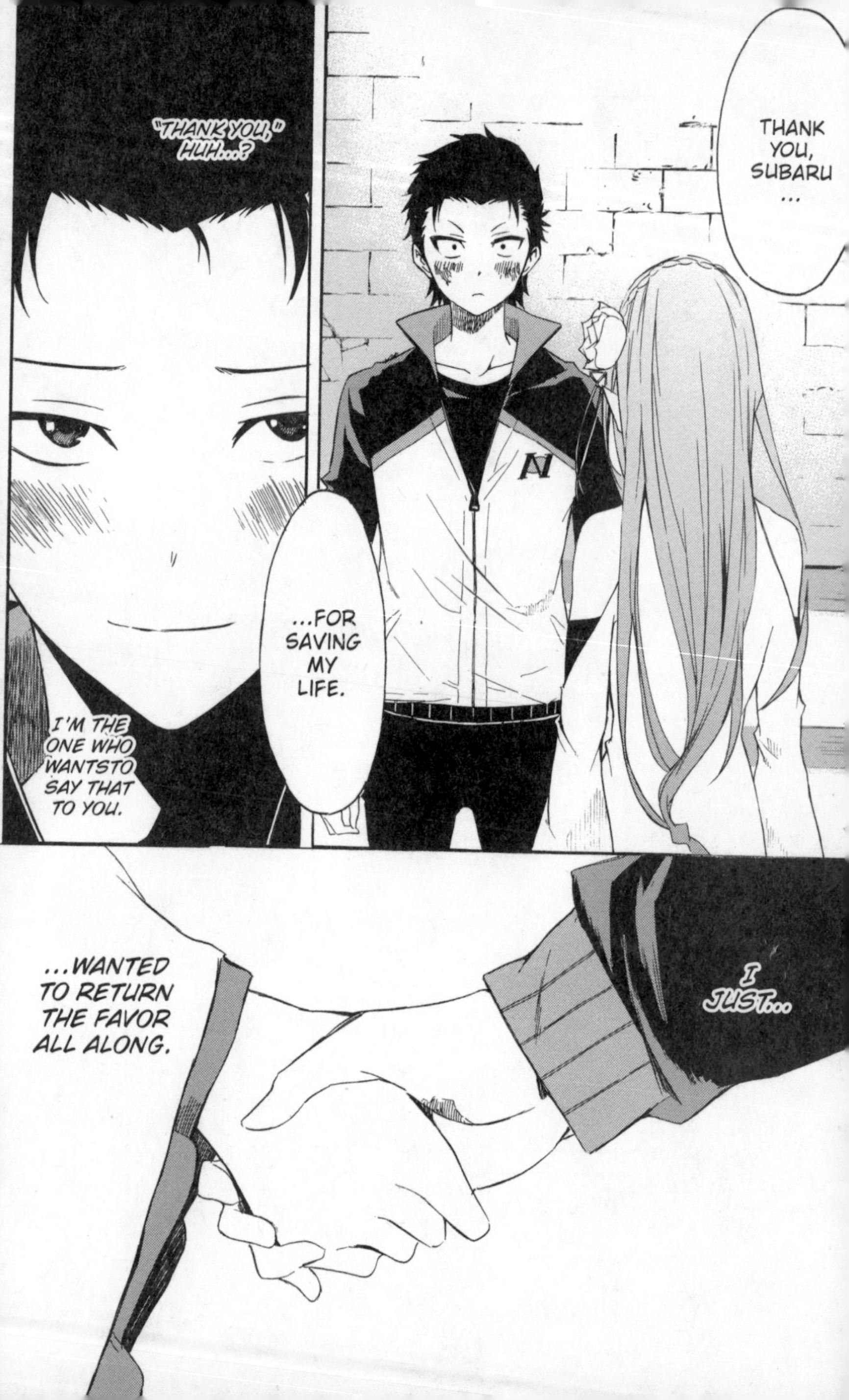
THANK YOU, SUBARU ...
...FOR SAVING MY LIFE.
"THANK YOU," HUH...?
I'M THE ONE WHO WANTSTO SAY THAT TO YOU.
I JUST...
...WANTED TO RETURN THE FAVOR ALL ALONG.

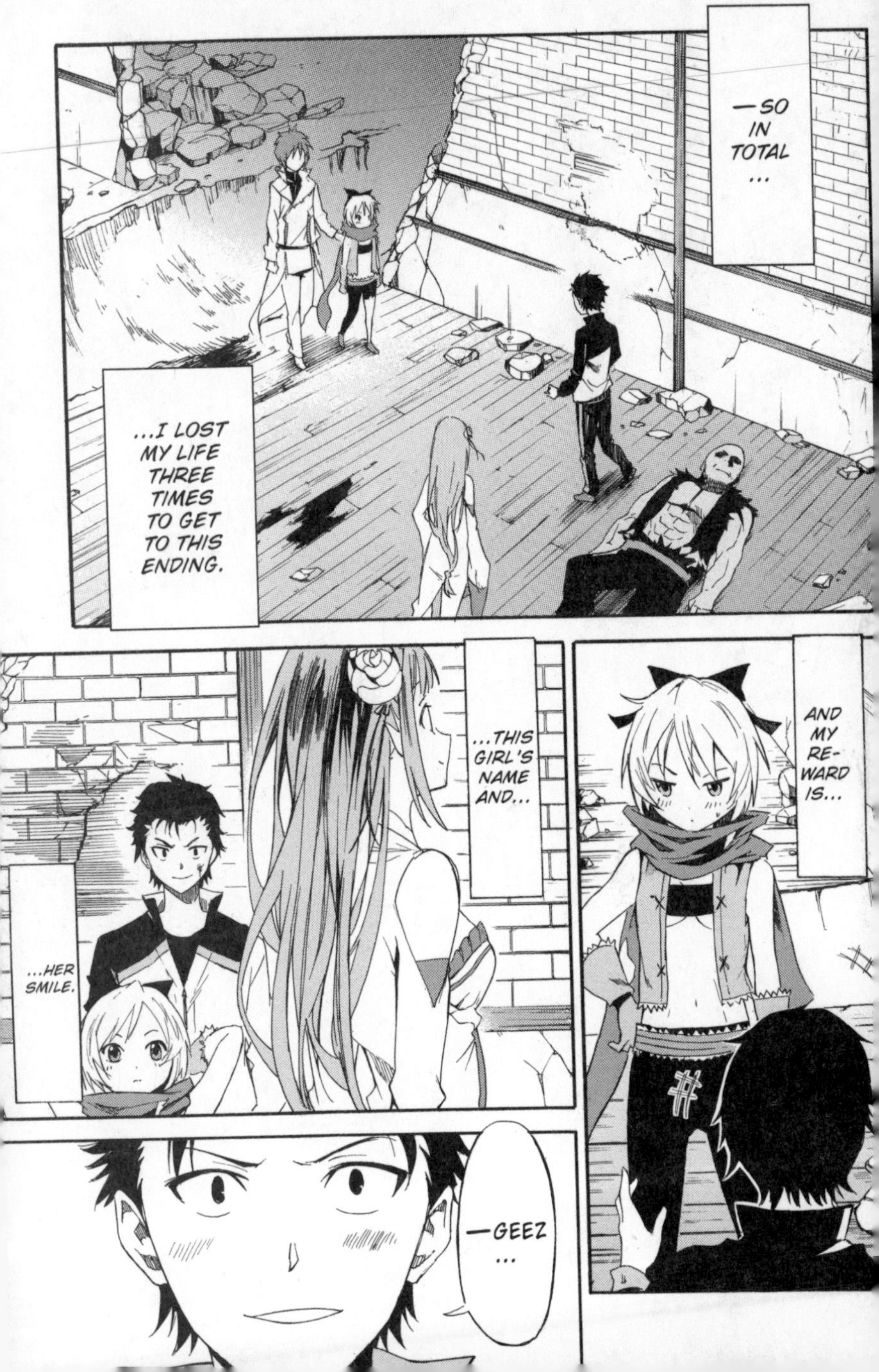
—SO IN TOTAL ...
...I LOST MY LIFE THREE TIMES TO GET TO THIS ENDING.
AND MY RE-WARD IS...
...THIS GIRL'S NAME AND...
...HER SMILE.
—GEEZ ...

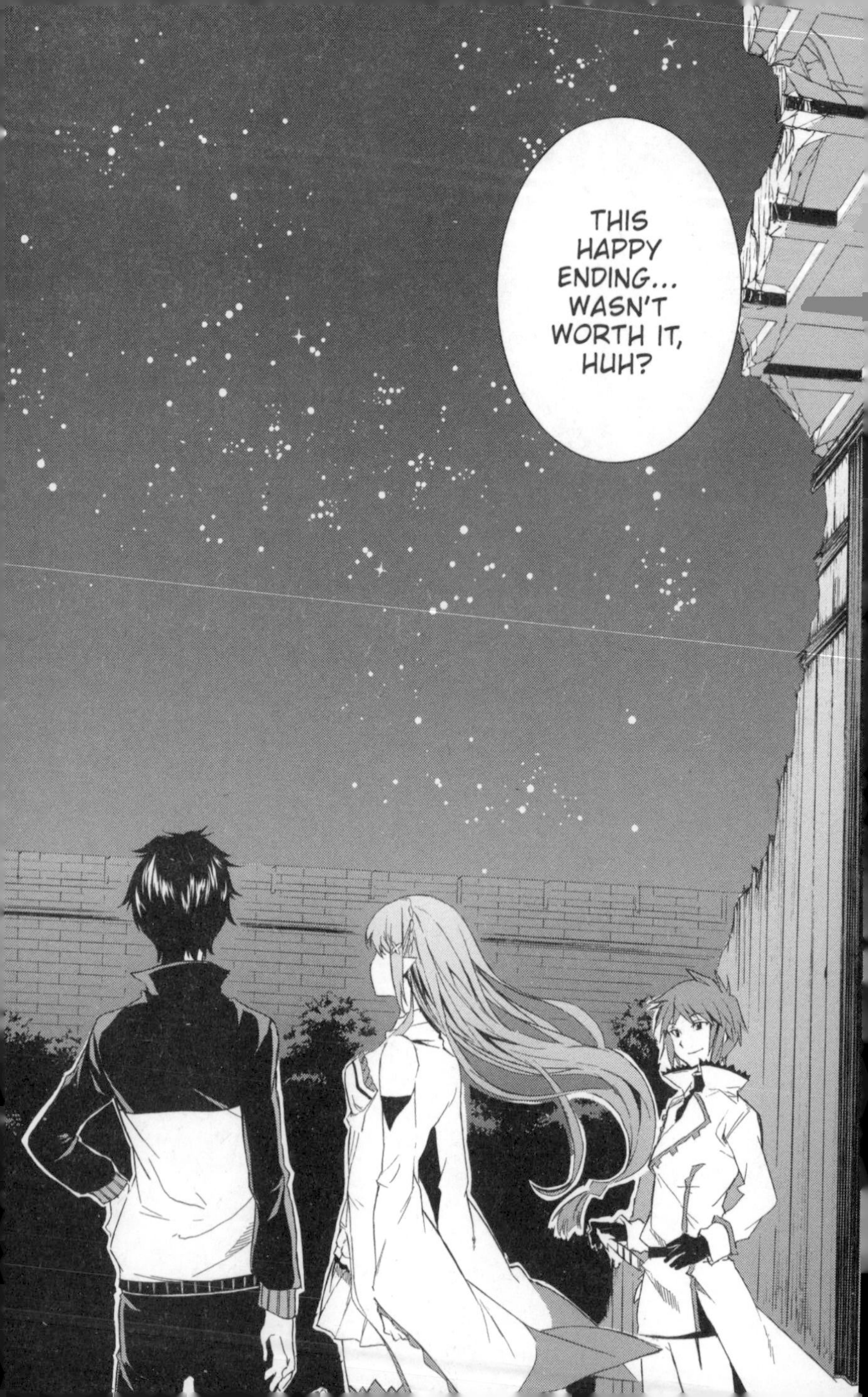
THIS HAPPY ENDING... WASN'T WORTH IT, HUH?

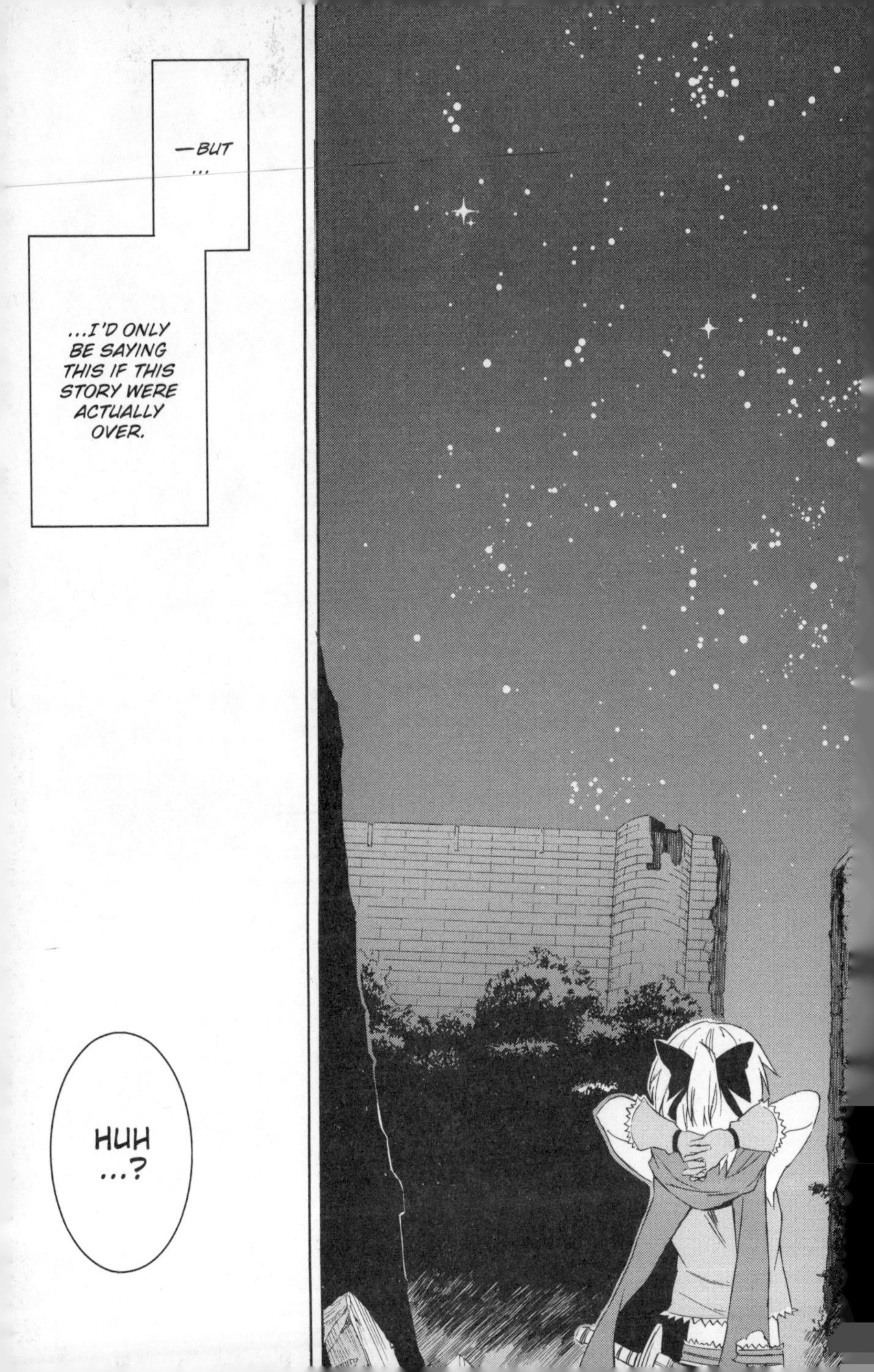
—BUT ...
...I'D ONLY BE SAYING THIS IF THIS STORY WERE ACTUALLY OVER.
HUH ...?

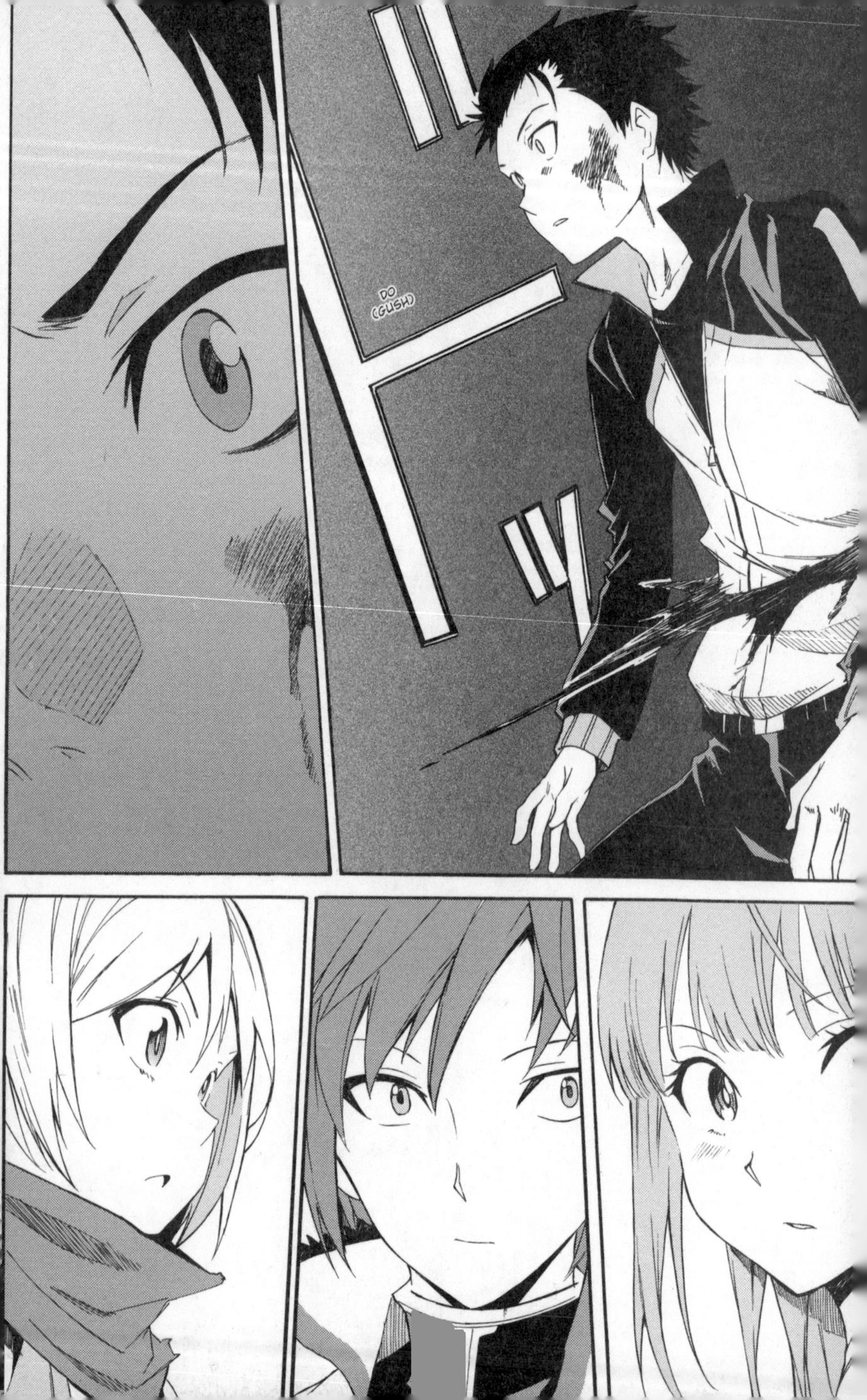
DO
(GUSH)

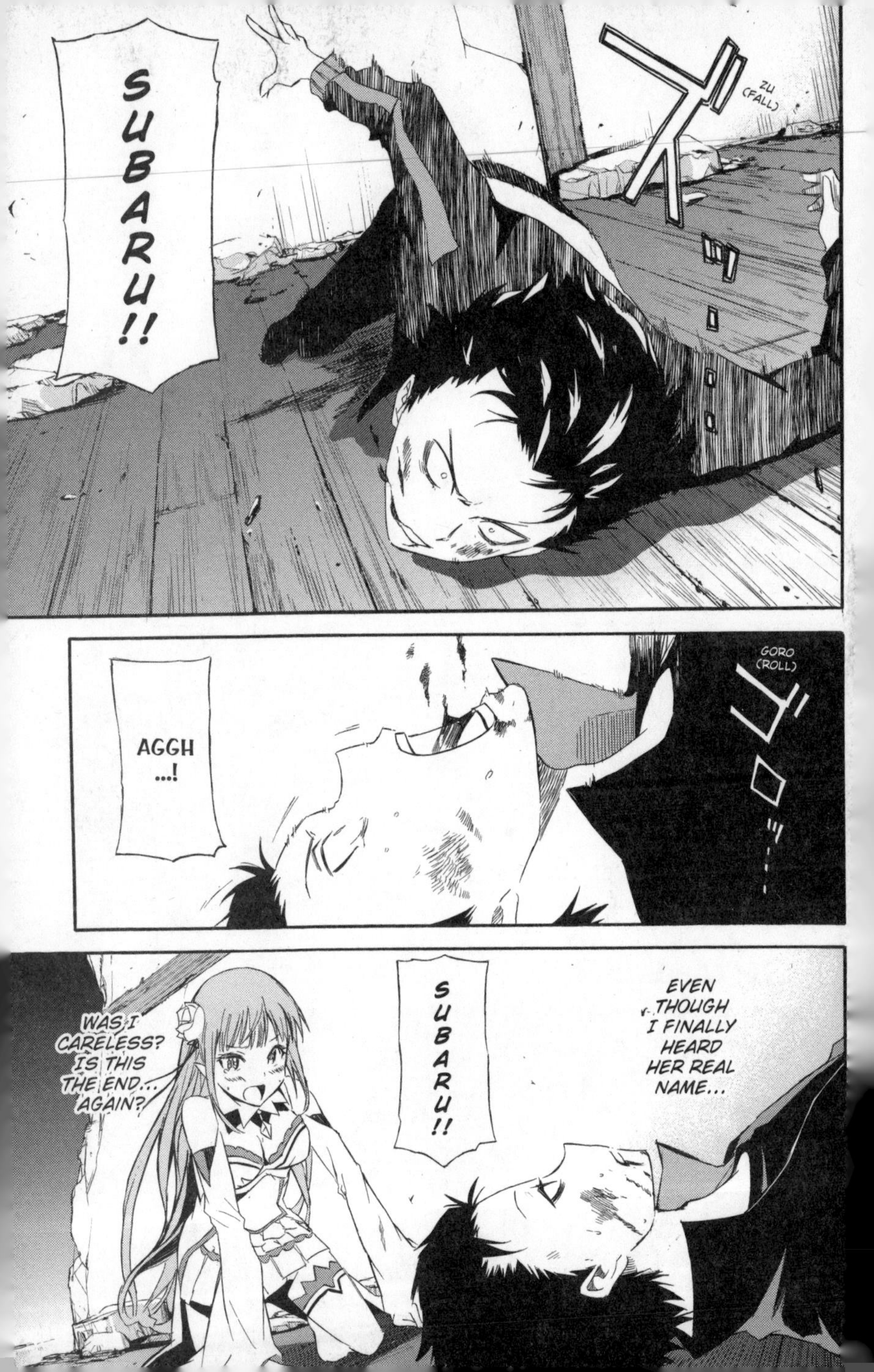
ZU (FALL)
SUBARU!!
GORO (ROLL)
AGGH ...!
EVEN THOUGH I FINALLY HEARD HER REAL NAME...
SUBARU!!
WAS I CARELESS? IS THIS THE END... AGAIN?

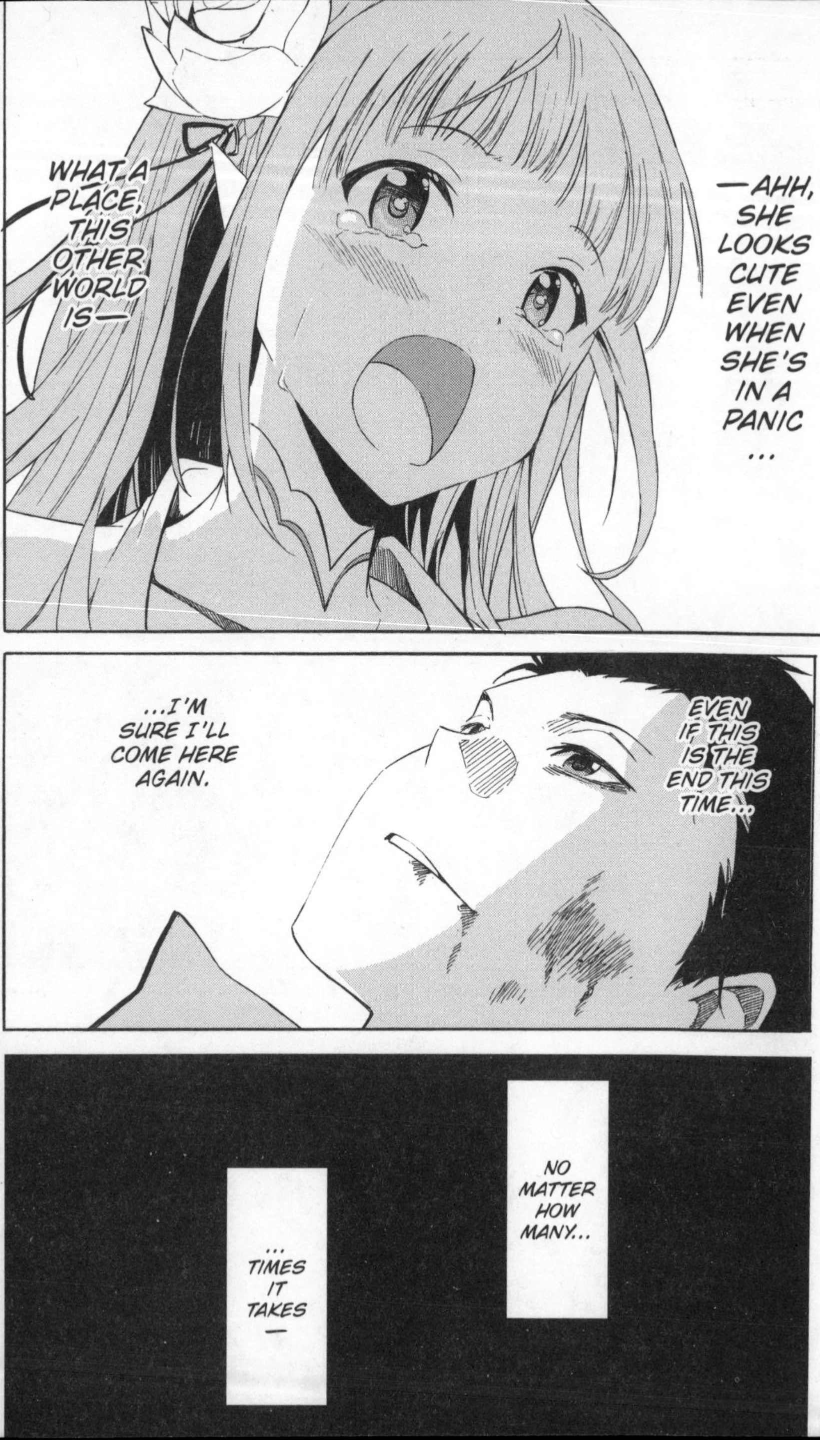
—AHH, SHE LOOKS CUTE EVEN WHEN SHE'S IN A PANIC ...
WHAT A PLACE, THIS OTHER WORLD IS—
EVEN IF THIS IS THE END THIS TIME...
...I'M SURE I'LL COME HERE AGAIN.
NO MATTER HOW MANY...
... TIMES IT TAKES —

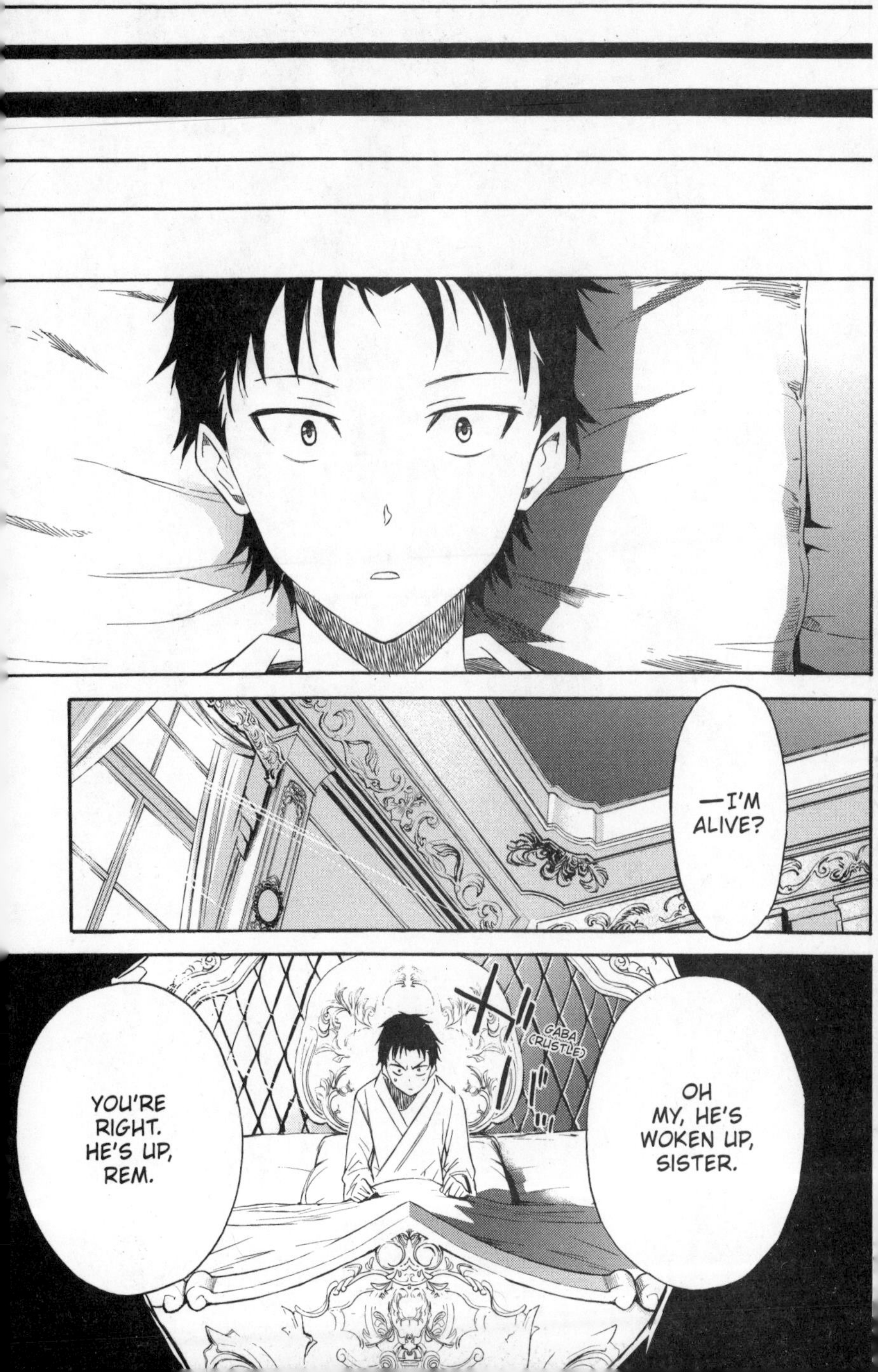
—I'M ALIVE?
OH MY, HE'S WOKEN UP, SISTER.
GABA (RUSTLE)
YOU'RE RIGHT. HE'S UP, REM.

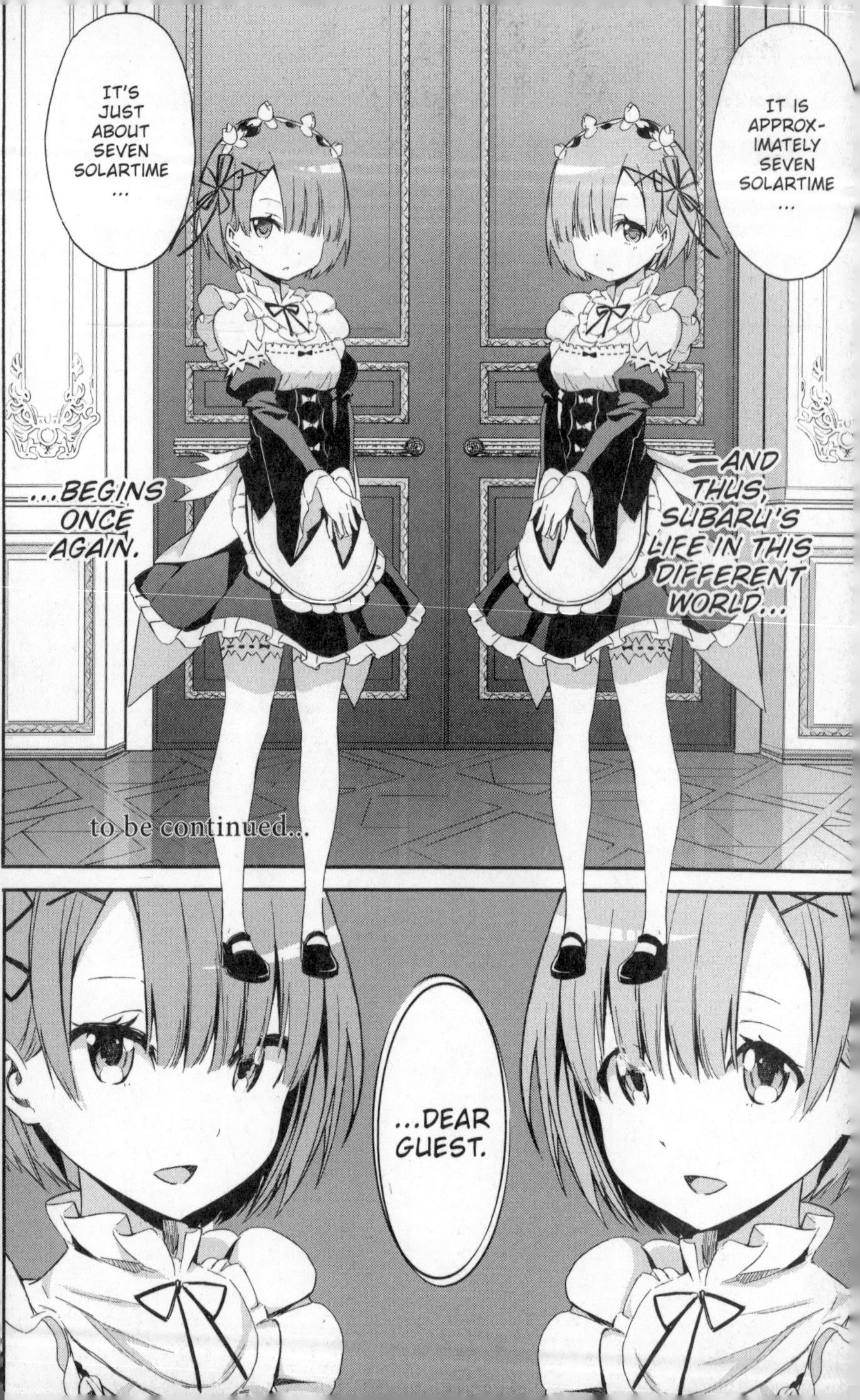
IT IS APPROX-IMATELY SEVEN SOLARTIME ...
IT'S JUST ABOUT SEVEN SOLARTIME ...
—AND THUS, SUBARU'S LIFE IN THIS DIFFERENT WORLD...
...BEGINS ONCE AGAIN.
to be continued...
...DEAR GUEST.

Re:ZERO -Starting Life in Another World-

Chapter 1: A Day in the Capital

The only ability Subaru Natsuki gets when
he's summoned to another world is time
travel via his own death. But to save her,
he'll die as many times as it takes.

Re:ZERO -Starting Life in Another World-

Chapter 1: A Day in the Capital

The only ability Subaru Natsuki gets when he's summoned to another world is time travel via his own death. But to save her, he'll die as many times as it takes.

Illustration by Shinichirou Otsuka
(Character Designer)

Re:ZERO -Starting Life in Another World-

Supporting Comments from the Author of the Original Work, Tappei Nagatsuki

Congratulations, Daichi Matsuse-sensei, on the release of Volume 2 of the *Re:ZERO* manga!
Ever since the beginning, I've been waiting to see Matsuse-sensei's battle scenes! In the second
volume, there are a lot of scenes with characters moving about, and it made me really excited!
Of course, there's Reinhard and Elsa's superhuman climactic battle, but there's also the scene
where Emilia and Puck were coordinating their magic attacks together! Even Subaru, who
didn't move much, got a chance to save face! (Ha-ha.)
In a time loop story, where the sense of time is all scrambled, relationships come together and
characters change with each recursion. Those subtle transformations as the circumstances
differ are hard to express in prose but were very energetically illustrated in the manga,
and I am certain that the *Re:ZERO* world has expanded a great deal!
Seeing that scene with Subaru's wish and Emilia's smile in the final run,
I thought it really showed what makes comics wonderful.
Well done, Matsuse-sensei, and thank you very much!

Re:ZERO -Starting Life in Another World-

Afterword

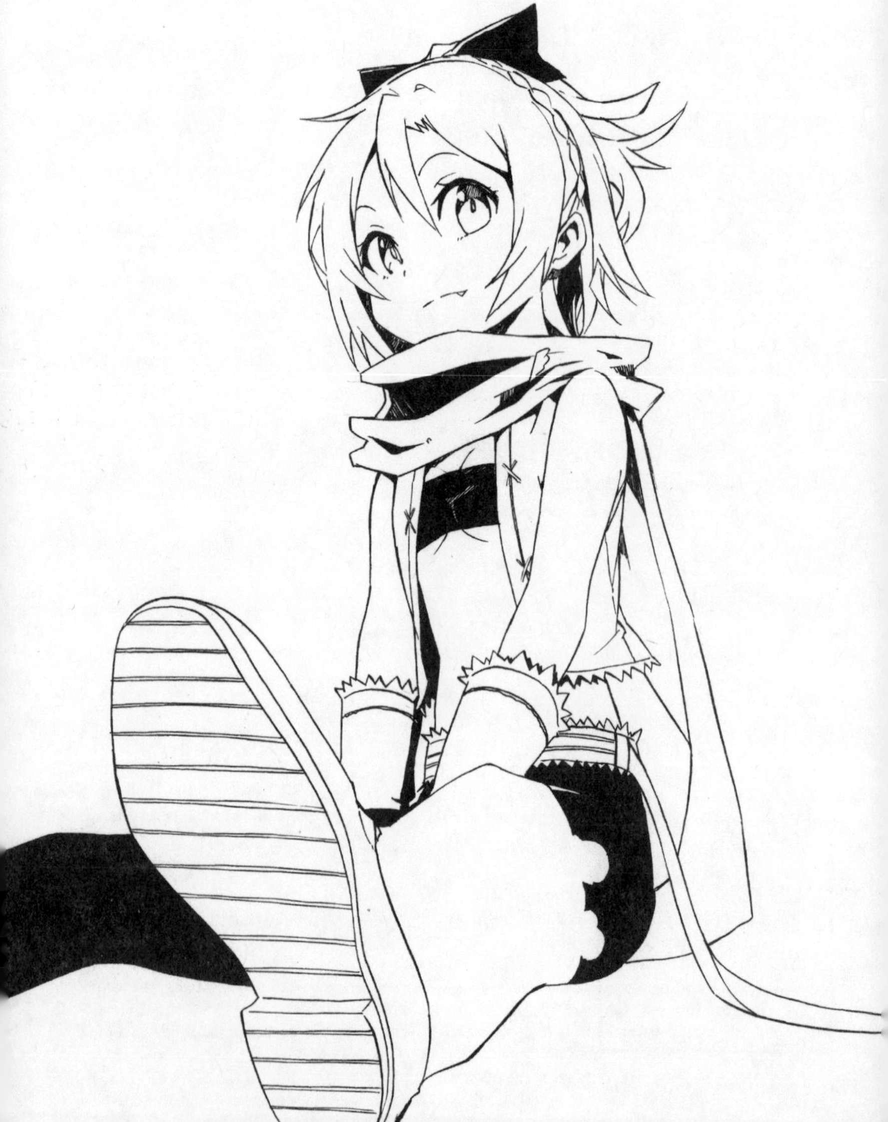

AFTERWORD

THANK YOU FOR READING *RE:ZERO -STARTING LIFE IN ANOTHER WORLD-*. THIS VOLUME MARKS THE END OF CHAPTER 1, BUT OF COURSE, THE STORIES OF SUBARU AND HIS COMPANIONS WILL GO ON. THE MANGA OF THE SECOND CHAPTER, WHICH CONTINUES WHERE THIS ONE LEAVES OFF, WILL BE SERIALIZED IN *BIG GANGAN* BY MAKOTO FUUGETSU-SENSEI. THOSE OF YOU WHO ARE WONDERING WHAT HAPPENS NEXT, BY ALL MEANS, KEEP READING. NOW, IN REGARDS TO THE THIRD CHAPTER, WHICH IS EVEN FURTHER ON AHEAD, IT HAS BEEN DECIDED THAT I WILL BE IN CHARGE OF ADAPTING IT! I'LL POUR EVEN MORE EFFORT INTO DOING MY BEST, SO I HOPE FOR YOUR ONGOING SUPPORT!

マツセ ダイチ

DAICHI MATSUSE

ILLUSTRATION STAFF

SPOROGAMU-SAN
SAWANABE-SAN
KAIRAKU KANO-SAN
TSUKUNEE-SAN

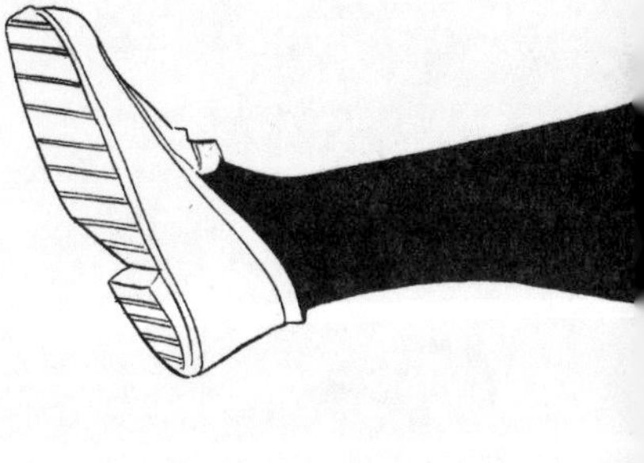

RE:ZERO -STARTING LIFE IN ANOTHER WORLD- ❷
Chapter 1: A Day in the Capital

Daichi Matsuse

Original Story Author: **Tappei Nagatsuki**

Character Design: **Shinichirou Otsuka**

Translation: **ZephyrRZ**
Lettering: **Bianca Pistillo**

RE:ZERO KARA HAJIMERU ISEKAI SEIKATSU
© Daichi Matsuse / Tappei Nagatsuki 2015
First published in Japan in 2015 by KADOKAWA CORPORATION, Tokyo.
English translation rights arranged with KADOKAWA CORPORATION, Tokyo.
through TUTTLE-MORI AGENCY, Inc., Tokyo.

English translation © 2016 by Yen Press, LLC

Yen Press
1290 Avenue of the Americas
New York, NY 10104

Visit us at yenpress.com
facebook.com/yenpress
twitter.com/yenpress
yenpress.tumblr.com
instagram.com/yenpress

First Yen Press Edition: October 2016

Yen Press is an imprint of Yen Press, LLC.
The Yen Press name and logo are trademarks of Yen Press, LLC.

The publisher is not responsible for websites (or their content) that are not owned by the publisher.

Library of Congress Control Number: 2016936537

ISBNs: 978-0-316-39854-1 (paperback)
       978-0-316-39855-8 (ebook)
       978-0-316-39856-5 (app)

10 9 8 7

WOR

Printed in the United States of America